Nationalism and Cultural Practice
in the Postcolonial World

In this wide-ranging study, Neil Lazarus explores the subject of cultural practice in the modern world system. The book contains individual chapters on modernity, globalization and the "West," nationalism and decolonization, cricket and popular consciousness in the English-speaking Caribbean, and African pop music. Lazarus analyzes social movements, ideas, and cultural practices that have migrated across the international division of labor – from the "first world" to the "third world" – over the course of the twentieth century. *Nationalism and Cultural Practice in the Postcolonial World* offers an enormously erudite reading of culture and society in today's world and includes extended discussion of the work of such influential writers, critics, and activists as Frantz Fanon, C.L.R. James, Edward Said, Gayatri Spivak, Samir Amin, Raymond Williams, Paul Gilroy, and Partha Chatterjee. This book is a politically focused, materialist intervention into postcolonial and cultural studies, and constitutes a major reappraisal of the debates on politics and culture in these fields.

NEIL LAZARUS is Professor of English and Comparative Literary Studies at the University of Warwick. He is the author of *Resistance in Postcolonial African Fiction* (1990) and numerous articles on postcolonial literature and theory.

Cultural Margins

General editor

Timothy Brennan
Department of English and Comparative Literature
University of Minnesota

The series **Cultural Margins** orginated in response to the rapidly increasing interest in postcolonial and minority discourses among literary and humanist scholars in the US, Europe, and elsewhere. The aim of the series is to present books (both contributory and by single author) which investigate the complex cultural zone within and through which dominant and minority societies interact and negotiate their differences.

Studies published in the series range from examinations of the debilitating effects of cultural marginalization, to analyses of the forms of power found at the margins of culture, to books which map the varied and complex components involved in the relations of domination and subversion. The books engage with expressions of cultural marginalization which might be literary (e.g. the novels of African or Caribbean or native American writers within a post-colonial context); or textual in a broader sense (e.g. legal or cultural documents relating to the subordination of groups under categories such as race and gender); or dramatic (e.g. subversive performance art by minority groups such as gays and lesbians); or in the sphere of popular culture (e.g. film, video, TV).

This is an international series, addressing questions crucial to the deconstruction and reconstruction of cultural identity in the late twentieth-century world.

For a list of titles published in the series, see end of book

Nationalism and Cultural Practice in the Postcolonial World

Neil Lazarus

CAMBRIDGE
UNIVERSITY PRESS

PUBLISHED BY THE PRESS SYNDICATE OF THE UNIVERSITY OF
CAMBRIDGE
The Pitt Building, Trumpington Street, Cambridge CB2 1RP, United
Kingdom

CAMBRIDGE UNIVERSITY PRESS
The Edinburgh Building, Cambridge CB2 2RU
UK http://www.cup.cam.ac.uk
40 West 20th Street, New York, NY 10011-4211
USA http://www.cup.org
10 Stamford Road, Oakleigh, Melbourne 3166, Australia

First published 1999

Printed in the United Kingdom at the University Press, Cambridge

Typeset in Palatino 9.5/12 pt [VN]

A catalogue record for this book is available from the British Library

Library of Congress cataloging in publication data

Lazarus, Neil, 1953–
    Nationalism and cultural practice in the postcolonial world / Neil
Lazarus.
        p.   cm. – (Cultural margins; 6)
    Includes bibliographical references and index.
    ISBN 0 521 62410 x (hardback) – ISBN 0 521 62493 2 (paperback)
        1. Nationalism.   2. Culture.   3. Postcolonialism.   I. Title.
II. Series.
    JC311.L3719   1999
    306.2'09172'409045–dc21   98–38084   CIP

ISBN 0 521 62410 x hardback
ISBN 0 521 62493 2 paperback

For Tamara and Anusha

Contents

Acknowledgments

I began this book while on sabbatical leave from Brown University in 1990. It has taken me seven full years to complete it. Over the passage of these years, as the study has changed shape and direction, assuming its current (final) appearance not only gradually but also – if I may say so – dialectically (so that I had almost finished writing before I began to sense what the overarching argument of the book was), I have accumulated an enormous number of intellectual and personal debts. I should begin by thanking my friends and colleagues at Brown. Without the generous encouragement of, and unflagging critical and material support provided by, Nancy Armstrong, Paul Buhle, Marianne Costa, Mary Ann Doane, Jim Egan, Annie Goldson, Roger Henkle, Paget Henry, Bill Keach, Richard Manning, Phil Rosen, Ruth Santos, David Savran, Bob Scholes, Len Tennenhouse, Elizabeth Weed, and especially Ellen Rooney, I would have lacked the resources, the space and freedom, to try out my ideas, to take intellectual risks without fear that my mistakes might have adverse professional consequences.

My friends in the world beyond Brown have been equally important in supporting and challenging my ideas, helping me to express myself more cogently and precisely, and enabling me to feel myself part of an active – and activist – community of left-wing intellectuals. Fran Bartkowski, Jenny Bourne, Hazel Carby, Laura Chrisman, Annie Coombes, Lisa Frank, Carl Freedman, Barbara Harlow, Isabel Hofmeyr, Peter Hulme, Cynthia Kros, Anne McClintock, Viet Nguyen-Gillham, Rob Nixon, Sonny San Juan, Naomi Schor, A. Sivanandan, and Gayatri Chakravorty Spivak have all commented searchingly on the typescript in part or whole; and without the commitment, humor, and passionate fellowship of Crystal

Acknowledgments

Bartolovich, Tim Brennan, Keya Ganguly, Benita Parry, and Khachig Tölölyan, I doubt that the study would ever have come to completion. Certainly, it would have been poorer than it is.

I owe an incalculable debt to my students at Brown over the past decade – graduate and undergraduate – whose radicalism, adventurousness, erudition, and intellectual virtuosity have amazed and delighted me, and from whom I continue to learn so much. It would be invidious to name students still completing their doctoral research. But I am proud to have worked with such young scholars as Anthony Arnove, Mark Cooper, Nick Daly, Bo Ekelund, Steve Evans, Rosemary Marangoly George, Kate Hammer, John Marx, Mark McMorris, Gautam Premnath, Helen Scott, Xiaoying Wang, and Alys Weinbaum, and I am honored now to count them among my friends. May they go on to enjoy great success in the years to come.

Beth Anderson, Nancy Armstrong, Anthony Arnove, Fran Bartkowski, Deryck Durston, Steve Evans, Peter Flinn, Liz Fodaski, Keya Ganguly, Penny Lewis, Jennifer Moxley, John Marx, Ellen Rooney, Len Tennenhouse, and Khachig Tölölyan all helped me, through various means – wit, wisdom, compassion, criticism, rock music, poker, New York City, and fabulous conversation – to get through a very difficult time in my life, and I would like to thank them formally for this.

Versions of individual chapters from the book have been given as papers at a number of different institutions in the United States and Europe. There are many people to whom I owe thanks for their invitations and organization of conferences, colloquia, and presentations: Patricia Alden (St. Lawrence University), Rita Barnard (University of Pennsylvania), Fran Bartkowski (Rutgers University, Newark), Charles Cantalupo (Pennsylvania State University), Rey Chow (University of Minnesota), Nicholas Dirks and Janaki Bakhle (University of Michigan), Bo Ekelund and Rolf Lunden (University of Uppsala), Keya Ganguly (Carnegie Mellon University; again at the University of Minnesota), Peter Hulme, Francis Barker, and Maggie Iversen (University of Essex), Debra Journet (University of Louisville), Gautam Kundu (Georgia Southern University), Scott McCracken (Salford University), Benita Parry (University of Warwick), Birje Patil (Marlboro College), Amrit Singh (Rhode Island College), Paul Smith (Carnegie Mellon University), Khachig Tölölyan (Wesleyan University), Betsy Traube (Wesleyan University), and Tim Watson (Columbia University).

My greatest debt is to Tamara Jakubowska, who has been a

critically important intellectual ally and, more important still, has shared her life with me. To her, and to her daughter Anusha, this book is dedicated, with love.

Introduction: hating tradition properly

Nationalism and Cultural Practice in the Postcolonial World is a book about the social trajectories of culture in the modern world system. The book comprises individual chapters on modernity, globalization, and the "West"; the conceptualization of nationalism in postcolonial studies; cricket and popular consciousness in the English-speaking Caribbean; and African pop music. It is intended as a self-consciously Marxist contribution to the academic field of postcolonial studies – one capable of suggesting a credible historical materialist alternative to the idealist and dehistoricizing scholarship currently predominant in that field in general. If I were asked to summarize the sustaining argument of the book – to say in a single sentence or less what the book as a whole was about – I would propose the rubric of "hating tradition properly."

I derive this notion of "hating tradition properly" from Theodor W. Adorno's fraught yet inexhaustibly rewarding work, *Minima Moralia*, which was first published in Germany in 1951 (although it had been written in exile during the dark war-era years of the 1940s). A particular fragment in *Minima Moralia* is entitled "Savages are not more noble" (*Die Wilden sind nicht bessere Menschen*: literally, "Savages are not better men"). At one and the same time smugly condescending and explosively radical, irretrievably Eurocentric and urgently anti-capitalist, it features Adorno at his most enigmatic and Olympian:

There is to be found in African students of political economy, Siamese at Oxford, and more generally in diligent art-historians and musicologists of petty-bourgeois origins, a ready inclination to combine with the assimilation of new material, an inordinate respect for all that is established, accepted, acknowledged. An uncompromising mind is the very opposite of primitivism, neophytism, or the "non-capitalist world." It

1

presupposes experience, a historical memory, a fastidious intellect and above all an ample measure of satiety. It has been observed time and again how those recruited young and innocent to radical groups have defected once they felt the force of tradition. One must have tradition in oneself, to hate it properly.[1]

"One must have tradition in oneself, to hate it properly" (*um sie recht zu hassen*). The proposition will no doubt strike many contemporary readers as being noteworthy chiefly for its elitism; and its unabashed cultural supremacism, too, will surely loom to politically progressive thinkers as a liability, embarrassing if not positively reactionary. Cosmopolitan German-Jewish intellectual that he is, Adorno clearly takes it for granted not only that he has "tradition" in him, but also that this "tradition" is the only one worthy of the name. For him, *there are no other traditions*. As Edward Said has observed, for mid-century Euro-American cultural critics like Auerbach, Spitzer, Blackmur – and Adorno – "their culture was in a sense the only culture." "Even in discussions concerning culture in general that seemed to rise above national differences in deference to a universal sphere, hierarchies and ethnic preferences (as between European and non-European) were held to."[2]

The elitism and Eurocentrism of Adorno's position cannot be gainsaid. Yet his standpoint is by no means as uncomplicatedly retrograde as it might initially seem. Indeed, my suggestion in *Nationalism and Cultural Practice in the Postcolonial World* will be that for all the various and ultimately crippling problems that attach to Adorno's own mobilization of it, the Adornian conceit of "hating tradition properly" in fact represents a uniquely illuminating and enabling rubric under which to think in a politically engaged fashion about intellectual and cultural practice today, not only or preeminently in the "First World," nor (correspondingly) merely or preeminently in the "Third World," but globally: athwart, rather than across, the imperial divide in the modern (more specifically: capitalist) world system.

Let me begin my commentary in this Introduction, then, by attempting to tease out some of the wider implications of Adorno's formulation. The problem, as he states it, is not only that "neophytes," intellectuals of "petty-bourgeois origins," and students from the "non-capitalist world" lack tradition, but also that *they fail to disavow it in the right way* even when they *are* belatedly exposed to it. We must be careful, as we rush to criticize the presumptuousness of the first of the claims made here, not to neglect the subversive thrust of the second, whose implicit logic, I believe, radically qualifies – perhaps even overturns – the elitism and Eurocentrism of what precedes it. As we shall see, the enigmatic reflexivity of Adorno's argument is quite remarkable.

In a characteristically cryptic and provocative formulation at the beginning of his essay "Cultural Criticism and Society," written in the 1950s, Adorno proposes that cultural critics must *in principle* presume themselves to be the bearers of "tradition." Such a presumption is, as it were, an objective precondition of critical practice: "the cultural critic can hardly avoid the imputation that he [*sic*] has the culture which culture lacks."[3] At first glance, this might seem a mere rationalization of the elitism of the critic's own standpoint. (It is quite clear, for instance, that Adorno himself is never led to doubt his own critical credentials.) But Adorno's argument is that while the presumption of cultural privilege is a *sine qua non* of criticism, the critic's task ought be to use this privilege *against* culture, to defetishize culture by way of puncturing its elitist pretensions.[4]

The same strategy in argument is also in evidence, I want to suggest, in the fragment in *Minima Moralia* on "hating tradition properly." Adorno insists upon the indispensability of "tradition" not for its vaunted civilizational attributes but because he believes that it is only from the ground of this tradition that the thoroughgoing, preservative yet emancipatory critique of its social conditions of possibility can be staged. The point for Adorno – as it is *not* for Auerbach, Spitzer, or Blackmur – is that while the tradition of European bourgeois humanism has always insisted upon its civility, has always gestured toward – even made a promise of – a universalistically conceived social freedom, it has never delivered on this promise, except, arguably, to the privileged few, and even then only on the basis of the domination of all the others. To hate tradition properly is in these terms very different from championing this exclusive (and excluding: what Raymond Williams called "selective"[5]) tradition; on the contrary, it is to keep faith with true universality, with the idea of a radically transformed social order, and to oppose oneself implacably to the false universality of modern (bourgeois) sociality. It is to use one's relative class privilege to combat all privilege, to shoulder the responsibility of intellectualism by "mak[ing] the moral and, as it were, representative effort to say what most of those for whom [one] say[s] it cannot see."[6] Adorno construes the privilege borne by intellectuals very solemnly. It is "false" inasmuch as it is premised on class domination. But it alone affords the social fraction of which intellectuals are comprised the freedom, the means, the institutionally sanctioned authority, to commit themselves to *thinking* as a sustained and systematic mode of social practice. An "uncompromising mind," we have already seen Adorno asserting, "presupposes . . . an ample measure of satiety." Intellectuals can see, hear, think, and say things that other social agents cannot, not because they are "better men" (*sic*) than they, but because they have been socially endowed with the resources, the status, the symbolic and social capital, to do so. Much the same argument has also been made recently by Pierre Bourdieu, who, like Adorno (from whom he is elsewhere concerned to mark an appropriate distance), pushes it home to a far-reaching conclusion:

among the specific products of the fields of cultural production are all the means of knowledge and objectification . . . which . . . offer to intellectuals the possibility of achieving self-consciousness and of inquiring into the principles of their own practices, interests, and distinterestedness, not least of all their interest *in* disinterestedness. These means of knowledge especially guarantee to them the *privilege* of being able to discover the particular economic and social conditions or, to be perfectly clear, the *privileges* (such as leisure, skholé) that form the basis of their claims to the universal. Thus, provided that they are able to pursue it to the very end . . . this *critical reflexivity* that they monopolize can offer them the means of justifying in practice their wildest claims to the collective monopoly of reason, truth, and virtue: by compelling them to discover the privilege on which their claim to the universal rests, it compels them, indeed, to associate the pursuit of the universal with the perpetual struggle for the *universalization of the privileged conditions of existence* which make the pursuit of the universal possible.[7]

The social figure of the intellectual as Adorno and Bourdieu address it is of course a paradigmatically *modern* one.[8] Bourdieu identifies the exercise of "critical reflexivity" as central to the practice of the intellectual; Adorno speaks of "historical memory" as a prerequisite of the "uncompromising mind." Both features – reflexivity and historical consciousness – are unthinkable outside of the universe of modernity. It is therefore something of a rich irony that, in the enigmatic passage upon which this Introduction is predicated, Adorno should characterize the bearer of these features as one who has *tradition* in him (or her). Clearly, "tradition" is not being used here in its conventional sociological sense, where it stands as the precise *antonym* of modernity. There can be no question about Adorno's familiarity with this standard sociological usagè. Indeed, he deploys the concept of tradition in just the conventional sense elsewhere, most notably in an essay entitled "On Tradition," which begins as follows:

Tradition comes from *tradere*: to hand down. It recalls the continuity of generations, what is handed down by one member to another, even the heritage of handicraft. The image of handing down expresses physical proximity, immediacy – one hand should receive from another. Such immediacy is the more or less natural relation of a familial sort. The category of tradition is essentially feudal . . . Tradition is opposed to rationality, even though the one took shape in the other. Its medium is not consciousness but the pregiven, unreflected and binding existence of social forms – the actuality of the past . . . Tradition in the strict sense is incompatible with bourgeois society.[9]

Anthony Giddens has correctly pointed out that tradition cannot think itself as such. "In traditional societies . . . especially in small oral cultures, 'tradition' is not known as such, because there is nothing that escapes its influence and, therefore, nothing with which to contrast it. 'History' is not understood as the use of the past to mobilize change in the future, but as the repetitiveness of 'reversible time'."[10] Elsewhere Giddens observes that the category of tradition "receives its identity only from the reflexivity of the modern."[11] The concept of "tradition," that is to say, is itself a modern(ist) concept. The point is well taken. But it is evident that in enjoining the critical intellectual to hate tradition properly, Adorno is *not* advocating hostility toward "the actuality of the past" as mediated through "the pregiven, unreflected and binding existence" of (rather than through the "consciousness" of) superseded social or cultural forms. On the contrary, measured along the continuum that stretches between tradition and modernity on the orthodox sociological plane, his injunction must be understood rather as being to hate *modernity* properly. For it is precisely *bourgeois* society, *bourgeois* humanism, *bourgeois* culture that Adorno wishes us to learn to hate in the right way, rigorously and thoroughly – that is to say, to redeem by totalization. And since, as he says, "tradition in the strict sense is incompatible with bourgeois society," it can only be a modern tradition – what we might, indeed, however paradoxically, call *the tradition of modernity* itself – that is for him the fitting object of the critical (or hating) intelligence. Adorno is not merely being perverse here, giving the name of "tradition" to what is conventionally termed "modernity" and distinguished categorically *from* tradition. On the contrary, as in *Dialectic of Enlightenment*, in which Adorno and Max Horkheimer argue that enlightenment reifies itself in (partially) realizing itself, so too in this instance his suggestion is that in the modern era, the social logic of modernity has taken on the attributes of "tradition"; its structures and tendencies have sunk so deeply down into the fabric of social life as to have ceased to be spontaneously intuitable. What tradition is said to have been, modernity has now become – a medium that is no longer reflected upon but is instead uncritically received as pregiven and unalterable.

"[E]nlightenment can only make good its deficits by radicalized enlightenment."[12] Jürgen Habermas's lapidary formulation from *The Philosophical Discourse of Modernity* is anticipated in Adorno's scrupulously Marxist argument that it is only on the basis of a dialectical critique (one that is simultaneously immanent and transcendental in its focus) that the particularism of bourgeois ideology can be exposed and its concrete totalization plausibly imagined. For those opposed to bourgeois class domination, it is necessary, on Adorno's reading, to think *with* modernity *against* modernity. For no other kind of thinking possesses the capacity to drive the historically actualized globality of the existing social order beyond its own ideological limits.

I make this point by way of suggesting that, as with Marx – and Georg Lukács, for whom Marxism represents "the self-knowledge of capitalist society"[13] – the dialectical aspect of Adorno's work resists and confounds the cynical or genealogical supposition that the radical contingency or situatedness of thought (historical, ideological, strategic) serves to render all and any *particular* ideas conformist, in the sense of being so inextricably "of their time" that they are of necessity *internal* to its categorical logic. As Fredric Jameson has cogently pointed out, in an explicit rejoinder to those, like Foucault, who have tended to construe Marxism in suffocatingly historicist terms as "a nineteenth-century philosophy" pure and simple, it would be just as plausible (and might in fact make better sense) to argue that "the dialectic is itself an unfinished project, which anticipates modes of thought and reality that have not yet come into existence even today."[14] The point can be generalized: to hate tradition *properly* is not at all to hate it on its own terms. "Properly," as Adorno uses the term, does not mark a plea for conformity, orderliness, civility, or good manners. Adorno calls for something far more profoundly ruptural, far less contained or, indeed, containable, than this. By the same token, however, the specification that tradition be hated "properly" obviously indicates that it is not enough merely to hate it *thoroughly* (in the sense, for example, that the Luddites might

6

be said to have hated machinery). To hate tradition properly is rather to mobilize its own protocols, procedures, and interior logic against it – to demonstrate that it is only on the basis of a project that exceeds its own horizons or self-consciousness that tradition can possibly be imagined redeeming its own pledges.

Capitalism paradoxically creates the material conditions of possibility for socialism. But it also creates the grounds for, and renders thoroughly irrepressible, a *socialist imaginary*, whose conception of emancipation both negates and preserves the bourgeois conception: preserves it in the sense of affirming what, following Hegel, we might still term its "rationality" and "universalism"; negates it in the sense of recognizing that neither this rationality nor this universalism – henceforth unforgoable – are feasible on the soil of bourgeois society.[15] What is at issue here is, at one level, what Habermas has identified as the "ambivalent content" or, more accurately, the "utopian-ideological double character of bourgeois culture." "In its claims to autonomy and scientific method, to individual freedom and universalism, to radical, romantic self-disclosure," Habermas writes, bourgeois culture

is on the one hand, the result of cultural rationalization – having ceased to rely on the authority of tradition, it is sensitive to criticism and self-criticism. On the other hand, the normative contents of its abstract and ahistorical ideas, overshooting as they do existing social realities, not only support a critically transforming practice by providing some initial guidelines, but also support an affirming and endorsing practice by providing a measure of idealistic transfiguration.[16]

I have suggested that the *de facto* referent of Adorno's injunction to hate tradition properly is not the *pre-modern* world but that of *capitalist modernity*. Conceived thus, the injunction seems to me to serve quite superbly as a heuristic device, making possible a boldly integrative theory of the social logic of contemporary cultural practice at the level of the world system. Yet it is precisely in this latter respect that the weaknesses of Adorno's own mobilization of the idea of "hating tradition properly" become clear-cut. The problem is twofold. First there is the fact that, despite his recognition of the *globality* of capitalist social relations, Adorno tends to view *modernity* as corresponding only to developments in the metropolitan formations of Euro-America. (In a strict sense, indeed, he is so resolutely Eurocentric in his focus as to neglect the significance or irreducibility of developments even in America.) This means that for him, only European subjectivity can be said to be truly modern. Related to this,

7

second, Adorno tends to construe the relationship between theory and practice in somewhat ultra-leftist terms, with the result that the Western working-class's failure to sustain or even consolidate a revolutionary socialist politics in the years and decades following 1917 (or the World War of 1914–18) is taken to signify the definitive miscarriage of the Marxist project.[17]

The great irony of the specifically Adornian (as distinct from the more generally Marxist) notion of "hating tradition properly" might then be said to consist in the fact that between Adorno's time and our own its truth has *manifestly* decentered itself, following the social logics of decolonization and "globalization." My suggestion in the pages that follow will be that recent historical developments have definitively stripped the burden of speaking in the name of humanity at large from such Eurocentrically limited figures as Adorno, and invested it in differently situated intellectuals – those capable of grappling, as Said puts it in *Culture and Imperialism*, with the "new integrative or contrapuntal orientation in history that sees Western and non-Western experiences as belonging together because they are connected with imperialism."[18] When George Orwell wrote in *The Road to Wigan Pier* that "[i]n order to hate imperialism you have got to be part of it," he was writing about himself.[19] Said focuses, however, on such figures as C.L.R. James, Aimé Césaire, George Antonius, S.H. Alatas, Ranajit Guha, Amilcar Cabral, Anouar Abdel-Malek, and Frantz Fanon, radical politico-intellectuals committed to "an imaginative, even utopian vision which reconceives emancipatory . . . theory and performance." Other names could easily be added, starting with that of Said himself: such *novelists*, for instance, as Assia Djebar, Toni Morrison, V.Y. Mudimbe, Gabriel Garcia Marquez, Alejo Carpentier, Nadine Gordimer, Wilson Harris, Pramoedya Ananta Toer, Chinua Achebe, George Lamming, Salman Rushdie, Kazuo Ishiguro. What is striking about the cultural and critical practice of such writers and intellectuals as these is their simultaneous commitment to the "philosophical discourse of modernity" *and* to its urgent critique, their extraordinary command of and respect for the European humanist (or bourgeois) canon existing alongside an equally extraordinary knowledge (and critical endorsement) of other cultural works, social projects, and historical experiences, the necessary consideration of which cannot be accomplished on the provincial soil of the European (or bourgeois) canon. Might it not be *these* figures in whom, paradoxically – since this was the last thing that imperialism was meant to achieve – contemporary history has encoded "tradition," and they, therefore, who, enjoined to find ways to hate it properly, are uniquely placed to do so? This, at least, is my hypothesis.

Nationalism and Cultural Practice in the Postcolonial World is, very obviously, premised upon the conviction that it is more useful to reconstruct by totalization the generative Adornian rubric of "hating tradition properly" than to jettison or relinquish it in any sense. The general point is that for all its admirable criticism of just the kinds of Eurocentrism and cultural supremacism casually exemplified by Adorno, most of the work in the subfields of postcolonial studies and "colonial discourse theory" (and also, I would say, "ethnic studies" and "cultural studies") currently being produced in cutting-edge intellectual circles of Europe and North America seems to me to compare very unfavorably with Adorno's own work, paying a huge price for its own premature repudiation of systematic theory.

It is a commonplace that postcolonial studies – a formation that has emerged and consolidated itself within the Anglo-American academy over the course of the past decade and a half – has from the outset existed in a relationship of supplementarity to that of critical theory in its postmodernist and/or poststructuralist incarnations. This has meant not only that access to the field and – even more – visibility within it, has tended to be contingent on the presentation and display of the appropriate "post-" theoretical credentials, but also that the specific methodological and ideological investments of scholars in the field have tended to be attuned to those of "post-" theory. Hence, for example, Homi Bhabha's asseveration that

the postcolonial perspective resists attempts to provide a holistic social explanation, forcing a recognition of the more complex cultural and political boundaries that exist on the cusp of the . . . often opposed political spheres [of "First" and "Third" Worlds] . . . It is from this hybrid location of cultural value – the transnational *as* the translational – that the postcolonial intellectual attempts to elaborate a historical and literary project.[20]

In its institutionally consecrated forms, at least, the field of postcolonial studies is deeply and constitutively informed by "post-" theoretical protocols and procedures. Such prominent figures in the field as Bhabha, Robert Young, Sara Suleri, and Trinh T. Minh-ha have all written at length to condemn as naive or, worse, tacitly authoritarian, any commitment to universalism, metanarrative, social emancipation, revolution.[21] Yet as Edward Said has recently pointed out in a thought-provoking commentary, the tendential thrusts of "postmodernism" and "postcolonialism" really gesture in quite different directions:

The earliest studies of the post-colonial were by such distinguished thinkers as Anwar Abdel Malek, Samir Amin, C.L.R. James; almost all were based on studies of domination and control made from the standpoint of either a completed political independence or an incomplete liberationist project. Yet whereas post-modernism, in one of its most famous programmatic statements (by Jean-François Lyotard), stresses the disappearance of the grand narratives of emancipation and enlightenment, the emphasis behind much of the work done by the first generation of post-colonial artists and scholars is exactly the opposite: the grand narratives remain, even though their implementation and realization are at present in abeyance, deferred, or circumvented. This crucial difference between the urgent historical and political imperatives of postcolonialism and post-modernism's relative detachments makes for altogether different approaches and results. [22]

As a Marxist critic whose research interests have turned, methodologically, on the articulation of literature and culture with wider social processes, and whose substantive area of focus has mostly been cultural production in the modern "Third World," with a particular emphasis on Africa, my own politico-intellectual investments lie with the definition of "postcolonialism" which Said presents in this passage. The obligation to frame what Henry Louis Gates, Jr., in a felicitous phrase, has termed global "counternarratives of liberation"[23] seems to me, at least, quite transparently as pressing today as it has ever been (if, indeed, it is not more so). In specific terms, accordingly, my ambition in this book is to try to alter somewhat the existing balance of forces in the field of postcolonial studies, by way of making the field as a whole accountable to philosophical and political claims, interests, and demands, to which (to its own detriment) it is currently little attuned. To this end, a few further preliminary observations about the field in general and my own work in this field in particular might be in order.

First, it seems to me that precisely to the extent that the field of postcolonial studies *does* exist in a relationship of supplementarity to "post-" theory, it follows that the steepling and accumulating critiques that have been adduced in recent years against such theory are cogent and telling, too, in the narrower sphere, against what we might call "pomo-poco" scholarship. Over the course of the past six or seven years, especially, there has been a veritable burgeoning of materialist and/or realist and/or Marxist critiques of "post-" theory in its various forms. In detail and in their cumulative thrust, these critiques appear to me to be decisive.[24] At the very least, I believe, they have served to make it incumbent upon "post-" theorists – their own avant-gardist self-understandings notwithstanding – to take cognizance of and attempt to defend their own positions and assumptions against them.

It no longer remotely suffices for "post-" theorists to proceed as though all of their realist opponents were empiricists, all of their materialist opponents essentialists, all of their Marxist or systematizing opponents totalitarians. To argue thus today is chiefly to betray the attenuated nature of one's *own* philosophical understanding. The time is past, I believe, when *anti-* "post-" theoretical (or indeed *post-* "post-" theoretical) initiatives can be dismissed sight-unseen as *pre-* "post-" theoretical.

A second observation concerns the contemporary *trajectory* of postcolonial studies as a field of academic inquiry. This is a subject that has received surprisingly little attention in the voluminous metacritical discourse on "postcoloniality." It is my impression that the field has tilted sharply just recently, as scholars have turned increasingly to the subjects of metahistory and representation, tending to insist upon the epistemological indispensability of the former and the ethico-political undesirability of the latter. It is *Foucault*'s name that one is likely to see cited talismanically in postcolonial criticism these days, whereas a decade ago he would have been obliged to fight for space alongside Lacan and Derrida. Somewhat ironically – given that it was *Orientalism* that may be said to have brought Foucault into the field of postcolonial studies – this late-breaking ascendancy of genealogy does not bespeak the consolidation of Edward Said as the field's dominant critical figure. On the contrary, Said himself seems in his recent work to have retreated somewhat from the overt Foucauldianism of *Orientalism* (which was, in any case, never quite as thoroughgoing as some of his champions and some of his critics have supposed). In fact, *Orientalism* now looms, to me at least, as a relatively atypical Saidian text. Certainly the influence of such figures as Lukács, Adorno, and Williams is much stronger than that of Foucault in the long-awaited *Culture and Imperialism*, which eventually appeared in 1993. But if Said has ceased to be the standard-bearer of a Foucauldian problematic in postcolonial studies, others have stepped forward to to assume this role – among them Ann Laura Stoler, Timothy Mitchell, Nicholas Dirks, Mary Louise Pratt, and, above all, the historians associated with the Subaltern Studies project in its newest, reterritorialized avatar.[25] Moreover, Gayatri Chakravorty Spivak and Homi Bhabha – who might be said to have been co-present with Said at the inception of postcolonial studies in the early 1980s – have both failed to produce any new work of particular significance in the last four or five years.[26] This, too, has enabled genealogy to emerge assertively as the privileged analytical mode in the field today, tending progressively to disturb the purchase of psychoanalysis and deconstruction, with which, respectively, Bhabha and Spivak were closely identified. It is specifically because of this genealogical surge, it seems to me, that the ineluctably (if not exclusively) *historical* questions of modernity and the "West" have latterly begun to bulk large within postcolonial criticism.

This brings me to a third observation, which concerns the conspicuous absence, until very recently, of any credible or legitimated *Marxist* position within the field of postcolonial studies. It is possible to make this point in a number of different ways. One such might be to register the disjuncture that obtains between the reception afforded the work of the major Marxist figures in the wider field of critical theory and that afforded these same figures in the field of post-colonial studies. (The supplementarity of the latter field to the former obviously does not entail the complete heteronomy of its dispositions and discriminations.) Raymond Williams, Terry Eagleton, and Fredric Jameson, for instance, who command considerable prestige within the wider "theory" field, are all severely *deprivileged* in the field of postcolonial studies: there, Williams looms preeminently as a cultural nationalist whose neglect of race and empire are sufficient, on Paul Gilroy's severe reading, to align his work willy-nilly with the reactionary and racist chauvinism of an Enoch Powell;[27] Eagleton positions himself (or at least is said to) as an unreconstructed Irish nationalist, yet to be disabused of his jejune commitment to the project of national liberation; and Jameson, of course, is the author not of a far-reaching and consequential body of work stretching back to the late 1960s, but only of the infamous essay on "Third World Literature in the Era of Multinational Capitalism,"[28] with its scandalous hypothesis concerning the national-allegorical form that *all* "Third World literature" must necessarily assume. The contrast here with Said is instructive: for while Said is unquestionably of the *left*, his repudiation of *Marxism* as a dogmatism is unambiguous. And in the case of Spivak, I shall risk saying that she seems to me "more of a Marxist" in the wider field of critical theory than she is in the narrower field of postcolonial studies: I mean that her pointedly Marxist writings seem to me to situate themselves, for the most part, as interventions into the "theory" field; within the field of postcolonial studies, by contrast, it is as a feminist exponent of deconstruction that she is most visible. (We might speculate, indeed, that her early prominence within this field derived at least partly from her ability to transfer or commute into it the academic capital that she had gained as a deconstructive critic and as the translator into English of Derrida's *Of Grammatology*.)

The fact that postcolonial studies should have constituted itself as an arena of scholarly production within which Marxism occupies a very marginal status obviously poses a special problem for Marxist readers and writers, whose specific investments and stockpiles of knowledge tend to remain unrecognized and undervalued in the field. The temptation, under these circumstances, to repudiate the field *tout court*, to insist upon its fundamental irrelevance, is sometimes irresistible. Hence Aijaz Ahmad begins a recent article on "The Politics of Literary Postcoloniality" by "confessing that the current discussions of postcolonialism in the domain of *literary* theory produce in [him] a peculiar sense of *déjà vu*, even a degree of fatigue."[29] Observing – correctly – that "postcolonialism" used to be a rubric under which, within the disciplines of sociology and political science, questions of social reconstruction in the newly decolonized states of Africa and Asia were discussed, he writes that

Now as this same term resurfaces in literary theory, without even a trace of memory of that earlier debate, I am reminded of something that the Cuban-American critic, Roman de la Campa, said to me in conversation, to the effect that "postcoloniality" is postmodernism's wedge to colonise literatures outside Europe and its North American offshoots – which I take the liberty to understand as saying that what used to be known as "Third World literature" gets rechristened as "postcolonial literature" when the governing theoretical framework shifts from Third World nationalism to postmodernism.[30]

Now I have already published an extended critique of this argument that the trajectory of metropolitan literary theory from the 1960s to the present corresponds to a passage from Third Worldist cultural nationalism to postmodernism, an argument that Ahmad develops and seeks to defend in his controversial, powerful, but deeply flawed book, *In Theory*. I do not plan to rehearse that critique here: suffice it to say that I am not persuaded by the general case that Ahmad lays out for the symmetry between Third Worldist cultural nationalism and the contemporary projections of "post-" theory, a symmetry that turns, on his reading, on their status as modal alternatives within the same broadly Maoist problematic.[31] Instead, I want to note that Ahmad is the notable exception to the case I have just been making about the relative invisibility of Marxism within the field of postcolonial studies. *In Theory*, an avowedly Marxist work, was published to considerable fanfare by Verso in 1992 (its back cover embossed, incidentally, with Eagleton's encomium to the effect that "some radical critics may have forgotten about Marxism; but Marxism, in the shape of Ahmad's devastating, courageously unfashionable critique, has not forgotten about them"). The book itself took on the very public figures of Said and Salman Rushdie in the most spectacularly polemical manner, and sparked something of a firestorm of controversy in Britain and the United States. A whole issue of the influential journal, *Public Culture*, was devoted to a discussion of it.[32] It is not only my students, graduate and undergraduate, who today read Ahmad alongside Said, Spivak, and Bhabha in their courses on postcolonialism. Ahmad has come to stand *for* Marxism in the field of postcolonial studies.

But precisely *this* seems to me to intensify the problem of Marxism in this field. It is a problem that I have found it particularly difficult to think myself beyond. The point is that while I, too, write explicitly as a Marxist, and therefore share many general assumptions with Ahmad and identify with a good number (though by no means all) of his specific judgments, I find the *mode* of his position-taking deeply troubling, which means that – to the degree that Ahmad is held to *represent* Marxism in the field – I find not only the marginality but also the objective registration of Marxism there unsatisfactory. The more I think about Ahmad's mode of position-taking – with its polemicism, its sweeping reductionism, its cultural insiderism, its romantic, not to say masculinist, rhetoric of purity and contamination – the more convinced I become as to its strategic ill-advisedness, and the less attractive it seems to me either as a model worthy of emulation or even as a pole of ideological identification.

In "East Isn't East," Said proposes (against the grain of postcolonial criticism's *own* self-understanding, to be sure) that we might read the heavy "emphasis on the local, regional, and contingent" that we find "in much of the best post-colonial work that has proliferated so dramatically since the early 1980s" as being "connected in its general approach to a universal set of concerns, all of them relating to emancipation, revisionist attitudes towards history and culture, a widespread use of recurring theoretical models and styles. A leading motif has been the consistent critique of Eurocentrism and patriarchy."[33] Unlike Ahmad, it seems to me that the Marxist theorist in the field of postcolonial studies would be best served were he or she to begin both by conceding to the field the authentic insights and advances that have been generated within it, and to committing himself or herself never to fall behind these. But on the basis of new work that has appeared over the course of the past few years – by such theorists as Tim Brennan, Laura Chrisman, Annie Coombes, Arif Dirlik, Peter Hulme, Geeta Kapur, Neil Larsen, Satya P. Mohanty, Supriya Nair, Benita Parry, Modhumita Roy, E. San Juan, Jr., Michael Sprinker, Achin Vanaik, and others[34] – I believe that it has today become possible, *for the first time since the field was instituted in the early 1980s,* for Marxist scholars to engage postcolonial studies on its own ground. It has today become possible, that is, for Marxist scholars to *oblige* the field to tilt in the direction they favor: the burden is to demonstrate, through means of a concerted critical performance that even non-Marxists in the field will have no choice but to acknowledge and grant credence to – in other words, through means of what Habermas has famously dubbed "the unforced force of the better argument" – that the conceptual reach of Marxism is superior to that of the problematics currently prevailing in the field. This, at least, is the *aspiration* that fires my project in the pages that follow. Whether I have succeeded in any respect, and to what extent, I must leave it to my readers to determine.

Modernity, globalization, and the "West"

In *Postmodernism, or, the Cultural Logic of Late Capitalism*, Fredric Jameson suggests that with its propensities toward "infinite expansion," capitalism "may be said to reinvent history in a new way, and also to constitute an incomparable and hitherto novel form of social imperialism."[1] My argument in this chapter takes as its point of departure this inherited Marxist understanding that capitalism – from this standpoint the foundational category for *any* credible theory of modern society[2] – is unprecedented as an historical formation both in its global *extension* as a mode of production and in its *intensive* saturation of social relations, in terms of which the logic of abstract equivalence (a logic corresponding to the material instance of generalized commodity production) writes itself upon social practice in general. What Jameson calls the "social imperialism" inaugurated by capitalism entails the progressive integration of the world system as such – along the axes of both "breadth" (combined and uneven development, the articulation of modes of production) and "depth" (the traversing not only of the sphere of production and the civic domain, but also of what Stuart Hall, in an arresting metaphor, once referred to as "the Maginot Lines of our subjectivities")[3] – under the dominant rubrics of commodity production and socialized wage labor.[4] The singularity of capitalism as an historical formation consists precisely in this relentless and almost irresistible tendency toward *universalization*.

My commitment to this received Marxist understanding – both systematic and totalizing – will doubtless strike at least some of my prospective readers as counter-intuitive or even perverse. Nor am I thinking in purely abstract terms here, of "readers in general." On the contrary, I have in mind a quite specific set of interlocutors: readers, clustered for the most part in social science, humanities, and cultural studies departments in the universities of Europe and North America, who would be likely to define themselves as politically progressive, and who might even be willing to endorse my initial emphasis on the universalizing propensities of capitalism (above all with respect to capitalism in its contemporary, putatively "globalized," avatar), but who would emphatically *not* be prepared to concede either that the global character assumed historically by capitalism *requires* that we develop concepts adequate to its systematicity, or – even more pointedly – that the Marxist concepts of "totality" and "universalism" are concepts of just this kind, bespeaking a social imperative that drives beyond capitalism in its historical and actually existing forms. For if there is any single assumption that can plausibly be said to command a consensus level of assent among this particular imagined community of readers, it must be that, as Agnes Heller and Ferenc Feher have put it, we have come to the "twilight of radical universalism,"[5] the end of the road for all universalistically conceived projects of social and political emancipation. From the standpoint of these readers, recent world developments – most notably the economic restructuring of the years since the late 1960s and the political events of 1989 – are taken to have marked a rupture of epochal proportions. "According to a certain apocalyptic litany," as Gregory Elliott has written in a spirited critique of this widely accepted assessment, "the final decade of the second millennium AD signals the death of Communism and socialism, the passing of the working class, the waning of industrial society, even – most portentously of all – the end of history."[6] In their wake, we are told, it is now necessary to recognize the obsolescence of the received modes not only of political practice but also of social analysis, not least the established critiques – whether liberal or Marxist – of capitalism.

Such claims find ready representation in every quarter of the academy today, not least in the work of avowedly progressive writers. In responding to them, one might plausibly begin at the level of metatheory, by pointing to the irony of the fact that, notwithstanding its own avant-gardist pretensions, the rhetoric of "New Times" or of "post-" or "endist" thought in its various guises (postmodernism, postindustrialism, the end of ideology, the end of history, etc.) tends to recapitulate a dominant theme in the self-understanding of *modernity*. If, as Jürgen Habermas has shown, the basic figure in the "philosophical discourse of modernity" is a conception of the present as dislocated from the past and open to the future, this figure tends to reproduce itself and proliferate *within* the horizon of "the modern" itself, inasmuch as the present is under constant pressure to (re-)imagine itself as a new beginning:

> Because the new, the modern world is distinguished from the old by the fact that it opens itself to the future, the epochal new beginning is rendered constant with each moment that gives birth to the new. Thus, it is characteristic of the historical consciousness of modernity to set off "the most recent [*neuesten*] period" from the modern [*neu*] age: Within the horizon of the modern age, the present enjoys a prominent position as contemporary history. Even Hegel understands "our age" as "the most recent period." He dates the beginning of the present from the break that the Enlightenment and the French Revolution signified for the more thoughtful contemporaries at the close of the eighteenth and the start of the nineteenth century . . . A present that understands itself from the horizon of the modern age as the actuality of the most recent period has to recapitulate the break brought about with the past as a *continuous renewal.*[7]

From the outset, there has been a latent tendency in modern(ist) thought to overstate both the radical novelty and the consequentiality of contemporary events, to annunciate these in the light of an epochal rupture that splits past irrevocably from present, stripping the former of continuing relevance and the latter of precedent. Hence Walter Benjamin, for example, whose "Theses on the Philosophy of History" labor so urgently to will the present into being as a messianic "time of the now," in which the continuum of history is exploded and the present stands suspended in mid-air, as it were, between the now irrevocable ground of developmental time and the as-yet-unknowable place to which its own "dialectical" "leap in the open air of history" has propelled it.[8] In much of the scholarship being produced today, this recurrent modernist gesture is repeated – but (in strict though apparently unwitting accord with modernity's own conventions) *as though for the first time.* Thus Martin Albrow (to reference just one figure in a broad and internally differentiated intellectual movement with literally hundreds of adherents) proposes in his recent book, *The Global Age,* that "modernity" has today been supplanted by "globality," and that this development entails "an overall change in the basis of action and social organization for individuals and groups."[9] For Albrow, "globalization, far from being the latest stage of a long process of development," might best be grasped as corresponding to "the arrest of what was taken for granted, a transformation arising out of a combination of different forces which unexpectedly changes the direction of history." It marks "the transition to a new era rather than the apogee of the old."[10] Or consider Eric Hobsbawm's suggestion, in a 1992 article entitled "The Crisis of Today's Ideologies," that the "events of recent years" have been not only "spectacular and world-changing," but altogether without historical precedent:

Never before in history has ordinary human life, and the societies in which it takes place, been so radically transformed in so short a time; not merely within a single lifetime, but within part of a lifetime . . . [H]uman societies, and the relations of people within them, have undergone a sort of economic, technological and sociological earthquake within the lifetime of people who have barely got beyond middle age. There has never before been anything like it in world history, for . . . these are not localized or regional changes but global ones – even though their specific impact differs from one country to another.[11]

Conspicuously absent from Hobsbawm's analysis is the category of *capitalism*. "What I am saying," he writes, "is that the crisis we find ourselves in is not specific to this or that economic or political or ideological system, but general."[12] In Hobsbawm's account of the current conjuncture (which is widely representative in just this respect), transformation is ubiquitous, but appears to have no material foundation. Against this presentist and discontinuist vision of history, I want to propose the strict *commensurability* of recent developments with the distinctive social logic of capital as already described by Marx and Engels in the *Communist Manifesto* of 1848: the "[c]onstant revolutionizing of production, uninterrupted disturbance of all social conditions, everlasting uncertainty and agitation [that] distinguish the bourgeois epoch from all earlier ones."[13] The point is that the years since 1968 – so often cited as the year zero of "endism" and "post-" thought alike – seem to me to have borne witness not to any putative transcendence or leaving behind of capitalist modernity but, on the contrary, to a *consolidation* of the historical patterns of bourgeois class domination. This consolidation is indexed by such features as the expansion of inter-imperialist conflict and the rise of new sub-imperialist powers, the sharpening of market coercion in the former Soviet bloc and elsewhere through means of the imposition of IMF- or World Bank-managed austerity or "structural adjustment" programs, and the so-called "race to the bottom" – the ongoing capitalist-sponsored downward leveling of living conditions on a world-wide scale – which has brought in its wake heightened instability and political conflict (often crystallizing around ethnic nationalist, neo-traditionalist, and fascist movements) and the restructuring of the international division of labor.[14]

We will need in this chapter to examine in some detail the structural and historical determinants of the current conjuncture. Before moving on to do so, however, it might be helpful for us to dwell a little longer on the question of "modernity" as a philosophical category. In particular, I would like to discuss the analysis of modernity that we encounter in the work of the influential British sociologist, Anthony Giddens. For Giddens's presentation – above all in his 1990 book, *The Consequences of Modernity* – holds profound implications for debates about Marxism, universalization, and "the West" that are currently taking place in the fields of social, cultural, and postcolonial studies. The first point that we must register about *The Consequences of Modernity* in this respect is already signaled by its title: the object of Giddens's investigation is not *capitalism*, and not even *capitalist modernity*, but rather *modernity* as such. It is not that Giddens neglects the role of capitalism in the constitution of modern society. But he situates it as only one of a constellation of relatively autonomous instances that together determine the trajectory of the modern age:

Do we now live in a capitalist order? Is industrialism the dominant force shaping the institutions of modernity? Should we rather look to the rationalised control of information as the chief underlying characteristic? I shall argue that these questions cannot be answered in this form – that is to say, we should not regard these as mutually exclusive characterisations. Modernity, I propose, is *multidimensional on the level of institutions*, and each of the elements specified by these various traditions plays some part.[15]

On any Marxist reading, as Achin Vanaik has recently pointed out, *capitalist* industrialization would be held to constitute "the fundamental process of modernity."[16] Giddens, however, thinks of capitalism and industrialization (and rationalization) as comprising distinct institutional clusters. He defines modernity through reference to them all: for him, the term names the historically specific sociocultural matrix shaped by the emergence, diffusion, and interpenetration of these institutional clusters. He refers, thus, to "modes of social life or organisation which emerged in Europe from about the seventeenth century onwards and which subsequently became more or less worldwide in their influence" (*Consequences*, p. 1); and he observes of these modes of social life that they:

have swept us away from *all* traditional types of social order, in quite unprecedented fashion. In both their extensionality and their intensionality the transformations involved in modernity are more profound than most sorts of change characteristic of prior periods. On the extensional plane they have served to establish forms of social interconnection which span the globe; in intensional terms they have come to alter some of the most intimate and personal features of our day-to-day existence. (pp. 4–5)

Giddens emphasizes the singularity and world-historical significance of the advent of "modernity." In *The Nation-State and Violence,* he writes that while he does not wish "to deny the importance of transitions or ruptures in previous eras," he *does* want to argue that

> originating in the West but becoming more and more global in their impact, there has occurred a series of changes of extraordinary magnitude when compared with any other phases of human history. What separates those living in the modern world from all previous types of society, and all previous epochs of history, is more profound than the continuities which connect them to the longer spans of the past.[17]

He insists, accordingly, that the modern order "is *not* just one civilisation among others" (*Consequences*, p. 51). The *qualitative* claim being made here (concerning the unprecedentedness and radical difference of the modern order) strikes me as being of indispensable value. But I want to put pressure here on Giddens's rather Weberian supposition that modernity can indeed be addressed adequately as a "civilization." My feeling is that the inevitable result of this supposition is a dematerialized understanding of modernity as being in a fundamental or primary sense a sort of *cultural* disposition.

It is with respect to the question of the "Western-ness" of modernity that the liabilities of Giddens's construction of modernity-as-civilization are most starkly apparent. In the famous opening lines of his Introduction to *The Protestant Ethic and the Spirit of Capitalism,* Max Weber had set up the problem as follows: "A product of modern European civilization, studying any problem of universal history, is bound to ask himself to what combination of circumstances the fact should be attributed that in Western civilization, and in Western civilization only, cultural phenomena have appeared which (as we like to think) lie in a line of development having *universal* significance and value."[18] Weber, of course, "answered" his own question by asserting the obviousness and integrity of the connection between "Western civilization" and "rationality." Following his general lead but breaking with his example, the "modernization theorists" of the 1950s and 1960s tended, as Habermas has pointed out in a brilliant analysis, to "perform . . . two abstractions on Weber's concept of 'modernity'." Modernization theory "dissociates 'modernity' from its modern European origins and stylizes it into a spatio-temporally neutral model for processes of social development in general. Further, it breaks the internal connections between modernity and the historical context of Western rationalism, so that processes of modernization can no longer be conceived of as rationalization, as the historical objectification of rational structures" (*Philosophical Discourse*, p. 2).

Hence modernization theory's propensity to cast modernity as a civilizational force – the "historical equivalent," as Jeffrey Alexander has written, of "a world religion, which relativizes it, on the one hand, and suggests the possibility of selective indigenous appropriation, on the other."[19] Alexander cites an exemplary passage in which S.N. Eisenstadt – a scholar of repute occupying a position close to the center of the modernization theory project – argues that

Instead of perceiving modernization as the final stage in the fulfillment of the evolutionary potential common to all societies – of which the European experience was the most important and succinct manifestation and paradigm – modernization (or modernity) should be viewed as one specific civilization or phenomenon. Originating in Europe, it has spread in its economic, political, and ideological aspects all over the world.[20]

Giddens, too, asks himself Weber's question about the "Westernness" of modernity. He sees it, however, as representing not one question but several, since it is necessary to consider "various analytically separable features of modernity" (*Consequences*, p. 174). If we consider the "organizational complexes" of the "*nation state*" and "*systematic capitalist production*," he observes, we can only answer the question as to whether modernity is "distinctively a Western project in terms of the ways of life fostered by these two great transformative agencies" in the affirmative (pp. 174–75). The question as to whether "the reflexive knowledge fundamental to [the] . . . dynamic character" of modernity is "distinctively Western" also "has to be answered affirmatively, although with certain definite qualifications" (p. 175). But modernity *cannot* be considered "peculiarly Western from the standpoint of its globalizing tendencies" because "we are speaking here of emergent forms of world interdependence and planetary consciousness," and "[t]he ways in which these issues are approached and coped with . . . will inevitably involve conceptions and strategies derived from non-Western settings" (p. 175).

These answers strike me as being patently insufficient. To begin with, Giddens's standpoint on the matter of modernity's *globalizing* propensities flatters only to deceive. Certainly, it might be said to represent an improvement on modernization theory insofar as it insists on the fundamental *difference* between the modern order and any historically prior universalizing project (such as Christianity or Islam). But because Giddens – like Weber but *unlike* the modernization theorists – continues to suppress or decenter the determining instance of capitalism *within* modernity, he proves incapable of accounting plausibly for this difference in structural-historical terms. And when he comes to speak about the *institutional* dimensions of modernity – the nation-state and "systematic capitalist production" – and the forms of social life engendered by them, he can, again like Weber, only read their globalization under the sign of the universalization of the *West*.

Such a reading can be faulted on several counts. Concerning capitalism, it is clear that for Giddens it has remained *essentially* a "Western" instance over the course of the past 500 years – and this notwithstanding its own ceaseless historical reconstruction and the vagaries, complexities, and contradictions that have attended its geographical dispersion across the globe (multiple and various forms of resistance, imposition, recuperation, accommodation, modification, etc.). The essentialist assumption here, as V.G. Kiernan, writing in a different context, once put it very succinctly, is that those who happen to be "first in the field with decisive innovations in technology are entitled to a perpetual primacy."[21] As Jameson has noted,

[t]he perfection of the grand machinery of capitalism (including its industry) is surely not some personal merit in the white (and often Protestant) northern Europeans: it is an accident of historical circumstances and structures (or conditions of possibility), about which it ought to be a tautology to add that in it "the educators" were by definition themselves already "reeducated," since among the other technologies capitalism produces and develops is also the human one: the production of "productive labor." (*Postmodernism*, pp. 381–82)

But we can criticize the conceptualization that underlies Giddens's glossing of "capitalist production" in terms of the category of the "West" more radically than this. We might insist, firstly, that if we *are* going to trace capitalism to its origins and argue for its *essential* constitution there, then we ought at least, for precision's sake, to parse it through reference to southeastern England rather than the "West," since, strictly speaking, capitalism had its origins not in "Europe," nor, more narrowly, in "*northwestern* Europe," nor even in "England," but rather in a specific and localized region *of* England. The selfsame process of universalization that produced the "West" as the orbit of "capitalist production" also produced the "trans-Western" form of the modern world system. There are no good reasons for arguing that while capitalism spread more or less "organically" from its point of origin in England to "Europe," its subsequent development must be referred forever to this continental locus. This is both counter-intuitive and historically distorting (inasmuch as it fails to reckon with the constitutive role of the "non-West" in the production of the "West" itself, that is to say, with the "always-already" integrated character of the world system as such): it amounts, in fact, to a fetishization of the "West." Hence Jan Nederveen Pieterse's recent observation that Giddens's theory of modernity (and other theories like it) is "[i]n effect ... a theory of Westernization by another name, which replicates all the problems associated with Eurocentrism: a narrow window on the world, historically and culturally. With this agenda it should be called Westernization and not globalization ... [It] turns into or becomes an annex of modernization theory."[22]

We might also object to Giddens's construction of modernity as a "Western" project, secondly, on the grounds that it runs together and confuses a formal social logic with a civilizational abstraction. As Giddens addresses the matter, capitalist modernity was, as it were, "Western" before it was global in its tendential social thrust. For him, in other words, the world beyond the boundaries of Europe was, for a time at least – and perhaps remains – *non-modern in the era of modernity*; or (to put it in spatial terms), modernity was "elsewhere" from the standpoint of the "non-West." In *The Nation-State and Violence*, Giddens approvingly cites Immanuel Wallerstein's observation (directed against modernization theory) to the effect that "[w]e do not live in a modernizing world but in a capitalist world"; and he adds that, for Wallerstein, "[t]he so-called 'modernizing societies' today are not countries that have not yet caught up with the processes of development witnessed in the West. They have been, and are, shaped by their involvement in global economic relationships stemming from the world-wide reach of capitalism."[23] But it is difficult to square this insight with Giddens's conclusions concerning the "Western-ness" of modernity. For the idea that underlies Wallerstein's project (and also that of Marx, I believe) is that capitalism must be understood as tendentially a *world system* from the outset: in other words, what it inaugurated was a concrete universality (structured in dominance and unevenness), without an "outside" – the point being that the "peripheries" of the world system are *intra*-systemic, not beyond its purview. Jameson insists that such a conception, which "posits and presupposes the absolute difference of capitalism itself,"

24

"no longer involves any kind of Eurocentrism" (*Postmodernism*, p. 382). This point is, obviously, hugely consequential. To conceptualize capitalism as a world system is to situate modernity as its action-horizon, such that, "even if before there were histories – many of them, and unrelated – now there is tendentially only one" (p. 380). This is a *modern*, but not a *Western* history. Nor does it suppose that the "development" that has marked the history of the West *within* modernity corresponds to the telos *of* modernity. On the contrary, (capitalist) modernity is characterized by unevenness: that is, by the dynamics of development and underdevelopment, autocentricity and dependency, the production and entrenchment of localisms (to a point approaching irreducibility) within larger processes of globaliz-ation, incorporation, and homogenization. In the capitalist world system, we are all modern subjects, which is not to say that we are all "modern*ist*" or "*Western*" ones.

The *locus classicus* of this conception of (capitalist) modernity is to be found in Marx's *Grundrisse*, of which Ranajit Guha gives a brilliant reading in his essay, "Colonialism in South Asia: A Dominance without Hegemony and Its Historiography."[24] Referring to the "uni-versalizing tendency of capital," Guha notes that it "derives from the self-expansion of capital. Its function is to create a world market, subjugate all antecedent modes of production, and replace all jural and institutional concomitants of such modes and generally the entire edifice of precapitalist cultures by laws, institutions, values, and other elements of a culture appropriate to bourgeois rule" (pp. 13–14). Read in isolation, this formulation might seem to confirm the Eurocentrism with which many contemporary critics have charged Marx and Marxism. Indeed, as Guha points out, it does not in itself even serve to distinguish Marx's position from that of "any of the myriad nineteenth-century liberals who saw nothing but the positive side of capital in an age when it was growing from strength to strength and there seemed to be no limit to its expansion and capacity to transform nature and society" (p. 15). A second step is therefore crucial, one that involves a cognitive break with the fundamental assumption of liberal analyses, namely, the assumption of the conti-nuity of capitalism and its extension into all possible futures. On Guha's reading, this step drives Marxist theory, via a rigorous theor-etical and practical commitment to universalization, beyond the limits of capitalist development. Marx's argument, he writes,

is not about expansion alone, but about an expansion predicated firmly and inevitably on limitations capital can never overcome; not simply about a project powered by the possibility of infinite development, but a project predicated on the certainty of its failure to realize itself . . . Nothing could be more explicit and indeed more devastating than this critique of the universalist pretensions of capital. It is a critique which distinguishes itself unmistakably from liberalism by a perspective extended well beyond the rule of capital. The continuity of the latter is a fundamental presupposition in every variety of liberal thought, whereas [the *Grundrisse*] . . . envisages the development of capital's universalist tendency to a stage where it "will drive towards its own suspension."

(pp. 15–16)

Guha points out that "the discrepancy between the universalizing tendency of capital as an ideal and the frustration of that tendency in reality" served Marx as "a measure of the contradictions of [the] Western bourgeois societies of his time" (p. 16). Samir Amin argues, similarly, that "capitalism has proposed a homogenization of the world that it cannot achieve."[25] Such formulations enable us not only to criticize the theorizations of those, like Giddens, for whom the question of the universalization of capitalist modernity is in the final analysis only answerable through reference to the universalization of "the West," but also to distance ourselves from the work of those contemporary scholars who respond to such theorizations by taking their authority at face value, only to infer that it is therefore necessary to disavow not just their problematic but the very episteme upon which it is predicated. In *The Philosophical Discourse of Modernity*, Habermas refers to an "anarchist" strain in contemporary thought which does not critique the partiality of rationalist or modernist thought but affirms such thought's own universalist pretensions, only in order immediately to disavow rationality and modernity and, indeed, universalism themselves. For these "anarchist" theorists, Habermas writes, not just Weber's Occidentalism but reason itself "becomes unmasked as the subordinating and at the same time itself subjugated subjectivity, as the will to instrumental mastery." The misguided attempt then becomes to "pull . . . away the veil of reason from before the sheer will to power" (p. 4).

It is in these terms that I would situate the *most recent* work to have appeared under the historiographic imprimatur of "Subaltern Studies," for example. The situation is somewhat ironic, for Ranajit Guha himself stands as the central figure in the founding of the Subaltern Studies collective in the late 1970s and early 1980s. Yet the work being produced under the rubric of Subaltern Studies today is predicated upon historico-philosophical assumptions distinctly different from those that have animated all of Guha's work, from *Elementary Aspects*

26

of Peasant Insurgency in Colonial India (1983) onwards.[26] Consider, thus, the crusading 1992 article, entitled "Postcoloniality and the Artifice of History: Who Speaks for 'Indian' Pasts?" in which Dipesh Chakrabarty calls for a "provincializing" of the principle of "Europe" in the writing of history. Chakrabarty argues that "insofar as the academic discourse of history . . . is concerned, 'Europe' remains the sovereign, theoretical subject of all histories, including the ones we call 'Indian,' 'Chinese,' 'Kenyan,' and so on. There is a peculiar way in which all these other histories tend to become variations on a master narrative that could be called 'the history of Europe'."[27] As a critique of colonialist or elitist – or, indeed, Giddensian – historiography, this claim would be unimpeachable. But the distinctive force of Chakrabarty's argument derives from his determination to prosecute it against "history" (and "social science") *as such*. Like the Moroccan writer and critic Abdelkebir Khatibi, with whose deconstructive call for the "decolonization of Arab sociology" his own position has much in common,[28] Chakrabarty considers that "history" and "social science" are *constitutively* Eurocentric: the social philosophy that "read[s] into European history an entelechy of universal reason . . . [is] the self-consciousness of social science" as such ("Postcoloniality," p. 3). From the standpoint of "history" or "social science," Chakrabarty claims, "[o]nly 'Europe' . . . is *theoretically* (i.e., at the level of the fundamental categories that shape historical thinking) knowable; all other histories are matters of empirical research that fleshes out a theoretical skeleton which is substantially 'Europe'" (p. 3).

Concerning Marx and Marxism, Chakrabarty pays lip service to Guha's conceptualization of the radical *difference* of the *Grundrisse* – the degree to which Marx's concepts and methods break decisively with those of bourgeois science. "Marx's vision of emancipation," he concedes, "entailed a journey beyond the rule of capital, in fact beyond the notion of juridical equality that liberalism holds so sacred" (p. 4). Yet Chakrabarty expressly relegates this fact, which for Guha is of epochal significance, to the status of a "parenthesis." "Marx's methodological/epistemological statements have not always successfully resisted historicist readings. There has always remained enough ambiguity in these statements to make possible the emergence of 'Marxist' historical narratives" (p. 4). And it quickly becomes apparent that for Chakrabarty such "historicist" narratives are ultimately defining of Marxism: for he goes on to produce a reading of Marx's writings that collapses them seamlessly into (Eurocentric) "history":[29]

The coming of the bourgeois or capitalist society, Marx argues in the *Grundrisse* and elsewhere, gives rise for the first time to a history that can be apprehended through a philosophical and universal category, "capital." History becomes, for the first time, *theoretically* knowable. All past histories are now to be known (theoretically, that is) from the vantage point of this category, that is in terms of their differences from it. Things reveal their categorical essence only when they reach their fullest development, or as Marx put it in that famous aphorism of the *Grundrisse*: "Human anatomy contains the key to the anatomy of the ape." The category "capital" . . . contains within itself the legal subject of Enlightenment thought.　　　　　　　　　　　　　　　　　　　　　　　　　　　　(pp. 3–4)

Thus where Marx, in his Introduction to the *Grundrisse*, had written that "[b]ourgeois society is the most developed and the most complex historic organization of production,"[30] Chakrabarty responds: "For 'capital' or 'bourgeois,' I submit, read 'Europe'" (p. 4).

In this formulation (representative, as I have already hinted, not merely of Chakrabarty's own thought but of a leading strain within contemporary social and cultural theory), the idealist inclination to replace a concrete *ideological* specification ("bourgeois," "capitalist") with a pseudo-geographical one ("Europe," "the West") is elevated to the status of a methodological principle. Chakrabarty admits that his mobilization of the concept of "Europe" is, as he puts it, "hyper-real." "Europe" for him is the name not of a continent but of an epistemo-political imperative: this "Europe," he writes, "reified and celebrated in the phenomenal world of everyday relationships of power as the scene of the birth of the modern, continues to dominate the discourse of history" (p. 2). Indeed, on his reading, "Europe" more than *dominates* the discourse of history: it saturates it. There is no historical discourse that is not centered on this "Europe." Chakrabarty's argument is not, he explains, that "the reason/science/universals which help define Europe as the modern are simply 'culture-specific' and therefore only belong to the European cultures" (p. 20). Rather, his project is to document and explain "how – through what historical process – [Enlightenment] 'reason,' which was not always self-evident to everyone, has been made to look 'obvious' far beyond the ground where it originated." And what is true of Enlightenment reason is true, for him, of modernity itself: "If a language, as has been said, is but a dialect backed up by an army, the same could be said of the narratives of 'modernity' that, almost universally today, point to a certain 'Europe' as the primary habitus of the modern" (pp. 20–21).

But against Chakrabarty I want to insist that at least one crucial modern narrative of modernity – the Marxist one – does *not* point in this direction. Chakrabarty fails to accord the instance of capitalism *within* modernity due centrality: in this sense his argument is ironically reminiscent of Giddens's. But he also fails to reckon with the unprecedentedness, the *difference* of (capitalist) modernity from all previous universalizing projects: in this sense his argument is not the equal of Giddens's. To propose the "provincializing" of "Europe" is both to dematerialize capitalist modernity and to misrecognize its world-historical significance. (The identical mistake is made, in a different quarter, by Zygmunt Bauman when he characterizes "European civilization" as "that locally conceived civilization which in its global hubris and ecumenical ambition called itself 'modernity'."[31]) Chakrabarty wrongly assumes the internality of Marxism to (liberal) "modernist" narratives of modernity.[32] His critique is directed against a progressivist or historicist conception of modernity – one that privileges "the West" and views the "non-West" as its non-modern remainder. And such a conception, I have been trying to argue, sits very poorly with Marx's paradigmatic insistence on the globality of capitalism as an historical formation.

Let us turn, now, to the question of the structural determinants of the current conjuncture. There is widespread agreement among theorists of all political persuasions that any periodization of the half century between 1945 and the present needs to be hinged around the economic recession and attendant political crisis that set in toward the end of the 1960s. Few would disagree, for instance, with Immanuel Wallerstein's general suggestion that the economics of the period since 1945:

> are in broad outline easy to expound. There was a major expansion of the capitalist world-economy following the end of the Second World War. It came to an end perhaps in 1967, perhaps in 1973. It was the greatest single expansion in the history of this world-system going back to 1500 (measured by any of the usual criteria, except that of expansion of land area included within the world-economy) . . . For all the standard economic reasons, this expansion came to an end and has been followed by an economic stagnation.[33]

The question, however, of how *precisely* to characterize this sequence of expansion and crisis – and more particularly of how to theorize the articulation of the two phases – has been the subject of fierce debate. Wallerstein's evocation of "all the standard economic reasons" suggests his openness to a cyclical theory of capitalist development. He argues in fact that the period of expansion was "fueled by relative monopolies in a few leading products for which the rate of profit was high, and the surplus-value of which was very unequally distributed, socially and geographically" and that this period came to an end

because the relative monopolies were eroded by entry into the world market of a large number of competitors, seeking to get on the bandwagon. It came to an end as well because of declining profitability, caused by rising retention of the surplus-value, both by direct producers and by managerial strata. The result was a severe decline in profit rates . . . relatively high worldwide unemployment of wage workers; acute politicized competition among core countries for the tighter world market; increased economic suffering in many sectors and . . . a sense in many sectors that they are suffering by comparison with the previous . . . period; increased world concentration of capital . . . geographical relocation of production processes; and a search for product innovations.[34]

One fruitful approach to the periodization of postwar capitalism – "sociological" rather than "economic" in the strict, disciplinary sense – is that represented by the French "regulationist school" of political economy. The regulationists construe the postwar phases of expansion and crisis as relatively distinct modes of accumulation, each entailing its own specific regime of social reproduction. A key meta-theoretical premise of their approach is that, in Alain Lipietz's words, every regime of accumulation will be "materialized in the shape of norms, habits, laws and regulating networks which ensure the unity of the process and which guarantee that its agents conform more or less to the schema of reproduction in their day-to-day behaviour and struggles."[35] In general terms the regulationist argument is that the stabilization of capitalism in the core economies of Western Europe and the United States in the immediate postwar period was secured on the basis of a predominantly *Fordist* regime of accumulation. Postwar Fordism, as Simon Clarke has explained in surveying this line of argument, is understood by the regulationists as being based

on the mass production of homogeneous products, using the rigid technology of the assembly line with dedicated machines and standardized (Taylorist) work routines. Increased productivity is attained through economies of scale as well as the deskilling, intensification and homogenization of labor. This gives rise to the mass worker, organized in bureaucratic trade-unions which negotiate uniform wages that grow proportionately with productivity increases. Homogeneous consumption patterns reflect the homogenization of production and provide a market for standardized commodities, while rising wages provide growing demand to match the growing supply. The overall balance between supply and demand is achieved through Keynesian macroeconomic policies, while the overall balance between wages and profits is achieved through a collective bargaining supervised by the state. The education, training, socialization, etc. of the mass worker is organized through the mass institutions of a bureaucratic welfare state.[36]

The regulationist theorists' general suggestion is that Fordism, thus conceived, was able to consolidate itself in the core capitalist societies by the early 1950s, and that there then ensued the period of sustained economic growth to which Wallerstein and others refer – a period of relative class consensus, marked by low unemployment, low inflation, and widely dispersed social and economic benefits.

Beginning in the late 1960s, however, a series of related developments combined to put an end to the postwar boom and to bring to crisis the Fordist regime of accumulation. The immanent instability of the Keynesian welfare state – the final incompatibility between capitalist class relations and social democracy – caused the rate of growth to slow and then to stagnate.[37] The various socioeconomic contradictions that had been both masked and exacerbated by the social democratic class compromise of Fordism began (once again) in the late 1960s and early 1970s to stage themselves as the sites of open confrontation. Having developed as far as it was possible to develop within the framework of Keynesianism, capital began to chafe under the bit of the restrictions it had been obliged by the power of organized labor to accept. It was in this context, as such commentators as Nicholas Costello, Jonathan Michie, and Seumas Milne have noted, that

a consensus started to emerge among the ruling classes of the major western states that without the discipline of redundancy and mass unemployment on the workforce there was no possibility of overcoming the stagflationary crisis of the period and carrying out the economic restructuring necessary to meet the challenge from Japan and the Far East. In Britain, this ideology emerged in the form of monetarism which in due course turned into the free-market crusade of Thatcherism. In the US it started life as Reaganomics. In France it arrived in a dramatic form in 1983 when the socialist government conducted a U-turn strongly reminiscent of the British Labour government's capitulation to the IMF seven years earlier.[38]

From the standpoint of the ruling classes in the core capitalist nation-states, the required "economic restructuring" could not be achieved through any reconsolidation of the welfarist order of Fordism and Keynesian class compromise. Instead, as Michael Rustin has written, new strategies [began to be] developed by capital, both intellectually and in political practice. These included the internationalization of its operations, transferring "Fordist" forms of production to less developed countries, while maintaining crucial command and research functions in the metropolises; the imposition of more stringent market disciplines on capital and labour, through the international "de-regulation" of trade, movements of capital, and labour; the internal "marketization" of operations within large firms, through the institution of management by local profit-centres; the development of new technologies and forms of production and marketing . . . and a dispersal and reduction of the scale of production in order to elude the countervailing cultures and institutions of organized labour.[39]

It is in this general context that the subject of "post-Fordism" has tended to arise in the literature (regulationist and other), for the suggestion is that these "new strategies" developed by capital in the late 1960s and early 1970s – and intended both to restructure the social relations of production and to install new technologies and forms of production – might have been sufficiently consequential in their scope and tendency to oblige us to think of them as inaugurating a new regime of accumulation. According to David Harvey, it is probably still too early for theorists to make this determination with any finality. Yet so striking in his view is the new flexibility on capital's part "with respect to labour processes, labour markets, products, and patterns of production," and so pointedly at odds is it with "the rigidities of Fordism," that the contemporary commentator is more or less compelled to entertain the "hypothesis of a shift from Fordism to what might be called a 'flexible' regime of accumulation." At the very least, Harvey suggests, this hypothesis might stand as "a telling way to characterize recent history."[40]

There are, I think, good grounds for us to accept in broad terms the schematic narrativization of the political economy of capitalism in the post-1945 era outlined above – and loosely modeled on the regulationist analysis – *provided that we first introduce a couple of necessary caveats or qualifications*. First, it is important for us to counter the tacit First Worldism of the argument as I have thus far followed other commentators in presenting it. It is clear that the prosperity of the period from 1945 until the late 1960s was indeed substantially predicated upon the welfarist class compromise in the core capitalist nations of Western Europe and the United States. (It is worth reemphasizing that the welfare state was a political settlement, reflecting no "magnanimous" or "natural" aspiration on capital's part to harmonize its interests with those of labor but, on the contrary, the bitterly hard won ability of organized labor to constrain capital.) Yet the achievement of the welfare state – measured not only in terms of economic growth but also in terms of social democracy: as Samir Amin has recently written, class relations under the welfare state were "significantly more favourable to the working classes than ever before in the entire history of capitalism"[41] – needs to be properly situated. It is in fact complementary with, and indeed partially dependent on, two other world-historical social projects – those which, following Amin, we might term "modernization" (or "developmentalism") in the so-called Third World, and Sovietism or the "Soviet project of capitalism without capitalists, relatively independent of the dominant world system" (*Capitalism*, p. 17). These three social projects operated in tandem and – notwithstanding their structural and ultimately definitive limitations – initially met with considerable success in the postwar era. They

either unfolded within the framework of autocentric national economies or, in the case of the countries of the East and the South, aspired to construct such autocentric economies. They differed in their relationship ("interdependence") with the world economy: Atlanticism, the construction of Europe, in the case of the developed countries of the West; a "negotiated" opening to the world economy in the case of the countries of the South; quasi-autarky for the countries of the East.   (*Capitalism*, p. 93)

Growth with democratization in the West was therefore accompanied, on Amin's reading, by real gains in the East and South:

The victory of the Soviet Union and the Chinese revolution created internal and international conditions favouring the development of the countries of the East, and also those of the West, in so far as they contributed to pressures exerted on capital to engage in the historic social-democratic compromise . . . The simultaneous rise of national liberation movements in the Third World and the ability of postcolonial regimes to harness the benefits of East–West competition favoured economic growth in the south in a number of ways.   (pp. 94–95)

The net result of all these developments was a period, or interregnum, in which "capital was constrained to operate within structures relatively favourable to the peoples of the world" (p. 95).

It is this global dispensation that Amin sees as having collapsed in the years of crisis that set in during the late 1960s. Sometime between 1968–71, he writes, "the world system entered a phase of structural crisis, which continues to this day. The crisis manifests itself in the return of a high and persistent unemployment accompanied by a slowing down of growth in the West, the collapse of Sovietism, and serious regression in some regions of the Third World, accompanied by unsustainable levels of external indebtedness" (p. 94). The thirty years from 1968 to the present have borne witness, then, not just to the crisis of postwar Fordism and the collapse of the welfare state, but to the *global* reassertion and consolidation of "the logic of unilateral capital" (p. 95).

The second caveat that needs to be entered to the schematic account of the trajectory of postwar capitalism offered above centers on the impression of *discontinuity* that is likely to be conveyed by the analytical starkness of its juxtaposition of the epochs of expansion (1945 to 1968 or 1973, say) and crisis (1968/1973 to the present). I suggested earlier that in its attempts to resolve the crisis of profitability that set in toward the end of the 1960s, capital launched a new offensive against labor world-wide, dissolving the welfarist class compromise that had marked its dealings with the Western working class and accelerating or intensifying its rate of exploitation of workers in the peripheries and semi-peripheries. Yet the "strategies" aggressively deployed by capital during this period – among them the transnationalization of production, the development of new productive forces and technologies, the installation of newly rationalized productive regimes and new modes of marketing, the prioritization of speculative or financial over productive capital – were not new. On the contrary, every one of these strategies, generally conceived, has had a long and checkered career in the development of capitalism over the course of the past several hundred years. Salutary here is Wallerstein's characteristically macro-historical reading of the recurring drama of overproductionism: "[w]hat seems to have happened every fifty years or so" in the history of capitalist development, he writes,

is that in the efforts of more and more entrepreneurs to gain for themselves the more profitable nexuses of commodity chains, disproportions of investment occurred such that we speak, somewhat misleadingly, of overproduction. The only solution to these disproportions has been a shakedown of the productive system, resulting in a more even distribution. This sounds logical and simple, but its fall-out has always been massive. It has meant each time further concentration of operations in those links in the commodity chains which have been most clogged. This has involved the elimination of both some entrepreneurs and some workers . . . Such a shift also enabled entrepreneurs to "demote" operations in the hierarchy of the commodity chains, thereby enabling them to devote investment funds and effort to innovative links in the commodity chains which, because initially offering "scarcer" inputs, were more profitable. "Demotion" of particular processes on the hierarchical scale also often led to geographical relocation in part. Such geographical relocation found a major attraction in the move to a lower labour-cost area.[42]

It scarcely remains after this for Wallerstein to add, as the "clincher," that "[w]e are living through precisely such a massive world-wide relocation right now of the world's automobile, steel, and electronics industries. This phenomenon of relocation has been part and parcel of historical capitalism from the outset."

I cite Wallerstein here by way of endorsing his general assumption as to the processual and historical *typicality* of the restructuring of capitalist class relations over the course of the past twenty-five years – not in order to deny that there is anything to be gained from a concrete analysis of the specific forms assumed and generated in its course, but rather to insist that the assumption and generation of these specific (and sometimes new) forms be situated as *intrinsic* to our understanding of capitalism as a dynamic system. As Paul Smith has put it, the current restructuring

does not represent a radical rupture in the history of capitalism, but . . . is rather a sort of outgrowth of familiar capitalist concerns . . . It is in other words not some drastic new phenomenon but a historically explicable one whose peculiar forms are dependent on the specific series of crises that capitalism has engendered within and for itself in the continual process of revolutionizing the means of production. What can be said to vary or to be subject to reorganization with each and any such crisis is the internal relation of capital to labor, and the external relation of capital to the state.[43]

Such an insistence is called for, it seems to me, as a counter to those prominent theories of the current conjuncture which lay undue stress on the portentousness and "radical novelty" of contemporary social and economic developments. Consider, for example, the portrait of "New Times" that emerged in the pages of the influential left-wing British journal, *Marxism Today*, in the years of Thatcherite ascendancy during the 1980s. In a special (1988) issue of the journal devoted to a discussion of this topic, editor Martin Jacques wrote that "[o]ur world is being remade. Mass production, the mass consumer, the big city, big-brother state, the sprawling housing estate, and the nation-state are in decline: flexibility, diversity, differentiation, mobility, communication, decentralization and internationalization are in the ascendant."[44] In trying to think about the historical phenomenon or experience being addressed here, it is helpful first of all to examine the content of the term "our" that Jacques deploys so cavalierly in his

35

first sentence. For it is clear that the subjects of "our world" do not include those people in the core capitalist countries – a clear majority, demarcated by their class position, from "industrial heartland" to "rust belt" to "silicon valley" – whose livelihoods and security have been undermined by the new strategies of resurgent post-Keynesian capitalism. Nor does "our world" include the subaltern classes from the "Third World" – those "massed up workers," as A. Sivanandan has described them in his devastating and largely unanswerable critique of the social vision animating "New Times" – "on whose greater immiseration and exploitation the brave new western world of post-Fordism is being erected."[45] For in Thailand, Indonesia, Mexico, and Kenya, the tide of poor people – landless peasants or "rural proletarians" – flooding from the countryside to the cities in search of jobs continues to rise exponentially. In Rwanda, Eritrea, Korea, and El Salvador, the question of the nation-state has never before seemed so pressing or so central. In Brazil, Ghana, Bangladesh, and the Philippines, thoughts of "diversity," "flexibility," and "communication" are really of practical significance only to foreigners and indigenous elite classes: to the overwhelming masses of local people, they mostly spell out exploitation in new letters.

On Jacques's account, the changes that have been wrought by globalization over the course of the past generation are fundamental – indeed, world-historical – in their significance and qualitative in nature. There has been a decisive shift, he writes, "from the old mass-production Fordist economy to a new, more flexible, post-Fordist order based on computers, information technology and robotics."[46] Taking a leaf out of the book of the regulationist theorists, the "New Times" thinkers see the rise of a globalized "post-Fordist" order as having transformed the nature not only of production, but also of work, politics, leisure, consumption, sexuality, and subjectivity – in short, of social being as such. Thus Stuart Hall, the most prominent of the "New Times" intellectuals, speaks of the "actual recomposition of class itself," and argues that classical theories of social change – Marxism among them – linked to Fordist regimes of accumulation, are in the contemporary – global – age no longer faced with the traditional challenge of reconstructing themselves to meet the rigors of changing circumstances, but are instead simply obsolete, more or less wholly irrelevant to the form of contemporary society:

In the era of flexi-time and part-time work, with women and blacks constituting a growing proportion of those at work, with work in the service sectors rapidly overtaking those [*sic*] in so-called "productive industry," with the preponderance of women in the deskilled echelons of modern technology and with such a large preponderance of the workforce in some local or national state-related activity, the whole masculine imagery of the proletariat . . . simply doesn't make any sense, except as a historic recall. What we are referring to here is therefore more than the collapse of the traditional historic agencies of change. It is the erosion of the cultures of work, economic organization, social and sexual identities in which the left, in an earlier era, was unreflectively rooted.[47]

Hall's theoretical standpoint is, of course, profoundly invested politically. It is elaborated as part of an active intervention into ongoing debates about the future of socialism and radical democracy in (post-)Thatcherite Britain, and elsewhere in Europe and North America. This is enough to distinguish it categorically from a fully postmodernist standpoint such as Jean Baudrillard's, for instance, which styles itself as "post-political," promotes an Olympian disdain for political activism and is – in its ideological thrust, and despite its mannered avant-gardism – both elitist and deeply conservative. Yet in one formal particular, Hall's representation of "New Times" is precisely reminiscent of Baudrillard's representation of the postmodern world: like Baudrillard, Hall views the contemporary era as categorically different from that – the era of the "modern" Keynesian welfare state – which preceded it. And like Baudrillard, he concludes, on these grounds, that the "old" conceptual paradigms and the "old" political strategies of the left are obsolete. At the beginning of *The Hard Road to Renewal*, thus, he writes that Thatcherism can be comprehended only in terms of "the decisive break with the postwar consensus, the profound reshaping of social life which it has set in motion" (p. 2). What Thatcherism "really represents" is then spelled out as follows:

Politically, Thatcherism is related to the recomposition and "fragmentation" of the historic relations of representation between classes and parties; the shifting boundaries between state and civil society, "public" and "private"; the emergence of new arenas of contestation, new sites of social antagonism, new social movements, and new social subjects and political identities in contemporary society.

Ideologically, Thatcherism . . . constantly repositions both individual subjects and "the people" as a whole – their needs, experiences, aspirations, pleasures and desires – contesting space in terms of shifting social, sexual and ethnic identities. (p. 2)

These themes are emphasized again and again in *The Hard Road to Renewal*, as well as in Hall's other writings since the mid-1980s. The basic claim is that "a profound reshaping of the classes of contemporary British society is underway at the present time . . . This recomposition is transforming the material basis, the occupational boundaries, the gender and ethnic composition, the political cultures and the social imagery of 'class'" (p. 5). Now one notices in this particular formulation the self-conscious deployment of the progressive form of the present tense. It is clear that Hall means to indicate that the changes that he believes are underway have not yet run their course. In defending himself against the criticisms of Bob Jessop and others, accordingly, he insists that his intentions are not to represent the Thatcherite project as having *achieved* hegemony – an idea he describes as "preposterous" – but rather to suggest that Thatcherism was a project *aimed* at hegemony (pp. 154–55, 163, 167). The trouble is that on numerous occasions in *The Hard Road to Renewal* he tends, despite himself one must assume, to give an impression of Thatcherism as *precisely hegemonic*, that is, as having been all too consummately successful in realizing its social aims. In such passages Hall is given to suggesting that Thatcherism succeeded because, unlike Labour (actually, with the developments of the last five years in mind, one should, presumably, write "Old Labour" here), whose program of social democratic reformism was still hopelessly wedded to the anachronistic assumptions of the Fordist era, it was alert to the changed nature of capitalist social relations. If, therefore, Thatcherism managed to "shift . . . the parameters of common sense" and to "persuade . . . ordinary people" of the superiority of its political platform, this is because in a real sense it was more sensitive to new realities than Labour's traditionalist ideology, hence more capable of addressing itself to new popular aspirations (pp. 188, 190–91).

This might strike one as a strange way for an avowed socialist to be talking.[48] But Hall does not regard the (post-)Thatcherite order as being beyond political instrumentality. On the contrary, as noted earlier, his writing of the 1980s and early 1990s is animated above all by the desire to combat Thatcherism, and by his conviction that it *can* be defeated. But even here Hall's "presentism" reveals itself. For he insists that the British left in the (post-)Thatcherite era can only "renew" itself by "precisely occupying *the same world* that Thatcherism does, and building from that a *different* form of society" (*Hard Road*, p. 15). Hence he calls upon British leftists to

submit everything to the discipline of present reality, to our understanding of the forces which are really shaping and changing our world. As

Laclau and Mouffe put it, "accept in all their radical novelty, the transformations of the world we live in, neither to ignore them nor to distort
them in order to make them compatible with outdated schemas." Start
"from that full insertion in the present – in its struggles, its challenges, its
dangers – to interrogate the past and to search within it for the genealogy
of the present situation." And from that starting point, begin to construct
a possible alternative scenario, an alternative conception of "modernity,"
an alternative future. (p. 14)

Conceding far too much to (post-)Thatcherite ideologues – who of
course also like(d) to speak of "the transformations of the world we
live in" and of the obsolescence of such "outdated schemas" as
socialism – this genealogical formulation ultimately strikes me as
being *dehistoricizing* in its effects. In Hall's view, British socialists in
the Thatcher era can only challenge the grip she and those she
represents hold on power by junking all that they have previously
championed and stood for, and by reconstituting their movement
from scratch, taking care to address themselves to contemporary
popular aspirations as voiced by "real people" in their everyday lives
(*Hard Road*, pp. 215–16). Such a formulation might – especially with
the benefit of hindsight – be seen as having provided a blueprint of
sorts for Tony Blair's "New Labour" platform. But it seems to me to
have very little to do with the renovation or reanimation of *socialism*.
From Hall's standpoint as he here elaborates it, indeed, it is but a
short step to the trivialization of previous, class-based forms of political struggle as wasted efforts, and to a high-handed disregard of the
aspirations and achievements, the defeats and victories, of generations of workers and activists:

Especially today, we live in an era when the old political identities are
collapsing. We cannot imagine socialism coming about any longer
through the image of that single, singular subject we used to call Socialist
Man. Socialist Man, with one mind, one set of interests, one project, is
dead. And good riddance. Who needs "him" now, with his investment in
a particular historical period, with "his" particular sense of masculinity,
shoring "his" identity up in a particular set of familial relations, a particular kind of sexual identity? Who needs "him" as the singular identity
through which the great diversity of human beings and ethnic cultures in
our world must enter the twenty-first century? This "he" is dead:
finished. (*Hard Road*, pp. 169–70)

One appreciates the general point that Hall is making here, concerning the relative (and sometimes absolute) neglect of race, gender,
sexuality, and so on, in socialist practice and theory from the nineteenth century onwards. Even so, it little becomes a socialist intellec-

tual of Hall's stature and insight, it seems to me, to write so condescendingly, and with such apparent indifference, of the historic struggles waged in the cause of "Socialist Man" by working men and – for
all Hall's inference to the contrary – women throughout this passage
of 150 and more years.[49] But then it also seems to me that one
consequence of "submit[ting] everything to the discipline of present
reality" is inevitably to traduce the past in this way. Ernesto Laclau
and Chantal Mouffe (whose phrase this is) might *speak* of "establish[ing] with the past a dialogue which is organized around continuities and discontinuities, identifications and ruptures."[50] But, as even
a cursory examination of their major text, *Hegemony and Socialist
Strategy*, will reveal, they are interested almost exclusively in "discontinuities" and "ruptures," and pay scarcely any attention whatso-
ever to "continuities" and "identifications."[51] Generally speaking,
indeed, postmodernist and "New Times" views of the political culture of the industrial working class are woefully schematic. As Costello, Michie, and Milne have pointed out, "New Times" theorists
tend to "paint a picture of a past in which workers drank the same
beer, wore the same clothes, went to Blackpool for their holidays,
watched the same TV programmes and talked about them at work the
next day in huge factories and mines."[52] Hall's characterization of
"Socialist Man" fits this schema perfectly. His monolithic portrait of
working class life might accord with an ideal-typification of Fordism;
but it cannot pass muster as an *historical* representation.[53]

Equally important, the "presentist" degradation of the past also
causes the *present* to be misconstrued. In an important critique dating
from the mid-1980s, Bob Jessop et al. charge that Hall tends to neglect
the structural dimensions of (British) capitalism in the Thatcherite era
in his countervailing emphasis on Thatcherism as first and foremost a
political and *ideological* project.[54] More specifically, it seems to me,
Hall's emphasis on the disaggregation and pluralization of social
identities during the "Long Decade" (Paul Smith's phrase) of
Thatcherite ascendancy leads him to overestimate the transformative
importance of the socioeconomic restructuring of this period. Like the
other "New Times" theorists, he fails to attend to the *class* provenance of Thatcherism, that is, to the question of the precise sectors or
fractions of the capitalist class represented by it.

In his 1989 critique of the "New Times" intellectuals, Michael
Rustin argued that their conception of Thatcherism as inaugurating
and enforcing a categorical break with the Fordist–Keynesian welfare
state is both too extreme and too schematic. "Post-Fordism" – the

term functioning as a key signifier of Thatcherite Britain for the "New Times" thinkers – "is better seen as one ideal-typical model or strategy of production and regulation, co-present with others in a complex historical ensemble, than as a valid totalizing description of an emerging social formation here and now."[55] In these terms, post-Fordism cannot adequately be theorized outside of its relation to Fordism in the context of contemporary capitalism. Post-Fordist production is integrated with Fordist and other forms of production in both the core capitalist states and the peripheral formations of the world system: "without a grasp of this larger integration of capitalism . . . [n]ot even the position of the subordinate classes in the First World can be correctly theorized."[56] "New Times" and postmodernist theorists tend to underestimate the enduring *systematicity* of capitalism. What I would characterize as an integrated, if uneven, formation, they tend to theorize in terms of decenteredness, autarky, and discontinuity. And there is steadfast opposition not only to the idea of developing a global theory of these decentered forms (of considering them under the rubric of any category of totality), but also to any call for a properly sociological account of their emergence. The net result, as Smith has suggested, is a theory which "ignores a huge array of both the causes and the effects of the current restructuring" (*Dreams*, p. 157).

In his remarkable study, *Late Capitalism*, first published in 1972, Ernest Mandel offered a provisional enumeration of the "main characteristics" of what he termed "the third technological revolution" – his periodizing designation for the restructuring of capitalist class relations, beginning in the 1960s, that we have been discussing. Among these characteristics, Mandel listed the following:

A qualitative acceleration of the increase in the organic composition of capital, i.e., the displacement of living by dead labour . . .

A shift of living labour-power still engaged in the process of production from the actual treatment of raw materials to preparatory or supervisory functions . . .

A radical change in the proportion between the two functions of the commodity of labour-power in automated enterprises . . . [L]abour-power both creates and preserves value. In the history of the capitalist mode of production, the creation of value has hitherto obviously been the crucial function. In fully automated enterprises, by contrast, the preservation of value now becomes critical . . .

A radical change in the proportion between the creation of surplus-value within the enterprise itself and the appropriation of surplus-value produced in other enterprises, within fully automated enterprises or branches . . .

A change in the proportion between construction costs and the outlay on the purchase of new machines in the structure of fixed capital, and hence also in industrial investments . . .

A shortening of the production period, achieved by means of continuous output and radical acceleration of preparation and installation work (and transition to necessary repairs) . . .

A compulsion to accelerate technological innovation, and a steep increase in the costs of "research and development" . . .

A shorter life-span of fixed capital, especially machines . . . [57]

This list is striking for two, mutually entailing, reasons. First, there is the matter of its far-sightedness or prescience – which we can register quite simply by pointing out that all of the "characteristics" specified by Mandel are central to the debate that has subsequently emerged about economic globalization. Writing at the very beginning of the 1970s – that is, in advance of both the abandoning of the Bretton Woods currency system and the "oil crisis" of 1973–75 – Mandel was already able to identify and explain such developments as the emergence of what has since been termed the "service economy"; the advancing commodification of knowledge and the corollary importance of information technologies; the tilting of the balance from productive to financial capital; the rise of subcontracting and other "transnational" productive practices; the likelihood that capital – on the basis of its stockpiling of the value created by dead labor – would be selectively able in the short term to free itself from its need for living labor, and hence to launch a devastating new offensive against the political power of the organized working classes of the core capitalist states; and so on. Related to this far-sightedness, second, there is the matter of Mandel's *problematic*: we can scarcely fail to notice the classically and definitively Marxist provenance of his language and conceptual schema. His claim, in fact, is that "late capitalism" is *uniquely* amenable to Marxist analysis – more so even than the *laissez-faire* capitalism of Marx's own time or of the monopolist or imperialist phase that succeeded it at the beginning of the twentieth century.

In these terms Mandel's commentary might be taken to present itself as a counter-example – or, put more strongly, to pose a ground-level challenge – to the "strong" version of globalization theory that has today become a significant point of reference in scholarly debates in the fields of sociology and cultural and postcolonial studies. As Paul Hirst and Grahame Thompson observe in the opening sentences of their invaluable critical study, *Globalization in Question*,

> it is widely asserted that we live in an era in which the greater part of social life is determined by global processes, in which national cultures, national economies and national borders are dissolving. Central to this perception is the notion of a rapid and recent process of economic globalization. A truly global economy is claimed to have emerged or to be in the process of emerging, in which distinct national economies and, therefore, domestic strategies of national economic management are increasingly irrelevant. The world economy has internationalized in its basic dynamics, it is dominated by uncontrollable market forces, and it has as its principal economic actors and major agents of change truly transnational corporations, that owe allegiance to no nation state and locate wherever in the globe market advantage dictates.[58]

A very similar definition is offered by William Tabb, who writes that

> [t]he globalization hypothesis is that there has been a rapid and recent change in the nature of economic relations among national economies which have lost much of their distinct claim to separate internally driven development, and that domestic economic management strategies have become ineffective to the point of irrelevance. Internationalization is, in this view, seen as a tide sweeping over borders in which technology and irresistible market forces transform the global system in ways beyond the power of anyone to do much to change.[59]

With its emphases on transnational processes as the motive force of contemporary economic development, on the corresponding irrelevance of nation-statist policy to economic practice, and on the inscrutability – not to say, implacability – of the market (as transcendental signifier), the globalization hypothesis, thus defined, accords very obviously with the interests of a specific fraction of corporate capitalists. In the discourse of this class fraction (or in that of their intellectual representatives, such as Kenichi Ohmae or Peter Drucker), the mantra of "globalization" tends to be recited evangelically, to spread the good news of a "new world order" built in the image of a supercharged, universal free enterprise zone, likely to be of benefit to all.[60] On such usage, as Gregory Jusdanis has written,

> globalization signifies the transnationalization of capitalism, the breakdown of national economies, and the creation of a more interconnected world economic system. It also describes the emergence of new technologies of communication such as satellite, fax, and e-mail, which, along with the possibility of rapid intercontinental travel, alter the relationship of time and space. This spatial compression and temporal acceleration

allow people, ideas, and goods to move with great speed, while also making it possible for individuals, however far apart, to witness events simultaneously.[61]

Globalization is in these terms a dream: more concretely we might qualify it as the name given to the "reactionary utopia" – Samir Amin's term (*Capitalism*, p. 5) – which neo-liberal discourse is today inclined to project as an historical actuality, notwithstanding its profound immateriality as far as politics, administration, and government are concerned. I do not wish to be mistaken on this point: I am *not* arguing that the changes in the disposition of the global economy identified by globalization theorists *have not happened* (although I follow others in believing that they have been "overstated and poorly conceptualized"[62] in the globalization literature). On the contrary, I do believe that there is, to put it colloquially, a "there" there. But what renders neo-liberalism's proclamation of globalization realized as a "reactionary utopia" is the fact that, in making it, it must pretend to *have resolved* what cannot in fact *be resolved* in terms of the market. For Samir Amin, as for Guha, and already for Marx a century ago, it is clear that the tendency toward universalization is inherent in capitalism; its historical forms of expression are a matter of record, and cannot be gainsaid. "The tendency to create the *world market* is directly given in the concept of capital itself," Marx wrote in the *Grundrisse*. "Every limit appears as a barrier to be overcome" (p. 408). But for Amin, as for Marx (we have already seen Guha following Marx as he makes this point), this drive toward universalization is ultimately incapable of realizing itself on its own terms. For what ultimately proves insuperable is a barrier *internal* to capital itself, one progressively disclosed by and through capitalist development. Marx put it thus:

But from the fact that capital posits every . . . limit as a barrier and hence gets *ideally* beyond it, it does not by any means follow that it has *really* overcome it, and, since every such barrier contradicts its character, its production moves in contradictions which are constantly overcome but just as constantly posited. Furthermore. The universality towards which it irresistibly strives encounters barriers in its own nature, which will, at a certain stage of its development, allow it to be recognized as being itself the greatest barrier to this tendency, and hence will drive towards its own suspension.   (*Grundrisse*, p. 410)

And a few pages later we find this consolidation of the argument:

there is a limit, not inherent to production generally, but to production founded on capital . . . [C]apital contains a *particular* restriction of production –

which contradicts its general tendency to drive beyond every barrier to production . . . [C]apital is not, as the economists believe, the *absolute* form for the development of the forces of production – not the absolute form for that, nor the form of wealth which absolutely coincides with development of the forces of production. (p. 415)

Amin's argument is very similar to Marx's and Guha's. "Globalization," he writes, is not something that one can be "for" or "against"; it is "a fact of modern history" (*Capitalism*, p. 75). But whereas the ideologists of capitalism proclaim globalization an existent reality, Amin insists upon both the attenuated nature of what has in fact been realized and the categorical *unrealizability* of "globalization via the market." "Here the bourgeois and the socialist part ways," he writes. For

[t]he first wishes to fix evolution, more or less submitting it to the perspective of the unilateral action of capital. Socialism on the other hand permits one to see why this capitalist globalization remains truncated, generating, reproducing and deepening global polarization step by step. The historical limit of capitalism is found exactly here: the polarized world that it creates is and will be more and more inhuman and explosive. (p. 75)

The thrust of this argument becomes clearer elsewhere, when Amin observes that claims that capitalism has instantiated a global order are premature not only in the categorical sense just discussed. They are also premature inasmuch as they are to date subtended by no credible political, governmental, or administrative structures at the global level:

No economy exists without politics and without a state. Therefore, economic globalization logically requires the construction of a world political system able to respond to the challenge, a power system capable of managing social compromises at the worldwide level, just as national states manage them at their level. However, sufficient maturity does not exist in the area, not even among the group of dominant capitalist countries . . . In my opinion capitalism is unable to overcome the growing contradiction between its economic management in an increasingly globalized space, and its political and social management which remain fragmented among national spaces. (*Capitalism*, p. 22)

"Globalization," for Amin, thus refers at one and the same time to the tendency toward universalization that inheres within capitalism as a dynamic system but that is finally unactualizable on the terrain of capitalism itself, *and* to the ideological figure in terms of which the currently prevailing neo-liberal discourse (mis-)recognizes and justifies the social order that contemporary capitalism has brought into existence. "Neoliberal discourse cannot respond to [the] real challenge of globalization," he observes, "unless, according to its principles, it anticipates the simultaneous opening up of all frontiers, to commerce, to capital and to the migration of workers." But since no actually existing capitalist state has of yet put itself in a position to accommodate the last of these "openings," the "discourse remains truncated, suggesting the opening of frontiers to capital but their closure to human beings" (pp. 75–76). The reactionary utopia of "globalization" thus effects to displace and neutralize or cancel out the potential reality necessarily inscribed as the very telos of capitalist universalization as a social tendency. "The alternatives are still either (worldwide) socialism or barbarism" (p. 22).

The oneiric dimensions of the neo-liberal conception of globalization are most readily apparent in the outlandish, technophilic claims that are sometimes made for its defining modalities. As Paul Smith has observed,

Magical notions such as that of fully global space replete with an ecstatic buzz of cyber communication, or of an instantaneous mobility of people, goods and services, or of a global market place hooked up by immaterial money that flashes around the globe many times a minute: these are the kinds of images that are regularly projected in the opening phase of millennial capitalism. Such images have effectively become shibboleths, appearing to construe a kind of isochronic world wherein the constrictions of time and space have been overcome, where the necessary navigational and communicational means are so fully developed and supremely achieved that they can eclipse even reality itself. (*Dreams*, p. 13)

Smith's own hypothesis – according closely with that of Amin – is that we ought to construe "globalization" as in large measure "an ideological formation annunciating a fundamentalist version of capitalism which has not yet arrived" (p. 25). I find this formulation appealing, not least because it allows us to reckon with the counter-intuitive and otherwise inexplicable fact that this "millennial dream" is evidently as much a feature of the politically progressive as of the corporate capitalist imagination. Hence Smith's observation that "millennial zeal" today "infects not just the globalization cheerleaders but also many on the left." Millennial dreaming is tendentially indicated, one might say, whenever the perduring dialectic of capitalist development is ignored, that is, whenever it is forgotten that "particular historical changes within the capitalist mode of production can be grasped accurately only as functions of specific crises of capitalism and its continual need to reinvent itself" (*Dreams*, p. 22). Like Amin and such other theorists as Wallerstein and Ellen Meiksins Wood,[63] Smith wants "to stress the continuities represented by millennial capitalism within the history of capitalist formations." For only through means of this emphasis on continuity, he argues, are we able to establish and maintain grounds sufficient "to counter not just the discourse of the millennial dream's many proponents, but also the discourse of those parts of the left – what we might call the postmodern left – which want to see in globalization a huge rupture or historical break" (p. 26).

The suggestion here of a connection, on the progressive side of the political ledger, between what Smith terms the "shibboleth of globalization" and *postmodernism*, is provocative. The work of any number of theorists might be referenced in this respect: Stuart Hall, Nestor Garcia Canclini, Arjun Appadurai, Jan Nederveen Pieterse, Martin Albrow, Scott Lash and John Urry, and many others.[64] It is clear that in the work of such theorists as these, "globalization" and "postmodernism" stand as twin columns together buttressing an ambitious new theory of society. At the same time, however, I think it is important for us to problematize, as rather *too* snug, the identification that Smith's reading appears to encourage between globalization and postmodernist discourses. For various "strong" versions of the globalization thesis are also to be found in the work of a number of progressive or even avowedly socialist writers whose theoretical assumptions are either quite explicitly opposed to postmodernism or, at least, clearly at some remove from it.[65] While these progressive writers seem as fully convinced as the postmodernist theorists cited above that the contemporary restructuring of capitalist social relations has been of epochal significance, they cannot plausibly be classified under the rubric of the "postmodern" left. Nor, indeed, in most cases, can their representation of globalization be viewed as "zealous," if by that term one means to indicate enthusiasm: participants in the "millennial dream" they might be, but for nearly all of them this dream has the qualities of a nightmare.

I myself am skeptical of the claims made by these left-wing commentators, postmodernist and anti-postmodernist alike. The balance of the available evidence seems to me to tilt *against* the "strong" version of the globalization hypothesis. Let me take just two – but two very important – examples. First, concerning the matter of the transnationalization of trade and the market: advocates of the "strong" version tell us that inasmuch as it now possesses more or less "total mobility and access to every corner of the world," capital has been "liberated from any constraint on its global activity."[66] Countervailing documentation, however, suggests that the vast bulk of contemporary trade is not "global" but remains heavily concentrated within the core capitalist states;[67] that very few of the corporations involved are in any strict sense "transnational";[68] and that even where patterns of decentralization and denationalization *are* in evidence, it is for the most part only with respect to *production* that they are so.[69] The available evidence, that is to say, seems in general to point to the prematurity of the conclusions drawn by advocates of the "strong" version; and it lends support to those concerned to emphasize *continuities* in the capitalist system. The same conclusions might be drawn, second, with respect to the obsolescence of the nation-state form: proponents of the "strong" version tell us that "the nation-state no longer presides over anything approximating the concept of 'national economy',"[70] or, put differently, that national boundaries have been eroded, such that it is today "structurally impossible for individual nations to sustain independent, or even autonomous, economies, polities and social structures."[71] Again, though, countervailing documentation suggests a quite different reality. It is clear that we need to concede at least *some* truth to the claim that the power of nation-states to function autocentrically (a power that was never by any means universally dispersed, in the sense that only the core states had it to exercise in the first place) has been eroded or weakened over the course of the past thirty years by processes of "transnationalization." Yet it is equally true not only that, as Alex Callinicos puts it, "private capitals continue to rely on the nation state to which they are most closely attached to protect them against the competition of other capitals, the effects of economic crisis, and the resistance of those they exploit,"[72] but also that, in the core capitalist countries, at least, the nation-state still retains the capacity to act decisively to limit or otherwise regulate the operations of capital.

Many other features of the "strong" version of the globalization hypothesis strike me as being inadequately conceptualized. I would list in this context the disposition toward technological determinism on the part of many commentators; the tendency to generalize from information and communications technologies to the ensemble of contemporary productive forces as such; the homogenization entailed in the diverse but linked notions that "globalization" involves the subsumption of "society" by the capitalist "economy," or the overcoming of unevenness, or the de-differentiation of hitherto distinct and hierarchically articulated instances; the argument as to the emergence of a denationalized capitalist class fraction or elite, fully conscious of its own transnationality; and so on. But perhaps the most remarkable feature of the "strong" left-wing version of the globalization hypothesis consists less in its empirical or sociological unsupportability than in the fact that it is invariably attended by the most exaggerated, not to say apocalyptic, of philosophical riders. William Robinson does not only believe that capital today has been "liberated from any constraint on its activity"; that "for the first time in the history of the modern world system," there has been a replacement "of all pre- (or non-) capitalist production relations with capitalist ones in every part of the globe"; that "a new 'social structure of accumulation' is emerging which, for the first time in history, is global." He also believes that the process of globalization "is redefining all the fundamental reference points of human society and social analysis, and requires a modification of all existing paradigms."[73] The same is true for Martin Albrow: not only has "modernity" been supplanted by "globality," but this development entails "an overall change in the basis of action and social organization for individuals and groups."[74] Even Arif Dirlik believes that "[c]hanges in the contemporary world appear to be so drastic that they have raised questions about whether or not past ways of thinking about the world (Marxist or otherwise) are relevant at all in the present."[75]

This way of thinking has nothing to recommend it, in my view. Historically specious – in the sense that, as Craig Calhoun has rightly put it, the fundamental theoretical and political problems that "shape our lives and thought" today continue to be those that "have shaped them throughout modernity"[76] – the claims to theoretical postmodernity are merely sensationalist where they are not actively mystifying. I would direct this critique even against a writer like David Harvey, whose work I find, in other respects, sympathetic and powerfully suggestive. We last encountered Harvey, in our discussion of the political economy of postwar capitalism, mooting the idea of a shift from Fordism to a "flexible" regime of accumulation as a periodizing hypothesis. That was in his 1989 book, *The Condition of Postmodernity*. In some of his more recent work, however, in which – significantly – the regulationist vocabulary of "flexible specialization," "regime of accumulation," and "post-Fordism" is eschewed in favor of that of "globalization," Harvey seems finally to have become convinced that the "quantitative changes that have occurred" in recent times are indeed "great enough and synergistic enough when taken together to put us in a qualitatively new era of capitalist development, demanding a radical revision of our theoretical concepts and our political apparatus (to say nothing of our aspirations)."[77] It is true that Harvey immediately qualifies this judgment, allowing that

> there has not been any fundamental revolution in the mode of production and its associated social relations . . . [I]f there is any real qualitative trend it is towards the reassertion of early nineteenth-century capitalist values coupled with a twenty-first-century penchant for pulling everyone (and everything that can be exchanged) into the orbit of capital while rendering large segments of the world's population permanently redundant in relation to the basic dynamics of capital accumulation. This is where the powerful image, conceded and feared by international capital, of contemporary globalization as a "brakeless train wreaking havoc" comes into play.

But it is hard to know what to make of this qualification, since it seems to be undermined by most of the substantive claims in Harvey's exposition. For if there has *not* been a "fundamental revolution in the mode of production and its associated social relations," then by what criteria does Harvey conclude that "we" (?) are in "a qualitatively new era of capitalist development"? Moreover, if there has *not* been a fundamental revolution in the mode of production and its associated social relations, why is a "radical revision of our theoretical concepts and our political apparatus (to say nothing of our aspirations)" *demanded*? For Harvey is in no doubt that it is so demanded: later in the same essay he writes that "the traditional Marxist categories . . . – imperialism, colonialism, neocolonialism – appear far too simplistic to capture the intricacies of uneven spatio-temporal development. Perhaps they were always so, but the reterritorialization and respatialization of capitalism, particularly over the last thirty years, make such categories seem far too crude to express the geopolitical complexities within which class struggle must now unfold" (p. 14). The "[p]erhaps they were always so" is more than a little confusing. But I would like in addition to protest the weakness, in context, of Harvey's general claim itself – that the received Marxist vocabulary of "imperialism" and "colonialism" is too "crude" or "simplistic" to account for the contemporary complexities of "uneven spatio-temporal development." I do so not in order to impugn Harvey's Marxist credentials. On the contrary, it is precisely *because* of Harvey's commitment to Marxism that I find his claim so unsatisfactory.

For it is not only that it was precisely under the rubric of "imperialism" that the notion of "uneven development" (in the conjunct form of "combined and uneven development") was introduced into social theory in the first place. It is also that Harvey's supplement – the phrase "spatio-temporal" – welcome as it might be as an *elaboration*, contains, as I understand it, nothing that points either to an incompatibility with the received meaning of "imperialism" as a concept, or to its anachronism. Harvey announces the obsolescence of the Marxist theory of imperialism. But nothing that he subsequently proposes is not readily conceivable in terms of that theory; and, worse, nothing that he subsequently says even *begins* to compensate for the loss of that theory. Under the circumstances, I confess to much preferring Paul Smith's reading, which is diametrically opposed to Harvey's. For Smith,

the current restructuring is perhaps most relevantly seen as a particular historical development arising from the collapse of the North's colonial systems and of American mid-century hegemony over both economic and cultural realms in the global system. In that important sense, the contemporary, "globalized" form of capital accumulation derives from the moment of direct imperialism and is in many respects the continuation of colonialism and imperialism by other means.   (*Dreams*, p. 19)

I would like to conclude this chapter by considering the recent work of Paul Gilroy, above all his 1993 study, *The Black Atlantic*. For this book takes as its project nothing less than the formulation of a new and comprehensive theory of modernity (and of modern cultural practice). By insisting on the constitutive "internality of blacks to the West,"[78] this new theory effects to overcome the nation-centeredness, the Eurocentrism, and the rationalistic logocentrism that Gilroy believes to be common to the most influential theories of modernity from Hegel onwards.

Gilroy argues that "the history and expressive culture of the African diaspora, the practice of racial slavery, [and] . . . the narratives of European imperial conquest . . . require all simple periodisations of the modern and the postmodern to be drastically rethought" (p. 42). His suggestion, in fact, is that the presence and self-presence of blacks in the West constitute a "distinctive counterculture of modernity" (p. 36). "The distinctive historical experiences of [the African] diaspora's populations" he writes, "have created a unique body of reflections on modernity and its discontents which is an enduring presence in the cultural and political struggles of their descendants today" (p. 45).

This is a point that Gilroy has made, by implication at least, often enough before – for instance in his by now fairly extensive scholarly production on the subject of black music – and that he explicitly reaffirms in *The Black Atlantic* in his commentary on music (again) and the writings of such figures as Richard Wright, W.E.B. Du Bois, and Martin Delany. But he is at pains to suggest that he is not interested in mounting a case for the exceptionalism of black (African-American, Caribbean, etc.) sociality and cultural practice. On the contrary, his contention is that blacks in the West are not only integral to the unfolding of modernity but constitute, in fact, the paradigmatic bearers of its process. Thus he quotes Toni Morrison to the effect that "modern life begins with slavery," a statement that he glosses as follows: "It is being suggested that the concentrated intensity of the slave experience is something that marked out blacks as the first truly modern people, handling in the nineteenth century dilemmas and difficulties which would only become the substance of everyday life in Europe a century later" (p. 221). Elsewhere in *The Black Atlantic* he observes, similarly, that the "time has come for the primal history of modernity to be reconstructed from the slaves' points of view" (p. 55). He himself spells out the consequences of this emphasis as follows:

Pointing out aspects of the particularity of modern black experiences should not be understood as an occasion for staging the confrontation between the regional values of a distinct sector or community and the supposed universalism of occidental rationality. I am not suggesting that the contemporary traces of black intellectual history comprise or even refer to a lifeworld that is incommensurable with that of the former slaveholders. That would be the easy way out, for in focusing on racial slavery and its aftermath we are required to consider a historical relationship in which dependency and antagonism are intimately associated and in which black critiques of modernity may also be, in some significant senses, its affirmation. (p. 48).

Central to Gilroy's exposition is his conception of the Atlantic, and of Atlanticism, "as one single, complex unit of analysis" (p. 15). This is a conception that is developed against two dominant contemporary (mis-)understandings: first, that modernity is the achievement of white, Euro-American bourgeois society and that the populations of the African disapora therefore exist only in a relation of inessentiality to it; second, that the story of modernity is best understood when set against the backdrop of the nation-state and of nationalism. I have already touched on the terms of Gilroy's demolition of the first of these shibboleths; but he sets out, equally, to offer a sustained and rigorous critique of nation-centered thinking. It is not only that, as he puts it, there is today an

> urgent obligation to reevaluate the significance of the modern nation state as a political, economic, and cultural unit. Neither political nor economic structures of domination are still simply co-extensive with national borders. This has a special significance in contemporary Europe, where new political and economic relations are being created seemingly day by day, but it is a world-wide phenomenon with significant consequences for the relationship between the politics of information and the practices of capital accumulation. (p. 7)

The crucial point for Gilroy is rather that the nation-form has *never* been an adequate analytical mode for the conceptualization of modernity or modern social relations. (His stance in this respect is quite different from that of the "globalization" theorists, who tend to argue that the nation-state *is being rendered obsolete* by contemporary developments. William Robinson, for instance, proposes that "[n]ation-states are no longer appropriate units of analysis,"[79] which implies that they once were.) Modernity, in Gilroy's account of it, is – and has been from the outset – an ineluctably and unforgoably transcultural, international, diasporic, hybridic formation. The key words in Gilroy's theorization of modernity emerge early in *The Black Atlantic* and are never allowed to disappear from view. Already by the second page of the book, we have encountered a cluster of these privileged words – "creolisation, métissage, mestizaje, and hybridity" – and the thesis of "the inescapability and legitimate value of mutation, hybridity, and intermixture" is still being repeated in the last paragraph of the book (p. 223).

Gilroy focuses upon the question of nationalism because it enables him to explore "some of the special political problems that arise from the fatal junction of the concept of nationality with the concept of culture and the affinities and affiliations which link the blacks of the West to one of their adoptive, parental cultures: the intellectual heritage of the West since the Enlightenment" (p. 2). A good deal has been written about the intersection of the discourses of race, nation, and culture in the dominant institutions of the core Western capitalist states. (Gilroy himself has contributed substantially to this literature, most notably in his 1987 book, *"There Ain't No Black in the Union Jack"* and in his contributions to the Centre for Contemporary Cultural Studies's 1982 volume *The Empire Strikes Back*.)[80] In *The Black Atlantic*, however, he directs his attention rather to the persistence of what he deems an essentialist cultural nationalism in the work of many *pro-gressive* thinkers in the general field of cultural studies: a certain "quiet cultural nationalism" can be identified, he argues, in the otherwise extraordinarily rich and genre-defining scholarship of such British social historians and cultural theorists as E.P. Thompson and Raymond Williams; and he finds an analogous strain of national-ism in the work of many of the most influential contemporary Af-rican-Americanists too.

With respect to the British projection, Gilroy builds on his contro-versial critique of Williams in *"There Ain't No Black in the Union Jack"* to deplore the "crypto-nationalism" that, on his reading, works to disincline radical scholars "to consider the cross catalytic of trans-verse dynamics of racial politics as a significant element in the forma-tion and reproduction of English national identities" (p. 4). He ar-gues, thus, that the Marxist social historians of the British New Left "compounded and reproduced" a received tradition of ethnocentric nationalism by

denying imaginary, invented Englishness any external referents whatso-ever. England ceaselessly gives birth to itself, seemingly from Britannia's head . . . Their predilections for the image of the freeborn Englishman and the dream of socialism in one country that framed their work are both to be found wanting when it comes to nationalism. This uncomfortable pairing can be traced through the work of Edward Thompson and Eric Hobsbawm, visionary writers who contributed so much to the strong foundations of English cultural studies and who share a non-reductive Marxian approach to economic, social, and cultural history in which the nation – understood as a stable receptacle for counter-hegemonic class struggle – is the primary focus. (pp. 14–15)

With respect to African-Americanist scholarship, he offers a stinging rebuttal of the "ontological essentialist" assumptions that, he argues, lead many scholars to appeal to a vague, quasi-Negritudinous pan-Africanism while insisting simultaneously on the irreducible *Ameri-canism* of African-American sociality and expressive culture. The starkest example of this kind of essentialism is of course provided by the discourse of Afrocentrism, which Gilroy quite properly criticizes for its absolutist conception of race and ethnicity, its elitism, its ahistoricality, and, most tellingly (and ironically), its Eurocentric conceptual provenance. (It relies, he maintains, "on a model of the thinking, knowing racial subject" whose "European, Cartesian out-lines remain visible beneath a new lick of Kemetic paint" [p. 188].) Yet he discovers a similar essentialist predisposition in the work of a

number of other African-Americanist scholars, who would not identify themselves under the rubric of Afrocentrism, but who nevertheless commit themselves to the mystificatory (Gilroy even adds the
term "volkish") notion of "blacks as a national or proto-national
group with its own hermetically enclosed culture" (p. 33).[81] Gilroy
provides the example of scholars of hip hop culture who willfully
disregard its transnational, diasporic constituents, constructing hip
hop instead along the axes of an Americocentric black nationalism:

> The musical components of hip hop are a hybrid form nurtured by the
> social relations of the South Bronx where Jamaican sound system culture
> was transplanted during the 1970s and put down new roots. In conjunc-
> tion with specific technological innovations, this routed and re-rooted
> Caribbean culture set in train a process that was to transform black
> America's sense of itself and a large portion of the popular music indus-
> try as well. Here we have to ask how a form which flaunts and glories in
> its own malleability as well as its transnational character becomes inter-
> preted as an expression of some authentic African-American essence?
> How can rap be discussed as if it sprang intact from the entrails of the
> blues? Another way of approaching this would be to ask what is it about
> black America's writing elite which means that they need to claim this
> diasporic cultural form in such an assertively nationalist way? (pp. 33–34)

Gilroy criticizes the "nationalistic focus" of both English and African-American cultural studies on the grounds that nation-centeredness is an inadequate lens and, indeed, "antithetical to the rhizomor-
phic, fractal structure of the transcultural, international formation" of
the black Atlantic (p. 4). Black Atlanticism as he presents it is
not a unisonant but a plurivocal mode of sociality. It is governed by
the logics of overdetermination, diaspora, multiple-rootedness.
"[S]tereophonic, bilingual . . . [and] bifocal" (p. 3), black Atlanticism
is inherently resistant to the received procedures of sociological and
historical investigation, seeming to require, instead, something in the
nature of a "webbed" exposition.[82] Since it is "unashamedly hybridic" in character, it "continually confounds any simplistic (essentialist
or anti-essentialist) understanding of the relationship between racial
identity and racial non-identity, between folk cultural authenticity
and pop cultural betrayal" (*Black Atlantic*, p. 99). These features of
black Atlantic sociality enable Gilroy to theorize it as a "changing
same," that is to say, as a formation constantly in flux, constantly
reinventing, re-membering, retraditionalizing itself. He writes, thus –
with respect to "the different practices, cognitive, habitual, and per-
formative, that are required to invent, maintain, and renew identity"
– that they "have constituted the black Atlantic as a non-traditional

tradition, an irreducibly modern, ex-centric, unstable, and asymmetrical cultural ensemble that cannot be apprehended through the manichean logic of binary coding" (p. 198).

Gilroy uses the concept of "tradition" in a particularly interesting way in *The Black Atlantic*. As he explains with reference to the subject of music, he understands the concept of tradition "neither to identify a lost past nor to name a culture of compensation that would restore access to it. It does not stand in opposition to modernity, nor should it conjure up wholesome images of Africa that can be contrasted with the corrosive, aphasic power of the post-slave history of the Americas and the extended Caribbean . . . [T]he circulation and mutation of music across the black Atlantic explodes the dualistic structure which puts Africa, authenticity, purity, and origin in crude opposition to the Americas, hybridity, creolisation, and rootlessness" (pp. 198–99).

The concept that Gilroy proposes as a means of representing the structure of black Atlanticism is that of "double consciousness." This concept derives, of course, from the work of W.E.B. Du Bois, who opened *The Souls of Black Folk* with the observation that "One ever feels his twoness, – an American, a Negro; two souls, two thoughts, two unreconciled strivings; two warring ideals in one dark body whose dogged strength alone keeps it from being torn asunder" (quoted in *Black Atlantic*, p. 126). Du Bois's purpose in mobilizing the concept of "double consciousness" was "to convey the special difficulties arising from black internalisation of an American identity" (p. 126; Gilroy's gloss); but Gilroy wishes to generalize its applicability, according it authoritative status with respect to black Western subjectivity *tout court*:

I want to suggest that Du Bois produced this concept at the junction point of his philosophical and psychological interests not just to express the distinctive standpoint of black Americans but also to illuminate the experience of post-slave populations in general. Beyond this, he uses it as a means to animate a dream of global co-operation among peoples of colour which came to full fruition only in his later work. (p. 126)

In these terms, "double consciousness" serves to profile a form of subjectivity that – despite the fact that it is quintessentially modern – cannot be accommodated within the Procrustean logic of modernity's master narrative. It cannot be clothed "without remainder" in the official uniform of modernity, whose normalizing lines and contours were, after all, explicitly and quite self-consciously fashioned with its exclusion in mind. "Double consciousness," Gilroy writes, emerges from the unhappy symbiosis between three modes of thinking, being, and seeing. The first is racially particularistic, the second national-istic in that it derives from the nation state in which the ex-slaves but not-yet-citizens find themselves rather than from their aspiration towards a nation state of their own. The third is diasporic or hemispheric, sometimes global and occasionally universalist.   (p. 127)

The polemical thrust of Gilroy's deployment of the concept of "double consciousness" thus consists in the suggestion that no theory of modernity that fails to take centrally into consideration the coun-ter-discourse entailed in black Atlantic sociality and expressive cul-ture can be considered anything more than partial and tendentious (not to say strictly ideological). Gilroy develops this argument in the first instance against Hegel, whose work provides one *locus classicus* of the theory of modernity. But he also challenges the ideas of Jürgen Habermas, the most important living exponent and champion of the sociophilosophical projects of modernity and enlightenment.

Now many contemporary commentators have noted and moved to deplore the Eurocentrism of Habermas's work. In *Culture and Imperi-alism*, for example, Edward Said points out that the "stunning" silence of the first-generation Frankfurt School theorists on the sub-jects of "racist theory, anti-imperialist resistance and oppositional practice in the empire" is, if anything, compounded rather than revised in Habermas's contemporary writings: "[L]est that silence be interpreted as an oversight, we have today's leading Frankfurt theor-ist, Jürgen Habermas, explaining in an interview . . . that the silence is deliberate abstention: no, he says, we have nothing to say to 'anti-imperialist and anti-capitalist struggles in the Third World,' even if, he adds, 'I am aware of the fact that this is a eurocentrically limited view.'"[83] Gilroy's approach to Habermas is somewhat different, for he begins by conceding the resonance and value of Habermas's reconstructive critique of the dominant construction of modernity. While he points out, thus, that Habermas continues to believe that "the unfulfilled promise of modernity's Enlightenment project re-mains a beleaguered but nonetheless vibrant resource which may even now be able to guide the practice of contemporary social and political struggles" (*Black Atlantic*, p. 46), he freely acknowledges that Habermas's endorsement of modernity is neither positivistic nor naive. On the contrary, he notes approvingly, "modernity [in Haber-mas] is apprehended through its counter-discourses and often de-fended solely through its counterfactual elements" (p. 49).

Gilroy's own disagreement with Habermas does not therefore proceed from the bald fact of Habermas's blindness to the question of imperialism. Rather, it derives from what this blindness seems to Gilroy to entail: because Habermas fails to register even the existence of the black Atlantic, Gilroy writes, he cannot appreciate the degree to which "racial terror is not merely compatible with occidental rationality but cheerfully complicit with it" (p. 56; see also p. 213). On Gilroy's reading, Habermas's would-be emancipatory reconstruction of the problematic of modernity is as thoroughgoing in its logocentrism as that of modernity's master narrative. He argues in general that "the history of the African diaspora and a reassessment of the relationship between modernity and slavery may require a more complete revision of the terms in which the modernity debates have been constructed than any of its academic participants may be willing to concede" (p. 46). And with Habermas in particular in mind, he suggests that:

In the period after slavery, the memory of the slave experience is itself recalled and used as an additional, supplementary instrument with which to construct a distinct interpretation of modernity. Whether or not these memories invoke the remembrance of a terror which has moved beyond the grasp of ideal, grammatical speech, they point out of the present towards a utopian transformation of racial subordination. We must enquire then whether a definition of modern rationality such as that employed by Habermas leaves room for a liberatory, aesthetic moment which is emphatically anti- or even pre-discursive? (p. 71)

One should not by any means take Gilroy's critique of Habermas to indicate a sympathy on his part with the terms of the contemporary poststructuralist (or postmodernist) repudiation of modernity as an historical project. On the contrary, as his rhetorical question to Habermas in the passage just cited makes clear, his assumption is that what he calls "the historical memories of the black Atlantic" (p. 55) are often – and, indeed, most characteristically – sedimented in cultural forms and social practices that are not amenable to investigation under the auspices of discursive reason. In order to address the significance of black Atlantic sociality and expressive culture, it is therefore necessary to reorient one's hermeneutic interest: *away* from models of linguisticality, discursivity, and textuality; *toward* "the phatic and the ineffable" (p. 73). Gilroy takes his distance, thus, not only from Habermasian discourse ethics[84] but also, and more adamantly still, from poststructuralism. He insists, for instance, that the expressivity of black Atlantic sociocultural practice is unassimilable by the poststructuralist notions of the text and of textuality:

Urged on by the post-structuralist critiques of the metaphysics of presence, contemporary debates have moved beyond citing language as the fundamental analogy for comprehending all signifying practices to a position where textuality (especially when wrenched open through the concept of difference) expands and merges with totality. Paying careful attention to the structures of feeling which underpin black expressive cultures can show how this critique is incomplete. It gets blocked by the invocation of all-encompassing textuality. Textuality becomes a means to evacuate the problem of human agency, a means to specify the death (by fragmentation) of the subject and, in the same manoeuvre, to enthrone the literary critic as mistress or master of the domain of creative human communication. (p. 77; see also p. 36)

Throughout *The Black Atlantic*, Gilroy makes his case about modernity and black Atlantic sociality through reference to cultural practice. This emphasis is not to be understood as unwittingly betraying a culturalist bias. On the contrary, it indicates a self-consciously assumed position on the status and meaning of culture in the lives of blacks in the West. In consonance with his elaboration of the notion of "double consciousness," Gilroy makes three related points about the culture of the black Atlantic populations. First, he argues that through its staging of the act of remembrance, through its mediation of contemporary suffering into aesthetic form, black culture is able to constitute itself as a vehicle of consolation. Second, he identifies this consoling function as bearing (in the form of its dialectical shadow) the latently insurrectionary specter of a transfigured world. Remembrance, Gilroy quotes Adorno as suggesting, cannot but serve "to give flesh and blood to the notion of utopia" (p. 212). Third, he speculates that it is possible to read this utopianism of black culture *philosophically*, as embodying a critique of the given world.

It is the integrity, the comprehensiveness, of the movement outlined here – from consolation to redemptive critique – that requires special emphasis. Writing with respect to black music in particular, thus, Gilroy observes that its "obstinate and consistent commitment to the idea of a better future" positively obliges us to pay attention not only to its formal attributes but also to "its distinctive *moral* basis . . . In the simplest possible terms, by posing the world as it is against the world as the racially subordinated would like it to be, this musical culture supplies a great deal of the courage required to go on living in the present" (p. 36). Yet even this is not all. For it is necessary, in addition, to grasp the critical thrust of black culture's utopianism as establishing a set of claims that are not merely political but fully philosophical as well:

I am proposing, then, that we reread and rethink this expressive counter-culture not simply as a succession of literary tropes and genres but as a philosophical discourse which refuses the modern occidental separation of ethics and aesthetics, culture and politics . . . This [western] tradition had maintained the idea that a good life for the individual and the problem of the best social and political order for the collectivity could be discerned by rational means. Though it is seldom acknowledged even now, this tradition lost its exclusive claim to rationality partly through the way that slavery became internal to western civilisation and through the obvious complicity which both plantation slavery and colonial regimes revealed between rationality and the practice of racial terror.

(pp. 38–39)

Hence, ultimately, the significance of black Atlantic culture for Gilroy: born in modernity but denied by those who have spoken in its name; existing, therefore, in the cracks of modernity, as a counter-discourse to the prevailing ideologeme of the modern; flourishing there, despite everything; consolidating itself, regenerating itself; and possessing, initially as a latency, increasingly as a concrete potential, the capacity to explode the pretensions of "the modern." Like Adorno (whom he cites on numerous occasions) – but on the basis of cultural practices that Adorno in his Eurocentrism would actively have disparaged and condemned – Gilroy presents culture as a privileged medium of political action in the modern era. In the field of culture as nowhere else for the diasporic populations of the black Atlantic, expressive practice has been able to become "the means towards both individual self-fashioning and communal liberation. Poiesis and poetics [have] beg[un] to coexist in novel forms – autobiographical writing, special and uniquely creative ways of manipulating spoken language, and, above all, the music. All three have overflowed from the containers that the modern nation state [has] provide[d] for them" (p. 40).

A good place to start a critical assessment of the achievement of *The Black Atlantic* might be to register again the force and effectivity of its critique of nation-centered scholarship. The challenge that Gilroy delivers to the assumptions framing much of the work undertaken in the field of African-American studies strikes me as especially decisive. His suggestion that "the intellectual heritage of Euro-American modernity determined and possibly still determines the manner in which nationality is understood within black political discourse" (p. 30) seems counter-intuitive at first, but becomes more and more credible and, indeed, compelling, the more fully he elaborates his counter-concepts of "double consciousness," transculturalism, hybridity, and diaspora. As he puts it in his chapter "Black Music and the Politics of Authenticity," these and similar concepts are

indispensable in focusing on the political and ethical dynamics of the unfinished history of blacks in the modern world. The dangers of idealism and pastoralisation associated with the[se] concept[s] ought, by now, to be obvious, but the very least that [they] offer . . . is an heuristic means to focus on the relationship of identity and non-identity in black political culture. [They] can also be employed to project the plural richness of black cultures in different parts of the world in counterpoint to their common sensibilities – both those residually inherited from Africa and those generated from the special bitterness of new world racial slavery.

(pp. 80–81)

Clearly, Gilroy's insistence on the transculturalism, internationalism, and irreducible hybridity of black Atlanticism and – behind it – of modernity itself is vastly to be preferred over the essentialism and unidimensionality of nation-centered cultural studies. But for this very reason it seems extraordinary that *The Black Atlantic* should acknowledge no countervailing or alternative theories of transnationalism or globalization – not even in order to dismiss them. There is not a single reference, for instance, to world-system theory or to the work of such writers as Immanuel Wallerstein, Samir Amin, or André Gunder Frank. The crucial absence here is of any sustained or plausible engagement with *Marxism*. Such an engagement is unforgoable in a book of *The Black Atlantic*'s scope and pretensions, it seems to me, since Marxism can credibly claim to have been (for over a hundred years now) the source and inspiration of the most coherent and principled theories both of the advent of capitalist modernity and of the universalizing propensities and global reach (the systematicity) of capitalism as an historical formation. Central to these theories from the outset has been a critique of nationalism, an insistence that the determinants of social life are secured globally and not at the level of the nation-state, and that, therefore, the only form of politics capable of presenting a decisive challenge to the globalism of actually existing capitalism is an internationalist socialism. As Samir Amin has written:

A humane and progressive response to the problems of the contemporary world implies the construction of a popular internationalism that can engender a genuinely universalist value system, completing the unfinished projects of the Enlightenment and the socialist movement. This is the only way to build an effective front against the internationalism of capital and the false universalism of its value system.[85]

Gilroy betrays a notable ambivalence toward Marxism. In *The Black*

Atlantic, as in his earlier work, he maintains simultaneously that his own political and intellectual investments are compatible with those of Marxism *and* that Marxism is a relatively discredited theoretical enterprise, one whose methods and concepts (including that of capitalism as a world system) can be indicted as deriving squarely from the dominant (and dominative) problematic of modernity. Thus, on the one hand, he moves explicitly to position the concept of black Atlanticism alongside Marxism, as supplementary to it: "in what follows," he writes, "the critique of bourgeois ideology and the fulfilment of the Enlightenment project under the banner of working-class emancipation which goes hand in hand with it is being complemented by another struggle – the battle to represent a redemptive critique of the present in the light of the vital memories of the slave past" (p. 71). On the other hand, however, he makes clear that he regards Marxist claims concerning the centrality of class struggle, the logic of social determination, and the analytical priority of production over consumption (and distribution), among others, as either philosophically untenable or historically anachronistic (or both).

In *"There Ain't No Black in the Union Jack,"* Gilroy draws (very selectively) on contemporary debates about postindustrialism, post-Fordism, the service economy, the professional-managerial class, class consciousness, and so on – only to fault Marxism for its totalizing propensities, its productivism, its metaphysical and essentialist conception of the proletariat, and its economism. Not much is added to this fairly formulaic commentary in *The Black Atlantic*. What sense are we to make, then, of Gilroy's suggestion that his analysis of black Atlanticism is readily compatible with a Marxist theory of modern capitalist society?

I do not, myself, believe that it is so compatible. It seems to me that there is at least a latent antagonism between the concepts of the black Atlantic and the capitalist world system. I have already alluded to Gilroy's exhortation to cultural historians to "take the Atlantic as one single, complex unit of analysis in their discussions of the modern world and use it to produce an explicitly transnational and intercultural perspective" (*Black Atlantic*, p. 15). The question that we must ask here concerns the consequences that follow from Gilroy's choice of (black) Atlanticism over (capitalist) world system as the preferred unit of sociohistorical analysis. If his own work can be taken as indicative in this respect, it would seem that this choice involves the loss of a specifically *global* perspective. One way of noting this loss is to record that vast regions of the "non-West" are conspicuously absent from *The Black Atlantic*, notwithstanding Gilroy's focus upon the problematics of diaspora and transculturalism. Africa and Asia are strictly marginal to his exposition, leaving us to conclude that if *The Black Atlantic* clearly obliges us to revise our assumptions as to the *racial* provenance of modernity, it leaves assumptions as to the *Western* provenance of the modern potentially undisturbed. Blacks might be internal to the West, therefore; but modernity is still a Western, and not a global phenomenon. A world system perspective, one that insisted upon the dialectic of development and underdevelopment, as well as upon the analytic of combined and uneven development, would seek to counter this impression through its mobilization of the theory of imperialism (a theory for which Gilroy appears, revealingly, to have little use).

Inasmuch as he centers his analysis in *The Black Atlantic* on modern slavery, Gilroy obviously commits himself to the study of racialized, as distinct from class, consciousness. In itself this is unexceptionable; and Gilroy follows Stuart Hall in specifying race as the modality in which class is lived (p. 85). (It is striking, nonetheless, that he should make no reference whatsoever to Eric Williams's *Capitalism and Slavery*.)[86] Yet because he abstracts slavery from the development of capitalism, Gilroy seems to me also to overstate its significance with respect to the constitution of modernity. One consequence of construing Morrison's formulation, that "modern life begins with slavery," as strictly as he does is that Gilroy is obliged to accord blacks in the West analytical precedence over other groups (elite and subaltern) as bearers of modernity. Specifically, this has the effect of rendering "belated," so to speak, the vast and collective historical experiences – of indenture, wage labor, forced migration, colonization, etc. – that subtended and existed alongside slavery and that are as inextricably constitutive of the modern world as slavery is. Since such experiences are not theorized in relation to modernity, however, Gilroy's reader is left to wonder what he takes their historical status to be. Is it meaningful, though, in the contexts of Trinidad or Guyana, for example, to distinguish the historical experience of slavery from those of wage labor, migrancy, and indenture, *along the axis of modernity*? Why should the specifically racialized (and, of course, specifically spatialized) concept of black Atlanticism become the model for an understanding of social formations shaped as centrally by diasporic populations from South and East Asia as from Africa? Again, it seems to me that what might have been gained by the application of the concept of the capitalist world system is lost in the application of the concept of the black Atlantic. The latter concept keeps at arm's length, if it does not necessarily seek to displace, the premise of the determinative role of capitalism in the structuring of modernity.

One of the most suggestive features of *The Black Atlantic*, in my view, consists in its attempt to ground the materiality of historical memory. "How do black expressive cultures practise remembrance?" Gilroy asks at one point: "How is their remembering socially organised? How is this active remembrance associated with a distinctive and disjunctive temporality of the subordinated? How are this temporality and historicity constructed and marked out publicly?" (p. 212). I find salutary here the properly materialist identification of thought and consciousness as bearing social effects. Experience matters, for Gilroy; that is to say not only that it is significant but also that it sediments itself in forms and traditions and institutions. Yet two major problems attach to Gilroy's elaboration of this idea of historical memory as a material force: the first concerns the selectivity of his actualization of it; the second concerns the displacement of the question of truth by the question of lived experience in his analysis of modern black sociality.

We have seen that Gilroy positions slavery as the *fons et origo* of modern (black) social existence and that one of the strengths of his analysis resides in his ability to relate cultural practice in the post-emancipation period compellingly to the experience of slavery. The historical memories of slavery do not simply "haunt" subsequent cultural practice; rather, they contribute decisively to the shape that it assumes – they mark it, register themselves upon it, at the levels of both form and content. Slavery is phrased, in other words, as an elemental and indissoluble residue within social and cultural practice even in the post-slavery era. It is fundamental to the identity of modern black social being. Hence Gilroy writes, about Richard Wright, that "[p]erhaps more than any other writer he showed how modernity was both the period and the region in which black politics grew. His work articulates simultaneously an affirmation and a negation of the western civilisation that formed him. It remains the most powerful expression of the insider–outsider duality which we have traced down the years from slavery" (p. 186).

The trouble, then, is that in Gilroy's work this suggestive premise of the materiality of historical memory seems admissible only in certain contexts. Consider for instance the terms of his critique of Raymond Williams. In his 1983 book, *Towards 2000*, Williams had written that it is a serious misunderstanding ... to suppose that the problems of social identity are resolved by formal (merely legal) definitions. For unevenly and at times precariously, but always through long experience substantially, an effective awareness of social identity depends on actual and sustained social relationships. To reduce social identity to formal legal definitions, at the level of the state, is to collude in the alienated superficialities of "the nation" which are limited functional terms of the modern ruling class.   (quoted in *"There Ain't No Black,"* p. 49)

With its patient, materialist emphasis on the substantiality of "long experience" and the socially constitutive effects of "actual and sustained social relationships," this passage would seem to be predicated on assumptions about historicity and historical memory very similar to Gilroy's own. (One recalls also the statement in Williams's great essay "Culture is Ordinary" to the effect that "I was not, by the way, oppressed by Cambridge. I was not cast down by old buildings, for I had come from a country with twenty centuries of history written visibly into the earth."[87]) But far from celebrating such formulations in Williams, Gilroy excoriates them. Williams's words in *Towards 2000*, he writes, are meant to serve as a response

to anti-racists who would answer the denial that blacks can be British by saying "They are as British as you are." He dismisses this reply as "the standard liberal" variety. His alternative conception stresses that social identity is a product of "long experience." But this prompts the question – how long is long enough to become a genuine Brit? . . . [T]hese arguments effectively deny that blacks can share a significant "social identity" with their white neighbours who, in contrast to more recent arrivals, inhabit what Williams calls "rooted settlements" articulated by "lived and formed identities."
(*"There Ain't No Black,"* pp. 49–50; see also *Small Acts*, p. 30)

There is a contradiction here, it seems to me. It may well be, as Gilroy argues, that "Williams's discussion of 'race' and nation . . . is notable for its refusal to examine the concept of racism which has its own historic relationship with ideologies of Englishness, Britishness and national belonging" (*"There Ain't No Black,"* p. 50). But I do not see how Gilroy can insist that the historical experience of slavery remains materially constitutive of contemporary black Atlantic sociality while denying to Williams the right to make a similar claim about the determination of contemporary Welsh sociality by its "twenty centuries of history written visibly into the earth." Williams is not, of course (although Gilroy rather implies that he is), denying the indispensability of citizenship rights, etc., to black immigrants to Britain. Rather, he is suggesting that the production and reproduction of social life has to be seen to determine the forms of identity that a people can and do assume. Gilroy makes just this point with respect to the populations of the black Atlantic; his failure to do so "across the board" is troubling and inconsistent.

Related to this is the problem of truth and lived experience. Consider here the following passage, drawn from the final paragraph of the first chapter of *The Black Atlantic* – entitled "The Black Atlantic as a Counterculture of Modernity." Gilroy is referring, once again, to the "convergence" between his own project and "other projects towards a critical theory of society, particularly Marxism." The key difference, he argues, is that

> where lived crisis and systemic crisis come together, Marxism allocates priority to the latter while the memory of slavery insists on the priority of the former. Their convergence is also undercut by the simple fact that in the critical thought of blacks in the West, social self-creation through labour is not the centre-piece of emancipatory hopes. For the descendants of slaves, work signifies only servitude, misery, and subordination.
>
> (p. 40)

I would like to raise two issues in connection with this argument. First, I want to contend that it is not because of the historical memory of slavery that "[f]or the descendants of slaves [today], work signifies only servitude, misery, and subordination." Gilroy appears to overlook the obvious here: that if in the post-slavery era work has continued to signify only servitude, misery, and subordination to the descendants of slaves, this is because the kinds of work available to this population since abolition have been conducive only to servitude, misery, and subordination! In short, I cannot accept Gilroy's insistence upon the radical and constitutive singularity of racial slavery and its memory to the formation of modernity and black Atlantic sociality. Surely the vicissitudes of wage labor and the coercion of the market play an even larger role in this respect?[88]

Second, it seems to me that the effect of the quoted passage considered as a whole is to reduce to insignificance the epistemological distinction – one that I regard as crucial – between "lived" and "systemic" crisis. As I understand it, the former category refers to *experience*; the latter to that which *is experienced*. It is true that "systemic" crisis can never be experienced as itself (that is to say, that "systemic" crises are always apprehended as "lived" crises). But this does not affect in the least the epistemological distinction between the two forms. That "the memory of slavery" insists on the priority of the lived crisis does nothing to ground the adequacy of this perspective, any more than the injunction to "remember the Alamo" serves to ground the adequacy of the perspective of unrepentant Anglo-Americanism. Yet throughout *The Black Atlantic*, Gilroy argues that racial slavery is not only the founding but also the overdetermining instance of black Atlantic sociality, in the present as much as in the past. One understands the force of this argument when measured against those tendencies in what Gilroy calls "Africentric" thought, which tend to "forget" slavery and to invoke in its place "the duration of a black civilisation anterior to modernity" (p. 190). But when measured against the formulations of historical materialist theory, Gilroy's achievement begins to seem considerably less prepossessing. It is greatly to be regretted that Gilroy did not look both ways – toward Marxism as well as toward "Africentric" or nationalist scholarship – before committing *The Black Atlantic* to print.

2

Disavowing decolonization: nationalism, intellectuals, and the question of representation in postcolonial theory

Over the course of the past fifteen years or so, and – for very obvious geopolitical reasons – especially since 1989, there has been something of an obsessive return to the subjects of nationalism and the nation-state in Western-based cultural, historical, and social scientific scholarship. These subjects, which – as the mere mention of the names of Ernest Renan and John Stuart Mill might be sufficient to indicate – were already important to European thought in the latter half of the nineteenth century, had remained so well into the twentieth. Yet their prominence diminished quite sharply in the 1970s and early 1980s, as scholarly interest turned away from the nation toward the analysis and championing of other forms of political community (whether sub- or transnational).[1] But contemporary developments – in Eastern Europe and the former Soviet Union, in India, in southern and central Africa, and elsewhere – have had the effect of reversing this recent trajectory and directing scholarly attention once again to the "national question."

The scope and suddenness of these contemporary developments – the collapse of historical communism, the end of apartheid, the cataclysm in Rwanda, etc. – were nowhere predicted and tended to catch everyone unawares. Despite this – or precisely because of it, perhaps – most of the contemporary studies have continued to be pitched quite unreflexively upon the terrain of the unambiguously First Worldist interpretation of nationalism that has been predominant since at least 1918. Nationalism, that is to say, has been seen as constituting a kind of return of the repressed. The sheer destructiveness of developments in Rwanda, Liberia, Chechnya, the Caucasus, and in what only a few years ago was still Yugoslavia, has been taken to reveal a fundamental truth about nationalism in general: not merely that it is chauvinistic, but also that it only ever results in the violent intensification of already existing social divisions.[2]

There is, of course, something deeply disingenuous about this kind of commentary, emanating as it does from policy centers, media headquarters, and institutions of higher learning in the core capitalist *nations* of Britain, France, Germany, and the United States. The contemporary studies and reports that classify and deplore the adamantine "persistence" or volcanic "resurgence" of nationalism in Algeria or Serbia or Georgia or Afghanistan tend to be premised upon an expedient naturalization of the trajectories of nationalism in the metropolitan West. In what Tim Brennan terms "a conveniently European lapse of memory,"[3] "our" nationalisms – to the extent that they become visible at all as objects of inquiry – are typically classed as finished projects and are taken to have had benign effects: modernizing, unifying, democratizing. "Their" supposedly still unfolding nationalisms, on the other hand, are categorized under the rubrics of atavism, anarchy, irrationality, and power-mongering. Nationalism in the East or South is centrally on the research agenda today, in short, for the basically strategic reason that it is taken to pose a danger to the established social order of the West. As Partha Chatterjee puts it,

> nationalism is now viewed as a dark, elemental, unpredictable force of primordial nature threatening the orderly calm of civilized life. What had once been successfully relegated to the outer peripheries of the earth is now seen picking its way back toward Europe, through the long-forgotten provinces of the Habsburg, the czarist, and the Ottoman empires. Like drugs, terrorism, and illegal immigration, it is one more product of the Third World that the West dislikes but is powerless to prohibit.[4]

The sheer perversity of this dominant conception of nationalism is attested to by the fact that if there is any one thing upon which all of the most important theorists of nationalism since the time of Hans Kohn (if not, even earlier, of Lenin and Otto Bauer) have agreed, it is that nations and nationalisms are irreducibly *modern* phenomena. Any attempt to theorize them as elemental or even prehistorical forces or formations is therefore condemned in advance to error and incoherence. Eric Hobsbawm's blunt observation that "[t]he basic characteristic of the modern nation and everything connected with it is its modernity"[5] receives explicit confirmation, on the basis of copious evidence and documentation, in the work of Benedict Anderson, Etienne Balibar, John Breuilly, Basil Davidson, Ernest Gellner, Liah Greenfeld, Miroslav Hroch, Tom Nairn, and Immanuel Wallerstein – to name only a few of the more broadly influential contemporary writers on the subject. Yet "[t]he most widely held theory of nationalism" continues to be "the one that believes it to be not merely the reawakening of cultures, but the re-emergence of atavistic instincts of *Blut und Boden* in the human breast."[6] This dominant conception is proof, evidently, against all repudiation, no matter how definitive. It seems to make no difference how often, or with what authority, it is demonstrated that "nationalism is *not* the awakening of an old, latent, dormant force . . . [but] is in reality the consequence of a new form of social organization."[7] A majority of commentators will still take it for granted that "national identification is somehow so natural, primary and permanent as to precede history" (Hobsbawm, *Nations*, p. 14).

Commentators on the political left today are of course opposed to the dehistoricizing and triumphantly First Worldist (not to say, "Cold War-ist") quality of much of the mainstream commentary. Yet for them, too, the production of an adequate theory of nationalism is evidently proving a vexed matter. Consider, for instance, the account that Hobsbawm offers in his 1990 study, *Nations and Nationalism Since 1780.* Three aspects of the distinguished socialist historian's presentation are particularly worthy of note at this point, it seems to me: first, there is his conviction that in the late twentieth century, the nation-form has been rendered anachronistic; second, there is the deep-set Eurocentrism of his analysis; and third, there is the relatively undifferentiating quality of his treatment of specific nations, nationalisms, and national movements. I shall return to the question of Hobsbawm's Eurocentrism later in this chapter. Here, however, because of its representative quality, I would like to look briefly at his argument with respect to the other two aspects just delineated.

Hobsbawm echoes some of the progressive commentators whose work we examined in Chapter One in arguing that the contemporary restructuring of global capitalist social relations – ensuing from the more or less coeval collapse of the Stalinist state system (in the East), partial destruction of Keynesianism and the welfarist "class compromise" (in the West), and containment and dissipation of radical anti-imperialist movements (in the South) – has been such as to render the nation-form obsolete. (This argument also has its liberal and conservative proponents, of course.) The nation, he writes, "is no longer a major vector of historical development" (*Nations*, p. 163). It is not that Hobsbawm is blind to the continuing significance of nationalism in sparking events throughout the world. Rather, his argument is that in spite of its evident prominence, nationalism is historically less important [than it once was]. It is no longer, as it were, a global political programme, as it may be said to have been in the nineteenth and earlier twentieth centuries. It is at most a complicating factor, or a catalyst for other developments. It is not implausible to present the history of the Eurocentric nineteenth-century world as that of "nation-building," as Walter Bagehot did. We still present the history of the major European states of Europe after 1870 in this manner, as in the title of Eugene Weber's *Peasants into Frenchmen*. Is anyone likely to write the world history of the late twentieth and early twenty-first centuries in such terms? It is most unlikely. (pp. 181–82)

Hobsbawm is convinced that the political and economic conditions that brought the modern nation-state into existence in the first place, and that have continued to sustain it since then, are dissolving. One of the striking features of his presentation rests in the confidence with which he moves to identify and define current developments as constituting not merely a sociological trend but a categorical transformation, momentous and irreversible: the dissolution of the nation-state; the obsolescence of nationalism; the reconfiguration of class relations; etc. To derive such epochal conclusions is, as I have suggested generally in Chapter One, to "over-read" considerably the available sociological evidence. It is not only, as Michael Löwy has written in assessing Hobsbawm's argument, that the mistaken propensity to herald "the imminent decline of nationalism and of the nation-state, made anachronistic by the internationalization of the economy" has long been a bugbear of radical thought in general.[8] It is also that

one can hardly avoid the impression that the great historian is taking his desires for reality. One does not need to sympathize with nationalist ideologies in order to take into account their growing influence in Europe. It is difficult to predict what is going to happen during the next century, but now, and in the coming years, it is impossible to consider the role of nationalism in Europe (and elsewhere) as a minor or secondary factor.[9]

Hobsbawm clearly assumes that "globalization" (i.e., capitalist internationalization) and nation-statism are contradictory tendencies. However, both the historical and the sociological records seem to suggest that, if anything, the reverse is the case – the two tendencies are typically twinned, mutually supportive and entailing. Against Hobsbawm, indeed, I would want to insist *both* that the "tension" between nationalist (particularist) and internationalist (universalist) tendencies is scarcely unprecedented, having been (in Wallerstein's words) "a constant feature of the political and intellectual landscape of capitalist development,"[10] *and* that inter-nationalization is not (necessarily) secured at the expense of the national polity or economy.[11] The latter point has been made rather nicely by Chris Harman in his programmatic essay on "The State and Capitalism Today." Reviewing the contemporary debate about globalization, Harman concludes that the historically institutionalized relationship between capital and the nation-state

does not disappear with multinationalisation. The giant company does not end its link with the state, but rather multiplies the number of states – and national capitalist networks – to which it is linked. The successor to state capitalism is not some non-state capitalism (as is implied by expressions such as "multinational" or "transnational capitalism") but rather a capitalism in which capitals rely on the state as much as ever, but try to spread out beyond it to form links with capitals tied to other states – perhaps best described as "trans-state" capitalism.[12]

Harman adds that

The four functions the state has fulfilled for capital in the past continue to be important to each individual capital – the guaranteeing of supplies of skilled labour power and of some degree of protection of local markets, the orderly regulation of commercial relations with other capitals and the provision of a stable currency, the taking of measures to protect firms against the sudden dangers presented by the collapse of large suppliers and customers, and the provision of military might as a last resort protector of interests. These functions by no means "wither away." In fact, some of them grow more important. (p. 34)

By way of illustration, he cites the stock exchange crash of October 1987:

The continued dependence of capital on national states is borne out by the behaviour of finance capital in crisis. Historically . . . finance capital has been less tightly rooted in the national state than productive capital, and in the boom conditions of the mid-1980s it seemed to move very rapidly in the direction of globalisation. However, the financial crisis of October 1987 . . . and the onset of recession in 1989 both brought home very strongly its need for the state. State intervention – particularly in the US where the state poured tens of billions of dollars into the financial system – was central in preventing the financial crisis spilling over into a crisis of the rest of the system . . . What is more, individual finance capitalists responded to the crisis by rushing back to the relative security of their national states. (p. 36)

A related problem with Hobsbawm's commentary derives from the fact that he tends to present nationalism as a unitary phenomenon – one that, whatever else one might want to say about it, has generally been successful in realizing itself, almost invariably with ghastly consequences, over the course of the past 200 years. Failing to distinguish adequately between *different* nationalist projects, Hobsbawm construes nationalism as an inherently violent and destructive phenomenon, toward which, therefore, he feels justified in evincing a more or less undifferentiating hostility. Hence, of the vicious chauvinist nationalism that led central European polities in the post-1914 period to seek to "create . . . coherent territorial states each inhabited by a separate ethnically and linguistically homogeneous population," he writes not only that it had as its "logical implication" "the mass expulsion or extermination of minorities," but also that "[s]uch was and is the murderous *reductio ad absurdum* of nationalism in its territorial version, although this was not fully demonstrated until the 1940s" (*Nations*, p. 133). Hobsbawm's suggestion is that the exterminism of post-1914 European developments bespeaks the essential truth of nationalism. The fact that other nationalists in other times and places might beg to differ, or that the politics of other national movements (such as that of the African National Congress in South Africa, for example) might tend to point in completely different directions, counts for absolutely nothing in his eyes.[13] It is not to be wondered at, therefore, that he should begin his study by insisting that since "[n]ationalism requires too much belief in what is patently not so," "no serious historian of nations and nationalism can be a committed political nationalist" (p. 12). Hence, too, his insistence that nationalism can only be a nostalgic and reactionary ideological enterprise today – in strict terms, indeed, a decadent indulgence that no democratic consciousness can afford. *Nations and Nationalism Since 1780* concludes with its author's disparagement of nationalism in the post-1945 period as "a substitute for lost dreams," as he looks forward to the time – both imminent and inevitable, on his reading – when it will have withered away altogether (p. 178). Hobsbawm takes comfort from the fact that nationalism is being fiercely debated today among historians; this, he says archly, "suggests that, as so often, the phenomenon is past its peak. The owl of Minerva which brings wisdom . . . flies out at dusk. It is a good sign that it is now circling round nations and nationalism" (p. 183).

Hobsbawm commits himself to this wholesale disparagement of nationalism, arguably, because he projects as normative and globally representative the nationalist models characteristic of the imperialist, metropolitan social formations – that is, because he fails to distinguish at the least between imperialist and anti-imperialist nationalist projects and problematics. As Brennan has pointed out, imperialist nationalisms have typically taken the form of "project[s] of *unity* on the basis of conquest and economic expediency."[14] They tend to be appropriative enterprises, in which conquest is succeeded by subsumption, of land or resources or the conquered population itself. Hence not only modern British, American, Russian, and Israeli nationalisms, but also, in the present conjuncture, the nationalisms of Indonesia, Croatia, and "Greater Serbia." Anti-imperialist nationalisms, by contrast, tend either to be predicated upon the "project of consolidation following an act of *separation* from [an imperialist power]" or else to be oriented toward that goal. Theirs is "the task of reclaiming community from within boundaries defined by the very power whose presence denied community."[15]

This distinction between imperialist and anti-imperialist nationalisms draws implicitly on the Leninist formula concerning nationalist in relation to socialist politics. In his pamphlet on *The Right of Nations to Self-Determination*, Lenin argued that while in an absolute sense socialist politics entailed an opposition to nationalism as such, it was essential for socialists to recognize and *"unconditionally* support" the "democratic content" of those nationalist movements (including bourgeois nationalist movements) that were "directed *against* oppression."[16] Polemicizing against Rosa Luxemburg, *inter alia*, Lenin insisted that socialists' "unambiguous appeal to the workers for *international* unity in their class struggle" needed to be complemented by an "absolutely direct, unequivocal recognition of the full right of all nations to self-determination" (p. 43; italics in original). "At a time when bourgeois-democratic revolutions in Eastern Europe and Asia have begun," he wrote,

in this period of the awakening and intensification of national movements and of the formation of independent proletarian parties, the task of these parties with regard to national policy must be two-fold: recognition of the right of all nations to self-determination, since bourgeois-democratic reform is not yet completed and since working-class democracy consistently, seriously and sincerely . . . fights for equal rights for nations; then, a close, unbreakable alliance in the class struggle of the proletarians of all nations in a given state, throughout all the changes in its history, irrespective of any reshaping of the frontiers of the individual states by the bourgeoisie.   (p. 45)[17]

Now it may be that Lenin's formulation requires further elaboration to qualify it to bear stipulatively upon the overdeterminations of contemporary nationalisms and national movements. Thus

Michael Löwy writes in a recent article that while "it is vital to distinguish between the nationalism of domineering states and the nationalism of those resisting oppression," a bald reiteration of the Leninist doctrine "is clearly insufficient for responding to modern nationalisms."[18] The problem, for Löwy (he has in mind contemporary developments in Eastern Europe and the former Soviet Union, although the insight is generalizable), is that "[i]n recent times, oppressed nations, as soon as they are liberated, rush to institute an analogous oppression over their own national minorities." To accommodate such developments – which give rise to a tangled "web of mutually exclusive claims," Löwy advocates that the Leninist doctrine be supplemented by "a further universal criterion":

This criterion can only be that – common to socialists and democrats – of the right of self-determination (until separation) of each nation, that is, of each community which democratically decides it is a nation. The advantage of this criterion is that it refers not to ancestral or religious claims over territory but to universal principles of democracy and popular sovereignty. It also allows for a vital distinction between nation and state, recognising that national self-determination could take many different forms: state separation (independence), federation, confederation, or limited sovereignty or rights in a multinational or multi-ethnic state. Lenin once likened the principle of self-determination to divorce, saying that it did not imply the desirability of separation: in fact couples can only live together harmoniously if they have the right to divorce. [19]

Like many other socialist thinkers today, Löwy is concerned to refine and revise the classic Leninist doctrine. Yet what I find particularly salutary about his commentary is its clear conviction that it would be a mistake to abandon Lenin's commitment to distinguishing politically *between* different nationalisms or national movements: for him, as for Lenin, there can be no retreating from the view that *some* claims to nationhood are legitimate and emancipatory, and must be upheld by socialists. From the standpoint of socialism (still less of Marxism), that is to say, no abstract or *a priori* assessment of nationalist politics is credible. Hence Lenin's critique of Luxemburg in *The Right of Nations to Self-Determination*, for example, whose central charge is precisely that Luxemburg's opposition to nationalism is abstract and *a prioristic*. The same point has also been made by Aijaz Ahmad, who argues, correctly in my view, that "it is only from the prior and explicit socialist location that [the Marxist theorist] . . . select[s] particular nationalist positions for criticism, even at times very harsh denunciation; a critique of nationalism without that explicit location in the determinate socialist project has never made any sense for me, either politically or theoretically."[20] This way of viewing things, Ahmad adds, requires a recognition of "the actuality, even the necessity, of progressive and revolutionary kinds of nationalism."[21]

It is precisely this ideologically discriminating approach to nationalism that Hobsbawm seems unwilling to endorse. For him, evidently, there are no "progressive and revolutionary kinds of nationalism," only murderous kinds. On his reading, of course, it is in the name of the emancipatory "grand narratives" of the (post-) Enlightenment era that nationalism must be resolutely opposed. Hobsbawm's intellectual presuppositions and ideological commitments remain refreshingly different from those (Foucauldian, "post-Marxist," postmodernist, etc.) that have come to exercise such influence in cultural studies, history, and sociological theory in recent years. Not for nothing does he move to declare "an interest" in "Barbarism: A User's Guide," one of his recent essays in *New Left Review*:

I believe that one of the few things that stands between us and an accelerated descent into darkness is the set of values inherited from the eighteenth-century Enlightenment. This is not a fashionable view at this moment, when the Enlightenment can be dismissed as anything from superficial and intellectually naive to a conspiracy of dead white men in periwigs to provide the intellectual foundation for Western imperialism. It may or may not be all that, but it is also the only foundation for all the aspirations to build societies fit for all human beings to live in anywhere on this Earth, and for the assertion and defence of their human rights as persons. In any case, the progress of civility which took place from the eighteenth century until the early twentieth was achieved overwhelmingly or entirely under the influence of the Enlightenment . . . This era when progress was not merely supposed to be both material and moral but actually was, has come to an end. But the only criterion which allows us to judge rather than merely to record the consequent descent into barbarism, is the old rationalism of the Enlightenment.[22]

In its abstraction and *a priorism*, however – that is to say, considered *formally* – Hobsbawm's construction of nationalism is identical with that which has latterly come to prevail in these avowedly progressive quarters of the metropolitan academy.

One might have thought that the sheer volatility of nationalism would be enough to prompt progressive intellectuals today to view it with cautious optimism, as a relatively open site of political and ideological contestation – since, as Ahmad states, "[w]hether or not a nationalism will produce a progressive cultural practice depends, to put it in Gramscian terms, upon the political character of the power bloc which takes hold of it and utilizes it, as a material force, in the process of constituting its own hegemony" (*In Theory*, p. 102). Nations, after all, as Anne McClintock has written, "are contested systems of cultural representation that limit and legitimize people's access to the rights and resources of the nation-state."[23] Yet progressive scholars today are more usually to be found emulating Hobsbawm in his blanket repudiation of all nationalisms. To these scholars, as McClintock suggests, nationalisms typically loom as "dangerous," not "in the sense that they represent relations to political power and to the technologies of violence" but in "Hobsbawm's sense of having to be opposed."[24] Significantly, however, most of these contemporary progressive critics of nationalism write from a quite different ideological and epistemological standpoint than Hobsbawm. Stranded upon the perceived ruins of Marxism, with their commitment to any kind of internationalist solidarity shaken and their confidence in the feasibility of anti-capitalist revolution undermined, they are evidently unable to credit that there could be *any* fundamental challenge to the prevailing order. Intellectually predisposed, as Ahmad puts it, to "debunk . . . *all* efforts to speak of origins, collectivities, determinate projects," they "no longer distinguish, in any foregrounded way, between the progressive and retrograde forms of nationalism with reference to particular histories, nor do they examine the even more vexed question of how progressive and retrograde elements may be (and often are) combined within particular nationalist trajectories" (*In Theory*, p. 38).

This tendency on the part of "progressive, cosmopolitan intellectuals . . . to insist on the near-pathological character of nationalism, its roots in fear and hatred of the Other, and its affinities with racism,"[25] receives a distinctive stamp in the field of postcolonial studies. Not so long ago, in the historical context of decolonization, there seemed little reason to doubt the liberationist credentials of at least some anti-colonial nationalist movements. To speak during those years of Vietnam or Cuba or Algeria or Guinea-Bissau – to evoke the names of such figures as Ché, Fidel, Ho, Amilcar Cabral, no matter how fetishistically – was to conjure up the specter of national liberation, that is, of a revolutionary decolonization capable, in Frantz Fanon's memorable phrase, of "chang[ing] the order of the world."[26] Today things are very different. It is not so much that the setbacks and defeats that have had to be endured throughout Africa and Asia and the Americas have been bitter and severe, though this is certainly true. Rather, contemporary theorists seem increasingly given to suggesting that the national liberation movements never were what they were – that is, that they were always more concerned with the consolidation of elite power than with the empowering of the powerless, with the extension of privilege rather than with its overthrow, and so on.

We might begin to interrogate – and, indeed, combat – these contemporary "second thoughts" about anti-colonial nationalist ideology and practice by anchoring ourselves in the work of Fanon. Not only was Fanon a direct participant in the struggles of the decolonizing era, of course; his writings are today the site of major controversy and investment in the field of postcolonial studies. Readers familiar with Fanon's work will recall that in his essay on "The Pitfalls of National Consciousness" in *The Wretched of the Earth*, he produced an excoriating critique of bourgeois anti-colonial nationalism, an ideology aimed at the (re)attainment of nationhood through means of the capture and subsequent "occupation" of the colonial state, and which on his reading represented only the interests of the elite indigenous classes. Fanon characterized bourgeois anti-colonial nationalism as "literally . . . good for nothing" (*Wretched*, p. 176). Its specific project, he wrote, was "quite simply . . . [to] transfer into native hands" – the hands of bourgeois nationalists – "those unfair advantages which are a legacy of the colonial period" (p. 152). The social aspirations of the bourgeois nationalists were geared toward neocolonial class consolidation: this meant that their "historic mission" was to constitute themselves as functionaries, straddling the international division of labor between metropolitan capitalism and the subaltern classes in the peripheries. The "mission" of the national elites, Fanon argued, "has nothing to do with transforming the nation; it consists, prosaically, of being the transmission line between the nation and a capitalism, rampant though camouflaged, which today puts on the mask of neo-colonialism" (p. 152).

Some contemporary theorists of "postcoloniality" have attempted to build upon Fanon's denunciation of bourgeois nationalism. Yet Fanon's actual standpoint poses insuperable problems for them. One fundamental difficulty derives from the fact that far from representing an abstract repudiation of nationalism as such, Fanon's critique of bourgeois nationalist ideology is itself delivered from an *alternative nationalist standpoint*. To theorists whose broad commitment to poststructuralist intellectual procedures inclines them to a mistrust of what Homi Bhabha rather dismissively calls "naively liberatory" conceptions of freedom,[27] this cannot but seem unassimilable.

Bhabha himself tends to "solve" this problem by, in Benita Parry's words, "annex[ing] Fanon to Bhabha's own theory,"[28] maintaining, for instance, that Fanon's political vision does "not allow any national or cultural 'unisonance' in the imagined community of the future" ("Question," p. 102). In truth, however, Fanon commits himself to precisely such a "unisonant" view of the decolonized state in distinguishing categorically between bourgeois nationalism and another would-be hegemonic form of national consciousness – a liberationist, anti-imperialist, nationalist internationalism,[29] represented in the Algerian arena by the radical anti-colonial resistance movement, the *Front de Libération Nationale* (FLN), to whose cause he devoted himself actively between 1956 and 1961, the year of his death. Of this latter, "nationalitarian" (the term is Anouar Abdel-Malek's[30]), form of consciousness, Fanon wrote that it "is not nationalism" in the narrow sense; on the contrary, it "is the only thing that will give us an international dimension . . . [I]t is national liberation which leads the nation to play its part on the stage of history. It is at the heart of national consciousness that international consciousness lives and grows" (*Wretched*, pp. 247–48).

For Fanon, in short, the process of decolonization brings the future of *capitalism* radically into question. In the decolonizing context, nationhood can be secured under different auspices. If the state that emerges from colony to nation comes to be dominated by the national middle classes, capitalist social relations will be extended. This is the "neocolonial" option: a capitalist world system made up – "after colonialism" – of nominally independent nation-states, bound together by the logic of combined and uneven development, the historical dialectic of core and periphery, development and underdevelopment. But for Fanon the *national* project also has the capacity to become the vehicle – the means of articulation – of a *social*(ist) demand which extends beyond decolonization in the merely technical sense, and which calls for a fundamental transformation rather than a mere restructuring of the prevailing social order.

Although Bhabha explicitly predicates his theory of colonial discourse upon Fanon's work, he contrives to read him "back to front," as it were – that is, from *The Wretched of the Earth* (published posthumously, but containing work produced immediately prior to Fanon's death) to *Black Skin, White Masks* (published in 1952, before Fanon had ever been to Algeria) – thereby distorting the testimony of Fanon's own evolution as a theorist. Bhabha's influential essay, "Remembering Fanon," was initially written as a Foreword to a new British edition of *Black Skin, White Masks*. The subtitle of the essay, "Self, Psyche, and the Colonial Condition," does justice to the *situation* (the term of course is Sartre's) of that text, but not to the work of Fanon as a whole. Bhabha, however, reads *Black Skin, White Masks* not merely tendentiously but more specifically *against* Fanon's subsequent intellectual production, using it to disavow Fanon's political commitments and his theorization of "the African Revolution." The strengths of *Black Skin, White Masks* are seen by Bhabha, thus, to derive from the related facts that it "shift[s] . . . the focus of cultural racism from the politics of nationalism to the politics of narcissism"[31] and that it "rarely historicizes the colonial experience. There is no master narrative or realist perspective that provide a background of social and historical facts against which emerge the problems of the individual or collective psyche" ("Remembering," p. 136).[32]

Bhabha's "re-membering" of Fanon inverts the historical trajectory of Fanon's thought in order to propose a vision of him as preeminently a theorist of "the colonial condition," of the interpellative effectivity of colonial discourse. Fanon's "search for a dialectic of deliverance" emerges on this reading as "desperate" and "doomed" ("Remembering," p. 133). Bhabha concedes the existence of a revolutionary-redemptive ethic in Fanon, of course, grounded in an existentialist and dialectical Marxist humanism, but he insists that the real value of Fanon's work lies elsewhere, in a psychoanalytic interrogation of the problematics of colonial desire. Fanon's constant utilization of existentialist, dialectical, and Marxist–humanist categories is therefore cast in the light of a sequence of unfortunate lapses, or as a determinate failure of vision:

In his more analytic mode, Fanon can impede the exploration of the . . . ambivalent, uncertain questions of colonial desire. The state of emergency from which he writes demands more insurgent answers, more immediate identifications. At times Fanon attempts too close a correspondence between the *mise-en-scène* of unconscious fantasy and the phantoms of racist fear and hate that stalk the colonial scene; he turns too hastily from the ambivalences of identification to the antagonistic identities of political alienation and cultural discrimination; he is too quick to name the Other, to personalize its presence in the language of colonial racism. These attempts, in Fanon's words, to restore the dream to its proper political time and cultural space can, at times, blunt the edge of Fanon's brilliant illustrations of the complexity of psychic projections in the pathological colonial relation . . . Fanon sometimes forgets that paranoia never preserves its position of power, for the compulsive identification with a persecutory "They" is always an evacuation and emptying of the "I". (p. 142)

Inasmuch as Bhabha wishes to construct a portrait of Fanon as a poststructuralist *avant la lettre*, his writing is full of such passages. The procedural logic of these passages is curious. Their thrust is to represent Fanon's ideas as according fundamentally with Bhabha's own epistemological and methodological program. To the extent that Fanon's explicit formulations seem to render such a construction implausible, however, they need to be reproved for preventing Fanon from saying what he would have said, had he been able – that is, had he had the right words, or the time to reflect, or the courage to follow through his best insights. For example, the real strength of Fanon's thought is said by Bhabha to consist in his attention to "[t]he *anti-dialectical* movement of the subaltern instance";[33] but since it cannot be denied that his characteristic mode of conceptualization is profoundly dialectical, Fanon "must sometimes be reminded that the disavowal of the Other always exacerbates the 'edge' of identification, reveals that dangerous place where identity and aggressivity are twinned" ("Remembering," p. 144). Similarly, Fanon is said by Bhabha to "warn . . . against the intellectual appropriation of the culture of the people (whatever they may be) within a representationalist discourse that may be fixed and reified in the annals of History";[34] but since it has to be admitted that Fanon's discourse is for the most part emphatically "nationalitarian," and therefore both historicist and representationalist, Bhabha bids us understand that his (Fanon's) preeminent claim to our attention is not as a theorist of decolonization or revolution, but of the "subversive slippage of identity and authority":

Nowhere is this slippage more visible than in [Fanon's] work itself, where a range of texts and traditions – from the classical repertoire to the quotidian, conversational culture of racism – vie to utter that last word that remains unspoken. Nowhere is this slippage more significantly experienced than in the impossibility of inferring from the texts of Fanon a pacific image of "society" or the "state" as a homogeneous philosophical or representational unity. The "social" is always an unresolved ensemble of antagonistic interlocutions between positions of power and poverty, knowledge and oppression, history and fantasy, surveillance and subversion. It is for this reason – above all else – that we should turn to Fanon. ("Remembering," pp. 146–47)

And again, Fanon's thought is said by Bhabha to tend toward theoretical anti-humanism; but since it has to be admitted that his language is more or less unwaveringly humanistic, Bhabha is obliged to proffer the rationalization that, for various reasons,

> Fanon is fearful of his most radical insights: that the space of the body and its identification is a representational reality; that the politics of race will not be entirely contained within the humanist myth of Man or economic necessity or historical progress, for its psychic effects question such forms of determinism; that social sovereignty and human subjectivity are only realizable in the order of Otherness. (pp. 142–43)

According to Bhabha, in short, Fanon's "deep hunger for humanism, despite [his] insight into the dark side of Man, must be an overcompensation for the closed consciousness or 'dual narcissism' to which he attributes the depersonalization of colonial man" (p. 143)!

With the tendentiousness of Bhabha's appropriation of Fanon in mind, perhaps, other anti-socialist theorists in the field of postcolonialism have tended to respond *critically* to Fanon's palpable commitment to a would-be hegemonic national-liberationist theory and practice. Debunking Fanon's writings and political engagements, they have charged that his ideas are as authoritarian as those of his bourgeois nationalist antagonists – or, indeed, of the colonialists themselves. Perhaps the most interesting, and symptomatic, of these repudiations is that advanced by Christopher Miller, in his book *Theories of Africans*.

Partly because Fanon addressed himself with such insistence to the question of *national* liberation, some *Marxists* have envisioned him as a nationalist – no matter how progressive – rather than as a revolutionary socialist, and have moved to criticize him on these grounds. Miller, conversely, takes Fanon's commitment to the question of national liberation to be indissolubly linked to his commitment *to* Marxism; and he attacks Fanon simultaneously for his national liberationism *and* his Marxism. Arguing in general that "the Marxist approach tends too much toward projection of a Eurocentric paradigm onto Africa, a continent in reference to which terms such as 'class struggle' and 'proletariat' need to be rethought,"[35] Miller claims to find the same irreducible Eurocentrism in Fanon's use of the language of nation and national liberation:

> by placing the word at the center of his concern for evolution, without questioning the complexities of its application to different geographical and cultural environments, Fanon winds up imposing his own idea of nation in places where it may need reappraising . . . Far from being "natural national entities" or cohesive nation-states, the modern nations

of black Africa must make do with borders created to satisfy European power brokering in the "scramble for Africa," borders that often violate rather than reinforce units of culture . . . In Fanon's essay on national culture, there is no analysis of what a nation might be, whether it is the same in reference to Algeria as it is in reference to Guinea, Senegal or, most notoriously, the Congo (now Zaire). The single most important fact of political existence in black Africa, the artificiality of the national borders and the consequent problem of cultural and linguistic disunity, receives no attention. (*Theories*, p. 48)

Let us start by conceding the validity of some of what Miller says here. It is indeed true that Fanon fails to question the purchase of the idea of the nation on African hearts and minds. In this respect he simply takes for granted the unforgoability and even the world-historical "appropriateness" of what has been imposed upon Africa by the colonial powers. He also summarily privileges the nation as not only an "obvious" but also a *decisive* site of anti-imperialist struggle. Certainly, his commitment to internationalism is such that he does not theorize the acquisition of nationhood as an historical terminus: on the contrary, he insists that "the building of a nation is of necessity accompanied by the discovery and encouragement of universalizing values" (*Wretched*, p. 247). But this is only to confirm Miller's general observation that Fanon's thinking follows the course of much post-Enlightenment social thought in subordinating "history . . . to History, particular to universal, local to global" (*Theories*, p. 50).[36]

It is also clear that Fanon's conceptualization of the nation is often derivative of the discourse of metropolitan romantic nationalism. In an essay entitled "Nationalism: Irony and Commitment," Terry Eagleton has argued that

[t]he metaphysics of nationalism speak of the entry into full self-realization of a unitary subject known as the people. As with all such philosophies of the subject from Hegel to the present, this monadic subject must somehow curiously preexist its own process of materialization – must be equipped, even now, with certain highly determinate needs and desires, on the model of the autonomous human personality.[37]

It is relatively easy to demonstrate the applicability of this formulation to Fanon's national liberationism. Fanon's discourse is full of references to the self-realization of the Algerian people-as-nation through their struggle against colonialism. And on at least one occasion, he moves explicitly to figure the relation between individuality and nationhood in an essentialist language of particular and universal:

Individual experience, because it is national and because it is a link in the chain of national existence, ceases to be individual, limited, and shrunken and is enabled to open out into the truth of the nation and of the world. In the same way that during the period of armed struggle each fighter held the fortune of the nation in his hand, so during the period of national construction each citizen ought to continue in his real, everyday activity to associate himself with the whole of the nation, to incarnate the continuous dialectical truth of the nation and to will the triumph of man in his completeness here and now. (*Wretched*, p. 200)

Yet Miller's fundamental argument against Fanon is less that his discourse is Eurocentric than that it is inapposite – not to say hostile – to African realities. Pointing to numerous passages in *The Wretched of the Earth* in which Fanon speaks of the African peasantry in what Miller interprets as "massively ethnocentric" terms as being "stuck in time, outside of history, 'plunged . . . in the repetition *without* history of an immobile existence'," he claims that Fanon "leaves no room for local knowledge": Fanon's national liberationist historicism commits him to viewing "precolonial history as no history at all" (*Theories*, p. 50).

This reading strikes me as being deeply misconceived. In the first instance, Miller fails to acknowledge numerous passages in *The Wretched of the Earth* and elsewhere, in which – even though his focus falls fairly unremittingly on *colonial* culture – Fanon does quite clearly address the specificity and interior adequacy of precolonial social and cultural forms. I have always been struck, for instance, by the passage in the essay, "Concerning Violence," in which Fanon celebrates as profoundly democratic the "traditional" protocols of public culture in Africa. Referring to "the substance of village assemblies, the cohesion of people's committees, and the extraordinary fruitfulness of local meetings and groupments," he maintains that

Self-criticism has been much talked about of late, but few people realize that it is an African institution. Whether in the *djemaas* of northern Africa or in the meetings of western Africa, tradition demands that the quarrels which occur in a village should be settled in public. It is communal self-criticism, of course, and with a note of humor, because everybody is relaxed, and because in the last resort we all want the same things. (*Wretched*, pp. 47–48)

Similarly, in the essay "On National Culture," there is a good deal of informed and appreciative discussion of the styles, themes, tonalities, and registers of various precolonial cultural practices. Stating quite explicitly that there is "nothing to be ashamed of in the [African] past," thus, Fanon remarks that one will encounter there only "dignity, glory, and solemnity" (*Wretched*, p. 210). He also refers freely to the "wonderful Songhai civilization," observing, however, that no number of such references can compensate for or alter "the fact that today the Songhais are underfed and illiterate, thrown between sky and water with empty heads and empty eyes." To suggest, in the face of passages such as these, that Fanon had nothing but contempt for precolonial African cultures, or that he regarded the social universe that they registered and to which they constituted a response only as "a primitive stage to be transcended, or . . . 'liquidated'" (Miller, *Theories*, p. 49), seems indefensible. Certainly, such a reading does not in my view find much warrant in Fanon's work.

The fundamental error committed by Miller, I believe, is to (mis-)read Fanon's representation of African culture in the era of colonialism as a representation of a history-less, culture-less *precoloniality*. Miller fails to reckon with Fanon's construction of *colonialism* as a total and elemental rupture within African history. Already in *Black Skin, White Masks*, Fanon had viewed colonialism in these terms: "Overnight the Negro has been given two frames of reference within which he has had to place himself. His metaphysics, or, less pretentiously, his customs and the sources on which they were based, were wiped out because they were in conflict with a civilization that he did not know and that imposed itself on him."[38] We need to pay attention here to the *time frame* implicated: "[o]vernight"; and to the *effect* of colonialism as Fanon sees it: "customs . . . wiped out." Fanon does not say that precolonial customs were *suppressed* under colonialism, or that they went into decline. On the contrary, he insists that they were *obliterated*, and that this obliteration was instantaneous. Elsewhere in *Black Skin, White Masks*, he uses this conception to ground a *definition* of the experience of colonization. A colonized people, he writes, is one "in whose soul an inferiority complex has been created *by the death and burial of its local cultural originality*" (p. 18; emphasis added). Again, colonialism is phrased as utterly destructive of precolonial culture.

In *The Wretched of the Earth* – as the passage cited above on the subject of the reflexivity of public cultural fora attests – Fanon occasionally seems prepared to soften this position slightly, to allow that *in some areas* and *to a limited degree* it is meaningful to speak of precolonial cultural forms surviving into the colonial era. Yet the same general understanding as before continues to underpin his analysis of colonialism. In "Concerning Violence," thus, he argues that "[t]he appearance of the settler has meant in the terms of syncretism the death of the aboriginal society, cultural lethargy, and the petrification of individuals" (*Wretched*, p. 93).

We come close, here, to sensing both *why* Fanon should refer to the culture of the colonized in the disparaging terms that so offend Miller, and *what is at stake for him* in doing so. Miller has it that Fanon holds African culture in contempt. The truth is quite different. For in a significant sense Fanon does not regard the culture of the colonized in Africa as "African culture" at all! On the contrary, the culture of the colonized is for him a starkly colonial projection, bespeaking a colonial logic that, from the standpoint of the colonized masses themselves, cannot be redeemed except through the destruction of colonialism itself: "The immobility to which the native is condemned can only be called in question if the native decides to put an end to the history of colonization – the history of pillage – and to bring into existence the history of the nation – the history of decolonization" (*Wretched*, p. 51).

Rather like Edward Said's concept of the "oriental" or Gayatri Chakravorty Spivak's concept of the "subaltern" – figures within colonial discourse that are imposed upon and, subsequently, taken up under duress and "lived" by colonized populations – Fanon's concept of the "native" or the "Negro" is not to be thought of as merely *descriptive* of independently existing (African) subjects. This is a point absolutely insisted upon by Fanon: he notes time and again that the figure of the native is not autochthonous, but is rather a construct of colonialism – actually, of the settler: "The settler and the native are old acquaintances. In fact, the settler is right when he speaks of knowing 'them' very well. For it is the settler who has brought the native into existence and who perpetuates his existence" (*Wretched*, p. 36); and, elsewhere:

The settler makes history; his life is an epoch, an Odyssey. He is the absolute beginning: "This land was created by us"; he is the unceasing cause: "If we leave, all is lost, and the country will go back to the middle ages." Over against him torpid creatures, wasted by fevers, obsessed by ancestral customs, form an almost inorganic background for the innovating dynamism of colonial mercantilism. (*Wretched*, p. 51)

In addressing himself to "native" culture, therefore, Fanon is not addressing himself to "traditional" African culture. On the contrary, he is addressing himself to a culture fabricated (almost) entirely by colonialism, a culture that positions the native as its degraded other:

The native is declared insensible to ethics; he represents not only the absence of values, but also the negation of values. He is, let us dare to admit, the enemy of values, and in this sense he is the absolute evil. He is the corrosive element, destroying all that comes near him; he is the deforming element, disfiguring all that has to do with beauty or morality; he is the depository of maleficent powers, the unconscious and irretrievable instrument of blind forces. (*Wretched*, p. 41)[39]

Pace Miller, then, Fanon does not argue that *precolonial* African culture is "plunged . . . in the repetition *without* history of an immobile existence." This statement refers, for Fanon, to the world of *those who have been made into "natives"*; it is a *product of colonialism*. Nor is precolonial culture held to be "primitive"; rather, it is held to have been destroyed, if not totally then very nearly so. For this reason, Fanon maintains that colonialism can only be combatted on its "own terrain," as it were – that is, on the basis of the struggle for national liberation. The materiality of colonialism must be reckoned with, and cannot simply be wished away, by its antagonists. As Patrick Taylor has put it, although perhaps too much in the subject-centered vocabulary of existentialism: "[o]ne has to define oneself in terms of one's opposition to the colonial system."[40] Colonialism cannot be overturned except through anti-colonial struggle; and in a world of nations, the colonial state cannot be captured and appropriated except as a *nation*-state. It only remains to be asked what *kind* of nation-state. Hence Fanon's critique of bourgeois nationalism, and his insistence that the anti-colonial struggle has brought national liberationist consciousness into existence as a fundamental practical reality:

The Algerian people, that mass of starving illiterates, those men and women plunged for centuries in the most appalling obscurity have held out against tanks and airplanes, against napalm and "psychological services," but above all against corruption and brainwashing, against traitors and against the "national" armies of General Bellounis. This people has held out in spite of hesitant or feeble individuals, and in spite of would-be dictators. This people has held out because for seven years its struggle has opened up for it vistas that it never dreamed existed. (*Wretched*, p. 188)

One notes some imprecision on Fanon's part as to the relationship between this decolonized world that the Algerian people are said to be bringing into existence and the precolonial social order. Fanon speaks at one point of the "*tabula rasa* which characterizes at the outset all decolonization," adding that "the proof of success lies in a whole social structure being changed from the bottom up" (*Wretched*, p. 35). This tells us about the relationship between the *decolonized future* and the *colonial present*, but not whether the former is to be understood as amounting in any sense to a restitution of precolonial sociality. The claim that the liberation struggle is opening up vistas that the people "never dreamed existed" suggests not, but there are other passages in *The Wretched of the Earth* – particularly those concerning national culture – that seem to encourage a different reading. We have already glanced at Fanon's affirmative characterization of such traditional legislative fora as the *djemaas* or the village assembly (with respect to southern Africa, one thinks here of institutions like the *kgotla* in Botswana), which seem to provide models for the future to emulate. And consider also the following passage, in which Fanon celebrates the emergence of new storytelling practices under the auspices of the national liberation movement, and argues that, where the colonial order had rendered oral traditions "inert" and reduced precolonial cultural forms to a state of petrification, these new practices operate in accordance with, and offer to redeem, the vibrant and communitarian cultural practices of the precolonial era:

> the oral tradition – stories, epics, and songs of the people – which formerly were [*sic*] filed away as set pieces are now beginning to change. The storytellers who used to relate inert episodes now bring them alive and introduce into them modifications which are increasingly fundamental. There is a tendency to bring conflicts up to date and modernize the kinds of struggle which the stories evoke, together with the names of heroes and the types of weapons. The method of allusion is more and more widely used . . . The contact of the people with the new movement gives rise to a new rhythm of life and to forgotten muscular tensions, and develops the imagination. Every time the storyteller relates a fresh episode to his public, he presides over a real invocation. The existence of a new type of man is revealed to the public. The present is no longer turned in upon itself but spread out for all to see. The storyteller once more gives free rein to his imagination. (p. 240)[41]

I have been arguing that Fanon's thinking about culture in the colonial era is premised upon a preliminary assumption as to the decisiveness of the transformation wrought by the colonial encounter. For him, scarcely anything of precolonial African culture is able to survive into the colonial era. Since Christopher Miller fails to recognize this initial assumption, he is obviously in no position to put pressure upon it. Yet it is precisely here, ironically – and not with respect to any supposed trivialization of precolonial African culture on his part – that Fanon's theorization is legitimately susceptible to criticism. For the plain fact is that, throughout Africa and elsewhere in the colonial world, precolonial social, cultural, and ideological forms survived the colonial era meaningfully. Indeed, they continue to survive meaningfully today, in the "postcolonial" present.

The significance of this point cannot be overestimated. However central the idea might be to his analysis, Fanon is simply incorrect when he maintains that the imposition of colonialism entails "the death of the aboriginal society, cultural lethargy, and the petrification of individuals" (*Wretched*, p. 93). Reports of "the death of the aboriginal society" in Fanon, one is tempted to say, are greatly exaggerated. The necessary corrective to Fanon is provided by Amilcar Cabral in an address, entitled "National Liberation and Culture," initially delivered in 1970. In this address, Cabral points out that "[w]ith certain exceptions, *the period of colonization* was not long enough, at least in Africa, for there to be a significant degree of destruction or damage of the most important facets of the culture and traditions of the subject people" (*Return*, p. 60).

At the *theoretical* level, Fanon's error consists in a confusion of *dominance* with *hegemony*. The distinction between these two concepts was, of course, first elaborated by Antonio Gramsci.[42] Within postcolonial studies, a distinctly Third-Worldist reading of the relationship between dominance and hegemony in the context of imperialism is offered by Abdul JanMohamed in his influential article, "The Economy of Manichean Allegory." Where Gramsci had articulated these concepts around the axis of *class*, JanMohamed suggests that they refer rather to *different historical periods*. "Dominance" is defined by him in a more or less orthodox fashion, in terms of the "exercise [of] direct and continuous bureaucratic control and military coercion of the natives."[43] However, as a mode of subjugation, dominance is historically delimited: the "dominant phase . . . spans the period from the earliest European conquest to the moment at which a colony is granted 'independence'." Within this period, "the indigenous peoples are subjugated by colonialist material practices (population transfers, and so forth), the efficacy of which finally depends on the technological superiority of European military forces."[44] This "dominant phase" is then to be set against the "hegemonic phase," marked by the moment of independence, within which "the natives accept a version of the colonizers' entire system of values, attitudes, morality, institutions, and, more important, mode of production. This stage of imperialism does rely on the active and direct 'consent' of the dominated, though, of course, the threat of military coercion is always in the background." I do not find this conceptualization convincing, not least because it clearly has the effect of minimizing, if not of denying, the significance of class divisions among the colonized in both the "dominant" and the "hegemonic" phases.[45] While the moment of independence might be taken to mark the acceptance by the indigenous elite of "the colonizers' entire system of values," for example (although to claim even this seems to me to claim too much), it is surely implausible to argue that the lives and cultural forms of the subaltern populations of Africa in the post-independence period betoken a conversion to bourgeois ideology. Nor, it seems to me, can it be plausibly maintained that these subaltern populations have "accepted" the colonizers' "mode of production," even when cash crop farming, wage labor, land rent, etc. have been imposed upon them.

A far better theorization of the relationship between dominance and hegemony is to be found in the reconstruction of Gramsci's basic concepts in the work of Ranajit Guha, especially his essay "Colonialism in South Asia: A Dominance without Hegemony and Its Historiography."[46] For a majority of the colonized, Guha suggests, and above all for those (mostly peasant) members of the subaltern classes living at some remove from the administrative and increasingly urban centers of colonial power, colonialism was experienced preeminently in terms of dominance, that is, along the lines of material, physical, and economic exaction: conquest, taxation, conscription, forced labor, eviction, dispossession, etc. There was comparatively little attempt on the part of the colonial establishment to seek *hegemony* among these subaltern classes, that is, to win their ideological, moral, cultural, and intellectual support for the colonial enterprise. The explicit targets of colonial hegemonization were the national or (sometimes) regional elites. One consequence of this was that although the subaltern classes could on occasion be recruited to the campaigns of the colonial government or the indigenous elites – and although the imposition and consolidation of colonial rule obviously had cumulative and long-term effects on the way in which subaltern populations lived, worked, and thought – inherited subaltern cultural forms (language, dance, music, storytelling) were able to retain both their traditionality and their autonomy from most forms of elite culture (colonial and "national"). The point is made thus by Taylor:

The colonizer's culture and his or her language, in particular, is the medium through which European values and life-style can be presented as the norm and the good, and in relation to which the colonized begin to define themselves. Still, the majority of the colonized, unlike the colonial bourgeoisie, are able to maintain a certain distance from these norms by resisting them and recreating traditional cultural patterns. (*Narrative*, p. 60)

Now it is not as though Fanon is altogether blind to this distinction between the forms of subjugation undergone by different classes among the colonized. It can certainly be argued that in *Black Skin, White Masks*, at least, he tends to generalize unwarrantedly from the ideological experience of his own class-fraction – that of the colonized intelligentsia – to the experience of the colonized population at large.[47] But even in this text, he does finally move to differentiate between the motivations that underlie "the quest for disalienation by a doctor of medicine born in Guadeloupe" and that of "the Negro laborer building the port facilities in Abidjan" (p. 223). In the former case, "alienation" is described as being "of an almost intellectual character"; in the latter, "it is a question of a victim of a system based on the exploitation of a given race by another, on the contempt in which a given branch of humanity is held by a form of civilization that pretends to superiority" (pp. 223–24).

Unlike Taylor, however – who concedes that in *Black Skin, White Masks*, "it is the colonized intermediary and elite classes in general whose story is told," but who argues that the text is less an analysis of colonialism as such than an impressionistic and semi-autobiographical working-through of the problematic of "racial alienation" in an attempt to "overcome" it (*Narrative*, p. 44) – I do not find Fanon's formulation of the distinction between elite and masses convincing. What is at issue, for me, is not merely whether Fanon *recognizes* that what is true of the colonized elite is not necessarily true of the majority of the colonized population. Rather, it is a matter of the way in which, on the basis of this recognition, he then proceeds to think about the social existence and the forms of consciousness of this colonized majority. And here, it seems to me, Fanon's supposition that – in Taylor's words – "[i]n the creation of a colonial world, precolonial life and horizons were totally transformed and shattered" (*Narrative*, p. 47) begins to loom as a decisive liability. For inasmuch as he severely underestimates the resilience and vitality of inherited cultural forms and practices in the colonial era, Fanon renders himself incapable of understanding exactly what is at stake for the subaltern classes in their involvement in anti-colonial nationalism.

Fanon has, in general, an insufficient grasp of what Guha, in the context of colonial India, refers to as the autonomous "politics of the people":

parallel to the domain of elite politics there existed throughout the colonial period another domain of Indian politics in which the principal actors were not the dominant groups of the indigenous society or the colonial authorities but the subaltern classes and groups constituting the mass of the labouring population and the intermediate strata in town and country – that is, the people. This was an *autonomous* domain, for it neither originated from elite politics nor did its existence depend on the latter.[48]

In the specific case of Algeria, Fanon's failure to credit the degree to which subaltern consciousness in the colonial period is still governed by vital "traditional" protocols causes him to misread the mass recruitment of the Algerian peasantry to the FLN as testifying to their embrace of the FLN's platform. In *The Wretched of the Earth*, thus, he speaks of the "upward thrust of the people" and declares that the people have "decided, in the name of the whole continent, to weigh in strongly against the colonial regime"; and he refers to the "coordinated effort on the part of two hundred and fifty million men to triumph over stupidity, hunger, and inhumanity at the same time" (p. 164).

In my 1990 book, *Resistance in Postcolonial African Fiction*, I argued that this tendency on Fanon's part to project a unity and coordinated political will onto the masses of the Algerian population in the late 1950s could not withstand close historical scrutiny. For it is impossible, on Fanon's reading, to account for the wholesale demobilization and disenfranchisement of "the people" in the years immediately following the acquisition of independence in Algeria in 1962, after an anti-colonial war that had lasted for eight years and claimed a million Algerian lives. Such a development cannot be reconciled with Fanon's evocation of a disciplined and progressively unified population coming closer and closer to self-knowledge as the struggle against the French colonial forces intensified. It seems inconceivable that, having been decisively and world-historically conscientized during the anti-colonial struggle (as Fanon claims they had been), this population would have permitted itself to be so easily and so quickly neutralized after decolonization. The truth, rather, would seem to be that as a class the Algerian peasantry was *never* fully committed to the vision of the FLN, even when it was fighting under the FLN's leadership.[49] Thus Ian Clegg, on the basis of his research into peasant politics and state formation in Algeria in the years following independence in 1962, claims that

[t]he involvement of the population of the traditional rural areas in the independence struggle must be clearly separated from their passivity in

face of its revolutionary aftermath. The peasants were fighting for what they regarded as their inheritance: a heritage firmly rooted in the Arab, Berber, and Islamic past. Their consciousness was rooted in the values and traditions of this past, and their aim was its re-creation.[50]

Now the specific political gloss that Clegg gives to this analysis no longer seems compelling. He argues – plausibly, in my view – that while the Algerian peasantry might well have committed themselves to a struggle for the restitution of their "homeland," they lacked the ideological resources to transform this struggle into a full-fledged social revolution. But he then proceeds to follow the bad precedent of much orthodox Marxist (and, of course, liberal elitist) theory in attributing this determinate historical limitation to the inherent fatalism of peasant consciousness. "Revolution, as a concept, is alien to the peasant consciousness, while the peasants' relationship to the environment remains one of passive endurance rather than active transformation" ("Workers," p. 239). The credibility of this sort of reading, and above all the supposition that peasants' relationship to their world can be characterized in terms of passivity, has been demolished by ethnographic and social-historical scholarship produced since around 1980.[51] As Allen Isaacman notes, even if most of the accounts of peasant consciousness produced by scholars in recent years are still "fragmentary and largely descriptive," they "offer . . . ample evidence of peasant-organized social movements."[52] At the very least, he concludes, this new scholarship obliges us to reassess "the vast literature which saw peasants either as inherently conservative and bound to ingrained habits or as inevitable victims of false consciousness or ruling-class hegemony."[53]

Yet Clegg's analysis rings true for all this. It enables us to account both for the Algerian peasantry's *commitment* to the struggle for independence, on the one hand, and, on the other, for its lack of concerted militancy in face of the FLN's (anti-socialist) policies of the years immediately following decolonization, when "[n]either the peasantry nor the subproletariat played any other than a purely negative role in the events" ("Workers," p. 239). The general theoretical conclusion to be drawn here has been spelled out, in a different context, by James Scott as follows:

[Peasant] [r]esistance . . . begins . . . close to the ground, rooted firmly in the homely but meaningful realities of daily experience . . . The *values* resisters are defending are equally near at hand and familiar. Their point of departure is the practices and norms that have proven effective in the past and appear to offer some promise of reducing or reversing the losses they suffer. The *goals* of resistance are as modest as its values. The poor strive to gain work, land, and income; they are not aiming at large historical abstractions such as socialism . . . Even when such slogans as "socialism" take hold among subordinate classes, they are likely to mean something radically different to the rank and file than to the radical intelligentsia.[54]

In this light, Clegg's complaint that Fanon "lacks a critical and dialectical analysis of the process of the formation of consciousness" ("Workers," p. 239), rings as plausible and judicious. For Fanon's formulations *are* consistently intellectualist in tone, often phrasing subaltern thought and practice in the elitist-idealist vocabulary of negation, abstract totalization, and self-actualization.

It is worth noting in this respect that to the extent that Fanon's contemporary followers remain faithful to his ideas about decolonization and popular consciousness, their writing tends to echo his in its intellectualism. Consider the following two passages from Patrick Taylor's *The Narrative of Liberation*, for example. In the first, Taylor is glossing Fanon's theorization of decolonization:

Decolonization, Fanon writes, is the process whereby "spectators crushed with their inessentiality" are transformed into "privileged actors, with the grandiose glare of history's floodlights upon them" [*Wretched*, p. 36]. The colonized rise above the Manichaean conception of the world as a tragic drama to assume a historical conception of the world as infinite possibility. They recognize human agency and responsibility in an open and unknowable history. Fanon's notion of the entry into history must be understood, not in Manichaean terms, but in terms of the stepping out of drama (mythical, tragic understanding) and the assumption of historical, national, and human responsibility.   (p. 70)

In the second passage, Taylor is referring to Fanon's theory of the role of violence in the anti-colonial struggle:

It is not the act of violent struggle that is the key to decolonization but, rather, the revolutionary leap, the "willed" entry into history, the consciousness of the categorical imperative. What moves the Hegelian dialectic from a situation of mutually exclusive protagonists to one of mutual recognition, is the recognition of the other and the recognition of oneself as an active, freely creative being.   (p. 85)

I cite these passages both because I believe that they provide a reliable (if, perhaps, one-sided) account of Fanon's own conception of decolonization, and because I believe that their weaknesses as representations of popular anti-colonial struggle are very clearly marked. Concerning the subject of reliability, Taylor quite correctly reads Fanon's thought in the light of an existentialist Marxist-humanism. Thus he constructs the Fanonian distinction between national liberationist and bourgeois nationalist ideologies in terms of a distinction between "the humanistic national consciousness brought about by the revolutionary movement" and "the degenerate consciousness of a dependent bourgeoisie" (*Narrative*, p. 10). He argues that "[u]nderneath the roles into which they are forced, the colonized preserve a human identity and temporal being through the recollection of the past in terms of a vision of the future" (p. 49). And he proposes that "the task" confronting radical intellectuals is "to tell the story of human freedom totalizing its situation in such a way that freedom is communicated and the oppressive situation transformed" (p. 19). Intellectually, and in their own terms, I do not find these theorizations particularly compelling. Yet I believe that the representation they offer of *Fanon's own problematic* is considerably more accurate than that proferred by such theorists as Bhabha or Robert Young, who would claim Fanon for a distinctly contemporary poststructuralism. In his book *White Mythologies*, for example, Young attempts to distinguish between "the Marxist-humanist attempt, by Lukács, Sartre, and others, to found a 'new humanism' which would substitute, for the Enlightenment's conception of man's unchanging nature, a new 'historical humanism' that would see 'man as a product of himself and of his own activity in history',"[55] and Fanon's own position, which Young characterizes as "new 'new humanism'." Young maintains that Fanon (and other "non-European writers" such as Aimé Césaire) were as critical of the "historical humanism" of Lukács and Sartre as they were of Enlightenment humanism; and he claims Fanon's standpoint as a theoretical anti-humanism, one rooted in "the realization of humanism's involvement in the history of colonialism, which shows that the two are not so easily separable."[56] Certainly, there is a critique of certain aspects of Sartre's philosophy in Fanon's work; but I do not accept that Sartre's *humanism* is ever the object of these critiques. I am not persuaded, in fact, that Fanon's humanism distinguishes itself in any meaningful way *as a humanism* from that of Sartre. On my reading, Fanon never places a "new 'new humanism'" on the agenda. On the contrary, the new humanism of which he speaks in concluding *The Wretched of the Earth* – "For Europe, for ourselves, and for humanity, comrades, we must turn over a new leaf, we must work out new concepts, and try to set afoot a new man" (p. 316) – strikes me as being manifestly Sartrian, and therefore just as *Taylor* (rather than Young) represents it.

Yet the fact that Taylor "gets Fanon right" at the level of philosophy merely throws into broad relief some of the *political* liabilities of the Fanonian standpoint. (Not that Bhabha or Young have anything worthwhile to contribute in this respect, let it quickly be said.) Briefly put, the problem emerges from the fact that Fanon as radical intellectual positions subaltern thought and action as the *exact* substantification of his revolutionary theory. Theory and practice are so closely aligned that it almost seems as though the latter exists principally to confirm the former. One is reminded of those passages in the early Marx – the Marx of the *Contribution to the Critique of Hegel's Philosophy of Right* (1844) – that give the impression that the European proletariat will soon be rising up to smash private property and the capitalist system because, as an emergent class, it represents the negation, "the *effective* dissolution of this order."[57] Seamlessly theorized in this way, how could the proletariat *fail* to overthrow capitalism, and, with it, class society as such? By the same token, Fanon (and, following him, Taylor) is often tempted to "overread" anti-colonial militancy, to construct it as the objective correlative of a revolutionary philosophy.

That the masses act; that they act *against* the colonial order; that they act *under the banner of* the national liberation movement – all of these statements are true. But the interpretation of these mass actions as corresponding to "the consciousness of the categorical imperative" or to a recognition of "human agency and responsibility in an open and unknowable history" seems appropriative in its externality. One does not have to doubt the legitimacy of Fanon's authority as a spokesperson of the masses in the anti-colonial struggle in Algeria to believe that a certain unwarranted "speaking for" – that is, ventriloquizing, speaking "in the place of" or "instead of" – is involved here.

It is, moreover, precisely in this context that Gayatri Chakravorty Spivak's warning about the need to "watch out for the continuing construction of the subaltern" seems especially timely.[58] One of Spivak's insistent contentions, after all, is that the "genuinely disenfranchised" among the colonized are represented as subaltern not only in the texts of empire, but also in "the great narratives of nationalism, internationalism, secularism, and culturalism" whose unfolding marks the trajectory of anti-colonialism and, indeed, of capitalist modernity itself.[59] In Fanon's world, the "genuinely disenfranchised" are plainly the peasant classes, of whom he writes that they are "systematically disregarded for the most part by the propaganda put out by the nationalist parties" (*Wretched*, p. 61). Fanon's own work distinguishes itself sharply from bourgeois nationalist propaganda in this respect. But even in *his* representations of the Algerian peasantry as a revolutionary force, there is no sustained consideration of the ways in which the peasants' views *fail* to match those of the FLN leadership, or aim at *different* ends, or reflect *another* social logic.

Let us, in the light of these considerations, return to *Theories of Africans* and give further thought to the thrust of Christopher Miller's commentary on Fanon.[60] For Miller, as we have seen, Fanon's weakness consists not in an underestimation of the *persistence* of "traditional" political practices and forms of thought in the colonial era, but in a contempt for tradition. Miller's general suggestion is that this "contempt" is characteristic of Marxist theory, which is held to "lack . . . relativism." Operating with a universalizing optic, Marxism, according to Miller, is constrained to gesture conceptually toward a "totalizing unity," in the name of which it must inevitably "overlook or 'liquidate'" difference, that which it cannot assimilate or subsume (p. 64). Marxism invariably claims "to possess the only fully integrated political . . . vision" (p. 32).

With respect to Fanon, Miller advances this argument as aggressively and tendentiously as possible, even claiming at one point that Fanon's ignorance about precolonial African history is reminiscent of that of Hegel or Hugh Trevor-Roper (p. 50)! (Hegel, of course, is responsible for having written in his Introduction to *The Philosophy of History* that "Africa proper, as far as History goes back, has remained – for all purposes of connection with the rest of the World – shut up; it is the Gold-land compressed within itself – the land of childhood, which lying beyond the day of self-conscious history, is enveloped in the dark mantle of Night . . . The Negro . . . exhibits the natural man in his completely wild and untamed state. We must lay aside all thought of reverence and morality – all that we call feeling – if we would rightly comprehend him; there is nothing harmonious with humanity to be found in this type of character."[61] Trevor-Roper, for his part, is notorious for having opened his study, *The Rise of Christian Europe*, with the observation that history in the non-West corresponded to little more than the "unrewarding gyrations of barbarous tribes in picturesque but irrelevant corners of the globe."[62]) Nor is this extreme statement resorted to casually. On the contrary, having introduced us to a conception of "ethnicity" – tentatively defined, following Jean-Loup Amselle and others, as "a sense of identity and difference among peoples, founded on a fiction of origin and descent and subject to forces of politics, commerce, language, and religious culture" (*Theories*, p. 35) – Miller maintains that Fanon's *imposition* of the category of "nation" upon African cultures organized around "ethnic" modes of self-understanding has to be accounted an act of epistemic violence, of such colossal proportions that it invites comparison with the violence of colonial ideology itself. "What matters most, what is most impressive in reading Fanon," he writes, "is the sheer power of a theoretical truth to dictate who shall live and who shall be liquidated" (pp. 50–51). And just as colonial ideology is undergirded by the repressive power of the colonial state, so too Miller casts Fanon's discourse as the official ideology of an empowered regime. This seems implausible, since Fanon died in 1961, with the struggle for independence still to be won in Algeria. Miller, however, brushes this mere historical fact aside in constructing an image of Fanon's political philosophy fully consonant with bourgeois nightmares of Robespierre or Lenin or Mao. When, for instance, Fanon calls for the "liquidation of regionalism and of tribalism" and, addressing himself to the collaborative role played by many local rulers (the deliberate wooing of whom by colonial regimes, in an attempt to facilitate the "pacification" of local populations, is well documented), suggests that "[t]heir liquidation is the preliminary to the unification of the people" (*Wretched*, p. 94), Miller draws the conclusion that: "Fanon's response to local resistance is to call out the firing squad" (*Theories*, p. 50). The statement *reverses* the vectors of power in the colonial context. That liberation movements should themselves have been responsible for egregious abuses is undeniable and deplorable, if scarcely surprising. But it remains the case, even so, that it was in general not the national liberation movements but *the colonial regimes* that tended to resort to the firing squad; and it was not "local resistance" but *the official suppression of local resistance* that mandated the liberation fronts' "response."

Miller then goes even further: in an extraordinarily idealist and dehistoricizing analysis, he attempts to implicate Fanon in Sékou Touré's execution of poet-politician Kéita Fodéba in Guinea in 1969. Rhetorically, his question as to whether "the fact that Sékou Touré wrapped himself in Marxist and Fanonian discourse ma[kes] Fanon responsible for the reign of terror in Guinea" is already answered in being asked. But Miller is careful to affect scrupulousness: he states that Kéita Fodéba's execution cannot be read as a "*necessary* outgrowth of either Marxism or Fanon's theories" (p. 62; emphasis added). However, this ostentatious circumspection is surely compromised by being positioned between an earlier observation that, when alive, Fanon often cited Sékou Touré as "a practitioner of what . . . [Fanon] preache[d]" (p. 52), and the subsequent suggestion that Fanon's "discourse on liberating violence inevitably [leads] to thoughts on the violence of discourse" (p. 63). In his analysis, Miller resolutely ignores the imperialist pressures, threats, intrigues, and exactions that – in conjunction with the long history of colonial underdevelopment – contributed decisively to the formation of Sékou Touré's regime even if they did not by any means make it inevitable. Instead, he presents the developments of the post-independence era in Guinea as corresponding to the instantiation of Fanon's anti-colonialist ideology – a strikingly Hegelian understanding if ever there was one!

One notes a superficial overlap here between Miller's position and that advanced by the Moroccan writer and critic, Abdelkebir Khatibi, in his influential article, "Double Criticism." Khatibi (who is not cited in *Theories of Africans*) argues that to the extent that Marxism is a "Western system of thought," it is prone to a reductive and otherizing construction of non-Western societies even though it "presents itself as, claims to be, and is applied – in one way or another – against imperialism."[63] It thus becomes possible to "read Marx in the following manner: the murder of the tradition(s) of the other and the liquidation of its past are necessary so that the West, while seizing the world, can expand beyond its limits while remaining unchanged in the end." Unlike Miller, however, Khatibi does not finally accept this reading – "which would reduce Marx's thought to a murderous ethnocentrism" – as defensible. For it falls foul both of the progressive thrust of Marx's own ideas and of the historical effects of Marxism as an institutionalized politics: "Who can deny that [Marx] was against colonialism and imperialism, that his thought has helped and continues to help the Third World in overthrowing imperialism and local powers?" The divergence between Miller and Khatibi here tells entirely to Miller's disadvantage, in my view, even if it also seems necessary to add that in its rather fetishistic binarization of the categories of "the West" and "the Third World," Khatibi's own position is scarcely immune from materialist critique.

In constructing Sékou Touré's Guinea as a model of Fanonism realized, Miller completely disregards a central feature of Fanon's analysis of "the pitfalls of national consciousness." In his essay of this title, Fanon had spoken with remarkable prescience of the evolution of precisely such a leader as Sékou Touré, a "man of the people" who might have had "behind him a lifetime of political action and devoted patriotism," but whose objective historical function it would become in the postcolonial era to "constitute a screen between the people and the rapacious bourgeoisie" (*Wretched*, pp. 167–68). No matter how progressive the role he played prior to independence might have been, Fanon argued, this populist leader, positioned between "the people" and the elite, would find himself thrust, in the postcolonial era, into the position of pacifier of "the people":

For years on end after independence has been won, we see [the leader] incapable of urging on the people to a concrete task, unable really to open the future to them or of flinging them into the path of national reconstruc-tion, that is to say, of their own reconstruction; we see him reassessing the history of independence and recalling the sacred unity of the struggle for liberation . . . During the struggle for liberation the leader awakened the people and promised them a forward march, heroic and unmitigated. Today, he uses every means to put them to sleep, and three or four times a year asks them to remember the colonial period and to look back on the long way they have come since then.   (pp. 168–69)

Far from being "responsible" in any way for the direction taken by Sékou Touré as the leader of Guinea after independence, Fanon had already foreseen its likelihood and tried to warn against it. Miller points to the contradiction between Sékou Touré's "ostensibly social-ist ideology" and the fact that "his Guinea was always dominated by multinational corporations," as though this tells in some way against Fanon and Fanonism (*Theories*, pp. 60–61). Fanon, however, does not need this lesson; before it had even entered the political vocabulary, he had already subjected "African socialism" to a blistering critique.[64]

Miller paints Fanon in the colors of despotism in order to suggest that all discourses that aspire to hegemony are effectively the same: even those that speak in the name of emancipation are necessarily predicated upon a will to power that cannot, in ethical terms, be distinguished from the will to power exemplified by the dominant discourse itself. Fanon's radical nationalism, on this reading, exists only as a latent recapitulation of colonialism: between it and colonial-ism there is little to choose. A European-derived import, Fanon's nationalism is without organic roots in African soil, and can be imposed upon Africa only by force. Because it is a totalizing dis-course, there can be no dialogue between it and the "local" discourses of "ethnicity."

In recoiling from Fanonism and nationalism, Miller calls for a new cultural relativism, "retooled as contemporary critical anthropology" (*Theories*, p. 66). Appealing to intellectuals to unlearn their privilege, to reimagine universalizing thought as "local knowledge" (p. 65), he goes to considerable lengths to disclaim *any* privilege for intellectuals, above all where the representation of subaltern populations is concerned. Indeed, he joins many other contemporary critical theorists in embracing a standpoint from which the very idea of speaking for others comes to be viewed as a discredited aspiration, and secretly authoritarian.[65] What is at issue here, it seems to me, is a kind of intellectualist anti-intellectualism, a premature (and unwarranted) Foucauldian disavowal of the project of representation as such.[66] It is one thing to concede, with Spivak, that unless intellectuals "watch out for the continuing construction of the subaltern," their work will tend to be "sustained" by the "assumption and construction of a consciousness or subject," and that this assumption/construction will "in the long run" assure that their work "cohere[s] with the work of imperialist subject-constitution, mingling epistemic violence with the advancement of learning and civilization" ("Subaltern," p. 295). It is quite another thing, however, to argue – as Trinh T. Minh-ha does, for example – that any attempt to distinguish in social terms between intellectuals (or members of social elites), on the one hand, and "the people" or "the masses," on the other, already contains an implicit justification of class-division:

Like all stereotypical notions, the notion of the masses has both an upgrading connotation and a degrading one. One often speaks of the masses as one speaks of the people, magnifying thereby their number, their strength, their mission. One invokes them and pretends to write on their behalf when one wishes to give weight to one's undertaking or to justify it . . . Guilt . . . is always lurking below the surface. Yet to oppose the masses to the elite is already to imply that those forming the masses are regarded as an aggregate of average persons condemned by their lack of personality or by their dim individualities to stay with the herd, to be docile and anonymous . . . One can no longer let oneself be deceived by concepts that oppose the artist or the intellectual to the masses and deal with them as with two incompatible entities.[67]

One does not want to deny, of course, that self-proclaimedly radical intellectualism is sometimes an exercise in bad faith, and that expressions of solidarity with "the masses" should therefore always be scrutinized carefully. One is reminded, in this context, of Theodor W. Adorno's devastating observation: "In the end, glorification of splendid underdogs is nothing other than glorification of the splendid system that makes them so. The justified guilt feelings of those exempt from physical work ought not to become an excuse for the 'idiocy of rural life.' Intellectuals, who alone write about intellectuals and give them their bad name in that of honesty, reinforce the lie."[68] But in Trinh's formulation, the baby of political representation is thrown out with the bathwater of ideological appropriation or "subalternization." The proposition that intellectuals cannot talk about "the masses" without guiltily romanticizing and/or implicitly disparaging them strikes me as being empirically indefensible. I cannot accept that all of the contemporary "postcolonial" novelists, poets, and dramatists who insist on the distinction between the masses and the elite in their work do so only to sanctify their own positions, or to assuage guilt. Nor can I accept that in the writings of all of the contemporary cultural critics, historians, and political theorists who – again – locate the distinction between elite and subaltern populations as indispensable, there is at work an implication that "the masses" are herd-like, docile, or anonymous.

What Trinh says about the representation of "the masses" in the totalizing discourse of intellectuals accords precisely with Christopher Miller's view of Fanon's intellectual practice. Yet if we return to *The Wretched of the Earth*, we find Fanon reiterating, time and again, that the relationship between "the masses" and "intellectuals who are highly conscious and armed with revolutionary principles" is not to be viewed from the standpoint of elitist assumptions about leaders and led, seekers and followers, shepherds and sheep. "To educate the masses politically," Fanon writes,

does not mean, cannot mean, making a political speech. What it means is to try, relentlessly and passionately, to teach the masses that everything depends on them; that if we stagnate it is their responsibility, and that if we go forward it is due to them too, that there is no such thing as a demiurge, that there is no famous man who will take the responsibility for everything, but that the demiurge is the people themselves and the magic hands are finally only the hands of the people. In order to put all this into practice, in order really to incarnate the people, we repeat that there must be decentralization in the extreme. (pp. 197–98)

It is easy to be cynical in face of such formulations as these. Miller sneers that "[e]veryone gives lip service to dialectics" (*Theories*, p. 64). Actually, dialectical theory is almost universally *discredited* in the various subfields of cultural studies today; but even if there were something to Miller's complaint, the fact would remain that not everybody who evokes dialectics is a hypocrite, or merely giving lip service to it.[69] And in a remarkable passage in "The Pitfalls of National Consciousness," Fanon points to the implications that follow from his understanding of the relation between intellectuals and "the masses" as dialectical:

> If the building of a bridge does not enrich the awareness of those who work on it, then that bridge ought not to be built and the citizens can go on swimming across the river or going by boat. The bridge should not be "parachuted down" from above; it should not be imposed by a deus ex machina upon the social scene; on the contrary, it should come from the muscles and the brains of the citizens. Certainly, there may well be need of engineers and architects, sometimes completely foreign engineers and architects; but the local party leaders should be always present, so that the new techniques can make their way into the cerebral desert of the citizen, so that the bridge in whole and in part can be taken up and conceived, and the responsibility for it assumed by the citizen. In this way, and in this way only, everything is possible. (*Wretched*, pp. 200–01)

Miller (and Trinh) would, of course, seize on the characterization of the citizens' intellect in this passage as a "cerebral desert." I have tried to demonstrate above that in deploying such language, Fanon was describing colonial culture rather than "local knowledge." Taken as a whole, moreover, the passage is remarkable for its *refusal* to sanction the imposition of ideas or technologies upon people who have not first "internalized" them, who have not first made them their own. The very thing that Miller accuses Fanon of doing, in fact, turns out to be the thing that Fanon refuses above all to do! Even if the citizens' intellect does amount to a "cerebral desert," even if the citizens are – from the point of view of the cosmopolitan radical intellectual – intransigent, narrow-minded, stubborn, wrong, nothing can proceed without them. The "fighting" intellectual can "shake the people" or try to "turn . . . himself [*sic*] into an awakener of the people" (*Wretched*, pp. 222–23). Ultimately, however, "he" "must realize that the truths of a nation are in the first place its realities" (p. 225). And these realities neither necessarily follow, nor can they forcibly be made to follow, "his" script.

One finds these emphases in the work of Amilcar Cabral as well. In his essay, "National Liberation and Culture," Cabral speaks of the need for revolutionary intellectuals and leaders of the national liberation movement to live with and among "the masses" as the liberation struggle unfolds:

> The leaders of the liberation movement, drawn generally from the "petite bourgeoisie" (intellectuals, clerks) or the urban working class (workers,

chauffeurs, salary-earners in general), having to live day by day with the various peasant groups in the heart of the rural populations, come to know the people better. They discover at the grass roots the richness of their cultural values (philosophic, political, artistic, social and moral), acquire a clearer understanding of the economic realities of the country, of the problems, sufferings and hopes of the popular masses. The leaders realize, not without a certain astonishment, the richness of spirit, the capacity for reasoned discussion and clear exposition of ideas, the facility for understanding and assimilating concepts on the part of population groups who yesterday were forgotten, if not despised, and who were considered incompetent by the colonizer and even by some nationals.
(*Return*, p. 54)

Writing a decade after Fanon's death, Cabral's thought is such that one would have supposed that he could not possibly be represented as undervaluing the richness and sophistication of precolonial African sociality. After all, he refers explicitly to the "richness of the . . . cultural values" of the "rural populations," and notes that "the accomplishments of the African genius in economic, political, social and cultural domains, despite the inhospitable character of the environment, are epic – comparable to the major historical examples of the greatness of man" (*Return*, p. 50). Yet in *Theories of Africans*, Miller contrives to read Cabral precisely as he reads Fanon. He quotes an observation of Cabral's, to the effect that although the peasantry – as the overwhelming majority of the population of colonial Cape Verde and Guinea Bissau – were indispensable to the armed struggle against Portuguese colonialism in those territories, the national liberation movement did not find it easy to mobilize them: "we know from experience what trouble we had convincing the peasantry to fight" (quoted in *Theories*, p. 44). Miller then proceeds to gloss this observation as follows:

Any revolution in Africa must have the support of the so-called peasants, who make up the vast majority of the population, yet the peasants do not lead but must be led . . . The Marxist leader must stand in a transcendent relation between the peasant and History. The peasant's destiny will be revealed to him by the leader, in a relation of active to "passive," literate to "illiterate," progress to tradition, knowledge to "ignorance." (p. 44)

It becomes apparent that for Miller, Cabral's fault is that he sought to prevail upon the Guinean peasantry to take up arms against Portuguese colonialism. Initially encountering among the peasantry views that were dissimilar from his own, Cabral ought, it seems, as a good, respectful cultural relativist, to have accepted their legitimacy and abandoned forthwith any aspirations to struggle for the overthrow of colonial rule! Miller reads Cabral's word "convince" as meaning to "impose." The fact, therefore, that Cabral was so successful in persuading the Guinean peasantry to take up arms against their colonizers that they were able, within a space of fifteen years, to topple the colonial regime, is interpreted by Miller as revealing only the degree to which the PAIGC (*Partido Africano da Independência da Guiné e Cabo Verde*) was able to inflict a "new" colonialism upon an already colonized people. It seems not to occur to Miller that the Guinean peasantry's struggle against the Portuguese might have reflected their own identification – however partial, mediated, uneven or belated – with the PAIGC's cause; nor, indeed, that the PAIGC's ideology might itself have been a barometer of popular aspirations.

At one point in his book, *The Black Man's Burden*, Basil Davidson evokes the dynamism and spirit of hopefulness that were experienced everywhere in Africa (and throughout the "Third World") during the decolonizing years. "[A]s the old imperial flags came down," he writes,

the mood was not euphoric but it was certainly optimistic. And there were many reasons for optimism. The old empires were falling fast and would not be restored. The social freedoms that had provided the real magnet behind nationalism were making themselves increasingly felt; and the grim silence of the colonial years was already shattered by a hubbub of plans and schemes for a more favorable future. People even talked of a "new Africa," and yet it did not sound absurd. A whole continent seemed to have come alive again, vividly real, bursting with creative energies, claiming its heritage in the human family, and unfolding ever more varied or surprising aspects of itself. The world became a larger and a happier place. (pp. 195–96).

This mood of optimism has of course been brutally punctured by the setbacks and defeats that have marked the years since independence. Nor have these setbacks been limited, by any means, to states that have followed the neocolonial path of "modernization" and dependent development. On the contrary, the record tells at least as decisively against avowedly revolutionary regimes in the postcolonial era: even where the anti-colonial war might be said to have been won, and quite literally so – as in Vietnam, Algeria, and Mozambique, for instance – the ensuing "peace" has clearly been lost.

A good portion of *The Black Man's Burden* is devoted to explaining why, in the case of Africa at least, this should have been so. David-

son's analysis centers on the fact that the nations that were inaugurated at independence were in all instances nation-*states*. His argument is that these states – "inherited" from the colonial powers in the
"transfer of power" that formally marked decolonization – were
states of a particular kind, scored and configured, both "internally"
and "externally," by their specific history as colonial dependencies in
the capitalist world system. "Externally," the states that were inherited by the representatives of the new nations at independence occupied dependent and cruelly circumscribed positions as peripheral
formations in the global economy. "Internally," they retained the
form of *colonial* states, that is to say, of *dictatorships*. As Davidson puts
it,

> for as long as these countries had been colonies, government had always
> been by rigid dictatorship . . . [C]olonial powers had invariably ruled by
> decree, and decree had been administered by an authoritarian bureau-
> cracy to which any thought of people's participation was damnable
> subversion . . . The systems that were "taken over" might vary in detail
> and culture, but all of them – from the British and French through to the
> Belgian and Portuguese and Spanish – supposed that the actual work of
> government, and all the crucial decisions depending on it and from it,
> would be exercised by a bureaucracy trained and tested in authoritarian
> habits and practices.   (*Burden*, p. 208)

Davidson salutes those political thinkers of the decolonizing era
"who understood that the colonial partition had inserted the continent into a framework of purely artificial and often positively harm-
ful frontiers," and who clearly foresaw "that a petty-bourgeois nationalism was bound to remain a nationalism subordinate to external
powers organized on a capital-owning and capital-commanding
basis" (p. 163). These radical thinkers might have shared with their
bourgeois nationalist antagonists the assumption that the appropriation of the colonial state represented a "necessary aim and achievement." Yet, unlike the bourgeois nationalists, they looked beyond this
moment of decolonization, "to the consummation of social struggles
which should be far more liberating for their peoples" (pp. 166–67).

Davidson argues, however, that the sheer intractability of the inherited *statist* dispensation in the postcolonial era has conspired to
thwart even such insistently liberationist aspirations. It is one thing to
defeat a colonial power militarily or to secure decolonization through
other means. In itself, this is already a vast achievement. But it is
another thing altogether to "devise and uphold a state such as citizens will accept and respect as the valid and therefore worthwhile

representative of their interests and protector of their rights" (p. 227). Even where their political conduct has been irreproachable (and it has most often been anything but, of course), the post-independence inheritors of the colonial state in Africa have found it extraordinarily difficult to take meaningful steps to fulfill the socially reconstructive demands whose articulation during the decolonizing era had been decisive in bringing the popular masses into the national movement. The valiant efforts of some of these leaders "to close the gap between People and State" (p. 241), and the partial successes they have won, should be noted and applauded.[70] More commonly, however, "social" demands have been subordinated to the narrowly "national" requirements of elite entrenchment – that is, where they have not been cynically jettisoned altogether. Not only, therefore, has "the extraction of wealth from an already impoverished Africa . . . in no way [been] halted by the 'transfer of power'" (p. 219). In addition, "the 'national conflict,' embodied in the rivalries for executive power between contending groups or individuals among the 'elites' . . . [has] take[n] priority over a 'social conflict' concerned with the interests of most of the inhabitants of these new nation-states" (p. 114).

The upshot of this, Davidson explains, is that the years since decolonization have borne witness to a profound loss of faith on the part of the bulk of the African population, not only in particular leaders, nor even in leaders as such (as representatives of elite class interests), but in *the very idea of the national state*. In the space of a generation or two, the credibility of the state as a political form capable of representing popular interests has all but evaporated:

At the outset of independence there had been a narrow gap in trust and confidence between the bulk of the population and the beneficiaries or leaders of anticolonial nationalism. The social aspects of the anticolonial struggle still retained primacy over all those aspects concerned with nation-statist self-identification. The welfare and advancement of the majority, one may even say, was still consciously accepted as an aim of policy more important than the interests of that necessarily small minority with access to political power and the economic fruits of political power. The gap existed but could be bridged if an attempt were made to bridge it . . . [But] after ten or twenty years, the gap had widened to an abyss: on one side, a great mass of resentful and impoverished rural people and, on the other, a small minority with quantities of wealth. Into that abyss there had plunged, more or less helplessly, the legitimacy and credit of the state which had allowed this gap to yawn.   (pp. 214–15)

The social and historical determinants of this crisis of legitimacy were (and remain) complex. As Davidson observes,

No simple explanation of such phenomena can ever be adequate. In this enormous invitation to disaster there were many contributory strands of action or inaction. But they all came together, visibly in the 1980s, in destruction of the accountability of the state upon which the nation was supposedly built. One of these strands was the territorial awkwardness of the state formed by the colonial partition and "transferred" to African hands. Another, in this legacy, was the contradiction between continued state dictatorship and the expectations of state democracy. A third was the growth of illegal trade, itself a product of the contradiction between the interests of the few and the interests of the many: in general terms, between the city and the countryside. There were other factors of disintegration, all working in the same direction . . . [e.g.] what may be called the ecological inheritance . . . [and] the international context.   (p. 215)

Davidson's analysis provides an exemplary contrast to the treatment of nationalism that one tends to encounter in the academic field of postcolonialism. The key concepts in Davidson's analysis are the state, the "social" and the narrowly "national" aspects of the anti-colonial struggle, and the class relationship between (elite) leaders and "the people" in the decolonizing and independence eras. Davidson approvingly quotes Thomas Sankara to the effect that "you cannot carry out fundamental change without a certain amount of madness . . . [W]e must dare to invent the future" (*Burden*, p. 241). Yet he points out that by the end of the 1980s even those African states with a genuine commitment to national liberationist ideals – like the Burkina Faso of Sankara, prior to his assassination in 1988 – had been forced to reconcile themselves to "reality," to accept that they lacked the resources *as nation-states* to defend themselves against the depredations of the world system. "Fundamental change" would have to be sought, and fought for, on the basis of *inter*nationalist solidarity, that is to say, in explicit opposition to the actually existing (capitalist) world system of nations.[71]

In postcolonial criticism, by contrast, the concept of the state is, by and large, conspicuous by its absence. Nor does one typically find in this criticism any echo, either of Davidson's carefully drawn distinction between "social" and "national" aspects of the anti-colonial struggle, or of the Leninist/Fanonian distinction – which might be said to underlie Davidson's – between bourgeois nationalist and national liberationist projects. What one tends to find, instead, is a culturalist emphasis on nationalism as *a mode of representation*. In terms of this emphasis, the ideological differences *between* various (and often competing) nationalisms – and the material consequences that follow from these differences – are downplayed in favor of an argument that all nationalisms are alike to the extent that they involve the attempt to secure consent for their claims to representativeness. All nationalisms, it is suggested, strive to represent themselves as the true – the legitimate – voice of the people-as-nation. All nationalisms are therefore appropriative, since they all claim unisonance, and since these claims necessarily involve speaking for – and therefore silencing – others. Specifically, nationalism is viewed as an *elitist* cultural practice in which subaltern classes are represented – spoken for – in the name of the nation which is, supposedly, themselves.

Postcolonial critics do not, of course, deny that there are differences – even profound differences – between what is claimed in the name of the nation by, say, Nelson Mandela as opposed to F.W. de Klerk, or Salvador Allende as opposed to General Pinochet. But they address themselves rather to the fact that all nationalists claim for their own nationalism that it corresponds, in Fanon's words, to "the all-embracing crystallization of the innermost hopes of the whole people" (*Wretched*, p. 148). Criticizing such claims as inherently "inappropriate" and "coercive,"[72] and directing their attention to the standing of those members of the population who, by virtue of their subalternity, are never authorized to speak within the elite-constituted sphere of "the nation" – that is, who cannot be heard within that sphere, no matter what its ideological provenance – they withhold their endorsement from all historical and actually existing nationalisms. Some even go on, as I have already noted, to inveigh against *representationalist discourse* in general.

Gayatri Chakravorty Spivak's writings on nationalism and subalternity provide an excellent basis for the further examination of these issues. For in Spivak's work we encounter what is perhaps *the* paradigmatic instance of an argument as to the elitism of nationalist discourse – *all* nationalist discourse, anti-colonial as much as colonial, liberationist as much as bourgeois – being integrally linked to an austere construction of the subaltern as a discursive figure that is by definition incapable of self-representation.

Spivak is comparatively uninterested in marking the differences between the ideological projects of colonialism and anti-colonialism. From the standpoint of the subaltern classes, as she tells us on numerous occasions, the two projects are relatively indistinguishable. In a characteristic formulation, thus – the context is a reading of Mahasweta Devi's short story "Douloti the Bountiful" – she urges us not merely to note in passing but to register the implications of the fact ("however hard it might be for us to imagine it") that Mahasweta presents "'Empire' and 'Nation' . . . [as] interchangeable names."[73]

The burden of Spivak's argument here, if I understand it correctly, is to suggest that anti-colonial nationalism is in all instances an elite configuration. In claiming to represent the aspirations of "the people," anti-colonial nationalists of all stripes posit the nation as an "imagined community" to which all classes and groups in the society have equal access and to which they all share the same allegiance. Spivak is perfectly willing to concede that, ideologically speaking, she finds some of these imaginings of the nation vastly more attractive than others; and that the political competition between them is hugely consequential. She insists, however, that this competition is, and remains, fundamentally a competition *between elites*. Authority in the representation of "the people" is for her more a function of the relative social power of the nationalist spokesperson than of any putative "identity" between nationalist discourse and popular consciousness.

Support for Spivak's position here can be found, rather improbably, in Pierre Bourdieu's short paper on "The Uses of the 'People'." Bourdieu writes that:

To throw some light on discussions about the "people" and the "popular," one need only bear in mind that the "people" or the "popular" . . . is first of all one of the things at stake in the struggle between intellectuals. The fact of being or feeling authorized to speak about the "people" or of speaking for (in both senses of the word) the "people" may constitute, in itself, a force in the struggles within different fields, political, religious, artistic, etc. . . . [T]he stances adopted towards the "people" or the "popular" depend in their form and content on specific interests linked first and foremost to belonging to a cultural field of production and, secondly, to the position occupied within this field.[74]

Later in this same essay, Bourdieu notes that

it is clearly in the political field that the use of "people" and the "popular" is most directly profitable, and the history of struggles within progressive parties or workers' unions bears witness to the symbolic effectiveness of workerism: this strategy permits those who can lay claim to a form of proximity with the dominated to set themselves up as holders of a sort of pre-emptive right over the "people" and, thereby, of an exclusive mission, at the same time as setting up as a universal norm modes of thought and expression that have been imposed on them by conditions of acquisition that are pretty unfavourable to intellectual refinement; but it is also what allows them to accept or to lay claim to everything that separates them from their competitors at the same time as concealing –

first and foremost from themselves – the break with the "people" that is implied by gaining access to the role of spokesperson.[75]

On Spivak's reading, to cast "the colonized" as such in a historical narrative is to privilege a certain kind of agency, a certain kind of subjectivity and of "speaking" – that of the *colonized subject* who "speaks" *as a national(ist)* – and to homogenize and bracket as incidental all other kinds. This mode of representation of popular social practice, she correctly points out, cannot be affirmed in any uncritical sense. There is now a large body of scholarly work demonstrating that – throughout the colonial world – local struggles and everyday forms of peasant resistance were often entirely divorced from and unassimilable to the "vertical" political concerns of (elite) anti-colonial nationalists. And even with respect to such manifestly "historical" events as peasant insurgencies, strikes, protests, rebellions, insurrections, acts of sabotage, etc., there are still good reasons to challenge the representation of them as struggles for *national liberation*. It is true that peasant insurgency is never "spontaneous" but, on the contrary, always "a motivated and conscious undertaking on the part of the rural masses," as Ranajit Guha has pointed out with reference to such diverse instances in the Indian context as the "Rangpur *dhing* against Debi Sinha (1783), the Barasat *bidroha* led by Titu Mir (1831), the Santal *hool* (1855) and the 'blue mutiny' of 1860 . . . the revolts of the Kol (1832), the Santal and the Munda (1899–1900) as well as . . . the jacqueries in Allahabad and Ghazipur districts during the Sepoy Rebellion of 1857–8."[76] But it does not follow from this that the *colonial order* was necessarily the antagonist in such events; nor, ideologically, that *nationalist* consciousness was necessarily implicated in their prosecution. Peasant insurgents in India during the colonial era, that is to say, did not necessarily think of themselves *as Indians*, and they did not necessarily believe themselves to be fighting for the liberation of India. The point has been made in general terms by Hobsbawm:

We know too little about what went on, or for that matter what still goes on, in the minds of most relatively inarticulate men and women, to speak with any confidence about their thoughts and feelings towards the nationalities and nation-states which claim their loyalties . . . We know what national parties and movements read into the support of such members of the nation as give them their backing, but not what these customers are after as they purchase the collection of very miscellaneous goods presented to them as a package by the salesmen of national politics. (*Nations*, pp. 78–79)

It is with such considerations as this in mind, no doubt, that Spivak moves to argue that the mobilization of the concept of the nation in nationalist discourse always entails the simultaneous "subalternization" of a variety of popular forms of self-understanding, social practice, and struggle – forms that do not articulate themselves in the language and syntax of national consciousness. The problem here, however, is that since Spivak defines subalternity very strenuously in terms of a structured inarticulacy at the elite levels of state and civil society – such that to occupy the station of the subaltern in any public discursive sphere is to be incapable of representing oneself within that sphere – she figures subaltern social and symbolic practice as programmatically inaccessible to elite actors. Subaltern practice, on her construction, cannot signify "as itself" across the social division of labor – a division overdetermined by the social operations of gender, sexuality, ethnicity, etc. Within the elite spheres, "[t]he subaltern cannot speak" ("Subaltern," p. 308); or, as Spivak puts it in a more recent essay, "[t]he gendered subaltern woman . . . can yield 'real' information as agent with the greatest difficulty, not the least because methods of describing her sympathetically are already in place. There is a gulf fixed between the anthropologist's object of investigation and the activist's interlocutor."[77]

In an important and challenging essay published in 1987, Benita Parry takes issue with this theorization of subalternity, charging that it "gives no speaking part to the colonized, effectively writing out the evidence of native agency recorded in India's 200-year struggle against British conquest and the Raj" ("Problems," p. 35). I find this an enabling formulation, but not quite for the reasons that Parry herself adduces.[78] For Parry evidently interprets Spivak's theory of subalternity in the light of a "translation" of the subject-centered concept of *agency* into the poststructuralist language of *interpellation*, such that the colonized come to be cast "passively" as constituted subjects-objects of colonial discourse rather than "actively" as colonialism's self-conscious resisters. As I read it, however, Spivak's theory of subalternity is not really a theory of "native agency" at all, but a theory of the way in which the social and symbolic practice of disenfranchised elements of the "native" population is *represented* (or, more accurately, *not represented*) in colonialist-elitist discourse. The subaltern is for Spivak not a *person* but a *discursive figure* in a battery of more or less integrated dominant social and cultural "texts." Intellectual practice – no matter what its ideological character – is, by virtue of its social conditions of possibility, ineluctably dependent upon these dominant "texts." (It is, in fact, predicated upon them even as it works to extend and reconfigure them.) To inquire, as an intellectual, into the forms of practice of the subaltern classes is therefore inevitably to ventriloquize these practices – to "translate" them, in the etymologically exact sense of carrying them across the social division of labor that separates the intellectual from "the people." It is in this light that Spivak writes in "Can the Subaltern Speak?" that "[r]epresentation has not withered away" (p. 295). She means "re-presentation," and we need to bear in mind that for her, following Althusser and others, all representation is mis-representation (*méconnaissance*). But precisely *because* representation has not withered away – it constitutes the very ground of intellectual practice – she argues that it is vitally important for intellectuals to remain alert at all times to the unbridgeability of the "gap" that separates the social practices and forms of consciousness of the classes and groups of people they are investigating from the representations of these practices in the elite spheres (including that of intellectual production itself). In her essay "Feminism and Critical Theory," accordingly, Spivak urges scholars in the field of postcolonial studies to analyze the production of subalternity at the same time as they research various forms of "native agency." Scholars today, she writes, need to study "not only the history of 'Third World Women' or their testimony but also the production, through the great European theories, often by way of literature, of the colonial object."[79]

How are we to assess this singular theorization of subalternity? Let us begin by noting that Spivak almost invariably fails to live up to her own injunction: while she clearly offers the examination that she calls for, of the mechanics underlying the "production . . . of the colonial object," an investigation of the "history of 'Third World Women'" is typically deferred in her own writings. She states explicitly that "[r]eporting on, or better still, participating in, antisexist work among women of color or women in class oppression in the First World or the Third World is undeniably on the agenda. We should also welcome all the information retrieval in these silenced areas that is taking place in anthropology, political science, history, and sociology" ("Subaltern," p. 295). In her own work, however, the deconstructive interrogation of subalternity is given precedence over the radical historiographical account of "native agency." Indeed, Spivak's emphasis upon the production of subalternity is so unmediated as to prevent her from turning her attention in any sustained fashion to an examination of the kinds of issues – concerning "native agency" in its insurgent aspects – that as a self-proclaimed Marxist she presumably deems of fundamental importance.[80]

Confronted, accordingly, with Spivak's answer – "No" – to her own famous question, "can the subaltern speak?" Benita Parry infers that "the lacunae in Spivak's learned disquisitions issue from a theory assigning an absolute power to the hegemonic discourse in constituting and disarticulating the native" ("Problems," p. 34). And she goes on to read Spivak as maintaining that it is up to the intellectual to "plot a story, unravel a narrative and give the subaltern a voice in history" – a conception that she duly criticizes as corresponding to an "exorbitation of the intellectual's role" (p. 35). I want to argue, however, that just the reverse is true: it is not because Spivak hypostatizes or otherwise exalts the work of intellectuals that her theory of subalternity runs into difficulties, but because *she claims too little for intellectual practice.* She concludes "Can the Subaltern Speak?" with the observation that "[t]he female intellectual as intellectual has a . . . task which she must not disown with a flourish" (p. 308). The formulation seems to promise a negotiation with the specificity and potential progressivism of intellectualism as a form of social practice. Yet – to restore the ellipsis – what Spivak actually writes is "[t]he female intellectual as intellectual has a *circumscribed* task . . . " (emphasis added); almost invariably when she comes to talk about intellectualism, the weight of Spivak's emphasis tends to fall on the question of circumscription, on the checks and constraints governing intellectual practice and on the severe limitations on what intellectuals – especially progressive intellectuals engaged in various ways in the struggle against imperialism – can hope to achieve politically as intellectuals.

The central problem with Spivak's theorization of subalternity is that in its relentless and one-sided focus on the problematics of representation as reading, it contrives to displace or endlessly defer *the epistemological question* – that concerning truth. As I have already indicated, Spivak freely admits that as a Marxist she prefers certain representations (of "the people," of particular events, etc.) over others. But she seldom (if ever) acknowledges that some representations might be more accurate – more adequate to their object – than others. On her reading, the actual contents of the social practice of "the people" are always, indeed definitionally, inaccessible to members of the elite classes. Whatever is read (that is, represented) as "subaltern" within elite discourse has for her always-already been made over, appropriated, translated, traduced. It is precisely the irreducible gap between popular practice and its (misrecognizing) construal in elite discourse that the term "subalternity" designates on her usage of it.

This conceptualization seems to me to come close to fetishizing difference under the rubric of incommensurability. Yet Spivak's argument – that the social aspirations and forms of consciousness of "the people" are inevitably displaced in their (mis-)representation at the elite levels of social discourse – finds a ready echo throughout postcolonial studies today. Consider, for instance, the terms of V.Y. Mudimbe's critique of the work of Marxist anthropologist Peter Rigby. In his 1985 study, *Persistent Pastoralists*, Rigby had offered an analysis of the social practice of the Ilparakuyo people of east Africa. (Rigby's status, interestingly, is that of consecrated cultural *insider* to the Ilparakuyo.) Criticizing Rigby's analysis in his own book, *Parables and Fables* (1991), Mudimbe writes that

[w]hat a competent translation such as Rigby's does is not to apprehend the being-there, not even to unveil it, but to organize a reflection and specify a commentary, a new order of meaning. I do not question the pertinence of specification. The point is to recognize the fact of a jump and, thus, understand the power of Rigby, that is, the power of the anthropologist. In reality, his interpretive practice witnesses to a meta-power: a capacity of transforming a place into a conceptual space and of moving from this space to the original place. In this context, to state that "the translation must be meaningful to all parties concerned," does not seem to make much sense. In effect, Rigby the anthropologist began by terrorizing everybody with his authority: he is the only perfect bilingual among his fellow anthropologists and his Ilparakuyo elders, *ilmurran*, and family.[81]

What is striking here is that although Mudimbe concedes "the pertinence of specification" – that is, the epistemological adequacy of Rigby's representation of Ilparakuyo social practice – this concession counts for nothing in his eyes. Like Spivak, he is more interested in "the fact of a jump," that is, in the formal (and unforgoable) gap between concept and object. He construes this gap preeminently as the locus of a power differential, such that – despite the fact that he "gets them right," so to speak – Rigby emerges as a terrorizer of the Ilparakuyo merely on the strength of his representation of them. To represent is to dominate. Thus Mudimbe goes on to argue that "Rigby seems to silence something . . . [His] text is interwoven with something like a terror of naming what is out there" (*Parables*, p. 173). And he explicitly identifies Rigby's project of representation as a colonizing enterprise, formally indistinguishable in this respect at least from that of colonialism proper (pp. 177–78).

The standpoint assumed here is, I believe, susceptible to criticism on a variety of grounds. I have argued elsewhere that the characteristic poststructuralist eschewal of the question of truth in favor of the specification of the conditions of possibility of the generation of "truth-effects" is predicated upon anti-realist epistemological assumptions about conceptuality and objectivity that cannot be sustained in the face of the realist counter-critiques currently being expounded by such theorists as Roy Bhaskar, Andrew Collier, Sabina Lovibond, Christopher Norris, and many others. I will not rehearse this argument here – interested readers can consult it at their leisure[82] – but will instead refer readers to Satya P. Mohanty, who has recently issued an eloquent call for a "post-positivist" standpoint in postcolonial studies. Writing in an Epilogue to a special issue of the *PMLA* dedicated to the topic of "Colonialism and the Postcolonial Condition," Mohanty argues that what emerges in the work of such theorists as Spivak (to whom he makes explicit reference) and Mudimbe is

an overly generalized and unqualified suspicion of objectivity and explanation. Where such skepticism is conjoined with a relativism of some kind (as, say, in Lyotard), we are left in the uncomfortable position of seeking a noncolonizing relationship with the other culture but accepting a theoretical premise that makes anything that can be called a relationship impossible . . . If we adopt this stance or accept the skeptical or relativist premises on which it is based, it is difficult to make decolonization a meaningful project involving cross-cultural contact and dialogue.[83]

In a rejoinder to Mudimbe's critique of his work (and reprinted in Mudimbe's *Parables and Fables*), Peter Rigby reiterates his claim to be able "to 're-present' (or 'interpret') the Ilparakuyo social formation" (*Parables*, p. 197). He insists that theorists can achieve a "*true* dialectic of theory and practice" provided that, in the spirit of intersubjective "co-evality,"[84] they devise methods of analysis sensitive to (and capable of minimizing) "[t]he inequality, and hence the relation of power, established by both [spatialized and temporalized] forms of distancing" (*Parables*, p. 198). I share Rigby's convictions in this respect. So too, evidently, does Mohanty, who argues that while the study of social or cultural difference is "unavoidably difficult," it is by no means impossible: "What is required," he writes,

is the belief that "getting it right" is often important, for both "us" and "them" . . . Contrary to relativists, who emphasize almost exclusively the extent to which cultures are distinct, different, and incommensurable . . . we can understand both differences and commonalities adequately only when we approach particular cross-cultural disputes in an open-ended way: thus, a basic question to ask about particular disagreements is whether – and to what extent – they refer to the same things, the same features of the world . . . Vital cross-cultural interchange depends on the belief that we share a "world" (no matter how partially) with the other culture, a world whose causal relevance is not purely intracultural. It is possible, in this view, to provide more – or less – accurate accounts of these causal features . . . What emerges as an alternative to relativism and skepticism is thus a postpositivist conception of objectivity as a goal of inquiry that includes in it the possibility of fallibility, self-correction, and improvement.[85]

As this passage intimates, it is also possible to contest the standpoint assumed by Spivak and Mudimbe through *counterfactual* reason. Specifically, it seems to me, the conceptualization of ideological and/or intellectual representation as *méconnaissance* makes it impossible to account plausibly for the investment of the masses of the colonized historically in various kinds of nationalist struggle – the "involvement," as Ranajit Guha has put it, in the context of India, "of the Indian people in vast numbers, sometimes in hundreds of thousands or even millions, in nationalist activities and ideals" ("On Some Aspects," p. 3).

The point here is that if nationalism is conceptualized exclusively as an elite phenomenon, and if subalternity is defined in terms of a structured inarticulacy at elite levels – at which it cannot represent itself – then it follows that, whatever else might be expressed in nationalist ideology, it is never popular consciousness, never the will of "the people." On the contrary, even when "the people" act in very large numbers under the banner of the nationalist movement, what is involved is always the *subsumption* of subaltern practice by elite discourse, regardless of the specific ideological commitments of the nationalist movement in question.

Ironically, this self-consciously avant-gardist standpoint – which disparages the question of representational adequacy as an empiricist residue – turns out to have as its unwitting consequence the duplication of the established trajectory of liberal historiography, which also casts nationalism as an elite, homogenizing imposition upon more or less disunited "ethnically" (or "local knowledge") identified communities.[86] Guha's unanswerable critique of liberal historiography might therefore be said to tell just as decisively against the position adumbrated by Spivak and Mudimbe: "In this particular respect," Guha writes, "the poverty of this historiography is demonstrated beyond any doubt by its failure to understand and assess the mass articulation of . . . nationalism except . . . in the currently . . . fashionable terms of vertical mobilization by the manipulation of factions" ("On Some Aspects," p. 3). Referring to the Indian case, Guha argues that even on those occasions in which "the masses" were mobilized very self-consciously and willfully by bourgeois nationalist elites, they "managed to break away from their control and put the characteristic imprint of popular politics on campaigns initiated by the upper classes" (p. 6). He draws our attention to "the contribution made by the people on their own, that is, independently of the elite, to the making and development of nationalism" (p. 3). The central thrust of his argument is to remind us that while anti-colonial nationalism is indeed an *articulatory* form of politics, whose objective tendency is to recruit subaltern support for "campaigns initiated by the upper classes," it is inconceivable that "the people" would consent to presenting themselves under the aegis of the nationalist movement unless and until that movement had been transformed, at least to some degree, into an instrument capable of expressing their aspirations.

I am emphasizing the theoretical *differences* between Spivak and Guha here not chiefly for documentary reasons (although it is worth pointing out that these differences are rarely remarked upon by those working in postcolonial studies), but because it seems to me that Guha's theorization of subalternity allows for a more credible interpretation of anti-colonial nationalism than Spivak's. Particularly resonant in this context is Guha's commentary on what he terms "the failure of the Indian bourgeoisie to speak for the nation" ("On Some Aspects," p. 5). This failure emerges for him as an inability on the part of the Indian elite during the colonial era to forge an articulated national ensemble out of the relatively autonomous domains of elite and popular politics. The bourgeoisie were unable to win the consent of the people, whose interests they failed to recognize, let alone represent: "There were vast areas in the life and consciousness of the people which were never integrated into the . . . hegemony [of the Indian bourgeoisie]" (pp. 5–6). Moreover, the political dominance of the dominant classes could not be challenged effectively by any counter-hegemonic alliance of workers and peasants:

the initiatives which originated from the domain of subaltern politics were not, on their part, powerful enough to develop the nationalist movement into a full-fledged struggle for national liberation. The working class was still not sufficiently mature in the objective conditions of its social being and in its consciousness as a class-for-itself, nor was it firmly allied yet with the peasantry. As a result it could do nothing to take over and complete the mission which the bourgeoisie had failed to realize. The outcome of it all was that the numerous peasant uprisings of the period, some of them massive in scope and rich in anticolonialist consciousness, waited in vain for a leadership to raise them above localism and general-ize them into a nationwide anti-imperialist campaign.   (p. 6)

Although Guha's suggestion, that the Indian nationalist movement failed to represent the interests of the people, becomes a central inspiration for Spivak's own critique of nationalist discourse, her position is revealingly different from his. For on Guha's interpreta-tion, the social "mission" that the Indian bourgeoisie failed to realize – the "mission" that the Indian working class movement for its part was too weak to appropriate and bring to fruition in "anything like a national liberation movement" – is to be characterized as an "historic failure of the nation to come to its own" (p. 7). The distinction implicitly drawn here, between the practical ideology of the "nation-alist movement" and the ideology that might have characterized a working class-identified "nationwide anti-imperialist campaign," finds an echo also in Edward Said's differentiation between the "insufficient" moment of "nationalist anti-imperialism" and "liber-ationist anti-imperialist resistance."[87] Like Said – and, behind him, of course, Fanon – Guha emerges in his work as an open advocate of the project of national liberation. This commits him to a nationalitarian politics – that is, to a socialist and representationalist politics predicated on the assumption that it is indeed possible for a move-ment or alliance or party to "speak for the nation." It is at this claim that Spivak seems to balk. She seems reluctant to follow Guha, Said, or Fanon in drawing nationalitarian conclusions from her critique of the pretensions of bourgeois nationalism. An air of hesitancy tends to mark her response to any claim for political representation – repre-sentation in the sense of *Vertretung* or "speaking for" as she analyzes it in "Can the Subaltern Speak?" Despite the critique of Foucault in that essay and her declaration (which we have already examined) to the effect that "[r]epresentation has not withered away," Spivak continues to grant what I view as an overly sympathetic hearing to arguments for a post-representationalist politics; and, conversely, she continues to evince a real disinclination to affirm the assumption of the burden of representation on the part of politico-intellectuals, even where – as in the case of anti-imperialist struggle – her ideological solidarity with them is freely admitted. Much the same critique can be leveled, too, at R. Radhakrishnan, whose important recent writings on anti-colonial nationalism address the volatility of nationalist discourse with great clarity, but whose belief that "the strategy of locating any one politics within another is as inappropriate as it is coercive" nevertheless leads him to characterize nationalist discourse undifferentiatedly as "an example of a 'bad totality'."[88] It is not that Radhakrishnan fails to register the distinction between bourgeois anti-colonialist and socialist or insurgent nationalisms. On the contrary, he refers explicitly to Fanon's theorization of national consciousness, describing it as "genuinely representative" in character. Yet the implications of this concession are not thought through in the analysis that follows, in which Radhakrishnan sets out to forge an alliance between a poststructuralist politics of difference and a nationalitarian politics of the universal. Why this should be necessary if Fanon's conception of national consciousness is indeed "genuinely representative" is left unexplained.

Enough has already been said, I hope, to enable us to recognize that what Benita Parry terms the "disparaging of nationalist discourses of resistance" is indeed a central feature of the contemporary field of postcolonial studies ("Problems," p. 35). In much of the work currently issuing from within this field, the massive nationalist mobilizations of the decolonizing years are thoroughly disavowed. Emphasis tends to be placed instead, as Aijaz Ahmad has critically observed, on "the failures, the distortions, the bureaucratization; that there [were] also . . . other kinds of solidarities no longer matter[s]" (*In Theory*, p. 33). Even the remarkable achievement of political independence is viewed less as an ineradicable, if inevitably limited, advance than as a strengthening and confirmation of "Western" hegemony.

In the face of such cynical and anti-political representations – which concede nothing, incidentally, to the ultra-leftist discourse of 1970s Third-Worldism[89] – it is important to try and keep alive the memory of the "revolutionary heroism" that was everywhere in evidence in the struggle for national liberation (*In Theory*, p. 28). Even more important, it seems to me, is to insist that the concrete *achievements* of this struggle are still intact and continue to provide a vital resource for present-day social and cultural practice. It is not only that the lives of hundreds of millions of people throughout the world were changed decisively by the experience of anti-colonial struggle. It is also that *these changes are irreversible*. No matter how great have been the defeats that have had to be endured *since* decolonization, the perduring solidaristic significance of the anti-colonial struggle has not been erased. Nor can it be: not in Vietnam, nor in India, nor in Zimbabwe. Hence, I take it, Basil Davidson's assessment that "not even the worst news has been able to cancel out the tremendous central gain of anti-colonial independence" (*Burden*, p. 196). And the same point is also made by Masao Miyoshi:

> At the darkest moment of despondence, we should try to remember that no matter how the history of the 1960s may be rewritten, it was the resisters and protesters, together with the Vietnamese, who ended the war in Vietnam. All the follies and errors of the time and the nostalgic, patriotic, and bored renarrativizations do not alter the history one bit. Likewise, apartheid was felled solely by those who struggled and sacrificed for justice and independence, and by their supporters. The future of South Africa might be bloody again, political suppression may only be replaced by economic domination, or apartheid might be forgiven, even eulogized. But it does not alter history: white rule was defeated by those who fought back.[90]

Many contemporary postcolonialist scholars, however, view anti-colonial nationalism (whether bourgeois or liberationist) as not only an elitist and authoritarian but also a *mimetic* discourse – that is, as a metapractice, one modeled – in certain key aspects, at least – on diverse metropolitan nation-projects and subordinate, for this reason, to their forms and protocols. Two lines of argument are typically adduced in this respect. Sometimes it is suggested that the "derivativeness" of nationalism in the colonial theater is sufficient to guarantee its fundamental externality – and, indeed, alien-ness – to the actual modes of social identification of the majority of the colonized. We have already encountered versions of this line of reasoning in the work of Miller and Spivak. A comparable analysis is advanced by Hobsbawm, who proposes that "[t]he leaders and ideologues of colonial and semi-colonial liberation movements sincerely spoke the language of European nationalism, which they had so often learned in or from the west, *even when it did not suit their situation*" (*Nations*, p. 136; emphasis added). One of the remarkable features of Hobsbawm's formulation is that he *himself* identifies its provenance as imperialist. "[I]mperial observers," he notes, tended to view nationalism in "the dependent world" as "an intellectual import, taken up by minorities of *évolués* out of touch with the mass of the countrymen, whose ideas of community and political loyalty were quite different" (p. 152). But he then goes on to offer cautious endorsement of this imperial assessment, writing that it was "often just, even though [it] tended to cause imperial rulers or European settlers to overlook the rise of mass national identification when it did occur, as Zionists and Israeli Jews notably did in the case of the Palestinian Arabs." I confess to finding this concession of justness or accuracy to the imperialist perspective more or less wholly unconvincing – not least because it follows hard upon the heels of a passage in which Hobsbawm has exposed the manifest cultural supremacism that underlies the imperialist construction of nationalism in "the dependent world":

Virtually all the anti-imperial movements of any significance could be, and in the metropoles generally were, classified under one of three headings: local educated elites imitating European "national self-determination" (as in India), popular anti-western xenophobia (an all-purpose heading widely applied, notably in China), and the natural high spirits of martial tribes (as in Morocco or the Arabian deserts). In the last case imperial administrators and intellectuals, not unmindful of the possibility of recruiting such sturdy, and usually unpolitical, fellows into imperial armies, tended to be indulgent, reserving their real hostility for urban agitators, especially those with some education.   (p. 151)

A second, complementary, line of argument is to suppose that the "mimeticism" of anti-colonial nationalism bespeaks its fundamental *internality* to the sociocultural project inaugurated by colonialism. On this reading, the discourse of anti-colonial nationalism is assumed to exist within or alongside colonial discourse – from which it is certainly distinct, but to which it poses no radical or epochal challenge. Writing under the auspices of what he calls "post-Orientalist historiography," Gyan Prakash, for instance, maintains that while at one level "nationalist historiography's narrativization of Indian nationalism" clearly opposes itself to Orientalist (that is, colonial) representations of Indian history, at another level its own ideologically and institutionally determined procedures and protocols insure that it merely replicates Orientalist reason. In two respects especially, according to Prakash, the "nationalist writing of history – both before and after independence" – proves itself incapable of surpassing Orientalism:

First, the nationalists, like the Orientalists, also assumed that India was an undivided entity but attributed it a sovereign and unitary will that was expressed in history. India now emerged as an active and undivided subject that had found its expression in the nation-state and transcended class and ethnic divisions, rather than being the inert object of Orientalist representations. Second, India was given an ontological presence prior to and independent of its representations which followed the procedures of Orientalism.[91]

Typologically, this way of thinking receives its imprimatur from

Foucault's plangent (mis-)representation of Marxism in *The Order of Things* as a discourse that coexists seamlessly alongside bourgeois ideology:

> At the deepest level of Western knowledge, Marxism introduced no real discontinuity; it found its place without difficulty, as a full, quiet, comfortable and, goodness knows, satisfying form for a time (its own), within an epistemological arrangement that welcomed it gladly (since it was this arrangement that was in fact making room for it) and that it, in return, had no intention of disturbing and, above all, no power to modify, even one jot, since it rested entirely upon it. Marxism exists in nineteenth-century thought like a fish in water: that is, it is unable to breathe anywhere else.[92]

In a recent account of the intellectual trajectory of the "Subaltern Studies" project, Dipesh Chakrabarty insists that "[u]nlike in the Paris of the poststructuralists, there was never any question in Delhi, Calcutta or Madras of a wholesale rejection of Marx's thought. Foucault's scathing remark . . . may have its point, but it never resonated with us with anything like the energy that anti-marxism displays in the writings of some postmodernists."[93] This defensive claim seems eminently disputable, however: for the terms of Foucault's construction of Marxism recur precisely, *mutatis mutandis*, in the accounts of anti-colonial nationalism put forward by Chakrabarty, Prakash, Chatterjee, and other contemporary theorists in postcolonial studies whose epistemological dispositions can broadly be described as poststructuralist. For these theorists, the (sometimes revolutionary) clash between the national movement and the colonial order is to be accounted a mere "controversy" rather than an event of any overarching historical importance: while it might – as Foucault wrote of the Marxist challenge to the bourgeois social order in the nineteenth century – have "stirred up a few waves and caused a few surface ripples," it ultimately amounted to "no more than storms in a children's paddling pool."[94] There is, accordingly, no pertinent distinction to be drawn between different nationalist projects – whether conservative or revolutionary, bourgeois or socialist. The moment of decolonization corresponds in all instances to a mere restructuring of "Western" hegemony. There is simply no passage from the social logic entailed in and by nationalism (or nationalist struggle) to that implied in the concept of "postcoloniality." Indeed, "nationalism" and "postcoloniality" (or "post-Orientalism") are on this reading definitively counterposed concepts. Hence Partha Chatterjee's argument that – at the level of what he calls its "thematic," at least (a level that is for him both constitutive and untranscendable) – "nationalist thought accepts the same essentialist conception based on the distinction between 'the East' and 'the West,' the same typology created by a transcendent studying subject, and hence the same 'objectifying' procedures of knowledge constructed in the post-Enlightenment age of Western science" as Orientalist thought.[95]

In Chapter One I tried to suggest that in their hypostatization – their groundless de-differentiation – of "the West," such representations as this tend to render the structurality of the modern world system either arbitrary or unintelligible. Here let us note further that for theorists like Prakash and Chatterjee, what is true of nationalism in the historical context of colonialism is *also* true of Marxism in the historical context of capitalist modernity. One does not have to look especially hard to see the light of Foucault's critique of Marxism shining behind the "post-Orientalist" critique of nationalism in the colonial world. Prakash is always very quick, thus, to observe that what he has said in criticism of nationalist historiography can and must be applied equally to Marxist historiography. In his view both modes of historical practice are foundationalist, which means that they assume "that history is ultimately founded in and representable through some identity – individual, class, or structure – which resists further decomposition into heterogeneity" ("Post-Orientalist," p. 397). Such an assumption, Prakash explains further, "excludes a critical return to the scene of writing history and carries an objectivist bias with it, however provisional." The full charge against foundationalist historiography is then drawn up as follows:

[T]he tenuous presence and the very historicity of class structures that anchor the transitional narrative cannot be fully acknowledged without the rejection of the stability occupied by the theme of transition in the discourse of historians. Without such an acknowledgement, the Marxist and social historians can only envision that India's "third worldness" consists of its incomplete or underdeveloped development. India, which is seen in this history as trapped in the trajectories of global modernity, is doomed to occupy a tragic position in these narratives. Such a vision cannot but reproduce the very hegemonic structures that it finds ideologically unjust in most cases, and occludes the histories that lie outside of the themes which are privileged in history.   (p. 398)

Prakash does not, in this formulation, go quite as far as Chakrabarty, who claims that the very enterprise of "history" is inextricably collusive with "the modernizing narrative(s) of citizenship, bourgeois public and private, and the nation state."[96] But insofar as we take Chakrabarty's central contention to be that, as a *modern* intellectual practice, "history" is incapable of assuming a critical standpoint on modernity, it is clear that Prakash's views accord closely with his. "Take . . . the narrativization of Indian history in terms of the development of capitalism," Prakash writes. "How is it possible to write such a narrative, but also contest, as the same time, the homogenization of the contemporary world by capitalism? How can the historians of India resist the totalizing claims of the contemporary nation-state if their writings represent India in terms of the nation-state's career?" ("Post-Orientalist," pp. 397–98).

As Prakash presents them, these are rhetorical questions, and strictly unanswerable. In fact, a lucid and perfectly plausible answer to them is given by Ranajit Guha in his essay, "Colonialism in South Asia: A Dominance without Hegemony and Its Historiography." Guha begins by affirming the premise of the historicality and social contingency of thought: "it is not possible," he argues, "to write or speak about the past without the use of concepts and presuppositions derived from one's experience and understanding of the present, that is, from those ideas by which the writer or speaker interprets his own times to himself and to others" ("Dominance," p. 6). One specific implication of this, he then suggests, has been the failure of liberal discourse to offer a credible or far-ranging critique of the projects of colonialism or of bourgeois nationalism. As he puts it:

To commit a discourse to speak from within a given consciousness is to disarm it insofar as its critical faculty is made inoperative thereby with regard to that particular consciousness. For no criticism can be fully activated unless its object is distanced from its agency. This is why liberal historiography, cramped as it is within the bourgeois consciousness, can never attack it vigorously enough as the object of its criticism. Since the paradoxes characteristic of the political culture of colonialism testify to the failure of the bourgeoisie to acknowledge the structural limitations of bourgeois dominance itself, it is hardly surprising that the liberal historical discourse too should be blind to those paradoxes. This is a necessary, one could say congenital, blindness which this historiography acquires by virtue of its class origin. (p. 7)

At first glance this formulation might seem to set well with Prakash's and Chakrabarty's strictures concerning the inability of anti-colonial nationalism, or of Marxism, or of historical discourse itself, to differentiate themselves from Orientalist reason. Guha indeed notes that

The knowledge systems that make up any dominant culture are all contained within the dominant consciousness and have therefore the latter's deficiencies built into their optics. The light of criticism emitted by such systems can, under no circumstances, be strong enough to penetrate and scan some of the strategic areas of that consciousness where dominance stores the spiritual gear it needs to justify and sustain itself. (p. 7)

Yet as soon as we look closely at Guha's terminology, we see that unlike Prakash or Chakrabarty he does not speak of "history" or "modernity" *as such*. On the contrary, his language is notably precise in its ideological thrust and provenance: "bourgeois consciousness"; "liberal historical discourse"; "class origin." Certainly, Guha agrees with Prakash and Chakrabarty that, as he puts it, "no discourse can oppose a genuinely uncompromising critique to a ruling culture so long as its ideological parameters are the same as those of that very culture" (p. 11). To the question to which this formulation inevitably gives rise: "Where then does criticism come from?" he first offers a general answer: "From outside the universe of dominance which provides the critique with its object, indeed, from another and historically antagonistic universe" (p. 11). But where Prakash and Chakrabarty follow Foucault's idealist lead in construing the *inside* of the "universe of dominance" so totalistically as to render the notion of any *outside* of it more or less moot – and certainly unrealizable in any concrete sociological sense – Guha particularizes his answer by way of clarifying it. The question is no longer: "Where does criticism come from?" It now becomes: "Where . . . does the critique of liberalism . . . come from?" (p. 13). And here Guha's answer is decisively opposed to that of the Foucauldians:

It comes from an ideology that is antagonistic towards the dominant culture and declares war on it even before the class for which it speaks comes to rule. In rushing thus in advance of the conquest of power by its class, this critique demonstrates, all over again, a historic décalage characteristic of all periods of great social transformation when a young and ascendant class challenges the authority of another that is older and moribund but still dominant. The bourgeoisie itself had dramatized such décalage during the Enlightenment by a relentless critique of the *ancien régime* for decades before the French Revolution and anticipating it in effect. And yet, for all the appearance of being in a hurry and arriving before its time, that critique was true to the real contradictions of the epoch in seizing on the feudal mode of production and its power relations as the object of its criticism.

In much the same way, the critique of the dominant bourgeois culture arises from the real contradictions of capitalism and anticipates its dissolution. (p. 13)

The allusion here is quite explicitly to Marxist thought, which Guha conceptualizes in properly dialectical terms both as an effect of capitalist sociality and as the social philosophy that anticipates the determinate supersession of capitalist by socialist social relations. (Prakash repudiates the "Hegelian" dialectics of the early writings of the Subaltern Studies historians, which he describes as "teleological" in tendency ["Post-Orientalist," p. 400]. But Guha's dialectics are surely *Marxist rather than Hegelian* in provenance. In a gesture that perfectly exemplifies the attenuated nature of the poststructuralist understanding of post-Enlightenment thought in general, Prakash conflates the two modes.[97]) For Guha, Marxism possesses a clear externality to the bourgeois "universe of dominance" (which does not, of course, mean that it does not hold any assumptions in common with bourgeois thought). Indeed, the bourgeois "universe of dominance" provides Marxism with its critical object. But to say this is immediately to understand why the Foucauldian critique of nationalism in the colonial world should also have to become, at the deepest levels of its articulation, a critique of Marxism. For it follows from Guha's reading that no de-differentiated characterization of "nationalism" (or of "modernity" or of "history") is justified. It is necessary, instead, to situate every particular movement or discourse in terms of its ideological and political tendency, its practical bearing with respect to the total (that is, local and global) social order within which it unfolds. Consider, for example, the language of the following formulation of the enabling sociocultural conditions and emergent trajectories of anti-colonial nationalism, drawn from Halim Barakat's very useful book, *The Arab World: Society, Culture, and State*:

Nationalism developed as a strong force in response to structural changes as well as to the need of Arab countries to free themselves from repressive Ottoman rule and to counter the onslaught of an aggressive European imperialism and colonization. For the eastern Arab world, particularly the Fertile Crescent, nationalism provided an alternative to divisive communal arrangements. Since the middle of the nineteenth century, the call for nationalism has been central to the process of social, political, and cultural renewal – that is, the achievement of the *nahda*. In the beginning, some conceived of nationalism as a movement to redress Arab grievances through decentralization and the creation of a new balance of power in the area. Others conceived of it as a secular alternative to the caliphate and a way to achieve full independence. Since the end of World War I, the latter view has become a strong, and ultimately dominant, political force. There have, however, been divergent orientations: nationalism is defined by local versus regional versus pan-Arab referents. It has been given either secular or apologetically religious overtones. It carries socialist versus capitalist or leftist versus rightist or progressive versus conservative implications. Nationalist goals can be reactionary or reformist or revolutionary.[98]

"These developments and others," Barakat continues, "disprove the notion that nationalism was borrowed from the West. They demonstrate, instead, the emergence of nationalism as a genuine result of the internal and external dynamics of Arab society." Barakat is concerned to demonstrate that the social logic borne in and by nationalism in the colonial world is irreducible to the form of sociality embodied in and enforced by colonial rule. He rightly sees no logical contradiction between the insistence that the *differentia specifica* of nationalism in the Arab world derive as profoundly from internal as from external dynamics, and the suggestion that the contours and lines of development of Arab nationalism can only be plotted comprehensively – that is, in all their real complexity – on a map of the modern capitalist world system. Hence the categories that frame his reading: "local versus regional versus pan-Arab"; "secular or apologetically religious"; "socialist versus capitalist or leftist versus rightist or progressive versus conservative"; "reactionary or reformist or revolutionary." For the Foucauldian theorists of "postcoloniality," however, all commentaries of this kind – regardless of their politics – are modernist-universalist and, by implication therefore, Eurocentric. Thus Prakash specifically writes of Guha that, like the "older Marxist historians," he deploys a "global mode-of-production narrative" that does not "fully confront the universalism of the post-Enlightenment order of Reason" ("Post-Orientalist," p. 404). On Prakash's reading, only a "post-Orientalist historiography" – post-Marxist, postmodernist, anti-universalist – is capable of "challeng[ing] . . . the hegemony of those modernization schemes and ideologies that post-Enlightenment Europe projected as the *raison d'être* of history" (p. 404).

Much the same position is adumbrated in the work of Partha Chatterjee. In his influential study, *Nationalist Thought and the Colonial World* (1986), Chatterjee seeks to outline and defend the "hypothesis" that anti-colonial nationalism constitutes a "different discourse, yet one that is dominated by another" (p. 42). Chatterjee frames his hypothesis as follows:

Pitting itself against the reality of colonial rule – which appears before it as an existent, almost palpable, historical truth – [anti-colonial] nationalism seeks to assert the feasibility of entirely new political possibilities . . .

[It] succeeds in producing a *different* discourse. The difference is marked, on the terrain of political-ideological discourse, by a political contest, a struggle for power, which nationalist thought must think about and set down in words. Its problematic forces it relentlessly to demarcate itself from the discourse of colonialism. Thus nationalist thinking is necessarily a struggle with an entire body of systematic knowledge . . . Its politics impels it to open up that framework of knowledge which presumes to dominate it, to displace that framework, to subvert its authority, to challenge its morality.

Yet in its very constitution as a discourse of power, nationalist thought cannot remain only a negation; it is also a *positive* discourse which seeks to replace the structure of colonial power with a new order, that of national power. Can nationalist thought produce a discourse of order while daring to negate the very foundations of a system of knowledge that has conquered the world? How far can it succeed in maintaining its difference from a discourse that seeks to dominate it?

A different discourse, yet one that is dominated by another: that is my hypothesis about nationalist thought.   (*Nationalist Thought*, pp. 40, 42)

This hypothesis, which certainly constitutes a cogent rebuttal of the arguments of those contemporary Third-Worldists who posit anti-colonial nationalism as a shadow discourse pure and simple, is not on the face of it radically at odds with that proposed by Barakat.[99] Yet both in *Nationalist Thought* and, even more starkly, in *The Nation and Its Fragments* (1993), Chatterjee goes to elaborate lengths to distinguish his position categorically from that of historians and philosophers who write about nationalism from within the inherited conceptual frameworks (liberal and Marxist) of modern social theory. Chatterjee's particular *bête noire* in this respect is Benedict Anderson – a discrimination that makes perfect sense if we bear in mind that it has been Anderson's signal achievement to have offered a non-Eurocentric Marxist theory of nationalism that situates nationalism's modern emergence within the global context of capitalist development. In *Imagined Communities*, Anderson suggests that the first truly *modern* nationalisms developed as *anti-colonial* nationalisms, in the various creole-led independence movements throughout the Americas in the latter half of the eighteenth and the first half of the nineteenth centuries. For Anderson, the nationalisms of Western Europe, whose emergence in some instances predated the development of nationalism in the New World, tended to be marked by their commitment to the political values of the *ancien régime*: "the 'observable reality' of France until after 1870," for instance, "was restored monarchies and the ersatz dynasticism of Napoleon's great-nephew" (*Imagined*, p. 78). By contrast, "[o]ut of the American welter came

these imagined realities: nation-states, republican institutions, common citizenships, popular sovereignty, national flags and anthems,
etc., and the liquidation of their conceptual opposites: dynastic empires, monarchical institutions, absolutisms, subjecthoods, inherited
nobilities, serfdoms, ghettoes, and so forth." "Populist" nationalisms
in Europe developed in staggered response to these developments in
the colonial world, as also – somewhat later – did the "official"
top-down nationalisms of Russia, Eastern Europe, and elsewhere. All
three "models" of modern nationalist development became – in
Anderson's resonant phrase – "available for pirating" by nationalist
movements in the twentieth century. It is necessary, according to
Anderson, to register the decisive influence often exerted upon the
trajectories of specific nationalist movements in the twentieth century
world by these historically engendered "models." Yet this is not in
the least to deny the irreducibility of the later developments: for as
Anderson explicitly and unequivocally notes, the "new states of the
post-World War II period have their own character" (*Imagined*, p.
104).

The tendentiousness of Chatterjee's reading of Anderson is remarkable. He begins by inverting the terms of Anderson's narrative
of nationalist development; and he follows this by dramatically over-
stating the case that Anderson makes for the modularity of the forms
of nationalism that developed in the eighteenth and nineteenth centuries. We have just seen that for Anderson, the "story" of modern
nationalism begins in the colonial Americas and travels thence to
Western Europe and on to Russia; and that the models of nationalist
development historically generated in this process become "available
for pirating" by later nationalist activists. Chatterjee, however, represents Anderson as arguing "that the historical experience of nationalism *in Western Europe, in the Americas*, and in Russia . . . supplied for
all subsequent nationalisms a set of modular forms from which
nationalist elites in Asia and Africa . . . chose . . . the ones they liked"
(*Nation*, pp. 4–5; emphasis added). By placing "Western Europe"
before "the Americas" in this formulation, Chatterjee falsifies the
historical logic of Anderson's account, a sleight-of-hand that then
enables him to detect in Anderson the same Eurocentrism that he also
claims to find in all of the most significant "area specialists" and
"historians of the colonial world." The overstatement of Anderson's
argument that the historically prior models of nationalist development subsequently became "available for pirating" works to the
same end. Here is how Chatterjee presents his case against Anderson:

I have one central objection to Anderson's argument. If nationalisms in the rest of the world have to choose their imagined community from certain "modular" forms already made available to them by Europe and the Americas, what do they have left to imagine? History, it would seem, has decreed that we in the postcolonial world shall only be perpetual consumers of modernity. Europe and the Americas, the only true subjects of history, have thought out on our behalf not only the script of colonial enlightenment and exploitation, but also that of our anticolonial resistance and postcolonial misery. Even our imaginations must remain forever colonized.

I object to this argument not for any sentimental reason. I object because I cannot reconcile it with the evidence on anticolonial nationalism. The most powerful as well as the most creative results of the nationalist imagination in Asia and Africa are posited not on an identity but rather on a *difference* with the "modular" forms of the national society propagated by the modern West. How can we ignore this without reducing the experience of anticolonial nationalism to a caricature of itself?

(*Nation*, p. 5)

Carried away by the righteousness of his indignation, Chatterjee fails to notice that his protest does not bear very telling witness against Anderson. Anderson never argues that "nationalisms in the rest of the world *have to choose* their imagined community from certain 'modular' forms already made available to them by Europe and the Americas." Nor, despite Chatterjee's solemn reiteration of the phrase "Europe and the Americas" (which again carefully misrepresents Anderson's own chronology), does anything that Anderson says remotely license Chatterjee's attribution to him of the assumption that "Europe and the Americas" are "the only true subjects of history." Most ironically of all, what Chatterjee himself finally produces, triumphantly, as "the evidence on anticolonial nationalism" is already more or less unproblematically entailed in Anderson's own treatment, in *Imagined Communities* and in other writings, of nationalism in Indonesia and elsewhere in southeast Asia! In *Nationalist Thought*, Chatterjee suggests that there is ultimately little to distinguish Anderson's theory of nationalism from that of Ernest Gellner:

What, if we look closely, are the substantive differences between Anderson and Gellner on 20th century nationalism? None. Both point out a fundamental change in ways of perceiving the social world which occurs before nationalism can emerge: Gellner relates this change to the requirements of "industrial society," Anderson more ingeniously to the dynamics of "print-capitalism." Both describe the characteristics of the new cultural homogeneity which is sought to be imposed on the emerging nation: for Gellner this is the imposition of a common high culture on the variegated complex of local folk cultures, for Anderson the process involves the formation of a "print-language" and the shared experience of the "journeys" undertaken by the colonized intelligentsia. In the end, both see in third-world nationalisms a profoundly "modular" character. They are invariably shaped according to contours outlined by given historical models. (p. 21)

The inference here is the Foucauldian one, with which we are already familiar: that Marxist discourse is really at one with liberal discourse within the circumambient episteme of modernity. It seems to me, however, that if Chatterjee cannot tell the difference between Gellner's position and Anderson's, this is not because of any deep-structural similarity between liberal and Marxist thought, but rather because of the difference-dissolving abstraction of Chatterjee's own methodological protocols. Already in *Nationalist Thought*, but much more obviously in *The Nation and Its Fragments*, Chatterjee tends to figure colonialism in insistently culturalist terms as a mode of discursive or ideological regulation, plotted along the axes of "Western-ness" and "modernity," and with respect to which the determining instance of capitalism is not only suppressed but explicitly denied. In *The Nation and Its Fragments*, as Achin Vanaik puts it, Chatterjee completes a

slide into culturalism and through it towards ever greater sympathy for indigenism. To the binary contrast of colonialism/indigenous commu nity, [he adds] . . . other polar contrasts such as material/spiritual, outer/inner, world/home. In each of these binaries, the second term . . . become[s] the more important, the realm of true autonomous thought and struggle, itself cultural as opposed to political or economic. Struggle on the terrain of the "material" or "outer" or "world" . . . become[s] a form of surrender to the defining principles of colonial discourse itself . . . [The] last chapter [of the book] constitutes Chatterjee's most sustained effort to date to theorize community and to counterpose the "narrative of community" (not of class) to the "narrative of capital," itself identified with and standing in for the narratives of universal history.[100]

Chatterjee seems to imagine that to reference capitalism is to commit oneself willy-nilly to a Eurocentric explanatory paradigm – a conception that, on my reading, simply fails to attend to the central feature of capitalism's emergence *as a world system*. In my view, Chatterjee fails to reckon adequately either with the historical singularity of capitalist globality or with the contradictions within the capitalist world system. In *The Nation and Its Fragments*, indeed, "capitalism" makes its appearance most notably as the name of a discredited narrative mode, mobilized in the work of the historians with whom Chatterjee wishes to disagree. "What is this theory? It is the familiar theme of capitalist development, which in one form or another has framed all discussions of modern history," he writes exasperatedly at one point (p. 30) – as though it were no longer very important to distinguish *between* these theories of capitalist development (between Marx's and Weber's, say, or Perry Anderson's and Francis Fukuyama's, or – in the context of Indian historiography – between Ranajit Guha's and Anil Seal's), and as though no account anchored in the "theme of capitalist development" could conceivably pretend to an adequate narration of the trajectories of modernity over the course of the past four hundred years.

One of the more celebrated uses of the idea of anti-colonial nationalism as a mimetic discourse is to be found in the work of Homi Bhabha. Bhabha casts what he takes to be the reiteration of metropolitan nationalism in anti-colonial nationalist practice as a displacement of sorts, a subtle articulation of difference within the semiotic space of the same. "Repeatability, in my terms, is always the repetition in the very act of enunciation, something other, a difference that is a little bit uncanny,"[101] he writes, expressing an insight that serves as a window onto his conception of colonial subjectivity at large. Repeatability (or mimicry) and ambivalence are indeed the two central categories mediating Bhabha's theory of colonial subjectivity. When he refers to colonial discourse as "ambivalent," he means to describe a certain slippage at the heart of the colonial episteme. In his essay, "Signs Taken for Wonders," thus, he argues that the colonial mode of authority is agonistic rather than antagonistic: "the colonial presence is always ambivalent, split between its appearance as original and authoritative, and its articulation as repetition and difference."[102] He adds that "[i]t is this ambivalence that makes the boundaries of colonial 'positionality' – the division of self/other – and the question of colonial power – the differentiation of colonizer/colonized – different from both the Hegelian master/slave dialectic or the phenomenological projection of Otherness." For Bhabha, "the effect of colonial power" is to produce not submission on the part of the colonized, nor "the silent repression of native traditions," but hybridization, or mimicry ("Signs," p. 173). Colonial "mimicry" is defined as "the desire for a reformed, recognizable Other, as *a subject of a difference that is almost the same, but not quite*. Which is to say, that the discourse of mimicry is constructed around an ambivalence; in order to be effective, mimicry must continually produce its slippage, its excess, its difference."[103]

In these terms, "hybridity" does not describe the identity of the "native" under colonial rule, but is rather "a *problematic* of colonial representation and individuation that reverses the effects of the colonialist disavowal, so that other 'denied' knowledges enter upon the dominant discourse and estrange the basis of its authority – its rules of recognition" ("Signs," p. 175). Bhabha's emphasis upon the incoherence of the colonial episteme, upon the "ambivalence at the source of traditional discourses on authority," leads him to insist upon the destabilizing propensities of colonial mimicry: he speaks of "a form of subversion, founded on that uncertainty, that turns the discursive conditions of dominance into the grounds of intervention" (p. 173). Bhabha's writing thus operates, as Benita Parry has put it, to render "visible those moments when colonial discourse already disturbed at its source by a doubleness of enunciation, is further subverted by the object of its address; when the scenario written by colonialism is given a performance by the native that estranges and undermines the colonialist script" ("Problems," p. 42).

Yet as Parry also notes, the effect of Bhabha's distinctive approach to colonial discourse "is to displace the traditional anti-colonialist representation of antagonistic forces locked in struggle with a configuration of discursive transactions." She adds that since, for Bhabha, "colonial power is theorized . . . as a textual function, it follows that the proper form of combat for a politically engaged critical practice is to disclose the construction of the signifying system and thereby deprive it of its mandate to rule" ("Problems," p. 42). Bhabha's textualism and his theoretical idealism prevent him from engaging adequately with the vastly differential thrusts, effects, and modes of domination/subjection of colonialism as practiced at different times by different powers in different parts of the world, or even within single colonies subject to the vicissitudes of uneven development.

I do not wish to be misunderstood here as denying altogether the cogency of Bhabha's intellectual production over the course of the past decade and more. Bhabha has contributed very significantly to the contemporary theorization of "postcoloniality" as a terrain of intellectual inquiry. But it is necessary to specify the precise *object* of Bhabha's theorization more circumspectly than he himself does. It might be supposed, on the grounds of his discussion of ambivalence and hybridization – "*Almost the same but not white*," he puns in "Of Mimicry and Man": "the difference between being English and being Anglicized"[104] – that Bhabha's real object was colonial elitism.

Bhabha's theorization of colonial discourse is, indeed, manifestly pertinent to a reading of the practice of colonial elites (including the leadership of nationalist movements). But I would like to suggest that the characteristic figure of Bhabha's work is the marginal subject of the "colonial encounter" – "marginal" not in the sense of being powerless or disenfranchised, but in the sense of existing at the margins, that is, of being "on the edge of the frame" of the dominant discourses, whether of colonialism or of anti-colonial nationalism.

A key assumption underlying Bhabha's work is that in the modern era, social identities – "strategies of identification and . . . processes of affiliation"[105] – are not only always compound and overdetermined, but also unstable at their origins, and incapable of being stabilized. On this reading, the problematics of exile, migration, and diaspora emerge as paradigmatic. Bhabha's cardinal concept-figures are the *mohajirs*, "emigrants" from the countries of their birth and "newcomers" in other countries (as Salman Rushdie puts it in his novel *Shame*),[106] multiply rooted subjects dwelling fully neither within the "First World" nor within the "Third World," but ranged across them, so to speak, athwart the international division of labor. The space of such subjectivity is labeled "postcolonial" by Bhabha: "The postcolonial space is now 'supplementary' to the metropolitan centre; it stands in a subaltern, adjunct relation that doesn't aggrandise the *presence* of the west but redraws its frontiers in the menacing, agonistic boundary of cultural difference that never quite adds up, always less than one nation and double" ("DissemiNation," p. 318).

As this formulation makes clear, Bhabha tends to use the concept of "postcoloniality," as he has defined it, *against* nationalism. In "DissemiNation," he praises Hobsbawm for writing "the history of the modern western nation from the perspective of the nation's margin and the migrants' exile" (p. 291). His general contention is that the problematic of nationalism is *exploded*, rendered both anachronistic and incoherent, by the questions that stem from any consideration of the situation of the marginal subjects of contemporary "postcoloniality." It is not only that "colonials, postcolonials, migrants, minorities" are "wandering peoples who will not be contained within the *Heim* of the national culture and its unisonant discourse, but are themselves the marks of a shifting boundary that alienates the frontiers of the modern nation" (p. 315). The "atonality" of the discourse of postcoloniality is in addition positively *disruptive* of "the powerful oratory of the unisonant" ("Question," p. 96). "Postcoloniality" – the standpoint of the migrant – is understood in these terms as being itself extremely powerful: Bhabha speaks, thus, of a "strange, empowering knowledge . . . that is at once schizoid and subversive" and which emerges as a function of the condition of exile, migrancy, diaspora ("DissemiNation," p. 319).

In his 1991 essay, "A Question of Survival," Bhabha offers a partial reading of Edward Said's book, *After the Last Sky*. On the basis of Said's poignant meditation on Palestinian identity in its contemporary guises, Bhabha draws the following conclusions, not only about Palestinian identity but about the "impossibility" of nationalist discourse in general:

The opaque silence of the atonal overwritten space of the Palestinian – Abandon the metanarrative! – petrifies the present, barring access to any . . . reflective, representationalist distance of knowledge, or time of return. The questions of the Other, "What do you Palestinians want?," cannot simply be answered in the images of identity or the narrative of historicism, because they are also asked in the language of Desire: *He is saying this to me but what does he want?* And that question cannot be replied to directly because it leads us past the place of meaning or truth and leads us to the enunciative level, to the moment that determines unique and limited existence of the utterance – the broken, fragmentary composition of the Palestinian: the atonal void . . . The silence or void dangerously decomposes the narrative of the national culture.   (p. 197)

Three points need to be made about this formulation. First, let me draw attention to the tendentiousness of Bhabha's reading of Said. As earlier with respect to Fanon, here too he seems simply to appropriate Said, to assimilate him to his own theoretical interests and preoccupations. Thus Said's longstanding commitment to a nationalist politics – evident in all his political work and writings on behalf of the Palestinian people – is not only ignored, but actually transmuted into its opposite, in Bhabha's commentary. The injunction to "[a]bandon the metanarrative," for instance, finds no sanction in Said's thought. Second, it is important to note that Bhabha's claims both for the representativeness and for the "disruptive" effectivity of the kind of subjectivity allegedly embodied in "the Palestinian" are considerably overstated. I do not mean merely that the Palestinian situation is socially and historically *sui generis*, and cannot be taken as a generative model, although this is clearly true. My point, rather, is that even if, in the contemporary world system, the subjects whom Bhabha addresses under the labels of exile, migration, and diaspora are vastly more numerous than at any time previously, they cannot reasonably be said to be paradigmatic or constitutive of "postcoloniality" as such. One cannot simply deem such subjects "true" postcolonials and leave out of account those hundreds of millions of people all over the world who – whether or not they would declare themselves *nationalists* – are manifestly centered in their national identities. Even if the category of the migrant or diasporic subject significantly complicates any easy espousal of nationalism in terms of belonging or territoriality, it is scarcely sufficient to undermine the credibility of those contemporary political movements – in Eritrea, East Timor, Armenia, and of course Palestine, for instance – that present themselves precisely as nationalist. Third, I want to protest the one-sidedness of Bhabha's treatment even of his theoretically favored categories of exile, migration, and diaspora. Bhabha fails to address the material circumstances of the vast majority of migrants from the peripheries of the world system to the core capitalist nations. He fails to register in any plausible manner the political, economic, and social dimensions of the lives of these millions of people. What Tim Brennan has recently observed in this respect of postcolonial and cultural studies in general is pointedly true of Bhabha's work in particular:

It is not so much the involuntary or coercive aspect of displacement that is forgotten but the one-sidedness of the conclusions drawn about the felt community of the nation. An overwhelming number of accounts look to reigning politico-emotive mythologies – ideological rituals of invented history and ethnic exclusion – while failing to analyze the reality of a simpler, more knifelike communal sense based upon the passport, the green card, and the open-ended residency permit. Since nationhood as residency in a wage setting plays almost no role in current theory, a simplistic coupling of formally cosmopolitan experience and transnational identity is facilitated.[107]

Bhabha contends that to open the question of the nation under the sign of "postcoloniality" is to push oneself "not merely to the edge of the discourse of a national culture, but to the limits of a metaphor of the modernity of Western Man at the point at which he encounters the Other" ("Question," p. 96). Let me, in attempting to rebut this position, turn again to Amilcar Cabral's essay on "National Liberation and Culture." Earlier, I cited a passage in which Cabral commented on the "realizations" and "discoveries" (about themselves and about "the people") that the leaders of the national liberation movement make in their interaction with "the various peasant groups in the heart of the rural populations." But Cabral focuses, too, on the transformations wrought on the consciousness of "the people":

On their side, the working masses and, in particular, the peasants who are usually illiterate and never have moved beyond the boundaries of their village or region, in contact with other groups lose the complexes which constrained them in their relationships with other ethnic and social groups. They realize their crucial role in the struggle; they break the bonds of the village universe to integrate progressively into the country and the world; they acquire an infinite amount of new knowledge, useful for their immediate and future activity within the framework of the struggle, and they strengthen their political awareness by assimilating the principles of national and social revolution postulated by the struggle. They thereby become more able to play the decisive role of providing the principal force behind the liberation movement. (*Return*, p. 54)

I am particularly interested, here, in the idea of a movement in popular consciousness from "local knowledge" to knowledge of "the principles of national and social revolution." For Cabral, of course, this is the desired consequence of the articulation of what he calls "converted" intellectuals and "the people." Within the modern era (and not only in the "Third World"), the nation has been one of the privileged sites – perhaps *the* privileged site – for the forging of this articulation between universalist intellectualism and popular consciousness. It is not only that "nation-ness," in Benedict Anderson's formulation, "is the most universally legitimate value in the political life of our time" (*Imagined*, p. 12). It is rather that it is at the level of the nation that the idea of unity in diversity has been given concrete form. As Achin Vanaik points out,

[t]he exceptional character of nationalism . . . lies in its unique combination of politics and culture, of civic power (e.g. the importance of citizenship) and identity. The nation-state for the first time invests ordinary people (through the principle of equal citizenship rights) with an authority and importance that is historically unique. To date the zenith of popular individual empowerment is political citizenship, whose frame of operation is the nation-state or multinational state.[108]

Nationalist discourse has enabled "nation-builders both to see a society as a fabric of complex patterns and to fit a national identity upon a population."[109] This fact enables us to understand why – for all its ultimate insufficiency – the moment of nationalism retains its indispensability not only to the struggle against colonialism but also, beyond that, to the struggle for socialism. It may be, as Rogers Brubaker follows the anti-essentialist lead of Bourdieu in insisting, that "[o]urs is not . . . a 'world of nations' . . . [but] a world in which nationhood is pervasively institutionalized in the practice of states and the workings of the state system."[110] Yet to the extent that this remains an accurate characterization of the contemporary world system, it suggests that it is only on the basis of nationalitarian struggle – that is, of a (global) struggle for socialist internationalism, but one centered (locally) on the terrain of the nation – that the overthrow of imperialist social relations can plausibly be envisaged. The point has been very well made by Ahmad in *In Theory*:

> to the extent that contemporary imperialism's political system takes the form of a hierarchically structured system of nation-states, it is only by organizing their struggles within the political space of their own nation-state, with the revolutionary transformation of that particular nation-state as the immediate practical objective, that the revolutionary forces of any given country can effectively struggle against the imperialism they face concretely in their own lives. In other words, the socialist project is essentially universalist in character, and socialism, even as a transitional mode, cannot exist except on a transnational basis; yet the *struggle* for even the prospect of that transition presumes a national basis, in so far as the already existing structures of the nation-state are a fundamental reality of the very terrain on which actual class conflicts take place. (pp. 317–18)

Because it obliges us to think of national liberation as a cultural (and not merely a political) project, Cabral's theorization allows us to appreciate the vital role that "converted" intellectuals can (and must) play in its promotion. It is important to insist on this truth, in opposition to both the anti-intellectualist discourse of ultra-leftism and the theoreticist discourse currently prevailing within the field of postcolonial studies. The work of Edward Said is a powerful resource here: for Said has for years written brilliantly about the indispensability of intellectual practice to anti-imperialist struggle. (His own political writings themselves provide an eloquent case in point, of course.) Consider, for example, the following statement, drawn from Said's essay, "Figures, Configurations, Transfigurations," in which he comments on the significance of the role that literature, as one specific medium of intellectual production, has been able to play in advancing the cause of anti-imperialism throughout the twentieth century:

> in the decades-long struggle to achieve decolonisation and independence from European control, literature has played a crucial role in the re-establishment of a national cultural heritage, in the reinstatement of native idioms, in the re-imagining and re-figuring of local histories,

geographies, communities. As such, then, literature not only mobilised active resistance to incursions from the outside, but also contributed massively as the shaper, creator, agent of illumination within the realm of the colonised.[111]

Obviously, some writers, some intellectuals, could have "contributed massively" to the decolonizing effort on the basis of their work as trade unionists or activists or coordinators of armed struggle. (One thinks for example of such figures as Sergio Ramirez or Ghassan Kanafani or Jose Luandino Vieira.) But Said's point seems to be that intellectuals have contributed most decisively to decolonization on the basis of their specific labor as intellectuals: by writing, thinking, speaking, reporting, etc. (The title of one of E. San Juan, Jr.'s essays captures this point brilliantly: "The Responsibility to Beauty: Toward an Aesthetics of National Liberation.")[112] It is on this basis, and not on others, that they have been able to constitute themselves as "agent[s] of illumination within the realm of the colonised." Nothing, therefore, could have replaced this kind of practice, whose effects have been both unique and indispensable.

Elsewhere, Said has moved to distinguish, within the broad field of cultural production, between *artists* and *intellectuals*. "In dark times," he has written,

an intellectual is very often looked to by members of his or her nationality to represent, speak out for, and testify to the sufferings of that nationality . . . To this terribly important task of representing the collective suffering of your own people, testifying to its travails, reasserting its enduring presence, reinforcing its memory, there must be added something else, which only an intellectual, I believe, has the obligation to fulfill. After all, many novelists, painters, and poets, like Manzoni, Picasso, or Neruda, have embodied the historical experience of their people in aesthetic works, which in turn become recognized as great masterpieces. For the intellectual the task, I believe, is explicitly to universalize the crisis, to give greater human scope to what a particular race or nation suffered, to associate that experience with the sufferings of others.[113]

It is true that a distinct whiff of modernist nostalgia – exilic, metropolitan, deracinated – sometimes emanates from Said's representation of intellectual practice. He is in my view considerably too much given to such pronouncements as that the intellectual life is "a lonely condition, yes, but it is always a better one than a gregarious tolerance for the way things are"[114] – pronouncements that, in general, suggest a suspiciously self-justifying romanticization of the intellectual vocation. It is in this mood, arguably, that Said most resembles the theorist of diasporic postcoloniality that Bhabha takes him to be. It is clear, for instance, that Bhabha would find much to applaud in the following passage from *Representations of the Intellectual*:

> Exile is a model for the intellectual who is tempted, and even beset and overwhelmed, by the rewards of accommodation, yea-saying, settling in. Even if one is not an actual immigrant or expatriate, it is still possible to think as one, to imagine and investigate in spite of barriers, and always to move away from the centralizing authorities towards the margins, where you see things that are usually lost on minds that have never traveled beyond the conventional and the comfortable. (p. 63)

Despite this propensity, however, Said's formulation of the role played by intellectuals in the struggle against imperialism strikes me as being of incalculable importance. For he does not only demonstrate that what intellectuals have been able to contribute to this struggle – the opening up of horizons, the crystallizing of memories and experiences as legitimate aspects of a cultural heritage, the discursive contestation of dominating paradigms of knowledge, the production of counter-truths, etc. – could not have been provided by any other form of labor-power, by any other social practice, in any other arena. He also allows us to recognize that in its essential gesture, such intellectual practice is fundamentally *universalistic*, directed through and beyond the nodal point of the nation to a proleptic space of *internationalism*. Hence his salutary reminder that many of the radical anti-colonial intellectuals and activists who are today usually thought of as nationalists were *at the same time* stringent opponents of any narrowly nationalist vision:

> [W]hat has not received as much notice as it should have from historians of Third World nationalism is that a clear if paradoxical antinationalist theme emerges in the writings of a fair number of nationalists who are wholehearted supporters of the national movement itself . . . [T]o cite a small number of examples: Tagore, very much the national poet and intellectual leader of early twentieth-century Indian resistance to the British, condemns nationalism for its state-worship, its triumphalism, and its militancy in his 1917 lectures on the subject. He also remains a nationalist. Césaire in his greatest poem explores *négritude*, hallmark of the African nationalist resistance, and finds it wanting for its exclusivism and ressentiment. Similarly, in the writing of C.L.R. James, great historian of what he called "negro revolution" and pan-Africanism, we find that over and over he warns against the nativism that would turn nationalism into a reductive and diminishing rather than a truly liberating effort. And who can miss in Fanon the intensity of his attack on "*mésaventures de la conscience nationale*," its febrile mimicry of colonial thought and practices, its imprisoning ethic, its brutalizing usurpations? In the annals of Arab nationalism a critique of exclusivism, sectarianism, and provincialism –

much of it associated with degradations in Arab and Islamic political life – is steadily present, from early thinkers like Shibley Shumayil to later figures like Rashid Rida, Abdel Rahman al-Bazzaz, Qunstantin Zurayk, and even the resolutely Egyptian Taha Hussayn. Finally, in the extraordinary pages of W.E.B. Du Bois's *The Souls of Black Folk*, we find repeated warnings against indiscriminate nationalism and reverse racism, the insistence upon careful analysis and comprehensive understanding rather than either wholesale condemnation of whites or futile attempts to emulate some of their methods.[115]

In these terms, Said's formulation might be said to combine the insight of Pierre Bourdieu, concerning symbolic power, with that of Samir Amin, concerning the specificity of intellectualism in the context of anti-imperialist struggle. Thus Bourdieu writes that

Cultural producers hold a specific power, the properly symbolic power of showing things and making people believe in them, of revealing, in an explicit, objectified way the more or less confused, vague, unformulated, even unformulable experiences of the natural world and the social world, and of thereby bringing them into existence. They may put this power at the service of the dominant. They may also, in the logic of their struggle within the field of power, put their power at the service of the dominated in the social field taken as a whole . . . The fact remains that the specific interests of cultural producers, in so far as they are linked to fields that, by the very logic of their functioning, encourage, favour or impose the transcending of personal interest in the ordinary sense, can lead them to political or intellectual actions that can be called universal.[116]

And Amin, for his part, observes that

The intelligentsia [in the periphery] is not defined by the class origin of its members. It is defined by: (i) its anticapitalism; (ii) its openness to the universal dimension of the culture of our time and, by this means, its capacity to situate itself in this world, analyze its contradictions, understand its weak links, and so on; and (iii) its simultaneous capacity to remain in living and close communion with the popular classes, to share their history and cultural expression.[117]

It is in this connection that I would like, in bringing this chapter to a close, to suggest that it is necessary for theorists working in the field of postcolonialism to think again about the valencies of both nationalism and radical intellectualism. Of course I have in mind Lenin's asseveration that "[w]ithout revolutionary theory there can be no revolutionary movement," an idea, as he put it, that "cannot be insisted upon too strongly at a time when the fashionable preaching of opportunism goes hand in hand with an infatuation for the narrowest forms of practical activity."[118] But it also seems to me that in the context of the contemporary capitalist world system, the need to construct a "counter-narrative . . . of liberation" is especially pressing.[119] Such a counter-narrative would necessarily derive from the narratives of bourgeois humanism and metropolitan nationalism, with their resonant but unfounded claims to universality. But it would not need to concede the terrain of universality to these Eurocentric projections. On the contrary, where postmodern and postcolonial theory have tended to react to the perceived indefensibility of bourgeois humanism and of colonial nationalism by abandoning the very idea of totality, a *genuinely* postcolonial strategy might be to move explicitly, as Fanon already did in concluding *The Wretched of the Earth*, to proclaim a "new" humanism, predicated upon a formal repudiation of the degraded European form, and borne embryonically in the national liberation movement:

Leave this Europe where they are never done talking of Man, yet murder men everywhere they find them, at the corner of every one of their own streets, in all the corners of the globe . . . When I search for Man in the technique and style of Europe, I see only a succession of negations of man, and an avalanche of murders . . . For Europe, for ourselves, and for humanity, comrades, we must turn over a new leaf, we must work out new concepts, and try to set afoot a new man.   (pp. 311–12, 316)

From *this* proleptically "postcolonial" standpoint, it is vital to retain the categories of "nation" and "universality." Hence, arguably, the specific role of anti-imperialist intellectualism today: to construct a standpoint – socialist, nationalitarian, liberationist, internationalist – from which it is possible to assume the burden of speaking for all humanity.

3

Cricket, modernism, national culture: the case of C. L. R. James

In an article on "C.L.R. James and the Politics of the Trinidadian Renaissance," published in 1988, Hazel Carby wrote that *Beyond a Boundary* was "one of the most outstanding works of cultural studies ever produced."[1] The judgment is likely to seem less remarkable today than it did ten years ago, for the years since James's death in 1989 have borne witness to a huge upsurge of interest in him on the part of scholars working in the fields of cultural and postcolonial studies.[2] Yet it is important to affirm the accuracy as well as the prescience of Carby's assessment, and I would like, in this chapter, to try both to build upon and to generalize from it. It is my conviction that in his writings about popular culture and philosophy, literature and politics, James reveals himself to be one of the truly decisive Marxist cultural theorists of our century. To neglect his writings would therefore, I believe, be to neglect a body of work whose stature rivals those of Georg Lukács, Mikhail Bakhtin, Walter Benjamin, and Raymond Williams. James is, moreover, almost unique among Marxist cultural theorists in taking up the question of intellectual practice as ideological representation in the explicit contexts of colonial and postcolonial social relations. A proper consideration of his work is therefore central to my concerns in this book.

A caveat needs to be entered right here at the outset, however. The problem is that James is in crucial respects unthinkable without cricket – his ideas about history and politics and culture all bear the decisive imprint of his encounter and lifelong fascination with the game. And cricket – or so one will often be led to infer by American commentaries that characterize it as a trivial if quaint game, aimless, foppish, and anachronistically genteel – simply makes no sense to an American audience. "[P]layed by eleven languid gentlemen in long

cream flannel trousers over interminable periods of time and to no
particular purpose," as Michael Manley (former Prime Minister of
Jamaica) summarizes this putatively standard American representation in his massive *History of West Indies Cricket*, cricket is typically
portrayed as more or less completely alien to the American way of
life.[3] In including a chapter centrally devoted to the work of C.L.R.
James in this book, which is intended to intervene in debates currently playing themselves out in the American at least as much as in other
academic contexts, accordingly, I feel myself under the shadow of an
inevitable objection. How to escape the conclusion that James is likely
to remain a dead letter where American readers are concerned? Some
have not tried to escape it: hence, for example, the British socialist
historian E.P. Thompson's observation, in a tribute to James published in 1981, that "I'm afraid that American theorists will not
understand this, but the clue to everything [in James] lies in his
proper appreciation of the game of cricket."[4]

I do not wish to underestimate the difficulty that those readers
unfamiliar with or uninterested in cricket – and this would of course
include many people in Britain and the Anglophone world in addition to mainstream American readers – are likely to encounter in
gaining access to James's thought. Yet because the claims that we are
entitled to make for James's significance as a theorist are, I believe,
considerable, it would be most regrettable were this difficulty to be
viewed as grounds not to engage with his work. I draw particular
encouragement, accordingly, from the twin facts that three of the full
length studies of James to have been published to date (those by Paul
Buhle, Aldon Lynn Nielsen, and Kent Worcester) *and* arguably the
best book on cricket to have been published since James's classic
autobiography, *Beyond a Boundary*, in 1963 (Mike Marqusee's *Anyone
But England: Cricket and the National Malaise*), have been written by
Americans. Particularly salutary for my purposes in this chapter is
Marqusee's dismissal of the claim that cricket is somehow unassimilable to Americans: "I shouldn't get irritated, but I can't help it. Every
time I'm asked, 'How can an American understand cricket?' I do a
bad job disguising my impatience. Why shouldn't an American understand cricket? It's a game like any other."[5] As Marqusee points
out, the presentation of cricket as alien to the American way of life is
an elaborate ideological production, serviceable on both sides of the
Atlantic:

Everything that English people take to be "American" – brashness,
impatience, informality, innovation, vulgarity, rapacious and

unashamed commercialism – is antithetical to what they take to be "cricket." For the English, it is a point of pride that Americans cannot understand cricket. They may imbibe American movies, music, hamburgers and nuclear missiles, but their national sport remains their own. As for the Americans, everything they took, until recently, to be "English" – tradition, politeness, deference, gentle obscurantism – seems to be epitomized in "cricket." The attitude was neatly put by the affable, pizza-eating vigilante Raphael in one of the Teenage Ninja Mutant Turtles movies. Assaulted by a mystery attacker with a cricket bat, Raphael protests, "Nobody understands cricket. To understand cricket you gotta know what a crumpet is."

The first encounter with James's writing about cricket is likely to induce a sense of shock or displacement in any contemporary reader with an interest in the field of cultural studies. It is not that such a reader will not have come across such prose before, although it is true that James's eloquence can sometimes be quite breathtaking. Rather, it is that he or she will seldom have seen it deployed with reference to the practice of sport – above all by a *Marxist* theorist. Consider the following passages, for instance – chosen not, of course, at random, but representing nevertheless only three of literally hundreds of passages that might have been cited:

There is nothing of the panther in the batting of Sobers. He is the most orthodox of great batsmen. The only stroke he makes in a manner peculiar to himself is the hook. Where George Headley used to face the ball square and hit across it, Denis Compton placed himself well outside it on the off-side, and Walcott compromised by stepping backwards but not fully across and hitting, usually well in front of and not behind square leg, Sobers seems to stand where he is and depend upon wrist and eyesight to swish the short fast ball square to the boundary. Apart from that, his method, his technique is carried to an extreme where it is indistinguishable from nature.[6]

A great West Indies cricketer in his play should embody some essence of that crowded vagueness which passes for the history of the West Indies. If, like Kanhai, he is one of the most remarkable and individual of contemporary batsmen, then that should not make him less but more West Indian. You see what you are looking for, and in Kanhai's batting what I have found is a unique pointer of the West Indian quest for identity, for ways of expressing our potential bursting at every seam.[7]

I haven't the slightest doubt that the clash of race, caste and class did not retard but stimulated West Indian cricket. I am equally certain that in those years social and political passions, denied normal outlets, expressed themselves so fiercely in cricket (and other games) precisely because they were games. Here began my personal calvary. The British tradition soaked deep into me was that when you entered the sporting arena you left behind you the sordid compromises of everyday existence. Yet for us to do that we would have had to divest ourselves of our skins. From the moment I had to decide which club I would join the contrast between the ideal and the real fascinated me and tore at my insides. Nor could the local population see it otherwise. The class and racial rivalries were too intense. They could be fought out without violence or much lost except pride and honour. Thus the cricket field was a stage on which selected individuals played representative roles which were charged with social significance.[8]

In the third of these passages, James identifies cricket as a privileged site for the playing out and imaginary resolution of social antagonisms in the West Indies in the era of colonialism. In the second passage, he suggests that only a sociopoetics of cricket will be able to do justice to its complexity and ideological resonance. Cricket, he writes in *Beyond a Boundary*, "is a game of high and difficult technique. If it were not it could not carry the load of social response and implications which it carries" (p. 34). We will return to these formulations in due course. Before we do, however, it will be necessary for us to reflect on the first of the passages cited above; for in this passage, crafted in the rhetoric of comparative aesthetics, and taking as its object the question of form – of cricketing *style* – James situates cricket unambiguously and unhesitatingly as art. The register of his descriptions of Garfield Sobers at bat, or of the technique of the great fast bowler Wesley Hall, derives unmistakably from the universe of high cultural criticism. What James writes about a glorious drive past point by Learie Constantine, off the canny bowling of Walter Hammond in 1926 – that the stroke had never been seen before, but that, having been made, it instantly entered cricket history as defining of the square drive – is not only reminiscent of, but strictly comparable with, Walter Benjamin's observation that "all great works of literature found a genre or dissolve one."[9] (One notes in passing that from James's own viewpoint, the more relevant comparison would have been to the writings about prize boxing, chess, or the game of fives, by the early nineteenth-century English essayist, William Hazlitt, to whom James refers admiringly on several occasions in *Beyond a Boundary*.)

Nor is this gesture on James's part remotely an accident. Cricket is in his view not an instance of "light" art, which he happens to find stimulating, nor an instance of a degraded "popular" culture, although it is certainly popular. On the contrary, James insists that cricket is a form of art to exactly the same degree as drama or opera or lyric poetry are forms of art. Attempting to specify the conditions of cricket's aestheticism, thus, he points, first of all, to the extraordinary balance within the game between structure and agency. Each cricket match consists of an indefinite number of discrete events, each with its own resolution, whose objective meaning can only be read at the level of the match as a whole; and yet the logic of the game is such that each and any one of these discrete events bears within itself the potential to shatter the substantive pattern of the match as it has unfolded (often over the course of several days) to that point. To win a cricket match, a team needs first to place itself in a position from which victory is possible. Time is involved, and imagination and application; advantages must be consolidated, opportunities seized, risks taken, mistakes capitalized upon. And yet for all its structurality, a cricket match balances on a hair-trigger. A single ball bowled, a single electrifying play by an agile fielder, can change its direction and outcome; a single batting stroke, in anger or defiance or disdain, can shatter and reconstitute the meaning of all that has preceded it. "The total spectacle," James writes

consists and must consist of a series of individual, isolated episodes, each in itself completely self-contained. Each has its beginning, the ball bowled; its middle, the stroke played; its end, runs, no runs, dismissal. Within the fluctuating interest of the rise or fall of the game as a whole, there is this unending series of events, each single one fraught with immense possibilities of expectation and realization . . . In the very finest of soccer matches the ball for long periods is in places where it is impossible to expect any definite alteration in the relative position of the two sides. In lawn tennis the duration of the rally is entirely dependent upon the subjective skill of the players. In baseball alone does the encounter between the two representative protagonists approach the definitiveness of the individual series of episodes in cricket which together constitute the whole.   (*Beyond*, p. 197)

Even baseball, however, cannot in James's view quite match the intensive quality of cricket's mode of representation. Like many games, he observes, "[c]ricket is first and foremost a dramatic spectacle. It belongs with the theatre, ballet, opera and the dance" (p. 196). Yet cricket's uniqueness consists not so much in its spectacularity – shared, obviously, by many other sports[10] – but in the manner in which its enactment of competition and struggle is conducted at the level of representative individuals – preeminently, bowler and batsman – whose individual performances emerge sustainedly and uninterruptedly as emblematic of the situation of their teams. Let us emphasize the phrase "sustainedly and uninterruptedly" here: for it is through reference to the relative temporal *limitlessness* of this encounter between representative individuals, perhaps, that cricket can most readily be distinguished from baseball. As Marqusee puts it, describing his own first encounter with cricket:

I recognized immediately in cricket the highly individualistic confrontation between bowler and batsman I knew from baseball. But in cricket the confrontation was so prolonged. It was not over in three strikes or four balls or a line drive to third base. It had no determinate end – but it could end at any moment. Like the game itself, it could go on and on, interrupted only for those civilized interludes dedicated to "lunch," "tea" and "drinks."   (*Anyone*, p. 7)

In speaking of cricket as a form of dramatic art, James does not mean that cricket *resembles* drama. He means that it *is* drama. Indeed, it is drama of a distinctly orthodox and historic kind. On numerous occasions throughout *Beyond a Boundary*, he draws an analogy between the spectacle of cricket in the West Indies and the spectacle of drama in classical Greek society: "Once every year for four days the tens of thousands of Athenian citizens sat in the open air on the stone seats at the side of the Acropolis and from sunrise to sunset watched the plays of the competing dramatists. All that we have to correspond is a Test match" (p. 158).[11]

The consequences that follow from this association of cricket and classical Greek drama are significant. Inasmuch as cricket's spectacularity emerges as an integral aspect of its aesthetic being, so too does its popularity. The role of the crowd is, in James's view, positively constitutive of cricket's meaning as a cultural form. In a brilliant passage in *Beyond a Boundary*, James exposes the elitism of the famous cricket commentator, Neville Cardus, who wrote about the game as an art form readily enough, but who insisted, at the same time, that its meaning as art was unavailable to the majority of those who made up its audience. On the one hand, James notes, "all [Cardus's] work is eloquent with the aesthetic appeal of cricket" (p. 195).[12] On the other hand, even as Cardus moved to grapple with this "aesthetic appeal" of cricket, he shied away from its democratic implications. For though cricket was to him a form of art, he would not allow that it might be so too for the millions who followed the game throughout the world. Art was not for the masses: "I do not believe that anything fine in music or in anything else can be truly understood or truly felt by the crowd" (quoted in *Beyond*, p. 195). To the extent that cricket was an art, therefore, its true meaning necessarily remained inaccessible to the overwhelming majority of those who watched and played it. To this latter sentiment, James takes strong and appropriate exception:

> Neville Cardus . . . often introduces music into his cricket writing. Never once has Neville Cardus . . . introduced cricket into his writing on music. He finds this "a curious point." It is much more than a point, it is not curious. Cardus is a victim of that categorization and specialization, that division of the human personality, which is the greatest curse of our time. Cricket has suffered, but not only cricket. The aestheticians have scorned to take notice of popular sports and games – to their own detriment. The aridity and confusion of which they so mournfully complain will continue until they include organized games *and the people who watch them* as an integral part of their data. (*Beyond*, pp. 195–96)

(Peculiarly, James follows this effective critique by lapsing into a rare contradiction. For having taken Cardus to task for his elitism, he goes on to concede that "Sir Donald Bradman's technical accomplishments are not on the same plane as those of Yehudi Menuhin. Sir John Gielgud in three hours can express adventures and shades in human personality which are not approached in three years of Denis Compton at the wicket" [p. 196]. It is difficult to know what to make of this concession, since James immediately undermines it by his insistence that cricket is "not a bastard or a poor relation, but a full member of the community" of arts. Certainly, James's point against Cardus is made: cricket is an art, not for the one or two "sensitive" souls among its viewers alone, but in its fundamental reality, that is, as it is ordinarily played and watched.[13] But, beyond this, it seems contradictory to maintain simultaneously that cricket is not a "poor relation" of the other arts *and* that the technique of Donald Bradman – to date, the most proficient batsman who ever played – is "not on the same plane" as that of Yehudi Menuhin. The thrust of James's work as a whole is along the lines of the affirmation – that cricket is indeed a fully articulated form of art – rather than of the concession.[14] This, accordingly, is the tendency I have chosen to emphasize as characteristically "Jamesian.")

James writes not only against the Neville Carduses of his world, exponents of a frankly confessed conservatism in cultural criticism, but also, implicitly, against such radical cultural theorists as Theodor W. Adorno, who also insist upon the "autonomy" of modern art from life. I want to emphasize the term "modern" here: despite the immensity of the political and philosophical differences between them (like those, in another field, between Adorno and Clement Greenberg), Adorno and Cardus share a certain conception of modernity.[15] This common conception of modernity is, moreover, paradigmatically *modernist*: this much can be inferred from the categorical opposition that underpins it, between an exalted "high culture" and a degraded "mass culture." High Culture *or* Mass Culture: this "or" is the dominant conjunction through which, in the bourgeois world at least, the politics of cultural production in the twentieth century have tended to be conceptualized. Of course, the opposition is in itself a modernist construction, what we might in fact call an *ideologeme* of modernism.[16] For from the outset, modernism tended to view mass culture as its spectral other.[17] The constituent dimensions of modernism as a cultural formation – above all, elitism and exilic metropolitanism – produced a self-justificatory rationalization of modernist practice as that alone which said "no" to modernity.[18] On the ideological *right*, this rationalization typically took the form of a neo-romantic and reactionary repudiation of capitalism (usually referred to as "industrial civilization"), of "modernization," of science, of democracy, of what was termed "progress" and what was termed "socialism," of "massification" and "proletarianization." In these terms, mass culture was to be disavowed on account of its popularity, its vulgarly democratic challenge to the proper refinement of the values of the cultivated few. And on the *left*, significantly, it was usually and in the first instance only the emphases here that changed. Thus from Adorno's standpoint, mass culture was to be disavowed not so much because its vaunted democratic appeal was vulgar, but more importantly because it was not truly democratic: it bespoke an unmitigated subordination to, and ratification of, capital logic. Mass culture, Max Horkheimer and Adorno wrote in their famous essay, "The Culture Industry: Enlightenment as Mass Deception," "is the triumph of invested capital."[19] It represents not the democratization of culture but the integration of all classes of society beneath the monopoly capitalist rubrics of standardization and conformism. Against the products generated by the culture industry, Horkheimer and Adorno cast modernism as the only contemporary mode of cultural practice with the determinate capacity to withstand subsumption to the dictates of capital. The tenuous autonomy of the modern(ist) artwork,[20] they argued, its fragile and only partial externality to a universalized logic of exchange, enables it to keep faith "with the idea of true generality," that is, with the idea of a realized socialism (*Dialectic*, 130). For Horkheimer and Adorno, only those cultural works that court incomprehensibility are in the modern(ist) era able to resist recuperation by the culture industry. Sport is specifically listed by

Adorno, along with film and popular music, as a wholly fetishistic cultural practice, disclosive only of the socially engineered regression of the working classes in modern capitalist societies.[21]

Horkheimer and Adorno do not confuse the advent of the culture industry with the *capitalization* of cultural production. The dominant forms of cultural production, as they well recognize, had already been capitalized by the mid-nineteenth century. "When mortally sick," they tell us, "Beethoven hurled away a novel by Sir Walter Scott with the cry: 'Why, the fellow writes for money,' and yet proved a most experienced and stubborn businessman in disposing of the last quartets, which were a most extreme renunciation of the market; he is the most outstanding example of the unity of those opposites, market and independence, in bourgeois art" (*Dialectic*, p. 157). What is new about the artwork in the era of the culture industry, therefore, "is not that it is a commodity, but that today it deliberately admits it is one"; it "renounces its own autonomy and proudly takes its place among consumption goods."[22] A second point is consequent upon this one: in order to emphasize the profundity and unforgoability of their distinction between modernism and mass culture – and it is, as they insist, this irreconcilable and historically determinate tension between between "light" and "serious" art that really needs to be attended to, not "serious" art alone or, still less, "light" art alone (*Dialectic*, p. 135) – Horkheimer and Adorno maintain that "between" or "beyond" modernist high culture and mass culture there is, in the twentieth-century world, nothing else. Specifically, *popular culture* is to them a concept without any contemporary referent. *Pleasure*, the use value of culture proper, has been commodified; and *amusement*, the use value of such traditional popular cultural forms as the circus, the fair, song and dance, mime, and the puppet show, has been obliterated, and along with it popular culture itself. Popular culture does not for them survive into the twentieth century. Indeed, it barely makes it into the nineteenth.

It is here, it seems to me, in their argument that popular culture has been destroyed, hollowed out from within by the social logic of monetization and exchange, that Horkheimer and Adorno's theory is both clinched and undermined. *Clinched*, because it enables us to see that their repudiation of mass culture and their insistence on the epochal significance of a modern(ist) practice that is obliged to risk unintelligibility and eschew pleasure in order to stave off incorporation is not merely another Spenglerian or Eliotian lament about falling standards or the decline of the West. But *undermined* because of its failure to contest, indeed its faithful reproduction of, the modernist episteme, which is altogether blind to the continuing vitality and autonomy of popular cultural forms. The point here is that modernism was (and, by virtue of its post-1945 canonization, still is) the name of a specific intervention into the universe of modern culture. Modernism is the name of a hegemonizing project which, directing its energies against the prevailing and received cultural formations of the late nineteenth and early twentieth centuries, not only displaced them but consolidated itself at their expense. In its proselytizing zeal, moreover, modernism overreached itself, constructing its own historically, socially, and culturally specific protocols, procedures, and horizons as those of the modern as such. As Raymond Williams puts it (with reference to the field of literary production), modernism recast, rewrote, and rearranged cultural history, producing a selective tradition whose selectivity was invisible to it: the authors and "theoretic contours" usually addressed under the rubric of "modernism" constitute "a highly selected version of the modern which then offers to appropriate the whole of modernity."[23]

To read modernism against the grain, in these terms – that is, from a standpoint not its own – it is necessary to contest its false universalism as a practice and a received tradition. Adorno's example does not suffice in this respect. Nor is *postmodernism* a solution. For like Adorno, the postmodernists adopt the modernist imaginary even as they undertake to work against or to supersede modernism.[24] Rather, it is necessary for us to begin to explore modernism, as Williams speculates,

with something of its own sense of strangeness and distance, rather than with the uncomfortable and now internally accommodated forms of its incorporation and naturalization. This means . . . seeing the imperial and capitalist metropole as a specific historical form, at different stages: Paris, London, Berlin, New York. It involves looking, from time to time, from outside the metropolis: from the deprived hinterlands, where different forces are moving, and from the poor world which has always been peripheral to the metropolitan systems. This need involve no reduction of the importance of the major artistic and literary works which were shaped within metropolitan perceptions. But one level has certainly to be challenged: the metropolitan interpretation of its own processes as universals . . . The formulation of the modernist universals is in every case a productive but imperfect and in the end fallacious response to particular conditions of closure, break-down, failure and frustration . . . At this level as at others . . . the supposed universals belong to a phase of history which was both creatively preceded and creatively succeeded.   (*Politics*, p. 47)

The suggestion here is that we look at modernism somewhat eccentrically, from its margins – even, to redirect a phrase of Edward Said's, from the standpoint of its victims.[25] Premised as it is upon Williams's conception of culture as a common inheritance, this is a suggestion that brings us back to James; specifically, it brings us very close to the pulse of James's thinking about West Indies cricket as a definitively modern (but *not* modernist) cultural practice. For James would have identified strongly with Williams's defense of the idea of "common culture," a phrase intended, as Williams has explained, to combat the elitist appropriation of the concept of "culture" for and by "high culture": "'Common culture' . . . was strictly a position against that. It was an argument that culture was both produced more widely than by the social elite which appropriated it, was disseminated more widely than this notion presumed, and that the ideal of an expanding education was that what had been restricted in distribution and access should be opened out" (*Politics*, p. 193).

Like Williams, James would have refused to concede the validity of either the Adornian principle of modern(ist) culture's autonomy, or the conception that, in Adorno's thought, makes that principle necessary – namely that life itself has become totalitarian, has been reduced to "the sphere of private existence and now of mere consumption" and, as such, is "dragged along as an appendage of the process of material production, without autonomy or substance of its own."[26] This is not to suggest that James was blind to what Georg Lukács once theorized as reification or to what Jürgen Habermas has recently identified as the advancing colonization of the lifeworld in contemporary capitalist societies.[27] On the contrary, James both acknowledged "the violence and ferocity of our age" (*Beyond*, p. 188) and, in his writings about cricket, traced changes in the ways in which the game had come to be played back to this violence. At no stage, however, did he commit himself to the hypostasized modernist conceit of art as an elite practice, whose (illusory) withdrawal from the social is the only thing that enables it to escape the debased, homogenizing, and ceaselessly recuperative waters of mass culture churning far below it.

Within the context of twentieth-century aesthetic theory, this modern(ist) and neo-romantic conception of culture has typically been mobilized in the service of an irreducibly *Eurocentric* anti-capitalism. Even where – as in the case of Western Marxism – this anti-capitalism has been insistently radical in tendency, it has invariably been sketched against the backdrop of "civilization." While "culture" has tended to be theorized as that which opposed the consolidation and extension of this "civilization" (that is, of *bourgeois* hegemony), so too, and paradoxically, the growing challenge to *Western* dominance (throughout the century, but above all in the post-1945 era) has very often been understood as signifying not the intensification and globalization of anti-capitalist struggle, but rather the end of history.

James is never disposed to think in these terms. Against those conservative critics who complain about "the envy, the hatred, the malice and the uncharitableness" of the modern (post-1920s) form of cricket, thus, he initially points out that it is not in cricket alone that a new ethic has come to prevail, but in "modern society" at large:

Modern society took a turn downwards in 1929 and "It isn't cricket" is one of the casualties. There is no need to despair of cricket. Much, much more than cricket is at stake, in fact everything is at stake. If and when society regenerates itself, cricket will do the same . . . The owl of Minerva flies only at dusk. And it cannot get much darker without becoming night impenetrable.   (*Beyond*, p. 192)

At first glance this might seem to support the Adornian reading of culture and society; and James is indeed unsparing in his denunciation of the rationalized "Keynesian" values (one-dimensional, ploddingly accumulative, cautious, productivist) that in his view came to prevail in Australian and English cricket in the 1920s and 1930s, and which, he argues, still tend to characterize cricket in these nations. But against Adorno's reading, in turn, James insists that it is only from a vantage point within the center(s) of the capitalist world system that the darkness seems all-encompassing. In James's view this darkness is not, in fact, the darkness of "night impenetrable" but rather of a world-historical eclipse, heralded, in the world of politics, by the rising tide of anti-imperialism, not least in the Caribbean, and, more narrowly, in one sector of the restricted field of culture, by the emergence, the sudden eruption in the late 1950s and the 1960s, of West Indies cricket onto the world's stage.

Hence the indispensability, for James, of a *sociopoetics* of cricket, an approach to the game that will make neither the mistake of supposing it to be less than a form of art, nor the mistake of supposing it, as a form of art, to be autonomous of society. In the trenchant "Introduction" to a selection of his writings on cricket that appeared in 1986, James writes that

An artistic, a social event does not reflect the age. It is the age. Cricket, I want to say most clearly, is not an addition or a decoration or some specific unit that one adds to what really constitutes the history of a period. Cricket is as much part of the history as books written are part of the history. (*Cricket*, p. xi)

Elsewhere, his tone is even more insistent – as when, in *Beyond a Boundary*, he asserts that "cricket and football were the greatest cultural influences in nineteenth-century Britain, leaving far behind Tennyson's poems, Beardsley's drawings and concerts of the Philharmonic Society. These filled space in print but not in minds" (p. 64).

A crucial point here, however, is that as James understands cricket, it is not merely as a form of culture that it assumes significance, but, very concretely and materially, as a form of *national* culture. It is for this reason that he can maintain that a biography of Donald Bradman will need, at the same time, to be "a history of Australia in the same period" (*Beyond*, p. 182).[28] Similarly, cricket, for James, has been *the* privileged arena for the playing out and imaginary resolution of social antagonisms in the Anglophone Caribbean. Accordingly, nobody ignorant of the play of Wilton St. Hill or Learie Constantine or Rohan Kanhai or Vivian Richards will in his view be able to grasp the historical trajectory of West Indian society over the course of the past 100 years.

To understand why this should be so – to equip us to appreciate the extent to which, and the different manners in which, cricket has figured as a constituent of national consciousness in England, Australia, India, Pakistan, Sri Lanka, New Zealand, South Africa, and the West Indies – it will be necessary for us to examine briefly James's social history of the game. He locates its institutionalization in the years between 1780 and 1840. Cricket was created, he writes

by the yeoman farmer, the gamekeeper, the potter, the tinker, the Nottingham coal-miner, the Yorkshire factory hand. These artisans made it, men of hand and eye. Rich and idle young noblemen and some substantial city people contributed money, organization and prestige. Between them, by 1837 they had evolved a highly complicated game with all the typical characteristics of a genuinely national art form: founded on elements long present in the nation, profoundly popular in origin, yet attracting to it disinterested elements of the leisured and educated classes. Confined to areas and numbers which were relatively small, it contained all the premises of rapid growth. There was nothing in the slightest degree Victorian about it. At their matches cricketers ate and drank with the gusto of the time, sang songs and played for large sums of money. Bookies sat before the pavilion at Lord's[29] openly taking bets. The unscrupulous nobleman and the poor but dishonest commoner alike bought and sold matches. (*Beyond*, pp. 160–61)

"There was nothing in the slightest degree Victorian about it." James goes to great lengths here to insist that the social logic of cricket as it was played in the early nineteenth century was the product of distinctively – if residually – pre-capitalist class relations: hence his emphasis on the ubiquity and openness of betting; on the excess, rudeness, and sentimentality of conduct on and off the field; on the rural (or at least non-urbanized) provenance of the game; etc. The emphasis is intended to anchor a stark contrast. For no sooner had cricket been socially consolidated, in these terms, as a game essentially outside the realm of (if not quite historically prior to) bourgeois social relations, than it became, during the Victorian era, the site of an ideological struggle. It was not, James writes, that the English national bourgeoisie, the "solid Victorian middle class" (*Beyond*, p. 161), consciously set out to appropriate the game, to lift it from its artisanal, regional, predominantly rural roots and to make it over in their own image. Yet it was precisely such an appropriation that began to be effected, and James describes it as "unerring" (p. 165). Cricket began to be transformed from a game expressing the social ethos of a residual and increasingly marginal combination of class fractions into a "moral discipline," disseminated above all in such public schools as Winchester (where, as Ashis Nandy reminds us, "the key words were manliness, stoicism, austerity, team spirit, loyalty and conformity to rules"[30]) and Thomas Arnold's Rugby, and serving the interests of the middle classes rising to hegemony:

The Victorians made it compulsory for their children, and all the evidence points to the fact that they valued competence in it and respect for what it came to signify more than they did intellectual accomplishment of any kind. The only word that I know for this is culture. The proof of its validity is its success, first of all at home and then almost as rapidly abroad, in the most diverse places and among peoples living lives which were poles removed from that whence it originally came. This signifies, as so often in any deeply national movement, that it contained elements of universality that went beyond the bounds of the originating nation.
(*Beyond*, p. 166)

In his stimulating critique of what he calls James's "materialist aesthetics of cricket" – a critique which I shall discuss in some detail below – Kenneth Surin provides a useful gloss of this passage:

[T]his "moment" of cricket is inescapably conjunctural, in that we have taking place here the coalescence of the sporting interests of a declining aristocracy, the moral outlook of an ascendant bourgeoisie, and the decisive contribution of an "actively" residual artisan and rural class in creating the forms and techniques that constitute the modern game. This, as James points out, made the game an inextricable constituent of English culture, and helped give the game an element of universality which made it easier for it to be taken beyond the place of its origin.[31]

If this transformation of cricket during the Victorian era must, retrospectively, be viewed in the light of an ideological struggle, it must be emphasized that the struggle was not always recognized or experienced as such. Indeed, in the person of W.G. Grace, the greatest exponent of cricket in the Victorian era, and one of the greatest players who ever lived, James identifies a figure whose astonishing aptitude for the game derived from the seemingly uncomplicated, if compound, presence within him of diverse residual elements of the national culture. Grace, he writes – and I do not apologize for the length of the quotation here, for James's formulation could neither be improved upon nor adequately summarized –

seems to have been one of those men in whom the characteristics of life as lived by many generations seemed to meet for the last, in a complete and perfectly blended whole. His personality was sufficiently wide and firm to include a strong Victorian streak without being inhibited. That I would say was his greatest strength. He was not in any way inhibited. What he lacked he would not need. All that he had he could use. In tune with his inheritance and his environment, he was not in any way repressed. All his physical and spiritual force was at his disposal to do what he wanted to do. He is said on all sides to have been one of the most typical of Englishmen, to have symbolized John Bull, and so on and so forth. To this, it is claimed, as well as to his deeds, he owed his enormous popularity. I take leave to doubt it. The man usually hailed as representative is never quite typical, is more subtly compounded than the plain up-and-down figure of the stock characteristics. Looking on from outside and at a distance it seems to me that Grace gives a more complex impression than is usually attributed to him. He was English undoubtedly, very much so. But he was typical of an England that was being superseded. He was the yeoman, the country doctor, the squire, the England of yesterday. But he was no relic, nor historical or nostalgic curiosity. He was pre-Victorian in the Victorian age but a pre-Victorian militant. (*Beyond*, pp. 177–78)

Little else that has been written on Grace can stand beside James's account. Marqusee, however – although he does not have much to say about "W.G." – offers the following evocative thumbnail sketch: "W.G. was indeed an anomaly, but not in his shamateurism, which was only an extreme example of common practice. Unkempt, unwashed, gluttonous, exuberantly competitive and a notorious cheat, W.G. brought into the urban world of the late nineteenth century a rural, yeoman aura – a hint of a past that was vanishing before people's eyes. For that, the elite patronized him and the public adored him" (*Anyone*, p. 77).

On the domestic stage – and, by osmosis, in Australia (especially), *pakeha* New Zealand, and white Anglophone South Africa – cricket began to be made over by the Victorian middle classes into an instrument of moral discipline. As Marqusee explains,

[t]he Victorian ethic of team sport was deeply paradoxical. The individual was subordinated to the team but the team itself was subordinate to the overriding dictates of "fair play." Winning was not all-important, even if the game itself was. "Playing the game," submitting to the Laws and the authority of the umpire, giving the benefit of the doubt to opponents, had nothing to do with not caring about winning or about personal success, both of which remained the driving forces in every game of cricket, then as now. Losing graciously was a way of saying not only that there were higher and more important games to win but that those who lost in those higher and more important games – economics, politics, empire – must also accept the verdict of the system. In this way a savagely competitive and unequal domestic and world order was cloaked in the mystical raiments of "fair play" and the rule of law.
(*Anyone*, pp. 73–74)

This refunctioning of cricket's social logic by the Victorian middle classes proved to be remarkably comprehensive and effective. Yet its ideological course never ran smooth; it remained fraught and contradictory. In part, this was because the structurality of cricket was intrinsically eccentric to bourgeois protocols. To quote Marqusee again:

Cricket bec[ame] the first modern sport at the dawn of the Industrial Revolution. Indeed, the same forces that changed a childish folk-game into modern cricket unleashed that revolution: the spread of the market economy, the domination of the state by a landowning bourgeoisie, the triumph of private property and law, the revenues from overseas trade and colonial conquest, the movement into the cities. But the creation of modern cricket was nearly complete when the Industrial Revolution was just beginning to gather pace. Cricket was not a product of that revolution but a by-product of the conjuncture of social and economic forces which set it in motion. (p. 53)

It is possible to focus on this historically engendered "eccentricity" of cricket to bourgeois sociality by way of registering the latent oppositionality to the emergent capitalist order in the early- and mid-nineteenth century of the rural and artisanal classes, whose work (and play) had not yet been subordinated to the laws of the market. Surin, for instance, writes that inasmuch as it conformed from the beginning to the rhythms and daily patterns of a largely pre-industrial way of life, cricket would require its practitioners to play matches that normally lasted from morning to evening, often extending over several days. Its ethos . . . would thus always be resolutely "anti-work." This, even for those who may not be lovers of cricket, is surely testimony to the deep and abiding sanity of the masses of ordinary human beings who played and watched the game as they were beginning to be dragooned into the factories and over-crowded tenements of England's manufacturing towns and cities. ("Materialist," p. 142)[32]

It is also possible to spool the formal "incongruity" between cricket's inner structure and bourgeois sociality out forwards in time, as it were – to focus on the ceaseless oscillation between "artisanal," "aristocratic," and "bourgeois" logics in the game as it has been played *in the twentieth century*. It is in just such terms that we might read the passage from the so-called "Golden Age" to the era of Bradman, for example. The former was marked above all by the cultivation of the off-drive and the majestic back-foot batting of Ranjitsinhji in England and Trumper in Australia:

In the "Golden Age" of 1895–1914, style was supreme. The model amateur batsman combined timing and power, grace and aggression. His play looked "effortless," a telling adjective. The off-drive, transmuting the pace of the bowler into its opposite through timing and footwork, was the consummate expression of this aesthetic. How you looked became as important as how many you scored. The aesthetic was counterposed to the utilitarian. (Marqusee, *Anyone*, p. 74)[33]

"Bradmanism," by contrast, undertook to reorganize batting in the interests of controlled aggression and efficiency. Pioneered, in the 1920s and 1930s, by the Australian team with Ponsford and Bradman at its helm, it was marked by its safety-first tactics, its humorlessness and lack of adventure, its "professional" resolve to insure that matches would not be lost, regardless of whether or not they were won.

James has a good deal to say about both the "Golden Age" and "Bradmanism" in his various writings on cricket. For the most part, however, he is interested in chronicling the social history of cricket in the West Indies in the years leading up to and immediately following decolonization in the 1960s. Here, a somewhat different canvas has to be used. For cricket was not introduced to the West Indies under the rubric of moral discipline alone. The social space of the West Indies was marked out as a *colonial* space, and cricket, imposed there (as it never really was in the settler colonies of Australia, New Zealand, or South Africa) upon a subject people from without, had a quite specific role to play in the consolidation and maintenance of colonial authority. As elsewhere in the Anglophone colonial world, "the growth and spread of cricket was coeval with the high noon of the British empire and derived part of its legitimacy from its association with Pax Britannica" (Nandy, *Tao*, p. 6). Nandy observes that

the culture of cricket was exported to the colonies as the basic model of sportsmanship, and as a "healthy, active pastime" which would be "a counter-attraction to praise and politics," as the fourth Lord Harris, an ardent cricket fan and once the Governor of Bombay, put it in the context of India . . . [T]he British gentry . . . took the lead; they were the most enthusiastic promoters of the game in the colonies through British army officers and bureaucrats. But the British middle classes were the most vociferous about the character-building potential of cricket in India. They were convinced that cricket typically nurtured British virtues and the spread of cricket would promote, albeit indirectly, Britain's civilizing mission. (p. 5)[34]

The same point has been made, with specific reference to the West Indies, by Hilary Beckles, who notes that cricket was introduced there as part and parcel of colonial governance – part and parcel of an ensemble that included "English Puritanism, English literature and cricket": the game

penetrated first the insecure and dependent cultural world of the proper-tied white creole elite who embraced it as a celebration of the tight, unbroken bond between themselves and their metropolitan "cousins." For this elite it served all intended purposes; particularly, it assisted in the social elevation of its members above "uncivilized" indigenes who lacked proper access to, or an informed appreciation of, things "English." By mid-[nineteenth] century it was clear that cricket was at once an instrument of imperial cultural authority as well as a weapon of class and race domination within the plantation civilization that still clung to the fabric of a dying slavery ethos . . . Cricket . . . imported into most West Indian territories by the beginning of the nineteenth century, and carry-ing the "made in England" hallmark, was marketed and consumed as a refined elite product in much the same way as was "high Church" Anglicanism . . . Within the recipient plantation world it reaffirmed the existing race/class division of labour while at the same time reassured supporters of empire that the central purpose of colonies in the industrial age was to consume with satisfaction things made at the centre.[35]

The special wonder of cricket in the Caribbean, in James's eyes, is that even in the face of these unpromising originary circumstances, it proved possible to transform the game into "a means of [West Indian] national expression" (*Cricket*, p. 171). West Indians have, over the course of the twentieth century, been able to pull cricket across the manichean divide of colonialism; they have been able to make it carry the weight of *their* social desires and speak *their* language – whether of emergent anti-colonialism, of nationalist affirmation, or since de-colonization, of international self-presence. In *Beyond a Boundary*, James remarks on "the grandeur of a game which, in lands far from that which gave it birth, could encompass so much of social reality and still remain a game" (p. 91). Over the years, the game has been fought for and fought over, made to vibrate with "the realism of West Indian life" (*Beyond*, p. 21). For James, as Manthia Diawara has written, "the mastery of cricket, a game representing Englishness, is, ironically, the West Indian's way of speaking for himself to the modern world."[36]

The "indigenization" (or "creolization"[37]) of cricket in the West Indies could never have taken place "unconsciously," beneath the level of popular consciousness, as, arguably, its "bourgeoisification" did in nineteenth-century England. James describes the ideologically resonant but psychologically unproblematical confluence of the old and the new in the person of W.G. Grace. Writing of himself, by contrast, he notes that while – as a boy exposed to colonial education and colonial culture, and believing what he was told – he was "a British intellectual long before I was ten," this subject position contrived to render him "an alien in my own environment among my own people, even my own family" (*Beyond*, p. 18). Where nativist intellectuals have tended to lament this sort of "alienation," however, regarding it as the ground of a "loss of self" from which they have never been able to recover, James suggests that its ideological implications were not fixed but volatile. Colonial subjection did not always produce obedient colonial subjects: "[I] found [myself] and came to maturity within a system that was the result of centuries of development in another land, was transplanted as a hothouse flower is transplanted and bore some strange fruit" (*Beyond*, p. 42). Since, in order to make cricket their own, the West Indian masses had to prise it loose from English culture; since English culture was precisely what, as a colonized population, they were struggling against; and since, by virtue of the specificity of the circumstances of their coloniz-ation, they were possessed of comparatively few institutionalized forms of cultural practice of their own, they bestowed upon cricket a privileged status in this respect. At the risk of oversimplification, we might say that in the West Indies, cricket became culture. Thus James, citing E.W. Swanton's 1957 observation to the effect that "in the West Indies the cricket ethic has shaped not only the cricketers but social life as a whole," comments that "[i]t is an understatement. There is a whole generation of us, and perhaps two generations, who have been formed by it not only in social attitudes but in our most intimate lives, in fact there more than anywhere else. The social attitudes we could to some degree alter if we wished. For the inner self the die was cast" (*Beyond*, p. 41).

In the colonial West Indies, cricket emerged as the cultural form most expressive of popular West Indian social aspirations. If, in being introduced to the West Indies, the game had seemed a perfect ideological foil for colonialism, it now began to represent a remarkably different sensibility. This sensibility was not a revolutionary one. It could not have been, in the absence of a revolutionary social movement. The ideological protocols of cricket were rebelled against and refashioned, not overthrown. West Indies cricket emerged entirely within the constraints of the conventions of the game. But where the predominant characteristics of the colonial game had consisted in orderliness, discipline, resolution, sacrifice, puritanism, and heroism of a "self-made" and individualist stamp, the West Indies game reflected a different rationality.

Writers on West Indies cricket since James have not, in general, been able to match his understanding of the fully dialectical nature of the historical process of indigenization at issue here. In his celebrated 1969 article, "The Ritual of Cricket," for instance, Orlando Patterson suggested that to the degree that cricket was "the Englishman's game *par excellence,*" it could not, ultimately, be decolonized. Usurpation, on this essentialist reading, was in the final analysis mimicry:

Cricket is the game we love for it is the only game we can play well, the only activity which gives us some international prestige. But it is the game, deep down, which we must hate – the game of the master. Hence it becomes on the symbolic level the English culture we have been forced to love, for it is the only real one we have, but the culture we must despise for what it has done to us, for what it has made of the hopeless cultural shambles, the incoherent social patchwork, that we have called Afro-Jamaican culture.[38]

Similarly, in an article on "The Elite Schools and Cricket in Barbados: a Study in Colonial Continuity," Keith Sandiford and Brian Stoddart seem to me to look past the emergent rationality or social logic of cricket in the West Indies in their emphasis on the question of *formal* continuity in the game. They contrast developments in the West Indies (or Barbados, at least) with those in other colonial territories in this respect. One of the striking features of the dissemination of the game in Barbados, they write, is that the game spread into mass appeal yet still followed the playing and moral codes established by the elites. In Samoa, Fiji and the Trobriand Islands, for example, love of the game certainly spread from the administrators, missionaries and educators who established it along with the imperial message, but the new converts soon subjected cricket to a quite radical reformulation so that it might better reflect the mass cultural customs. This never happened in Barbados . . . While the game was taken up almost fanatically by the island's lower classes . . . the codes and standards to which they aspired were those established and maintained by the culturally dominant cricketing products of the elite schools.[39]

It seems to me that Sandiford and Stoddart mistake a *formal* parallelism for an *ideological* identity here. The point that I am making here has also been very well made by Mark Kingwell, who proposes that the "civility" of cricket in the Caribbean should not be mistaken for ideological conformism:

I want to suggest a different interpretation of politeness . . . if civility is an expression of values that a ruling class considers desirable, or at least thinks it ought to, it is possible that civility may be turned to political advantage through colonial use – not by imitation, which gives the game away, but by selective internal application. The most effective colonial strategy will therefore not be a kind of gleeful surrender to hyper-competitiveness, the value that ignores civility, for this will only reinforce the colonial position. The most effective response will be an ironic maintenance of just those values that the ruling classes profess to admire, a maintenance that . . . will ultimately indicate how little in fact they live up to them.[40]

The social significance of the emergent rationality of cricket in the West Indies was, naturally enough, misrecognized by English commentators. They could see in the West Indies mode of play – which Manley summarizes under the rubrics of "style and humour: that aggressiveness that is somehow good-natured and which is the distinctively West Indian quality in all sport" (*History*, p. 52) – only indiscipline, excess, irresponsibility. Thus a correspondent for *The Times*, writing in 1928, had this to say about the West Indies batsman, Wilton St. Hill:

W. H. St. Hill . . . can be relied upon to provide the entertainment of the side. He is very supple, has a beautifully erect stance and, having lifted his bat, performs amazing apparently double-jointed tricks with his wrists and arms. Some of those contortions are graceful and remunerative, such as his gliding to leg, but some are unsound and dangerous, such as an exaggerated turn of the wrist in cutting. He will certainly play some big and attractive innings, but some others may be easily curtailed by his exotic fancy in dealing with balls on the off-side. (quoted in *Beyond*, pp. 96–97)[41]

164

James turns to Wilton St. Hill in discussing the emergence of a peculiarly West Indian brand of cricket because the Trinidadian was one of the truly decisive – and, for James, truly *representative* – figures in West Indies cricket in the pre-1939 years. It was on the strength of batting of the quality and style of St. Hill's that cricket proved its ability to shoulder the political burden of its popularity. I have already cited James's comment to the effect that "the cricket field was a stage on which selected individuals played representative roles which were charged with social significance" (*Beyond*, p. 66). The role played by St. Hill, in these terms, was a tragic one. It was tragic because, as a batsman, St. Hill carried all before him except for one season; but that one season – with the visiting West Indies side in England in 1928 – was historic. Not only did it become the yardstick by which the English public measured St. Hill's play, it was also read, by his devoted followers back in Trinidad, as a comprehensive set-back for the kind of cricket that he played, and for the social vision embryonically prefigured in this kind of cricket. To the Trinidadian crowds, James writes

the unquestioned glory of St. Hill's batting [in the years prior to 1928] conveyed the sensation that here was one of us, performing *in excelsis* in a sphere where competition was open. It was a demonstration that atoned for a pervading humiliation, and nourished pride and hope. Jimmy Durante, the famous American comedian, has popularized a phrase in the United States: "That's my boy." I am told that its popularity originates in the heart of the immigrant, struggling with the new language, baffled by the new customs . . . Wilton St. Hill was our boy. (*Beyond*, p. 93)

For years, St. Hill batted brilliantly, against any opposition. He was left out of the West Indies side to England in 1923 solely on racial grounds; he persevered and, in 1926, when the English side visited the West Indies, he was outstanding. When, finally, in 1928, he simply could not be omitted from another West Indies team bound for England, he left with the expectations of all Trinidad hanging on his performance. "We [were] . . . convinced in our own minds," James writes, "that St. Hill was the greatest of all West Indian batsmen and on English wickets this coloured man would infallibly put all white rivals in the shade" (*Beyond*, p. 94). The responsibility proved to be too much for St. Hill to shoulder. He did not only fail in England, he failed miserably: "He was a horrible, a disastrous, an incredible, failure, the greatest failure to come out of the West Indies" (p. 95). This collapse can only be read in ideological terms: St. Hill failed because no one person could have succeeded, at that time, in doing what he was asked to do. Although he never overcame the blow of this failure, it was not his alone, but that of all the Trinidadians whose social desires his batting represented. "For people of African descent," Diawara has written,

Blackness is . . . a way of being human in the West or in areas under Western domination. It is a compelling performance against the logic of slavery and colonialism by people whose destinies have been inextricably linked to the advancement of the West, and who have therefore to learn the expressive techniques of modernity: writing, music, Christianity, and industrialization in order to become uncolonizable.[42]

James concludes that St. Hill's "spirit was untameable, perhaps too much so" (*Beyond*, p. 97). Only when it is understood historically is this conclusion fully intelligible. It suggests that St. Hill's tragedy lay in the fact that although he played cricket as it would come to be played, and in such a way as to articulate the aspirations of the masses who adored him, he could not represent himself on the world's stage when it mattered most – on the only occasion, indeed, when it might truly have made a difference. His failure was therefore a failure to perform uncolonizability, that is, to bring forth in his batting an image of decolonized space, not merely "under Western eyes," but, more decisively, in England itself, and before English spectators.

To raise the issue of self-representation in the colonial context is to raise the issue of nationalism. In the history of West Indies cricket it is to move from Wilton St. Hill to Learie Constantine. James argues that St. Hill's failure in England in 1928 was not his alone, but a representative failure, reflecting a certain prematurity, a certain lack of cohesion in the social consciousness of the classes whose aspirations were expressed in St. Hill's batting. This argument can be cast counterfactually, in the form of a question: What would it have taken for St. Hill to succeed? The question finds its answer, for James, in the career of Constantine, for Constantine succeeded – and succeeded prodigiously – where St. Hill could not. Where St. Hill failed so desperately in 1928, Constantine, his near contemporary and fellow Trinidadian, took England by storm: "he took 100 wickets, made 1000 runs and laid claim to being the finest fieldsman yet known" (*Beyond*, p. 106).

James locates the difference between St. Hill and Constantine in class terms. St. Hill was born in 1893, into the Trinidadian lower middle class. He worked all his life as a salesman in a department store. His experiences as a cricketer simply underscored his experiences as a "brownish" (*Beyond*, p. 87) subject of the colonial order. With Constantine it was different. Born a few years later than St. Hill, he was a member of a cricketing family universally respected in the West Indies:

From the time young Constantine knew himself he knew his father as the most loved and most famous cricketer in the island. His mother's brother, Victor Pascall, was the West Indies slow left-hander, a most charming person and a great popular favourite with all classes. We cannot overestimate the influence of all this on young Constantine. He was born to the purple, and in cricket circles never saw himself as inferior to anyone or dependent for anything on anyone. (*Beyond*, p. 103)

Constantine received a good elementary education, but found himself incapable of securing a job commensurate with his qualifications. On the cricket field, he was first among equals; off it, and despite his family's reputation, he was "non-white" in a colonial society in which a strict color bar functioned to reserve preferential jobs for whites. In St. Hill's case, the encounter with discrimination in the social sphere was expected and, partly because of this, met with resignation. In Constantine's case, it was unexpected, and was bitterly resisted. James reads Constantine's success in England in 1928 in the light of a strike against colonial racism: "Constantine, the heir-apparent, the happy warrior, the darling of the crowd, prize pupil of the captain of the West Indies . . . revolted against the revolting contrast between his first-class status as a cricketer and his third-class status as a man" (*Beyond*, p. 106).

If the tour to England was a crushing defeat for St. Hill, it allowed Constantine to emerge as a national hero. In this fact, James locates the fundamental difference between the two players. St. Hill was idolized, revered by his followers; but he could never have been spoken of as a "national" hero. The social aspirations to which his batting gave eloquent voice were those of the popular masses, and they would come in due course to serve centrally as constituents of West Indian national consciousness. But they were not – or not yet – *national* in scope or tendency. Constantine, however, was a properly national hero. The irony was that, as it was then constituted politically, Trinidad was only a *colony*, and the West Indies only a *group of colonial islands*. Constantine's success on the cricket field, James argues, was therefore as instrumental as any other factor in laying the ground for the emergence of a national consciousness throughout the West Indies.

It is testimony to his extraordinary self-consciousness that Constantine recognized this. He recognized it, in fact, at a time – in the late 1920s and early 1930s – when even James himself did not do so. In *Beyond a Boundary*, James records some of the conversations that he had with Constantine during these years, when both men were living and working in the north of England – Constantine as a professional cricketer, James as a writer, journalist, and political activist. He recalls Constantine's insistence that despite the fact that West Indies teams seemed invariably to lose important matches to England, the standard of West Indies cricket was as high as that of its English counterpart. Constantine's repeated "They are no better than we" was, James notes, already a political demand: "It was a slogan and a banner. It was politics, the politics of nationalism" (p. 113). It was such, because Constantine's proposed solution to the problem was so demonstrably nationalist in tenor:

> They are no better than we, he used to say: we can bat and bowl and field as well as any of them. To my – as I thought – devastating query, "Why do we always lose and make such a poor show?" he would reply: "We need a black man as captain." I was stupid enough to believe that he was dealing with the question of race. I should have known that it was not so . . . What he used to tell me was that the West Indian players were not a team and to become a team they needed a captain who had the respect of the players and was able to get the best out of the team. Not too far from his argument was the sentiment that a good captain would respect all the men.　　　　　　　　　　　　　　　　　　　　　　(*Cricket*, p. 257)

The fact that this quotation is extracted from a 1970 essay on Frank Worrell, points to the direction assumed by James's social history of cricket in the West Indies. If the space between Wilton St. Hill and Learie Constantine is the space through which the problematic of nationalism entered West Indies cricket, that between Constantine and Worrell marks the moment of decolonization. What Constantine was prescient enough to be able to imagine, Worrell was able to make real – but not before conditions were ripe. Worrell's captaincy of the West Indies team in the late 1950s and early 1960s – like the play of individuals such as Garfield Sobers, Rohan Kanhai, Lance Gibbs, and Wesley Hall on this team – had everything to do with the current of West Indian politics. Not for nothing does James, in a passage I have already cited, speak of Kanhai's batting at this time as expressive of the "West Indian quest for identity."

It would be next to impossible to match the *quality* of James's insights about cricket, generated, as he himself points out, from a lifetime's study of the game.[43] But – drawing on Lukács's famous argument about "orthodox" Marxism – I would like to suggest that the validity of James's examination of West Indies cricket as a socially expressive practice consists in its *method*. In *Beyond a Boundary*, James himself writes extensively about Worrell, George Headley, Everton Weekes, and Clyde Walcott. Others have followed his lead with respect to these figures, with exemplary results. But it seems to me that his methods can readily and relevantly be applied, too, to an analysis of cricket in the West Indies (and elsewhere) in the years *since* the publication of *Beyond a Boundary* in 1963.

Consider, for instance, the remarkable climax of the Test series between the West Indies and England in 1967–68, in which, after three very dull drawn Tests, Sobers – who had acceded to the captaincy upon the retirement of Worrell in 1963 – astonishingly declared the West Indies second innings closed on the last afternoon of the Fourth Test, allowing England to seize an opportunity which they had not earned, but which they gladly took, to win the match. The importance of this declaration was magnified when, despite a brilliant personal performance from Sobers himself, England held on to draw the thrilling Fifth and final Test, thereby winning the series 1–0.

Sobers's declaration was deemed a blunder at the time and has continued to be thought of by almost all commentators as a disastrous miscalculation. Manley, for instance, articulates the majority view in concluding that Sobers must have "miscalculated, assuming perhaps that he could work another personal miracle." He goes on to argue that:

Miracles are fine when they succeed. When they fail, however, one is entitled to examine the question of probability. With the declaration that he made, there was at least an outside chance that England could make 215 runs in 165 minutes under the conditions. There was next to no chance that the West Indies could have bowled them out. The balance of probability therefore was all against the West Indies and this is why the decision was a mistake. As to the suggestion that it was a "sporting" declaration . . . the explanation does not wash. Sportsmanship does not mean inviting the other guy to a victory which is clearly beyond your own reach. (*History*, pp. 183–84)

Recently, however, Tim Hector has offered a persuasive Jamesian rebuttal of this conventional wisdom. As background, let us note that the England team had come to the Caribbean in 1967–68 expecting not to win. (They had been beaten comprehensively in England by the West Indies in 1963 and again in 1966.) They had resolved, under the circumstances, to play to a grimly defensive strategy – to lose, if necessary, in a war of attrition. The plan was to dull the edge of the West Indies bowling attack through ultra-cautious, safety-first batting; and to bowl not primarily to get the West Indies batsmen out, but rather to prevent them from scoring runs freely. In this context, Hector reads Sobers's declaration in the Fourth Test quite differently from most analysts. I quote from his article at length:

I agreed with [Sobers's] declaration then, and I agree with it now 26 years after. Let us call Sobers himself to the bar to testify on his own behalf. Sobers says "It was 1968 in the West Indies and we had reached stalemate. England even with two spinners in the side, somehow managed to bowl 11 and 12 overs an hour." Sobers was absolutely against this. He felt England should play up, play up and play the game. England had reneged on the basic principle of the game, and they were doing so openly and with vulgarity.

Sobers then makes one of the most profound cricket and political statements: "I felt we had an obligation to the people who paid to watch us, and in an effort to break the deadlock, I made that now infamous declaration in the fourth Test in Trinidad. It backfired, we lost and I've been criticised for it ever since. People forget that John Edrich was dropped behind the wicket in the first over and that, with a little more luck, the outcome could have been different . . . I was fed up with what was going on, set about doing something about it and have never regretted my decision" . . .

Sobers had launched an assault on what can only be termed the "Welfare State of Mind" in cricket. It is a state of mind, in which players play safe and dull, the duller the better, and devoid of all adventure. Never hitting against the break or across the line, refusing to get to the pitch, it plays not to lose. Sobers was fed up with it. To him cricket was art, but its artistry lay in entertainment for the ordinary people. It required daring, excitement, risk, *"dynamic explosions of individual and creative personalities expressing themselves to the utmost limit,"* as . . . C.L.R. James expressed it.[44]

Although it would have been very much to the point, Hector does not restate *Beyond a Boundary's* foundational question, "What do they know of cricket who only cricket know?" (p. xxi). Instead – and it amounts to the same thing – he insists that in the West Indies, at least, "cricket is a continuation of politics, by other means" ("West Indian," p. 122). The series between England and the West Indies in 1967–68 was not merely about cricket. It was about "postcoloniality," about national sovereignty and the forms of possible social expression in the West Indies. England brought Keynesian professionalism – the "Welfare State of Mind"[45] – to the Caribbean. By his declaration in the Fourth Test, Sobers forced them to abandon it. For in order to win the Test, England had to throw their gameplan to the winds, to bat adventurously, with imagination and ingenuity. That they did so (with Colin Cowdrey scoring a fluid and free-spirited 71) can be considered a triumph not of the "Welfare State of Mind" but of the ethic represented by Sobers – an ethic, significantly, that both sides then carried into the Fifth Test. (The fact that it should have been Cowdrey who led England's way to victory is not incidental. Already in 1957, in an article in *Cricketer* magazine [reprinted in *Beyond a Boundary*], James had identified Cowdrey as a batsman whose fundamental predilections for attacking, creative strokeplay were being curtailed by the safety-first ethic that had come to prevail in world cricket: "Cowdrey is a striking example of how an individual who in another age would have flourished like the green bay tree is profoundly affected by the contemporary pressures" [*Beyond*, p. 217].)

Nor is this all. The full meaning of Sobers's achievement in restoring a "West Indian" ethic to a Test series against England played in the West Indies can only be appreciated when situated in the context of the political and ideological situation at that time. The point is that while the stock of the West Indies cricket team had continued to rise throughout the 1960s, the progressive nationalist concept of a pan-West Indian political formation "had gone nowhere" (Hector, "West Indian," p. 122). The much-vaunted West Indian Federation of 1958, repository of so many progressive political hopes, had collapsed in 1963, dissolving under the weight of chauvinism and the opportunism of island leaders.[46] This collapse stripped pan-West Indian aspirations of any plausible political outlet in the form of a movement or party. Only at the level of cricket were these aspirations still meaningfully represented – not merely on the grounds that West Indians played Test cricket *as the West Indies* (and not as Jamaicans or Barbadians or Trinidadians), but above all because the team's mode of play was so attractive: daring, imaginative, and buoyantly confident. In these terms, Hector notes, West Indies cricket in the post-Federation years (i.e., after 1963) had served as the only "symbol of liberation and integration," despite the disintegration of the political initiative. "West Indian cricket alone, existentially, and in life, ke[pt] the idea and the practice of Caribbean nationhood alive" (p. 120). It was this legacy – the capacity of cricket to give expression to a pan-West Indian consciousness beyond the wreckage of the Federation – that was finally at stake in Sobers's declaration. And, notwithstanding the subsequent political failures of Carifta and Caricom, it has, arguably, remained at stake in the years since.[47]

In 1975–76, a West Indies team of which much was expected was routed by an Australian side spearheaded by the fearsome fast bowling of Dennis Lillee and Jeff Thomson, losing 5–1 in a six match Test series. Following that series – under the captaincy first of Clive Lloyd, then of Vivian Richards, and then of Richie Richardson – the West Indies enjoyed absolute and unbroken preeminence in world cricket until they were beaten at home by the resurgent Australians in 1995, compiling in the process a record which, as Manley observes, is unparalleled in the annals "of any internationally recognized sport in modern history" (*History*, p. 6). Manley compares the West Indies team under Lloyd (1974–84) with the only two other sides in the history of cricket that might be thought to have been its equal: Warwick Armstrong's Australian squad in two series against England in 1920–21; and Donald Bradman's Australians against England in 1948. He argues convincingly for the superiority of the West Indies team, and not merely on the grounds that its dominance was longer lasting (and, indeed, continued well beyond Lloyd's retirement). He also speculates that the dominance of Lloyd's West Indies side was more complete than that of any dynastic team in American sporting history – whether the New York Yankees in the days of Babe Ruth or, later, of Mickey Mantle; the Boston Celtics under the leadership of "Red" Auerbach; or Vince Lombardi's Green Bay Packers (*History*, p. 10).

I believe that a Jamesian reading of cricket in the "postcolonial" West Indies would be able to contextualize and render properly the significance of this defeat in Australia, as well as of such other nodal moments and developments as the following: the celebrated "blackwashes" of England in 1984 and 1985–86 (when the West Indies won every Test in two successive series against England); the West Indies' victory in the first and third World Cup finals (against Australia and England, respectively) in 1979 and 1987; the unscriptable defeat of South Africa in 1992, in the first ever Test match between the two teams, played in Barbados under extraordinary (and profoundly overdetermined) political and historical circumstances;[48] the emergence of Brian Lara, the brilliant left-handed batsman from Trinidad, and the glory of his batting in early 1994 when, in a matter of a couple of months, he broke both Sobers's record for the highest score ever made in a Test and Hanif Mohammad's record for the highest score ever made in any first-class match;[49] and so forth.

To argue for the *continuing* relevance of James's analytical method is, however, to take up a position in express opposition to Ashis

Nandy and Kenneth Surin, two contemporary theorists who seem willing – more or less[50] – to endorse James's representation of cricket in the colonial and decolonizing eras, but who insist that the game's social meaning has changed beyond all recognition since then, rendering it comprehensively beyond the reach of his allegorical and radical nationalist model. The encounter between James, on the one hand, and Nandy and Surin, on the other, is significant, since it takes the form of a debate between a Marxist theory representing cricket in the West Indies as a modern (but not modernist) cultural practice objectively aligned with national liberationist aspirations, and a theory – postmodernist in Surin's case, anti-modernist in Nandy's – asserting the obsolescence or irrelevance of the modern paradigm in all of its aspects, including those of Marxism and nationalism. It will therefore be useful for us, at this point, to consider in some detail the substance of the arguments advanced by Nandy and Surin.

On Nandy's reading, the historical narrative of cricket as an expressive cultural practice is articulated around four decisive instances (Nandy uses the topographical metaphor of "planes"):

traditional English cricket (which is in many ways a reflection of earlier social hierarchies but is also unwittingly a criticism of the values associated with modern industrialism), modern cricket (increasingly an endorsement of the hegemonic, urban-industrial managerial culture and a criticism of the pre-industrial values now associated with defeated ways of life), imported cricket (the cricket which was exported to non-western societies as a criticism of native life-styles from the point of view of the industrializing West but which, as reconstructed by the natives, brought out the latent function of the game in the West and became a criticism of the common cultural principles of capitalism, colonialism and modernity) and new cricket (the cricket which by its close identification with the industrial-managerial ethos is becoming increasingly an endorsement of the ruling culture of the world and a criticism of the victims of history).

(*Tao*, p. xi)

The initial schema here corresponds quite closely to James's own historicization of cricket as a sport: the "traditional" era, incorporating cricket from its origins, through the W.G. Grace years, to the "Golden Age" of Edwardianism; the "modern" era, associated with the name of Donald Bradman – roughly thirty years, from the late 1920s to the late 1950s[51] – and characterized by the restructuring of the game along the corporatist axes of professionalism, controlled aggression, opportunism, concentration, and the minimization of errors; and the era of "imported" cricket, in which the game in the colonial world is first indigenized and then refunctioned to bear the

burden of majoritarian social aspirations. Crucially, however, Nandy
adds a fourth instance to these initial three. It is the plane of what he
calls "new" cricket – a phenomenon that receives no theorization in
James, but that Nandy believes is increasingly definitive of the way in
which cricket is being played throughout the world today.

At various points in his analysis, Nandy evokes the specter of
"postmodernity." The problem with his description of "new" cricket
in this respect, however, is that it cannot really be distinguished from
his description of "modern" cricket. Consider the following formulation, for instance, drawn from the opening pages of *The Tao of Cricket*:

the ambience of cricket is under attack in the modern world which seeks
to make the game more scientific, faster, more professional, more obviously thrilling, combative and decisive – in other words, to make the
game fit in with the dominant worldview of our times. Cricket *is* being
turned into a synecdoche at last. Not because society is being altered to
suit the needs of cricket but because cricket is being altered to suit the
needs of contemporary consciousness. (p. 3)

Nandy is referring here to cricket in the contemporary era, the era of
the 1980s. But exactly the same description could plausibly – and,
indeed, accurately – be held to characterize developments within
cricket during the 1920s and 1930s. Nandy deplores the commodification of the game, its "internal" accommodations to the mass-media.
"Cricket," he writes,

is now more a paying entertainment than a game. On one side are the
spectators who see it as a consumable commodity, on the other are the
performers who aim to perform professionally and please. It is a business
deal with a difference. In new cricket, unlike on the stage or on the screen,
one entertains if one is successful; one does not succeed because one
entertains. (*Tao*, 41)

Above all he deplores what he sees as the increasing dominance of an
ethic of technocratic corporatism in cricket, whose sway, he argues, is
such that the flexible "conventions" that used to guide conduct in the
game are today being displaced by rigid "rules." Cricket is increasingly being played more to the letter than in accordance with the
spirit of its laws:

[the gamesmanship in] new cricket is increasingly the competitiveness
and success-hunt of the culture of modern management and business. In
it, as long as you obey the letter of the law, no hold is barred and no
quarter given: none is expected either. Cricket is now increasingly a game
which could well be taught in an institute of management studies. (p. 38)

Nandy goes on to draw some of the consequences that follow from this supposedly new corporatist ethic in cricket: the game – now less a game in his view than a commodity-spectacle – "is gradually taking on . . . the characteristics of the industrial sector: the same work ethic, the same principles of organization, the same criterion of productivity . . . Individuality resides not in the game, but in the measure of performance" (p. 116). Accordingly, "a less talented but more reliable player, according to the new culture of cricket, should always be preferred to a more talented but risky player. While the latter entertains, the former 'truly' entertains by ensuring the victory of his team. In other words, the culture of the gentleman-amateur has now been almost fully superseded by that of the professional" (p. 41). The net result is a hollowing out of the idiosyncratic (and, Nandy insists, essentially anarchic)[52] dimensions of cricketing performance and a transformation in the representative status of players: the contemporary cricketer

gradually begins to symbolize the idea of a hard-working, innocent, patriotic, law-abiding citizen whose exhibitionist narcissism, instrumental view of other human beings, and conventionality are justified by his conformity to the dominant social norms represented by the "rules of the game" . . . The good sportsman is now not a player who entertains himself and in the process entertains us; he is a person who gives a false sense of drama, success and victory to the conformist, self-hating, pseudo-politicized, potency-driven, over-socialized citizen. (pp. 118–19)

The attitude that Nandy expresses toward these supposedly new developments in the sociality of cricket is one of regret. "[C]ricket is a threatened species of play," he writes, "a Victorian pastime of leisurely seriousness and self-denying stoicism, about to die a natural death in the post-second-world-war-world . . . [W]hen cricket goes, it is bound to take away with it something of the meaning of life of many of my generation" (p. x).[53] But Nandy's representation of these supposed changes in cricket as "new" is undermined even by the words and concepts he deploys: the critique of instrumental reason, of narcissism, of conformism; the mobilization of the concepts of norm and self-hatred and pseudo-politicization – these are precisely the terms of the Frankfurt School's critique of mass society. As such, they have been a staple of critical social and cultural theory since at least the 1930s. Nandy approvingly cites James, who – protesting against the encroaching commodification of the game – had "ask[ed] for the de-expertization of cricket, and [had] plead[ed] for a return to adventure and creativity from the security-seeking of modern cricket" (*Tao*, p. 114). But he fails to observe that James's protest had been directed against *the "Bradmanian" mode of cricket* – precisely the mode that Nandy himself characterizes as "modern." To warrant a different label, today's "new" cricket would presumably need to be distinguishable from its 1930s "modern" counterpart.

We might speculate that by introducing the term "new" cricket to describe the *contemporary* game, Nandy intends to indicate the ultimate *supersession* of "imported" cricket as the form of the game to which (above all in the West Indies) anti-colonialism and the drive to decolonization bore witness. In these terms, "new" cricket might be said to correspond to the globalization of "modern" cricket – that is, to the recuperative metropolitan subsumption of "imported" cricket. The relationship of "modern" cricket to "new" cricket would, on this reading, be analogous to the relationship of "modernism" to "postmodernism" as Fredric Jameson theorizes it in the concluding chapter of his book, *Postmodernism, or, The Cultural Logic of Late Capitalism*. Jameson argues that modernism

must . . . be seen as uniquely corresponding to an uneven moment of social development, or to what Ernst Bloch called the "simultaneity of the nonsimultaneous," the "synchronicity of the nonsynchronous" (*Gleichzeitigkeit des Ungleichzeitigen*): the coexistence of realities from radically different moments of history – handicrafts alongside the great cartels, peasant fields with the Krupp factories or the Ford plant in the distance.[54]

So, too, "modern" cricket might be said to have existed, in accordance with the principles of "combined and uneven development," *alongside* "imported" cricket during the late colonial and decolonizing years. *Postmodernism*, by contrast, is defined by Jameson in terms of the definitive overcoming of unevenness, the final integration of the world system:

the postmodern must be characterized as a situation in which the survival, the residue, the holdover, the archaic, has finally been swept away without a trace . . . Ours is a more homogeneously modernized condition: we no longer are encumbered with the embarrassment of non-simultaneities and non-synchronicities. Everything has reached the same hour on the great clock of development or rationalization . . . This is the sense in which we can affirm, either that modernism is characterized by a situation of incomplete *modernization*, or that postmodernism is *more* modern than modernism itself.[55]

"New" cricket, thus conceived, would then correspond to the simultaneous and uniform modernization of cricket wherever it was played. In India as in England, in Sri Lanka as in New Zealand, "new" cricket would be played in the same way, would be governed by the same social logic, would reflect the same underlying premises.

As we shall see, this vision of homogeneous modernization is explicitly and self-consciously promulgated by Kenneth Surin in his postmodernist critique of James's reading of cricket. Nandy, however, is ultimately no postmodernist. For all his gestures in the direction of postmodernism, he remains committed to a thoroughgoing "Third Worldism," which causes him to insist upon the irreducible difference between cultural practices on the two sides of the international division of labor.[56] Thus he writes of Indian cricketers – and the example is generalizable to Pakistani and West Indian but *not* to Australian or English players – that "the responsibility . . . [they] carry in international matches is enormous. Eleven players, with an average age less than thirty and mostly innocent of politics and culture, are expected to recover the self-esteem of 800 million Indians and undo – in both the everyday and psychoanalytic senses of the term – colonial history in the southern world" (*Tao*, p. 108). A good deal could be said (mostly in refutation, but even in qualified support) of the Third Worldist dimension of Nandy's thought. Here, however, it is only necessary to point out that it cannot possibly be reconciled with the evocation of "new" cricket as a hegemonic form bespeaking the global social logic of managerial rationality. For one cannot maintain simultaneously, as Nandy attempts to do, both that "the culture of the gentleman-amateur has now been almost fully superseded by that of the professional" *and* that "[a]s a living game, cricket in the Third World is primarily a mode of expression shaped during the age of amateurism" (pp. 41; 6). Nor can one maintain simultaneously that cricket is today more or less exclusively governed by the ethics of instrumentalism and managerial rationality *and* that it continues to constitute a vital "source of human pride." Nandy cites this latter – Jamesian – phrase in support of his argument that Test cricket in the "Third World" still "represents the hopes, ambitions, fears and anxieties of countries caught within and humiliated by the modern nation-state system. For the millions seeking personal and collective dignity within the system, cricket is a compensation, a channel of mobility and a vision of the world which allows more equality or balanced competition than does the real world" (p. 108). To accept *this* argument, however – and it is, I believe, to Nandy's relative credit that he does so – it is necessary to believe that the social aspirations expressed by cricket in the "Third World" remain quite distinct from those expressed by cricket in the metropolitan societies.

177

This would imply at the very least, though, that one abandon the notion of "new" cricket as a global cultural dominant.[57]

Surin's analysis of cricket is quite free of the sorts of internal contradiction that, I have suggested, undermine the cogency of Nandy's presentation in *The Tao of Cricket*. The tension between modern and postmodern imperatives in Nandy's account is conspicuously resolved in Surin's reading, in favor of the latter. Like Nandy, Surin begins by reconstructing and affirming the broad lines of the "cultural history of cricket" that James sketches in *Beyond a Boundary*. James's periodization of the game, he argues, should be conceptualized in the light of "Max Weber's three-fold schema of charismatic inauguration, traditionalization, and routinization" ("Materialist," pp. 126–27). James's schema is reconstructed by Surin in terms of a narrative depiction of ideal-typical representatives: first, W.G. Grace as "the charismatic inaugural figure"; then, Pelham Warner, born in the West Indies, captain of the English side that toured Australia in 1903–04, and under whom "the game . . . attain[s] to its next historical stage, namely, that of its traditionalization" (these two phases together correspond to Nandy's first moment of "traditional" cricket); following this, in turn, Donald Bradman, an Australian – described by James as "the cricketer symbolical of the age which can be called the age of J.M. Keynes" – who presides over the routinization of the game, its transformation into what Nandy calls "modern" cricket ("Materialist," pp. 127–28). Nandy's third moment ("imported" cricket) is then read by Surin under the sign of "renewal," that is, of the reactivation of the tripartite Weberian schema through "the arrival of new resources of charisma from the newly independent West Indies":

Thus for James, Frank Worrell, the great West Indian captain of the 1960s, is the representative figure who more than any other stands for the repudiation of the legacy of Bradman and his routinized times . . . Worrell, the first black man to captain the West Indies, made West Indian self-government a reality on the cricket field by turning what had previously often been an assorted collection of gifted players – who alas lost frequently to English and Australian opponents – into a unit that managed to win and to play marvelously attractive cricket at the same time. (p. 129)

Like Nandy, Surin suggests that the Jamesian schema is unable to account for the sociality of cricket – even and especially in the West Indies – *since* the 1960s. I shall quote him at length here, since his formulation of what he calls the "aporias in James's historical scheme" is symptomatic:

unfortunately for the reader, James in his last years did not provide a sustained analysis . . . of Clive Lloyd's West Indian team, a team that acquired an unparalleled winning record in international cricket by, if anything, perfecting the methods James associates with Bradman and the deplorable "Age of Keynes." In a period which has ostensibly seen the demise of the Keynesian and the Bradmanian ethos, Lloyd and his team-mates scorned to take cricketing risks, primarily by relying in each match on a roster of four very fast bowlers (Roberts, Holding, Garner, Marshall, Patterson, Walsh, Benjamin, Ambrose, Bishop, Davis, Gray, *inter alia*) who would be ceaselessly rotated to wear down – "psychologically" as much as anything else – opposing batsmen; and by preferring cautious and unspectacular batsmen – e.g. Haynes, Gomes, and Murray (who was also an unobtrusively safe wicketkeeper) – to more aggressive but perhaps unreliable players. James never expressed much enthusiasm for this team, but he did not tell us why Lloyd's team would, in so striking a reversal, bear the mark of Bradman and not Worrell. Why would the most successful team, not only of the "postmodern" 70s and 80s but of all time, be one that has ostensibly espoused a playing philosophy hardly different from the one which James identifies with the brutal and stagnant 1920s and 1930s? Why would this team come, not from a metropolitan country (as was the case with the equally successful, dominant English and Australian teams in Bradman's time), but from the peripheries of the Wallersteinian world economic system? (pp. 129–30)

It is true that the success of the West Indian teams of the late 1970s and 1980s is unparalleled in world cricket. It is also true that James never provided a fully comprehensive analysis of the West Indies team during these years. Unlike Surin, however, I do not find anything especially portentous in the coexistence of these facts. (It is perhaps worth pointing out here that James was already well into his seventies, and rather infirm, by the time that Clive Lloyd came into the captaincy of the West Indies team. To read a great deal into his failure to produce a "sustained analysis" of Lloyd's team seems, under these circumstances, rather severe. James did indeed continue to write in his last years; but little that he wrote – about any subject, not just about cricket – was notable for being "sustained." Moreover, while it is certainly true that in his cricket writings of these years he did not focus exclusively or even centrally upon the achievements of Lloyd's team, he did write a fair amount about such outstanding players as Richards, Greenidge, Roberts, Holding, and Lloyd himself.) And more significantly, I find myself fundamentally at odds with everything *else* that Surin writes in this long passage. Whether empirical or conceptual, the claims made seem to me incapable of withstanding close scrutiny.

Surin's central empirical claim is that the West Indies under

Lloyd's captaincy abandoned the ethos of Worrell and instead embraced – and perfected – a "Bradmanian ethos." In their batting, he argues, the West Indies eschewed the attacking, adventurous, and ostensibly carefree style that had marked both the era of the "three W's" – Walcott, Weekes, and Worrell himself – in the 1950s and of Sobers and Kanhai in the 1960s, and embraced instead a defensive, steady, relentlessly acquisitive style. In their bowling, similarly, they abandoned the commitment to a multi-accented attack – speed, spin, medium-paced cut and swing – that had been their trademark in the halcyon days of Wesley Hall, Charlie Griffith, Sobers, and Lance Gibbs, and embraced instead a one-dimensional and mechanically rotated four-pronged pace attack.

Neither with respect to batting nor with respect to bowling can this representation be upheld. Surin seeks to substantiate his assertion that the West Indies team under Lloyd adopted the standpoint of caution and safety-first in *batting* by referring us to Desmond Haynes, Larry Gomes, and Deryck Murray. This is akin to characterizing the Victorian novel on the basis of the work of Anthony Trollope, Wilkie Collins, and Mrs. Humphrey Ward (as she still tends to be called). Surin simply suppresses in this instance the names of the most significant West Indies batsmen of the Lloyd era, every one of whom – Gordon Greenidge, Roy Fredericks, Viv Richards, Alvin Kallicharan, Lawrence Rowe, Lloyd himself – was a dazzling and audacious strokemaker. Even with regard to Haynes, Gomes, and Murray, Surin misleads. He himself admits that Murray was in the team primarily as a wicketkeeper who could also bat usefully, not as a batsman proper (in which capacity alone he would almost certainly not have been selected). By the same token, Haynes was an opening batsman, in whom, for this reason, a certain degree of circumspection could scarcely have been foregone – but an opening batsman whose style was in any event superbly matched and offset by that of his illustrious partner, Gordon Greenidge. As a pair – and it is above all as *partners* that great opening batsmen tend to be remembered – Greenidge and Haynes were both the most proficient *and* among the fastest-scoring in cricket history.[58] It is only one batsman, therefore – Gomes – who comes close to fitting Surin's description of West Indies batsmanship in the Lloyd era as cautious and unimaginative. And while Gomes was certainly successful – he played sixty Tests for the West Indies, scoring nine centuries and averaging just under forty runs per innings – it would hardly be correct to herald his style as "representative" of West Indies batsmanship in the Lloyd era. It was no more so than the solid, unspectacular style of Joe Solomon was "representative" of batsmanship in Frank Worrell's West Indies team of the early 1960s.

Nor does Surin do any better with respect to *bowling*. Offering us only an undifferentiated list of some of the bowlers who played for the West Indies during Lloyd's tenure, he suggests that these bowlers were effectively *indistinguishable*, owing their selection only to their blinding speed. Any four could, it seems, have been selected for any given Test match at any given venue: Lloyd would then have put them through their paces in mechanical fashion, bowling the first two until they were fatigued and replacing them without much thought with the next two, before returning to the opening pair, and so on. Thus Surin writes that Lloyd "handled the most formidable bowling side in the history of the game 'without surprises': where successful captains of past times had at least sought to give the appearance of changing their bowlers according to a strategy, he merely changed them according to a routine (or so it seemed)" ("Materialist," pp. 138–39). The "or so it seemed" is disarming, to be sure; but the untenability of this reading will be clear to anybody who gives due consideration to the vast differences in the bowling actions and capabilities of, say, Andy Roberts, Michael Holding, Malcolm Marshall, Joel Garner, and Colin Croft – the principal bearers of Lloyd's attack in the late 1970s and early 1980s. As Marqusee puts it, "[e]ach of the great West Indian quicks . . . worked to create his own style, experimentally varying height and angle of delivery, line and length" (*Anyone*, p. 148).[59] Surin's judgment was certainly not shared by the opposing batsmen who had to face these bowlers, and who often enough found them equally *unplayable*, but who never for a moment found it difficult to distinguish one from another! The fact that the West Indies pace attack was deadly and unrelenting does not indicate that it was one-dimensional.

As for the unimaginativeness of Lloyd's *captaincy*, it would be interesting to make a contextual examination of his decisions in the field: for many commentators have pointed out that, far from merely "rotating" his bowlers, Lloyd rung his bowling changes to exceptional effect.[60] Time after time, a new bowler would be called upon to bowl and would almost immediately achieve a breakthrough by taking a wicket or two, thus prompting a collapse in the opposing side's batting. This happened so frequently when Lloyd was at the helm that it could not possibly be attributed to luck. Nor was it a matter only of the relative freshness of the new bowler and the relative fatigue of the old: often enough, Lloyd would produce start-ling results by determining – against the better judgment of other players or of knowledgeable onlookers – *not* to replace a weary bowler whom he felt still had an edge over the batsmen, even when it seemed that there was a realistic risk of bowling him into the ground and thereby of impairing his effectivity for the next innings or even the next match. This happened most notably, perhaps, in the Fifth Test between the West Indies and England at the Oval, London, in August 1976. On an flat, even wicket affording little lift or movement to the bowlers, Lloyd kept Michael Holding on at full pace, unre-lieved, for hour after hour. Bowling 33 overs in the first innings alone, Holding took 14 wickets in the match in a performance that Manley describes as "one of the greatest displays of fast bowling in the history of the game" (*History*, p. 246).

Surin disregards the evidence of the creative, attacking, and intri-cately differentiated expressivity of the West Indian teams during the Lloyd era and since – simultaneously unfettered and yet concen-trated, it seems to me – in order to ground his contention that throughout the world over the course of the last couple of decades, cricket has become homogeneously modernized and instrumental-ized:

even the "subjectivities" of cricketers [have] become fungible. Hence the great Indian batsman Sunil Gavaskar is frequently likened to his English counterpart Geoffrey Boycott, who in turn is said to have been stylisti-cally indistinguishable from the Australian Bill Lawry; the Pakistani Imran Khan, the New Zealander Richard Hadlee, the Australian Dennis Lillee, and the West Indians Roberts, Holding, Garner and Marshall have acquired virtually identical Test Match records by each bowling with similar effect on just about any cricket ground in the world; and so forth.
("Materialist," pp. 120–21)

It is necessary, once again, to protest the empirical insufficiency of this account. For it is only by thinking in profoundly abstract or strictly statistical terms that it makes any sense at all to speak of Lawry, Gavaskar, and Boycott as batsmen of "similar" styles or means – and elsewhere in his article, Surin goes even further and adds Allan Border of Australia and Javed Miandad of Pakistan to his reductive list (p. 138). Let us consider just the cases of Lawry and Gavaskar, for instance: tall and angular, Lawry was an obdurate opening batsman in the "Bradmanian" mold, whose rock-solid de-fense, reinforced by his exceptional patience and ability to punish the bad ball, enabled him to anchor an Australian batting line-up which, if not quite the equal of that of the West Indies, was nevertheless formidable, and full of strokemakers: Bob Simpson, Ian Redpath, Norman O'Neill, Bob Cowper, Keith Stackpole, Doug Walters, Greg Chappell. Gavaskar, by contrast, was one of the great opening batsmen of all time: a small man, a good eight or nine inches shorter than Lawry, he was a wonderfully fluent, supple, and wristy striker of the ball, possessed of a magnificent eye and lightning-quick reflexes and footwork. The adjectives often used to describe his batting style – "graceful," "delightful," even "charming" – could never have been applied to the resolute but stolid Lawry. Like George Headley in the 1930s – nicknamed "Atlas" because he had so often to carry single-handedly the burden of run-making for the West Indies – so too Gavaskar's already luminous record (34 centuries and more than 10,000 runs in 125 Test match appearances) becomes even brighter if we take into consideration the fact that he stood for years as the only Indian batsman of world-class stature. Until the emergence of Dilip Vengsarkar and Kapil Dev at the end of the 1970s, it was often Gavaskar alone – or Gavaskar and such good but not quite top-flight batsmen as D.N. Sardesai, Gundappa Viswanath, and Mohinder Amarnath – who stood between India and complete rout at the hands of Test bowlers of the caliber of Lillee and Thompson of Australia, Roberts and Holding of the West Indies, and John Snow of England.[61]

Nor is it necessary to say much about Surin's unconvincing conflation of such *bowlers* as Imran, Holding, Lillee, Hadlee, and Garner – other than to note that it, too, seems premised upon severe decontextualization. Surin refers to the Test match records of these bowlers as "virtually identical." He does not say that these records are also exceptionally good, indeed among the best records ever compiled in Test match history. This, on the face of it, might be taken to indicate not the *standardization* of fast bowling but the *perfection* of it by a few of its contemporary exponents! This is how Marqusee, at least, sees the matter. He interprets the unprecedented success of the West Indian fast bowlers from the mid-1970s onward as testifying to their versatility and cricketing acumen: they have shown themselves, he writes, to be "among the most adaptable cricketers the world has ever seen" (*Anyone*, p. 148).

Ultimately, however, it is what prompts and motivates Surin's (mis)reading of discrete details – what underlies his analysis of the trends prevailing in contemporary cricket – that matters. In criticizing James for failing to recognize and take explicit stock of the supposed transformation in the social meaning of cricket between the 1960s and the 1980s, he asks: "What causes these apparent aporias in James' historical scheme?" (p. 130). Let us try to ask a similar sort of question of *Surin's* postmodernist reading of cricket in the contemporary world system: what are the assumptions that structure *it*, in turn?

The first such assumption is that capitalism as a world system has undergone an epochal transformation over the course of the past twenty-five years. Drawing upon the work of Antonio Negri,[62] Surin argues that, at some point toward the end of the 1960s, the world entered a new, systemic, globally extensive, and dominant phase of capitalist development. In this new phase, the "planned capitalism" that had been the motor of economic growth and political "stability" since 1945 (and whose contours had been shaped by Keynesianism, welfarism, nation-statism, and [neo-]colonialism) collapsed – or, rather, was rendered obsolete – to be superseded by a new, differently and more fully "modernized" configuration. Surin follows Negri in speaking of "the subsumption of society by capitalist development" (quoted in "Materialist," p. 139), by which he apparently means to indicate that the logic of capital has come not only to penetrate but to *saturate* all aspects and dimensions of society: still drawing on Negri, thus, he writes elsewhere that "[t]he current phase of capitalist expansion has created a social order in which all the conditions of production and reproduction have been directly absorbed by capital . . . Capital has . . . extend[ed] its logic of command over productive cooperation to envelop the whole of society . . ."[63]

This theory of the restructuration of contemporary capitalism is very similar to those that I have examined (under the rubrics of postmodernism, "post-Fordism," and globalization) and attempted to refute in the first chapter of this book and elsewhere.[64] I shall not restate the terms of that critique here but will focus, instead, upon two further premises that Surin derives from his theory of "late capitalism" in the contemporary world system. First, from his assumption that society has been subsumed by capital, Surin infers that cricket (and, by implication, all sociocultural practice) has lost its erstwhile capacity for relatively autonomous ideological expression. He argues that "[w]hat cricket does more and more is simply to 'express' its own situation as a commodity produced and consumed within a unitary and standardized flow of production and consumption which now straddles the world (and thus the entire cricketing world)" ("Materialist," p. 139). The significance of his emphasis upon the alleged homogenization and instrumentalization of cricket – even at "the peripheries of the Wallersteinian world economic system" – thus becomes clear: the intent is to construe this "flattening out" of the game as evidence of its subordination to the newly globalized and horizontally integrated social logics of standardization and productivism. A second consequence is structurally related to this first (indeed, the two are mutually entailing): it concerns what Surin calls the "internationalization" of cricket – although such is his argument that the terms "globalization" or even "post-nationalization" might have been more appropriate. The argument is that as world cricket has begun to "reflect" the subsumption of society to capital, it has ceased to be "a means of national expression." Surin explicitly evokes this Jamesian formulation in order to refute it: "[t]he claim that cricket is 'a means of national expression'," he writes, "is . . . untenable, especially [now] . . . when capitalism has moved into a globally integrated phase" (p. 120).

Surin devotes a good deal of space to arguing for these twin hypotheses, concerning cricket's homogenization and its post-nationalization. With respect to the former, thus, he maintains that the game is today played in the same "truly contemporary" way everywhere: "[t]he same mode of cricketing 'production' can . . . be found in economically and culturally disparate nations, say, England and Sri Lanka" (p. 139). He adds that "this is only to be expected in 'late capitalism.'" The suggestion is that inasmuch as cricket has "become a kind of engineering" (p. 138), it must be interpreted as having been fully capitalized – or, more specifically, postmodernized, since what is at issue is the belated rationalization or "completion" of the "Bradmanian" ethos of the modern era of the 1930s. "In these times when cricket (like capitalism) is in an integrated global phase," Surin argues,

it is not only a Bradman or a Hutton who can bat like an automaton: today a Hanif Mohammad (the Pakistani who holds the world record for the highest score in first-class cricket) or a Graeme Hick (the white Zimbabwean who in 1988 scored the first quadruple-century in English first-class cricket since 1895) are likely to bat as unrelentingly as any of the great Australian or English batsmen did in the 1930s. (p. 139)

In responding to this argument, it is perhaps necessary only to point to the telltale sleight-of-hand that is evident in Surin's quick reference to "today," when the Hanif Mohammads and Graeme Hicks of the cricketing world are said to be able to bat "as unrelentingly" as did Bradman, Ponsford, Kippax et al. in the 1920s or 1930s. Certainly, the uninformed reader would not know on the basis of Surin's formulation that Hanif Mohammad's record-breaking innings of 499 was made for Karachi against Bahawalpur *almost 40 years ago, in 1958–59* – that is, a full decade prior to the supposed transformations in capitalist social relations upon which Surin predicates his reading of the contemporary situation! Are we then to understand that cricket had already become globally homogenized in the late 1950s, prior to the contemporary integration of capitalism as a world economic system? This, of course, would make the extraordinary flowering of the West Indian team at precisely this point in time more or less incomprehensible. It would also render incomprehensible the subsequent emergence of such exciting strokeplaying Pakistani batsmen of the 1970s, 1980s, and 1990s as Majid Khan, Zaheer Abbas, Imran Khan, Aamir Sohail, Inzamam-ul-Haq, and Saeed Anwar. It is also worth noting, perhaps, that to describe Graeme Hick's batting as "unrelenting" seems generous in the extreme. The inadequacies of Hick's technique, his vulnerability against the fast short-pitched ball slanted into the body or outside the off-stump, have been repeatedly and definitively exposed by such bowlers as Curtly Ambrose and Courtney Walsh of the West Indies and Wasim Akram and Waqar Younis of Pakistan. One must also wonder, moreover, what Surin would have made of Brian Lara's world record innings of 501 not out for Warwickshire (against Durham) in May of 1994. While Lara has indeed revealed a prodigious appetite for run-making since his emergence as a world-class batsman a couple of years ago, his fluid and brilliantly intuitive batsmanship could not possibly be characterized as "unrelenting." There is nothing of the managerial capitalist in Lara's "mode of cricketing 'production'."

With respect to the post-nationalization of cricket, Surin suggests that the ways in which the game at the highest levels has come to be financed and marketed have changed fundamentally in recent years – a pattern of change, he argues, that has "progressively detached" the "economic base of international cricket . . . from the national economies of individual nation-states" ("Materialist," p. 135). At one level, this is a point that can be conceded very readily. Thus Marqusee informs us, with specific reference to the game in England, that the leading sponsors are typically affiliates of transnational corporations, and that the same sectors that dominate the sponsorship of cricket (retail and financial) also dominate the national economy at large:

Texaco chose cricket for its "quintessentially British" image: a "family sport with a diverse audience and one associated with fair play." The

US-based oil company is not the only sponsor for whom cricket's "Eng-lishness" is a prime asset. Cornhill Insurance plc is owned by Allianz AG Holdings in Germany. Fosters is a subsidiary of the Fosters Brewing Group, Australia, which also owns Courage, John Smiths, Websters and now even Watneys. Tetley Bitter is owned by Allied Lyons, a world-spanning food and drink conglomerate. Benson & Hedges is owned by BAT, an international retail giant. AXA Equity and Law is owned by a French-based multi-national . . . At relatively little expense, these trans-national enterprises lease an English national identity from the TCCB [Test and County Cricket Board]. (*Anyone*, p. 121)

For Surin, however, this state of affairs appears to have conse-quences that do not seem to be entailed for Marqusee. Such is the internationalization of the game today, according to Surin, that at the Test match level it "approximates to a well-organized global travel-ing circus," with players continually on the move, from one series in one country to another series in another country; and the upshot of this perpetual movement and season-less, year-round play is that

[t]eams are . . . not as likely to reflect particular national or cultural identities as they were in the past. Gone are the days when a major West Indian test cricketer would live most of the year in, say, Barbados or Antigua and play nearly all his cricket there. "Home" for such a player is now probably only a place for a "holiday" during the off-season. Indeed, after a cricketing career spent in other lands, "home" can become the country where that career was based: for example, Garfield Sobers now lives in Australia, and Sonny Ramadhin, Clairmonte Depeiaza, Alvin Kallicharan and Clive Lloyd (to pick out a few names randomly) are domiciled in Britain. Lloyd, having become a British citizen, even joined the English cricketers Gatting and Emburey in the Conservative Party's "celebrity" campaign during the 1987 General Election. ("Materialist," p. 133)[65]

At the core of the argument here is the claim that the (purportedly) advancing *atypicality* of the lifestyles and social situations of West Indian Test cricketers relative to the West Indian population at large renders them increasingly incapable of bearing the burden of national-popular expression. "On the whole," as Surin puts it,

players of international class today find themselves in a playing environ-ment less directly exposed to a specifically West Indian politics of race . . . to the politics of inter-island rivalry . . . to the struggle for self-govern-ment . . . to the everyday realities of poverty and deprivation in the islands . . . The relationship a top-class cricketer has to his West Indian "base" has thus been quite radically transformed in the course of two decades. (pp. 134–35)

This reasoning seems to me to confuse the problematic of *typicality* with that of political (or ideological) *representation*, as though to speak *for* "the people" (to represent their aspirations through one's own discourse or practice) it was necessary also to be *of* "the people," in the sense of sharing a *habitus* with them. Several points might be made in rejoinder to this conception. First, let us recall that nationalism is *always* an articulatory formation – one in which popular aspirations are both partially constructed and given voice by elite representations. Even if we take to heart Frantz Fanon's evocation of a nationalism that would be capable of standing as "the all-embracing crystallization of the innermost hopes of the whole people,"[66] it is still clear that popular consciousness needs to be thematized, organized, given coherence in nationalist ideology: hence Fanon's term "crystallization." No matter how militant the subaltern classes of a given population might be, nationalist ideology never emerges directly or unmediated from the ranks of "the people." Popular consciousness is central to nationalist ideology; but so too, and unforgoably, is elite discourse.

A second point follows from this first. Surin makes a great deal out of the fact that Sobers now lives in Australia and that Lloyd not only lives in England but has taken out English citizenship and has allowed himself to be associated with the British Conservative Party. The implication is that Sobers and Lloyd are deracinated figures, whose alienation from West Indian life is such as to render them incapable of representing popular West Indian aspirations. But surely it is necessary to distinguish here between "cultural" and "political" forms of expression? What makes Lloyd readable as "of the West Indies" is not his political sensibility, nor his social practice in strict terms, but his square drive, his cover fielding – in short, the way in which he plays cricket.

Let me say something more about the term "readable" here. Insofar as we are considering the matter of the expression of (nationalist) ideology through *cultural* means, the consciousness that is decisive is not that of the player (or players) but that of the crowd, the "people," the West Indian population at large – to which, significantly, Surin makes no reference at all. But one could even say that it is not so much a consciousness as an *intersubjectivity* or *relationship* that is finally at issue: not that obtaining between players and sponsors but that between players and the crowd – a structured relationship, mediated by the text or performance of the game.

Consider the following statement, for instance. The speaker is Curtly Ambrose, who is explaining his feelings after having bowled

West Indies to victory in the Fourth Test against England in Trinidad in March 1994:[67] "I understand how important it is to play my cricket hard. I do it for the people. They expect nothing less and we're very conscious of them whenever we go on to the field. Their love is very strong. It is demanding on you, but it also makes you strong" (quoted in Marqusee, *Anyone*, p. 150). One might, of course, respond that this is just the kind of unselfconsciously nationalist statement that one would *expect* a cricket player who has been chosen to "represent his country" to make. But what interests me is the possibility that Ambrose might be right – that is, that the claims that he makes concerning the complex and elaborately structured bond between representing players and represented "people" might be warranted. Certainly, this is how it seems to Marqusee, who comments that "[i]t is impossible to imagine any contemporary English cricketer speaking this language of solidarity. For Ambrose, as for many West Indies players, there is a living bond with a broader West Indian public. It may often be a fraught relationship, but it is felt by the players as an intimate and inescapable one" (*Anyone*, p. 150). Against Surin, I would want to insist that we carry through the recognition that cricket's social meaning emerges on the basis of its distinctive mode of *representation*. It is not only that the crowd is positively constitutive of the "speech act" of cricket. It is also that cricket's expressivity is formally mediated, which affords it a certain structured impermeability to the naked imperatives of the market.

James's own commentary seems to me to offer a quite decisive rebuttal of Surin's post-representational standpoint in this context. In *Beyond a Boundary*, we find the following passage:

What do they know of cricket who only cricket know? West Indians crowding to Tests bring with them the whole past history and future hopes of the islands. English people, for example, have a conception of themselves breathed from birth. Drake and mighty Nelson, Shakespeare, Waterloo, the Charge of the Light Brigade, the few who did so much for so many, the success of parliamentary democracy, those and such as those constitute a national tradition. Underdeveloped countries have to go back centuries to rebuild one. We of the West Indies have none at all, none that we know of. To such people the three W's, Ram and Val wrecking English batting, help to fill a huge gap in their consciousness and in their needs. In one of the sheds on the Port of Spain wharf is a painted sign: 365 Garfield Sobers. (p. 233)

"365 Garfield Sobers": the reference is to the highest score made by any one batsman in a single Test match innings, and to Sobers, who made it.[68] We have already encountered James's argument that in the West Indies cricket is not only *also* culture, that is, one cultural form among several, but culture itself. But notice too his foregrounding of the social *reception* of cricket: it was not only the rare cricket critic who, watching Sobers send a good length ball racing to the cover boundary with such effortless timing and pinpoint accuracy that the fielders were quite incapable of intercepting it, felt himself or herself to be in the presence of a national cultural treasure. Rather, this was the experience of the West Indian crowd as a whole, as explained by the fact that a popular phrase was coined to describe this very stroke: "Not a man move" (James, *Future*, p. 215). On James's reading, the West Indian crowd is to be understood as a sort of "collective intellectual," the knowing possessor of national culture. Inasmuch as this crowd still strains in its thoughts and actions toward a pan-West Indian consciousness, cricket in the West Indies will continue to be constructed as, and to represent, national culture.[69] As Michael Manley has written, "[t]he West Indies were unable to put a federation together and at times have difficulty in giving life and meaning to their regional economic institutions . . . But when the cricket team is playing the whole area surges together into a great regional hubbub of excitement and involvement" (*History*, 11). Note, however, that Manley's studied use of the term "regional" as distinct from "national" to describe pan-West Indian consciousness in this formulation would have drawn James's censure. For James insisted that what Manley describes as "separate sovereign territories" (*History*, 12) – Jamaica, Antigua, Barbados, and so on – have little viability as independent nation-states, and that pan-West Indian consciousness therefore exists as the only appropriate form of *national* consciousness in the Caribbean. In fact James advocated a federation of the whole Caribbean, explicitly including under this conception Cuba, Haiti, Martinique, Guadeloupe, the Guyanas, and the Dominican Republic, as well as the Anglophone West Indies.[70]

Let us take stock: Surin argues, as we have seen, that James is "somewhat at a loss when it comes to forming an estimation of the extraordinary achievements of Clive Lloyd's team" ("Materialist," p. 137). At the level of the historical narrative of cricket, this is because James is supposedly incapable of appreciating – that is to say, of making sense of – the "fact" that Lloyd's West Indians play the game in the "Bradmanian" style. Underlying this "incapacity" on James's part, however, is a deeper incapacity, namely that he has "no really 'productive' way of talking about capitalism beyond the point at which the European powers gave up the struggle to retain their colonies." This renders him unable, "in his cricketing writings at any rate, to register the full force of the new conjuncture which is integrated world-capitalism" (p. 137). He is

unable to conceive that once the energies released by [decolonization] . . . were stabilized or transmuted by a succeeding phase of capitalism, it would actually become possible for West Indian cricket, "after" Worrell and Sobers, to "complete" something that Bradman and the players of the 1930s were only just in the process of realizing, namely, that cricket could become a kind of engineering. (pp. 137–38)

Surin generously allows that most of James's writing on cricket was produced in the 1950s and 1960s, and that James was therefore only able to "glimpse . . . what Toni Negri and others have been describing to us in considerable detail in recent years" (p. 148). He was not able to "recognize" that one era of capitalist development had been definitively superseded by another. The inference here is that had James been born, say, twenty years later than he was, he would have agreed with Surin's own analysis of contemporary cricket. I do not believe this. On my reading, it is not because James could only glimpse what Surin now claims to be able to see clearly that he failed to produce his own postmodernist analysis of cricket. Rather, it is because his politics and philosophy were, and remained, quite different from Surin's. What is at issue between James and Surin, in other words, is less a matter of a temporal gap than of a sharp ideological divergence. James never accepted the sociohistorical premise of an epochal restructuration of capitalism in the contemporary era; nor would he do so today. He never accepted arguments for the obsolescence of class struggle, or for the redundancy of the received Marxist vocabulary of imperialism, core and periphery, labor, dialectics, and the like; nor would he do so today.[71] He never accepted that "the energies released by [decolonization] . . . were stabilized or transmuted by a succeeding phase of capitalism"; nor would he do so today. He never characterized the West Indies cricket teams "'after' Worrell and Sobers" as "Bradmanian"; nor would he do so today. To the end of his days, James continued to espouse world revolution; to evoke the specter of a vast uprising of the international(ist) working classes; and to hold true to the vision of "socialism or barbarism." He also insisted that, far from having been "stabilized or transmuted," the struggle against imperialism was alive and gaining momentum throughout the "Third World." In all of these contexts, but above all with respect to anti-imperialism, he saw cricket as playing a significant role at the levels of symbolic action and ideological mobilization.

In drawing this chapter to a close, I would like to step back for a moment from the subject of cricket, in order to reflect briefly on James's general significance as a theorist of culture in the modern era. Consider James once again in relation to Raymond Williams. In his 1958 essay, "Culture is Ordinary," Williams, the working class son of a Welsh railwayman, describes his undergraduate education at Cambridge University and writes:

> I was not, by the way, oppressed by Cambridge. I was not cast down by old buildings, for I had come from a country with twenty centuries of history written visibly into the earth: I liked walking through a Tudor court, but it did not make me feel raw. I was not amazed by the existence of a place of learning . . . Nor was learning, in my family, some strange eccentricity; I was not, on a scholarship in Cambridge, a new kind of animal up a brand-new ladder. Learning was ordinary; we learned where we could. Always, from those scattered white houses, it had made sense to go out and become a scholar or a poet or a teacher. Yet few of us could be spared from the immediate work; a price had been set on this kind of learning, and it was more, much more, than we could individually pay. Now, when we could pay in common, it was a good, ordinary life. (p. 5)

Twenty centuries of history there, in that place. Twenty centuries of cultivation and exploitation, of production and social reproduction. It is no wonder that, confronted by someone who boasts that he and his family "came over with the Normans," Williams could imagine himself responding: "Yes, how interesting; and are you liking it here?" (p. 15).

With James it is both the same and different. No twenty centuries of continuous, stably located history: instead, the historical experience of deracination, slavery, and struggle; of colonization, imperialism, and struggle. (West Indians, James observes in his essay "The Making of the Caribbean People," "have been the most rebellious people in history."[72]) And no opportunity, even formally, to claim for himself, a colonial subject, the "good, ordinary life" that Williams is able to put into perspective as *his* birthright. For in James's case it is not merely a matter of class and of the cost of education; it is a matter, too, of race and of colonial domination. There is a magnificent moment in "Culture is Ordinary" in which Williams argues that

> [T]o say that most working people are excluded from [the dominant institutions of bourgeois culture] is self-evident . . . But to go on to say that working people are excluded from English culture is nonsense . . . A great

part of the English way of life, and of its arts and learning, is not bourgeois in any discoverable sense. There are institutions, and common meanings, which are in no sense the sole product of the commercial middle class; and there are art and learning, a common English inheritance, produced by many kinds of men, including many who hated the very class and system which now take pride in consuming it. The bourgeoisie has given us much . . . But this is not to say that contemporary culture is bourgeois culture. (pp. 7–8)

It is a magnificent moment. But it is, so to speak, easy for Williams to say. I mean that it is easier for Williams to say than it would have been for James. And yet, I want to suggest, James often did say it, or something very like it. Culturally and ideologically, this is his central, astonishing achievement. He found a way to redeem this kind of formulation, to strip it of its Eurocentrism by appropriating it, dragging it across the colonial divide in order to make it do his insurrectionary bidding. And this not as a maverick or iconoclast, but as a way of mapping Caribbean identity, the identity, as he never tired of pointing out, of a – perhaps even *the* – paradigmatically modern people. What James does with respect to cricket, he does also with respect to Hegel and Marx, calypso and carnival, "liberty, equality, fraternity," Shakespeare and Thackeray and the Greek polis. It is sometimes observed that a residual Eurocentrism attaches to James's own valorization of Greece, of Shakespeare, and of the French Revolution.[73] This is true in one respect, but not in another. I think it is true that James undervalued the strength and integrity of the African cultural traditions that could not be broken by the middle passage or slavery or colonialism, that outlasted these depredations, and that continue to inform the cultural practices of African diasporic populations everywhere. It is not enough for him to argue that "[t]he Negroes who came from Africa brought themselves," and that this was "something of primary importance" (*Spheres*, 174). Yes, he uses this argument to ground his claim that

[w]here we have had an opportunity to work freely, there we have shown great distinction. Where we have not shown it, it is because we have been prevented. It is not the lack of capacity . . . If those on our backs get off our backs, we shall be able to rise: we have done pretty well with the burdens that we have always carried and are still carrying. (p. 175)

But this defense is pitched at the level of an *abstract* human resiliency and resourcefulness. There is a need to address the African dimensions of Caribbean identity more concretely and substantively than James seems capable of doing.

On the other hand, James's celebration of "Western civilization" (he calls it that himself) should not be mistaken for a fawning romanticism:

I denounce European colonialist scholarship. But I respect the learning and the profound discoveries of Western civilisation. It is by means of the work of the great men of Ancient Greece; of Michelet, the French historian; of Hegel, Marx and Lenin; of Du Bois; of contemporary Europeans and Englishmen like [Richard] Pares and E.P. Thompson; of an African like the late Chisiza, that my eyes and ears have been opened and I can today see and hear what we were, what we are, and what we can be, in other words – the making of the Caribbean people.   (*Spheres*, 179)

This is not only stated, as an intention. It is, I think, borne out in James's work. (He observes rather endearingly at one point that while some of us may believe that we have read *The Black Jacobins*, he did more than that. He wrote it! Yet he adds, and this is crucial: "But it is only in late years that I am able to understand and to appreciate the full significance of what I wrote in that book" [*Spheres*, p. 178].) The task is not to define oneself in relation to Marx and Hegel, Melville and Thackeray. It is to define Marx and Hegel, Melville and Thackeray in relation to oneself, to define cricket and "liberty, equality, fraternity," to define socialism in relation to oneself. It is the making of the *Caribbean* people that interests James, not the making of the English people, not even, despite James's admiration for E.P. Thompson, the making of the English working class.

Referring, in the Haitian context, to Boukman, Toussaint, Dessalines, and the slaves who made the revolution, James observes that "[t]hese are my ancestors, these are my people. They are yours too if you want them" (*Spheres*, p. 187). Elsewhere, as we have seen, he observes of himself that he was a "British intellectual long before I was ten . . . Somehow from around me I had selected and fastened on to the things that made a whole" (*Beyond*, p. 18). Between these two statements, I want to argue, there is not even the shadow of a contradiction. The category that governs their complementarity – their peculiarly contemporary complementarity – is that of totality, a dialectical and historically concrete category, not an abstract and purely philosophical one. In *History and Class Consciousness*, Lukács wrote that

if from the vantage point of a particular class the totality of existing society is not visible; if a class thinks the thoughts imputable to it and which bear upon its interests right through to their logical conclusion and yet fails to strike at the heart of that totality, then such a class is doomed to play only a subordinate role. It can never influence the course of history in either a conservative or progressive direction.   (p. 52)

The significance of James, in these terms, is that in what I think we can only call his *universalism*, he has been able to think the thoughts imputable to him through to their logical conclusion and *succeed* in striking at the heart of Lukács's totality. In common with such other Caribbean thinkers as Aimé Césaire, Frantz Fanon, Edouard Glissant, and Wilson Harris, he has been able to sketch the outlines of a global "counternarrative of liberation."[74] The whole point of the work of these thinkers, as Edward Said has observed of Fanon in particular, is to "bind the European as well as the native together in a new non-adversarial community of awareness and anti-imperialism."[75] Hence James's insistence that it is today impossible to "write of the history and literature" of "Western civilization" without mentioning the names of such figures as Toussaint, Garvey, Maran, Fanon, Carpentier, Padmore, and Sobers (*Spheres*, p. 190). One reads James, in these terms, to discover not only *that* the emancipatory project of modernity is unfinished, but more specifically *why* it is, and *how* – even and especially today – its totalization might be envisaged. For James, as for Lukács and Williams, this remains an urgent task.

4

"Unsystematic fingers at the conditions of the times": Afropop and the paradoxes of imperialism

I would like to begin this chapter, on contemporary African pop music, by referring to a scene from *The Healers*, a novel by the Ghanaian writer, Ayi Kwei Armah. Published in 1979, *The Healers* offers a perspective on the collapse of Ashanti military power and the formal institution of British colonial rule in Ghana in the 1870s. The novel's final pages describe an official ceremony, as the ranks of the British forces against the Ashanti, composed overwhelmingly of African conscripts drawn from the entire region of West Africa, are marshaled to attend the departure for England of the all-conquering British general, Wolseley. Here is how the novel ends:

West Indian soldiers had come with [Wolseley] to the bay, with their guns and musical instruments . . . [They] played solemn music to send the white general off. But once the ship had disappeared, their playing changed. The stiff, straight, graceless beats of white music vanished. Instead, there was a new, skilful, strangely happy interweaving of rhythms, and instead of marching back through the streets the soldiers danced. Others joined them . . . All the groups gathered by the whites to come and fight for them were there and they all danced . . . a grotesque, variegated crowd they made, snaking its way through the town . . .
"It's the new dance," Ajoa said, shaking her head. She spoke sadly, and her sadness was merely a reflection of the sadness of [the other healers] . . . as they watched.
But beside them they heard a long, low chuckle of infinite amusement. It came from Ama Nkroma . . . "It's a new dance all right," she said, "and it's grotesque. But look at all the black people the whites have brought here. Here we healers have been wondering about ways to bring our people together again. And the whites want ways to drive us farther apart. Does it not amuse you, that in their wish to drive us apart the whites are actually bringing us work for the future? Look!"
Together with Ama Nkroma's laughter, tears came to her eyes.[1]

In two respects, this scene is exemplary of the line of argument I shall follow in this chapter. First, there is the recognition, familiar in its structure to any reader of Marx, Fanon, or C.L.R. James, that colonialism creates the conditions of possibility of its own overthrow, since it brings the colonized into existence as a collectivity (however internally divided) whose objective interests are not only diametrically opposed to those of the colonial state, but are also incapable of realization on the terrain of colonialism. Second, there is the identification of a latently resistive dynamic of cultural indigenization. The regimental West Indian guard is spoken of as having appropriated "the white men's instruments." Instruments whose symbolic logic in this normative context is imperial and militaristic are domesticated and made over, refunctioned to bear the imprint of a different – and, indeed, opposing – cultural logic.[2]

In the pages that follow, I want to say something more about this subject of indigenization, taking as my primary example the case of pop music from Zimbabwe in the decolonizing and postcolonial eras. Before turning directly to this music, however, let me pause briefly to consider the concept of indigenization itself, as well as some of the theoretical and ideological implications of using it in cultural analysis.

Many ethnomusicologists and scholars of African culture would reject in principle the idea of taking as one's object of analysis a compound form like African pop music. Their argument would be that the putative "Africanity" of this music has been wholly overdetermined and compromised by "Western" compositional grammars and styles of performance. As Deborah James has recently pointed out, the work of ethnomusicologists of this persuasion "is most often associated with an interest in 'pure' traditional music, and a scorn for hybrid styles or those which have evolved out of the experience of proletarianized communities."[3] James refers especially to Hugh Tracey and his assumptions that "urban African music lacks the formal integrity of its 'traditional' forebears, and that it has been bastardized by its assimilation of Western forms."[4] But similar assumptions are shared by other prominent scholars of African music: the Cameroonian musicologist Francis Bebey, for instance, opens his classic study, *African Music: A People's Art*, with the pointed definition of "[a]uthentic African music" as "the traditional music of the black peoples of Africa."[5] On such definitions, contemporary urban-based African popular musics often find themselves being characterized as "non-traditional" and dismissed as "inauthentic." In general, as

Peter Manuel has observed, "[d]etractors of the new popular musics are apt to criticize what often appears [to them] to be the naive, indiscriminate borrowing of hackneyed Western clichés, and the simultaneous abandonment of rich traditional musical practice." Hybridic forms like highlife or *soukous* are frequently disparaged on the grounds that they lack both "the polyrhythmic complexity of traditional West African music" *and* "the sophisticated harmonies of [their] Western influences" (*Popular*, p. 21).

Several rejoinders to this kind of argument are possible. One can demonstrate – as David Coplan in the case of South Africa, and John Storm Roberts and others in the general case of sub-Saharan Africa, have done – that the "Western" forms by which urban African music has allegedly been compromised are themselves strongly marked by the "African" forms on which they, in turn, were substantially predicated.[6] To take just one example: since at least the 1930s, Latin American and Caribbean musics have extensively influenced playing styles in West and Central Africa. This influence is patently neither coincidental nor the result of any merely contingent factor. Rather it is a matter of what Weberians would call an elective affinity. It derives from the direct and concrete historical link between these cultures.[7] "The musical 'round trip' between Africa and the Caribbean," as Manuel observes in this context,

is particularly notable. Descendents of African slaves in the Americas developed dynamic hybrid musics synthesizing African-derived rhythms and Western melodic and harmonic patterns. Some of these styles – especially the Cuban *rumba* – became widely popular in the Congo and other parts of Africa from the 1950s on, and they generated new hybrids of native African and Afro-Caribbean music. These, in turn, excited the interest of Caribbean musicians in the seventies, stimulating the development of new pop forms like Haitian "mini-jazz." (*Popular*, p. 20)[8]

Similarly, one can put pressure on the essentialist notion of "tradition" that ethnomusicologists like Hugh Tracey and Bebey typically assume. Tracey's son, Andrew, who shares his father's general disapproval of popular and urban styles of African music, has lamented that "[i]n traditional African music these days, you almost never hear the original harmony. There's always someone putting in that third note and you have this sickly-sounding Western harmony all the time."[9] The point here is that the Traceys' idea of a "pure" traditional African music is resolutely unhistorical. As Simon Frith puts it, "there is no such thing as a culturally 'pure' sound."[10] Like all cultural forms everywhere at all times, African music has been cease-lessly in the process of transformation, as it has moved to assimilate, and to accommodate itself to, new sounds, new instruments, new tongues, and new social imperatives. "The 'purity' of third world music" therefore, as Andrew Goodwin and Joe Gore maintain, "must always be questioned not only for dangerous (we would say *racist*) ideological assumptions about the 'authenticity' of non-Western cul-tures, but also for empirical flaws in the argument."[11] To listen – even as a cultural "insider" – to a Mande song, sung in traditional style with kora and balafon accompaniment, is not and has never been to encounter unchanging tradition; rather, it is to grapple – necessarily – with culture as an historical palimpsest: here the phrasing and inton-ation will be melismatic, bespeaking an Islamic influence; here the kora's lyrical range will have been influenced by flamenco guitar, or, in the case of a contemporary musician like Toumani Diabate, by jazz and blues; here the reference will be to a specific historical event; and so on.[12]

It is instructive, in this context, to listen to the work of Salif Keita, on such albums as *Soro* (Mango, 1987), *Ko-Yan* (Mango, 1989), *Amen* (Mango, 1991), and *Folon* (Mango, 1995). By nationality and citizen-ship, Salif Keita is a Malian, born in 1949 into a dynastic lineage descending from the legendary Soundiata Keita, who founded the expansive Mali empire over 750 years ago. Because of his royal birth, his road to musicianship was difficult. As he put it in 1985, in an interview with Chris Stapleton, "I come from a noble family. We are not supposed to become singers. If a noble had anything to say, he had to say it through a griot."[13] Keita's decision to leave school in the late 1960s to become a musician caused an uproar both in his family and in the wider Malian society. Yet if he has set his back against a caste-system that has been upheld in Mali and elsewhere in West Africa for hundreds of years, his music itself demonstrates that he is far from abandoning his cultural roots. Even when his lyrics are addressed prescriptively to the arena of contemporary social exist-ence, thus, they tend to remain scrupulously attentive to Mande history; and a similarly nuanced reworking of traditional forms is evident in his musical arrangements, both with the band Les Ambas-sadeurs and, since 1985, as a solo artist. Built around his remarkably expressive voice, in which the rhythms of the Bambara language are infused with Islamic and Arabic registers, Salif Keita's music is "powered by horns, keyboards and electric guitars which carry the inflections of kora and balafon music" (Stapleton and May, *African*

All-Stars, p. 112). The total effect, as Nii Yamotei has written, is to provide a "powerful, seamless, and highly sensitive melting pot of influences; transplanting the traditional music of the griots into the present. He has blended in other West African influences from Guinea and Senegal, and influences from Cuba, Spain and Portugal, fusing his traditional vocal themes with modern instruments and style."[14] The album *Soro* was recorded at Studio Harry Son in Paris, on a 48-track digital machine. The title track, "Soro (Afriki)" features West African musicians on percussion (trap set drums, congas, djembes), guitars, and vocals, and French session musicians on saxophone, trumpet, trombone, and keyboards. The responsorial Bambara lyrics encourage Africans to "seek happiness in unity," an appeal embedded in the traditional Mande concept of "djibe":

> If a wife is a true partner
> In the home
> We call her "djibe"
>
> "Djibe" is the name we give
> The white horse and honesty
> Sincere and united neighbours
> We call "djibe" too
>
> Africans, let us be "djibe"
> Let's try and find
> Happiness in unity.[15]

The affirmative character of indigenization as a cultural dynamic should not be overstated, of course. In defining a position against essentialism, it is important to avoid an equally idealist theorization of indigenization as "hybridity" or cultural "dialogue." As Ella Shohat has written, a "celebration of syncretism and hybridity per se, if not articulated in conjunction with questions of hegemony and neocolonial power relations, runs the risk of appearing to sanctify the *fait accompli* of colonial violence."[16] We ought not to be in such a hurry to celebrate the syncretic tendencies of contemporary African cultural practice that we overlook the material workings of imperialism, or bracket imperialism as an exclusively "political" phenomenon without implications for the putatively autonomous sphere of culture. Chinua Achebe has pointed out that one cannot talk about "cultural exchange in a spirit of partnership between North and South," because "no definition of partnership can evade the notion of equality," and because there is precious little equality in prevailing North–South relations.[17] The point here is that if we wish to speak of at least some contemporary African music in the light of anti-imperialist cultural struggle, it is necessary to begin by conceding the effectivity and reach of imperialism. This reach is not total: if it were, there would be no countering it. But if it is not total, it is nevertheless extensive, both in political-economic and in ideological terms.

It is worth noting at the outset, for instance, that the six largest Western-based record companies – CBS, EMI, Polygram, Time-Warner, MCA, and RCA – are responsible for producing more than half of all the records, tapes, and compact discs sold in the world today. Together, they "control around two thirds of the world market."[18] "[W]ith their complex system of subsidiaries and licensing arrangements," as Billy Bergman has explained, these transnational corporations are able to exercise an extraordinary influence – both quantitative and qualitative – on the production and distribution of recorded music throughout the "Third World": "They record local music and distribute it to local and, sometimes, international markets. Then they also promote and distribute Top Forties American and British hits with the same fervor that such music is promoted in the United States and Europe" (*Goodtime*, p. 19). Even in countries like Nigeria, where pressure brought to bear by the nationalist Musicians Union eventually led the government in the late 1970s to legislate against the monopolization of the local recording industry by foreign companies, the "growth in Nigerian control over the means of mass-reproducing music" is, as Christopher Waterman has argued, attenuated and radically conditional:

the vigor of the record industry continues to be strongly affected by shifts in Nigeria's balance of trade and in import–export laws, which restrict the flow of raw materials and machinery. Indigenization has not shifted the balance of power between local and foreign concerns, rather it has served to "rationalize the relationship between the Nigerian bourgeoisie and its patron, international capital." It is very difficult for entrepreneurs without ties to foreign corporations to break into the record manufacturing business.[19]

The impact on African popular music of the metropolitan ownership and control of the means of musical production is often decisive. John Miller Chernoff observes that the appropriation of African pop music by transnational record companies is typically conducted "under the formulas of the business."[20] In Africa, as in Europe and the United States, the general process of the commodification of popular music entails "the reinforcement of passive consumption rather than communal performance, and the alienation of the performer from the musical product and the personal audience" (Manuel, *Popular*, p. 15).

In the African case, however, capitalist domination over the labor-power of musicians is secured transnationally, across the interna tional division of labor. Moreover, the marketing of African pop music is sharply oriented toward an "international" (that is, a Western-centered) audience. The music of the most widely publicized African performers has, therefore, characteristically been modified, doctored, finessed, edited, rationalized, and generally "made over" with this "international" audience in mind. As Chernoff notes, "[a] lot of things happen to the music itself" in the course of this appropriation:

We initially receive some predictable compilations, in which songs are shortened for radio slots. First to be edited out are the extended jams, which originally made the music a hit with dancers, as with music from Zaire. Lyric sections are placed first instead of following long instrumental introductions, as with Fela's music. Eventually some players start making shorter songs by themselves, as in the Antilles and in Zaire. Western-style funky passages are excerpted and African-style highlife passages are cut, as with Sunny Ade's early releases. If the songs themselves are not edited, then at least fuzzy and dirty mixes have to be cleaned up in mixing or remixing. The bass is moved back, along with rattles and bells. ("Foreword," p. xiii)

The adverse ideological consequences of this general state of affairs were starkly demonstrated in South Africa in the aftermath of the release of Paul Simon's album, *Graceland*, in 1986. In *Graceland*, as South African musician and musicologist Johnny Clegg observed at the time, Simon

has basically presented to the world an image of South African music that is sixteen, twenty years old. That music . . . you don't hear it any more . . . There's a time warp. And young black musicians are being told by the record companies, 'Look, guys, you've got to go back twenty years, because that's where the market is now.' They feel quite resentful.[21]

The crucial point here is that *Graceland* was so successful internationally that even though there was relatively little resurgence of interest among black South African musicians and audiences themselves in the dated style of music that it embodied, the big recording companies in the country spent a considerable amount of time and energy in the years following its release pressuring sometimes reluctant local musicians to put out music in the *Graceland* idiom, and making it difficult for them to get contracts otherwise. The net result was a restrictive channeling of creative energies, and a compounding of the already exploitative relations between black South African musicians and studio bosses or record producers in the country, the vast majority of whom were white.[22]

Of course it is not as though, prior to the release of *Graceland*, South African popular music had been autonomous in its development or – still less – free of market control and external determination. Helen Kivnick has pointed out that from the outset – and certainly well before 1986 – the marketing of *mbaqanga*, or "township jive," had always involved "at one end of [its] spectrum . . . pickup musicians hired cheaply by studios to record repetitious licks to duplicate a given label's last big hit."[23] By the same token, it is possible to see the history of popular music in South Africa as essentially a history of successive market-governed "importations" from without: big band swing jazz in the 1930s, bebop and rhythm-'n-blues in the 1950s, rock and soul in the 1960s, disco and funk in the 1970s, and so on. What is true of South Africa in this respect, moreover, is true, in the abstract, of the continent at large. Jazz and blues have been a massive shaping influence on the development of popular music in Ethiopia, for instance; and elsewhere, as Manuel has pointed out, audiences in East, West, Central and Southern Africa have danced successively to the Latin rhythms of "the *chachacha*, *rumba*, and the Dominican *merengue*" (*Popular*, p. 87).

Typically, however, it is only when these "imported" musical styles have found favor among significant sectors of the local population, and been "taken up" by them, that they have been able to institutionalize and consolidate themselves. In these terms "importation" has characteristically involved not simply passive reception, but dynamic recuperation. Thus Cuban *rumba* did not merely reproduce itself in Africa in the 1950s; rather, it "generated its own set of hybrid, re-Africanized derivatives" (Manuel, *Popular*, p. 87). Similarly, while rock has, over the course of the past twenty years, represented "the single most pervasive influence" on popular African music, "rock elements [have] not [been] imported indiscriminately"; on the contrary, "most current styles can be regarded as fusions of traditional elements with heavy rock rhythms and instrumentation" (*Popular*, p. 88).[24] In certain cases the "hybrid, re-Africanized derivatives," once institutionalized in a particular region, have themselves gone on to exercise a decisive (and, on some interpretations, damaging) influence on the development of popular music elsewhere on the continent. Thus the *rumba*-derived Congolese *soukous* (known in much of East Africa as *sungura*) is today a dominating cultural force throughout central Africa, and as far afield as Kenya, Angola,

Cameroon, Senegal, and the Ivory Coast. John Storm Roberts has written of *soukous*'s "immense force and flexibility," adding that although it "at first sounds somewhat Latin American . . . there is actually nothing like it in the New World. It seems to have grown partly from localizing techniques . . . and partly from the playing on guitar of lines that, in Cuban music, were brass or sax lines" (*Black Music*, p. 253). Manuel notes that "[s]ince the early 1960s, [*soukous*] has inundated West, East, and even South-Central Africa, often at the expense of local musics" (*Popular*, p. 97). Much the same could be said of South African *mbaqanga*, which has decisively informed – not to say swamped – the development of popular music in such nations as Botswana, Namibia, Malawi, Mozambique, and even Zambia. (For reasons I shall outline below, Zimbabwe represents something of an exception to this general southern African pattern.)

The situation with respect to *Graceland* is, however, decidedly different from the conventional pattern. For while the *Graceland* sound, like bebop and soul before it, served to disrupt and then reconfigure the shape and trajectory of the field of popular music in South Africa (its principles of hierarchization, distributions of value, structures of competition, logics of autonomy and heteronomy, etc.)[25] its intervention was more in the nature of a sudden imposition from above than of a gradual institutionalization, involving appropriation from below. What is objectionable here, in other words, is not the mere fact that the *Graceland* sound was visited upon South Africa from without, but rather that its dissemination throughout the country was so much a matter of top-down determination, more or less wholly indifferent to the response of local (black) musicians and listeners.[26]

The effect of *Graceland*, in short, was to contribute to the *underdevelopment* of South African music. The immanent trajectory of the development of this music was put under threat of destabilization from without, since industry managers within South Africa found themselves in a position from which they were able not only to call for, but actually to enforce, the production of local music in accordance with the world system's dominant consuming interests – those in Europe and the United States. It was this fact, more than any other, that served to render *Graceland* imperialist in its effects.

It might be appropriate at this point to comment briefly on the recuperation of African popular musical styles by Western performers. The work of some of the megastars in the pop music firmament

– among them Paul Simon, David Byrne, Paul McCartney, Brian Eno, Michael Jackson, Madonna, Mick Fleetwood, and Lionel Richie – reveals a profound insensitivity to the politico-ethical implications of cultural appropriation across the international division of labor. Even in the best of the work of these musicians – I am thinking, for instance, of the mordantly witty mock-lament, "Nothing But Flowers," off the 1988 Talking Heads album *Naked* (Fly/Sire), or of any of the tracks off *Graceland* – there is a distressing unilateralism of influence. While "Nothing But Flowers" features Abdou M'Boup on congas, Yves N'Djock on guitars, and Brice Wassy on shaker, and has a distinctly West African feel about it, it remains wholly and unrepentantly Euro-American in its lyric reference. The discrepancy between the self-conscious "One-Worldism" of the music and the unselfconscious "First-Worldism" of the lyrics is discomfiting, and not in a productive sense:

> Here we stand
> Like an Adam and an Eve
> Waterfalls
> The Garden of Eden
> *Two fools in love*
> So beautiful and strong
> The birds in the trees
> Are smiling upon them
> From the age of the dinosaurs
> Cars have run on gasoline
> Where, where have they gone?
> Now, it's nothing but flowers
> There was a factory
> Now there are mountains and rivers . . .
> We caught a rattlesnake
> Now we got something for dinner . . .
> There was a shopping mall
> Now it's all covered with flowers . . .
> If this is paradise
> I wish I had a lawnmower

It is hard to rid oneself of the suspicion that the organizing logic of this composition is that of advanced capitalist consumerism: as though from the center of the world system – his studio in Manhattan – David Byrne had selected diverse sounds, rhythms, and musical motifs from all over the world out of a catalogue, and blended them into an exotic and hi-tech backdrop for his parodic, postmodern, but paradoxically *stabilizing* play on nature and culture.[27] Similarly, while Simon draws his musical inspiration in *Graceland* not only from

Sotho, Shangani, Zulu, and other South African musics, but also from West Africa,[28] Cajun Louisiana, and Chicano Los Angeles, most of his lyrics reveal a complete lack of cultural dialogism. Here, for instance, is the improbable opening verse from the *mbaqanga*-based track, "Gumboots":

> I was having this discussion
> In a taxi heading downtown
> Rearranging my position
> On this friend of mine who had
> A little bit of a breakdown
> I said breakdowns come
> And breakdowns go
> So what are you going to do about it
> That's what I'd like to know
>
> You don't feel you could love me
> But I feel you could

There are even occasions on *Graceland* in which Simon's lyrics seem actively to contribute to imperialist assumptions about Africa and the "Third World." The album's opening track, "The Boy in the Bubble," begins as follows:

> It was a slow day
> And the sun was beating
> On the soldiers by the side of the road
> There was a bright light
> A shattering of shop windows
> The bomb in the baby carriage
> Was wired to the radio
>
> These are the days of miracle and wonder
> This is the long-distance call
> The way the camera follows us in slo-mo
> The way we look to us all
> The way we look to a distant constellation
> That's dying in the corner of the sky
> These are the days of miracle and wonder
> And don't cry, baby, don't cry

It could be maintained, perhaps, that these lyrics are addressed precisely to the mass-mediatization of "Third World" struggles and realities, and that they constitute an implicit critique of the kind of coverage typically extended to these struggles and realities by the Western media agencies. But even on these (heteronomous) terms, compare "The Boy in the Bubble" with the Police's "Driven to Tears," off their album *Zenyatta Mondatta* (1980):

Seems that when some innocent dies
All we can offer them is a page in some magazine
Too many cameras and not enough food
This is what I've seen.

It is revealing that where the Police track focuses on underdevelopment and the indifference with which wealthy states deny humani-
tarian assistance to populations in need, "The Boy in the Bubble"
broaches the subject of Western media coverage of the "Third World"
through the massively statist discourse of terrorism. Especially if we
situate Paul Simon's lyrics in the context of the "armed struggle" in
mid-1980s South Africa – in which the African National Congress
was scrupulously attempting to avoid attacks on civilian targets that
would have enabled P.W. Botha's regime to brand it unproblematically as a "terrorist" organization – they seem singularly inappropriate and ill-advised. And they are scarcely atypical. It is not for
nothing that the multiracial hard rock band, Living Colour, should
have chosen to spoof Simon in "Elvis is Dead," a track on their 1990
album, *Time's Up*. In *Graceland*'s title track, Simon had sung of having
"a reason to believe / We all will be received / In Graceland." In "Elvis
is Dead," we find what music critic John Pareles calls "a sly reversal"
of these lines. Living Colour sing "I got a reason to believe we all
won't be received at Graceland." The reference is both to the allegedly
racist nature of some of Presley's public statements and to Simon's
wholesale neglect of the question of race in the lyrics of *Graceland*.[29]

Graceland is produced by Warner Brothers Records. *Naked* is produced by Sire Records Company, but marketed by Warner Brothers.
Until fairly recently, transnational corporations were responsible for
almost all of the recording that took place in Africa, and it was only
the superstars in the African popular musical firmament – musicians
like Manu Dibango, Franco, and Tabu Ley – who were able to exercise
any creative control in the production, distribution, and marketing of
their music. Today the situation is somewhat different: on the one
hand, there has been a proliferation of small, predominantly private-
ly owned, recording companies in several African states; on the other
hand, a number of European- and American-based independent
companies have emerged to challenge the dominance of the transna-
tionals. It is these independents – labels like Sterns, Earthworks,
GlobeStyle, Oval Records, Shanachie, WOMAD, Rounder, Rykodisc,
and Discafrique – that have been largely responsible for the recent
explosion of interest in African music among Euro-American listeners. To date, as Ronnie Graham has written, their contribution has

been a positive one. Founded by individuals with "[e]nthusiasm, imagination, a background in Africa and, most of all, access to 'progressive capital,'" they "have been able to make significant contributions to the promotion of African music while, in the main, correctly interpreting trends originating in Africa and throwing their meager resources behind these innovations."[30]

Zimbabwe has been one of the African countries best served by the independent record labels. Doubtless this is partly a matter of luck: the emergence of the independents, and of Euro-American interest in African music, happened to coincide with Zimbabwe's acquisition of political sovereignty in 1980 and the subsequent burgeoning of the music industry in that country. But one should not underestimate the extent to which, reciprocally, Zimbabwe's widely publicized and internationally popular accession to sovereign statehood after years of struggle served as a catalyst, stimulating Western-based audiences to listen to music from that country.

The recent history of music in Zimbabwe makes for a remarkable narrative. One can glean the centrality of the national liberation struggle merely from a casual recitation of the names of leading bands: Thomas Mapfumo and the Blacks Unlimited, the Bhundu Boys,[31] the Marxist Brothers, Ephat Mujuru and the Spirit of the People, the Fallen Heroes, Zexie Manatsa and the Green Arrows, Susan Mapfumo and the Black Salutarys, Robson Banda and the New Black Eagles, and many others.

In the precolonial era, the music of the Shona people in what would become Zimbabwe was founded on the *mbira*, a legendary instrument found in many parts of Africa and consisting of a set of between eight and fifty keys laid over a usually flat soundboard, and typically placed in a box resonator or some other device for amplifying the sound.[32] Strongly associated with Shona religious and artistic practices, the *mbira* was ruthlessly disparaged, in the years following colonial conquest, by colonial officials and European missionaries. Performers often "found themselves subject to intense religious indoctrination as well as ridicule and abuse for being mbira players" (Berliner, *Soul*, p. 240). As a result of these pressures,

mbira music suffered a decline in popularity in certain parts of the country . . . It would appear . . . that for a period of time the older generation of mbira players had difficulty finding members of the younger generation to whom they could impart their knowledge of mbira music. Young Shona students . . . had had a negative image of traditional African culture instilled in them and they therefore shunned identification with the ways of the elders. Those individuals who showed musical skill gravitated toward the guitar rather than the mbira ... In a sense, for a generation of Africans the guitar and the mbira came to symbolize a dichotomy of life-styles and values. Africans associated the mbira with the poverty of the reserves and with things "unChristian" and "old-fashioned," while the guitar represented the wealth and glamor of the cities and things "modern" and "Western." (pp. 240–41)

This dichotomy, characteristic of the years between 1920 and 1960, and so obviously convenient for the purposes of colonial rule, was challenged and eventually shattered by the rise of nationalism and the coming of the liberation struggle in Zimbabwe. Anti-colonial nationalists began to pay attention to the *mbira* precisely *because* it was regarded with contempt by the colonial authorities; and when, during the liberation struggle, the countryside became the resistance movement's center of gravity, the cultural significance of the instrument was, however belatedly, once again recognized.

Remarkably, however, the return to the *mbira* did not in this case constitute a mere nativist gesture. On the contrary, as the struggle intensified, a remarkable fusion of *mbira* sounds and conventions, Western instrumentation, and modern means of communication took the war to the remotest regions of the country. The fusion was called *chimurenga*, the Shona word for struggle – and *chimurenga* came to refer both to the war of liberation and to the style of music that spread its message. From outside the country every evening at 8 p.m., Radio Mozambique broadcast the liberation movement's news program, "Voice of Zimbabwe" on short wave and medium wave. It was picked up throughout Zimbabwe, despite the efforts of the Rhodesian government to jam the signal, to restrict the ownership of transistor radios, and to market a new cheap transistor receiving only FM signals. The most popular feature of the "Voice of Zimbabwe" broadcasts was the "*Chimurenga* Requests" segment, in which listeners' written requests for *chimurenga* songs would be entertained. Most of these songs had been written by fighters in the various guerrilla bases in Mozambique and elsewhere. Usually traditional in structure and melody, they were sung in Shona, Sindebele, and other Zimbabwean languages and tended, as one might expect, to be explicit and direct in their lyric reference:

> People of Zimbabwe
> Living under oppression
> The world is changing
> Arise! Arise![33]

(Alex Pongweni offers a five-part typology of the *chimurenga* songs sung by "liberation choirs": songs of conscientization, songs of "argument by proxy"; songs appealing to ancestral spirits; songs appealing to the people for assistance and expressing gratitude to the people for assistance rendered; and songs addressing the past, present, and future. *"Muka! Muka!"* is listed by Pongweni as a conscientization song. His translation of the second verse of the song is rather different from that offered by Julie Frederickse, and cited above. Translating *"Muka! Muka!"* as "Wake up! Wake up!" Pongweni's version runs as follows:

> Sons and daughters of Zimbabwe,
> The whole world has left us in our troubles,
> The world is upside down,
> Wake up, oh please wake up.   [*Songs*, p. 32])

Music from the *"Chimurenga* Requests" program was, of course, banned in Ian Smith's Rhodesia itself. In the mid-1970s, however, Thomas Mapfumo began to develop an "internal" variant of the form. At that time, the dominant shaping influence on Zimbabwean pop music was Cuban-derived Congolese *rumba*. (Other major influences were American soul, funk, and rhythm-'n-blues, reggae, and South African township jive.) Instead of basing himself on the sounds of *soukous*, though, Mapfumo predicated his music on the ancestral rhythms and cadences of the *mbira*, utilizing guitars which, finger-picked, mimicked the *mbira* sound, producing driving guitar lines made up of discrete but cascading notes. Recording and performing in public in Zimbabwe, Mapfumo obviously could not duplicate the outspokenness of music from the Requests program. Here, too, however, confronted by the problem of censorship, he was able to formulate a tradition-based solution. For historically, as Paul Berliner has observed, ambiguity and innuendo have been central features in the performance of *mbira* music: "Since subtlety is an important element in the art of . . . [*mbira* playing], performers strive to express themselves indirectly at times, and members of the audience must guess at the meaning of their words. It is not uncommon for individuals listening to a performance of mbira music to derive differing meanings from the singer's lines" (*Soul*, p. 177). This customary motif was tailor-made for incorporation into the underground *chimurenga* music pioneered by Mapfumo. Mapfumo himself attained enormous popularity in Zimbabwe in the late 1970s on the strength of a string of releases that alluded indirectly to the liberation struggle. These tracks were never played on the radio; but their indirection and apparent apoliticality were for the most part sufficient to ensure that they were not banned outright; and despite the lack of radio play, and the total absence of publicity, several of them became best-sellers in Zimbabwe. One of these was *"Pamuromo Chete"* ("These Are Mere Words"), whose lyrics give some idea of the mode of address of Mapfumo's music in the 1970s:

> Some of our people, Lord,
> Live as squatters at the Market Square;
> Some of our people, Lord,
> Have no place to go;
> Some of our people, Lord,
> Are suffering;
> Some of our people, Lord,
> Are existing as strays.
>
> These are mere words.
> These are mere words.   (quoted in Frederickse, *None*, p. 107)

Mapfumo has said of this song that it

wasn't being sung directly. I was telling Mr. Smith that there were people in such trouble that all his talking was mere words, talk without substance. He was saying that never in a thousand years would we have a majority government. And I was saying that people will fight for the freedom they want . . . The people understood. They knew what I was talking about.   (quoted in Frederickse, *None*, p. 108)

Mapfumo himself was made to pay for his activism. He was continually harassed by the Rhodesian authorities. On one occasion he was detained for ninety days without trial. On another occasion he was kidnapped. He was forced to perform at political rallies for Bishop Abel Muzorewa, a conservative black political figure broadly aligned with the ruling white Rhodesian regime. And he was routinely summonsed to police stations and subjected to interrogation.

Mapfumo played alongside Bob Marley at Zimbabwe's independence ceremony in April 1980. Since then, his career has gone from strength to strength. The independence period itself saw the release of several songs glorying in the success of the national liberation struggle and, in more somber vein, attempting to weigh the continuing obstacles to prosperity. In *"Ndamutswa Nengoma"* ("Drums Have Woken Me Up"), for instance, Mapfumo sings that

> The sun has risen forever
> There will never be darkness again in Zimbabwe
> It has dawned forever

Let's work together – let's have socialism . . .
I have been asleep
Drums have woken me up.[34]

Similar sentiments are voiced in tracks like *"Kwaedza Mu Zimbabwe"* ("It Has Dawned in Zimbabwe") and *"Nyarai"* ("Be Ashamed") – the former purely celebratory, the latter urging "reactionaries" to abandon their opposition to Robert Mugabe's new government.[35] Already by independence, however, Mapfumo was beginning to turn his commitment and political vision to the problems of postcolonial development in Zimbabwe. In *"Chauya Chirizevha"* ("Rural Life Is Back"), composed before independence, for instance (and included on *The Chimurenga Singles*), he addressed the questions of reconstruction, and of the return of citizens to their homes in the countryside:

> The Chief was really saddened
> Seeing all his people come back
> To rural life
>
> Some lost their legs
> Some died there (in the bush)
> Some died in their homes
> Some fled their homes because of the war
>
> Today the war is over
> For sure the war is over
> And finished, Chief.

(A similar song, entitled "Communal Life Has Been Destroyed," is analyzed by Pongweni, whose translation runs as follows:

> War unleashes suffering,
> It opens the flood gates of hell,
> To swallow the innocent.
>
> Some of our people lost their limbs,
> Others their life on the spot,
> Some were roasted alive in their huts,
> While the lucky found refuge in the towns.
>
> It melts my heart to recount these things.
> My song is a chronicle of sad events.
> I cannot keep these happenings out of my mind,
> They haunt me!   [*Songs*, pp. 96–99])

This extension in the reference of Mapfumo's music has continued throughout the 1980s and into the 1990s. The results can best be appreciated on *Corruption* and *Chamunorwa* ("What Are We Fighting For?"), two albums by Mapfumo and the Blacks Unlimited, released – to considerable fanfare – by Island Record's Mango subsidiary in

1989 and 1991, respectively. *Corruption*, in particular, offers a superb example of politically committed popular music. Recorded at Shed Studios in Harare, the production values are extremely high. Mapfumo sings about the legacy of the liberation struggle in *"Chigwindiri"* ("A Very Strong Person"); but most of the tracks on the album are devoted to postcolonial issues of class division, political disunity, and public morality. Similarly, where some tracks, like *"Muchadura"* ("You Will Confess"), are still instrumentally reminiscent of the electric *mbira* sound of *chimurenga* music, others sample freely from reggae, *kwela*, *mbaqanga*, funk, and *sungura* styles.[36]

This tendency to reach out beyond the *chimurenga* sound to other musical styles, while retaining the political focus of *chimurenga*, typifies Zimbabwean pop music in the 1980s and 1990s. One observes it, for instance, in the music of such outfits as the Four Brothers, Stella Rambisai Chiweshe and the Earthquake, the Jairos Jiri Sunshine Band, the Sungura Boys, Oliver Mtukudzi, and the Bhundu Boys. Until their cohesiveness was undermined by the departure of Biggie Tembo and the untimely deaths, first of David Mankaba and then of his replacement, Shepherd Munyama, the Bhundu Boys were the only Zimbabwean band whose prestige and popularity, both within Zimbabwe and internationally, rivaled Mapfumo's. Like Mapfumo, they freely expressed in their lyrics their solidarity with anti-imperialist struggles in Zimbabwe and throughout Africa. Their outstanding third album, *True Jit* (Mango, 1988), for instance, was dedicated "to Robert Mugabe and the others who restored sanity to our country." Yet the sound of the Bhundu Boys is quite unlike that of Mapfumo and the Blacks Unlimited. After all, the *jit* to which their album title refers is the name of a young people's dance music, vibrant, heavily percussive, and vocally melodic. The band's commitment to *jit*-jive, as Stapleton has noted, puts them "at some distance from the elders of modern Zimbabwe pop, among them Thomas Mapfumo, who base their repertoire around the ancient mbira tradition" (*African All-Stars*, p. 221). Certainly, Mapfumo's damped *mbira* guitar style remains a heavy influence on a track like *"Chemedzevana"* off *True Jit*, where in counterpoint with the percolating bass line, it provides the rhythmic anchor for the song's explorations into different musical domains. Yet the track is more noteworthy, perhaps, for its incorporation of elements from other southern and central African popular musics, a true case of "South–South dialogue." The general pacing of the song, for instance, recalls the temper of *marabi* music from South Africa. By the same token, the jangling, bell-like guitar lines of the climax are reminiscent of the chromaticism of Congolese *soukous*, as is the recognizably Latin-derived brass section. One recalls Bergman's discussion of the similarities between *chimurenga* and *soukous*: "as in Congolese music . . . [*chimurenga*] harmonies are filled out by horn lines and the dance momentum is effected by a quasi-rhumba bass. But the guitars are even faster and more twangy than in Zaire" (*Goodtime*, p. 120).

Another track from *True Jit*, entitled "*Vana*" ("The Children"), is even more remarkable. Formally, like "*Chemedzevana*," the track is based not on the *mbira*-sound but on *soukous*, although it employs in addition the call-and-response chorus of male voices that, in various modes, accompanied and unaccompanied, represents one of the distinctive features of southern African music in general. Yet if the track therefore has a *transnational* feel to it, it is nevertheless clear that what is involved is not in any sense a post-Independence dissipation of *chimurenga* music into a depoliticized "Afropop." On the contrary, "*Vana*" might not at first *sound* like *chimurenga* music, but lyrically it is entirely *about chimurenga*. It is composed in Shona, but features one verse in English, declaimed over a solid rhythmic groove to the accompaniment of a tense, high-pitched, staccato guitar line, echoing like machine-gun fire:

> This song is dedicated to all our brothers and sisters
> Who were fighting for our liberation in Zimbabwe
> Who fought and died in the bushes of Zimbabwe
> The lions were eating the children
> They were left to be swollen by the sun
> When this song was sung, *vana* (the children)
> Of Zimbabwe were fighting for our liberation
> My friend Theo didn't come home
> But I knew we would overcome in the struggle.

The sustainedly melodic passages of this track are predicated on traditional melodies of the kind that were taken up and modified by fighters during the years of the liberation struggle. One notices also the characteristically indirect and metaphorical quality of the lyrics – "The lions were eating the children / They were left to be swollen by the sun" – and the self-conscious internationalism achieved not only through the use of English but, more specifically, through the allusion to globally current progressive slogans like "We shall overcome." Within the Zimbabwean context, in short, "*Vana*" – like the brilliant "*Viva Chinhoyi*" on *Pamberi!* (Mango, 1989) – might be said to repre-

sent an attempt to consolidate the gains of the revolution by extending the range of *chimurenga* music and broadening its musical vocabulary.

Pamberi! was the Bhundu Boys' fourth album, and the last before
the death of bassist David Mankaba and the departure of Biggie
Tembo from the band. The Bhundu Boys have continued to tour and
play concerts, and have released further albums, among them *Friends
on the Road* (Cooking Vinyl, 1993) – a disappointing venture, whose
good intentions and ideologically impeccable sentiments cannot
compensate for its listless and even banal sound – and the far more
successful *Muchiyedza* ("Out of the Dark," Cooking Vinyl, 1997). For
his part, Biggie Tembo has released *Out of Africa* (Cooking Vinyl,
1992), which, while manifestly not of the quality of the first four
Bhundu Boys albums, nevertheless features several intriguing tracks.
Among these are "Mozambique," with its affirmation of the role
played by the newly empowered FRELIMO government in that country in supporting and promoting the Zimbabwean liberation struggle
despite the brutal retaliation of the Rhodesian security forces; and
"Harare Jit," which celebrates the power of music (and, by implication, culture generally) to promote internationalist affinities and solidarities. Tembo now plays with the Ocean City Band.

One of the most interesting of the musicians to have emerged as a
popular force in Zimbabwe since independence is Stella Rambisai
Chiweshe, an accomplished *mbira* player who manages to wear the
twin hats of pop musician and *maridzambira* (she has been involved,
since independence, with the National Dance Company of Zimbabwe). As Florian Hetze notes, Chiweshe's work has spanned the
range from spirit worship to "weddings, funerals, all kinds of dances,
ceremonies, chief's courts, processions, business inaugurations, political gatherings, parties and concerts."[37] Chiweshe herself identifies
the liberation struggle as having created the conditions of possibility
for her own emergence as a *mbira* player. Underscoring the research
claims of Berliner, cited earlier, she recollects that

[t]he government made it possible for me to be free to play. Before
independence you weren't allowed to play mbira on stage. Before, we
were wrapping them up to hide them. Because the missionaries were
saying if you do these things, it's Satan's work, it's uncivilized, you will
go to hell. So we grew up to think that this was something dirty to do. But
because it is spiritual, in the people and in the soil, this strong feeling of
wanting to play keeps coming back. This feeling was stronger than their
words.[38]

Certainly, the 1990 album *Ambuya?* reflects Chiweshe's full endorsement of the general ideological problematic that has sustained popular musical production in Zimbabwe since the *chimurenga* years. The tracks "*Chachimurenga*" and "*Ndinogarochema*" ("I Am Always Crying") are strictly comparable to the best work of Thomas Mapfumo. The former assesses the gains and costs of the liberation struggle, and links this struggle to the campaign to end apartheid in South Africa. The latter pays tribute to Samora Machel of Mozambique. Chiweshe's music differs from Mapfumo's, however, in being more profoundly rooted in the received conventions of *mbira* playing in Zimbabwe. This "classical" dimension, already fundamental to Chiweshe's work on *Ambuya?* and *Shungu* – a live album recorded in Germany in 1992 (Piranha, 1994) – becomes even more pronounced on the two subsequent albums *Chisi* (Piranha, n.d.) and *Kumusha* (Piranha, n.d.). Besides the *mbira* of Chiweshe and Virginia Mukwesha,[39] *Chisi* features *marimba, hosho, ngoma*, and percussion in front of a support section comprising electric bass, guitars, and drums. *Kumusha*, for its part, is a solo album dedicated to traditional *mbira* music.

A certain irony attends the "traditionalism" of Chiweshe's *mbira* playing, since, as many commentators have noted, women have customarily been excluded from assuming the position of *maridzambira* in Zimbabwe. Here again we must note that if the liberation struggle enabled the *mbira* to be repositioned as a central component of the national culture, this repositioning did not amount to a return to the *status quo ante*. On the contrary, as with *rai* music in Algeria, so too with *chimurenga* in Zimbabwe: the forging of a national consciousness in the liberation struggle enabled some women to challenge their traditionally subordinate roles in the field of cultural production, and to assume commanding and directorial positions.[40] The specifically *feminist* dimension of Chiweshe's practice as a musician is significant and unambiguous. (As director of the Network of Female Artists in Zimbabwe, for instance, she has been a tireless campaigner for gender equity in the field of culture.) Yet there is no contradiction between her feminist commitments and her radical *nationalism*. On the contrary, as with the Algerian singer Djura, the South African Miriam Makeba, and the Malian Oumou Sangare, among many others, nationalist consciousness provides both a point of inspiration and a ground (or field of application) for Chiweshe's feminist politics.[41]

In the Western media, the mass-marketing of Afropop, and the recent incorporation of African, Caribbean, and Latin rhythms and styles into mainstream Euro-American rock music are often hailed as a welcome development, on the grounds that they have helped to breathe new life into an otherwise increasingly routinized cultural domain. A glance at Top Forty charts or radio playlists far from persuades one that "world music" has in fact helped to revitalize its Euro-American counterpart. Still, there is perhaps some validity to this claim. It is unquestionably true, for example, that many thousands of Western-based listeners with no previous exposure to South African music experienced the relatively unfamiliar and, to them, "exotic" sounds of *Graceland* as exhilarating. As Chernoff has observed, these listeners turned "to the music for new kinds of sounds, curious textures, intriguing rhythms, fresh harmonies. [They were] looking at African music as a source of new ideas, as an addition to what [they] ha[d], as a style to take parts of" ("Foreword," p. xii). From one vantage point, it might seem churlish and – worse – elitist for us to impugn or belittle this enthusiastic and, on the face of it, generously open-minded response. After all, as new world music fans have often reminded me over the course of the past decade, they would never have found out about such musicians as the Boyoyo Boys, Ladysmith Black Mambazo, Stimela, or Youssou N'Dour had it not been for Paul Simon and *Graceland*. Hence, arguably, the thrust of Martin Roberts's observation that "[t]he *Graceland* album and tour played an important role in launching the international careers of Southern African musicians such as Hugh Masakela [*sic*], Miriam Makeba, and the a cappella group Ladysmith Black Mombazo [*sic*]. Senegalese vocalist Youssou N'Dour gained similar recognition through recording projects with Peter Gabriel and Paul Simon" ("'World Music'," p. 232).

While the validity of Roberts's claim can freely be conceded with respect to musicians like N'Dour, Joseph Shabalala, or Ray Phiri, the "international careers" of Masekela and Makeba were "launched" years before *Graceland*, of course – as long ago, indeed, as the early 1960s. It also seems to me a remarkable fact that the fierce debates about cooptation and cultural imperialism that were occasioned by the release of *Graceland* evidently took Paul Simon himself by surprise. He attempted to defend himself by insisting that since he had paid all of the musicians who had worked on *Graceland* at the going American studio rates, he had not been guilty of exploiting anyone. This defense misses the point, of course: exploitation under capitalist social relations is rarely (and even then only incidentally) a matter of *personal* calculation or intent. Rather, it is *structural* in nature, simultaneously marked and masked by its relative *impersonality*. Racism (or cultural imperialism), as Tunde Jegede and Galina Chester have argued in a slightly different context, "stems from and is perpetrated by an authoritative system which only those few in positions of power can direct to advantage."[42] It is this argument, above all, that Simon seemed incapable of assimilating.

More significantly, I believe that to argue as Roberts does here is to assume an exclusively "First Worldist" perspective, one incompatible with a progressive, internationalist politics. Ultimately, it does not suffice to consider matters solely from the perspective of the Western-based pop music enthusiast. To do so is to consign *African pop music* in advance to secondary status, as an auxiliary phenomenon – paradoxically, indeed, as a phenomenon *within Euro-American pop music*. In this respect, as in others, it is necessary to think both globally and systematically.

Of course, thinking globally and systematically does not involve ignoring the fact that a lot of Afropop on the market today has been produced entirely *for* Western consumption and can therefore quite legitimately be categorized under the rubric of Euro-American pop music. What is true of the music of David Byrne or Paul Simon is true, too, of much contemporary Afropop. As Jane Kramer has written, with reference to the situation in Paris (a city sometimes referred to, only half-ironically, as "the capital of African music"), many of

the African groups that Parisians like so much are really ordinary rock groups – guitar, bass guitar, keyboard, and drums – with the native instruments thrown in like spice, for flavor. Certainly there is not much harmonic complexity in most of the African music you are likely to hear on [the radio] . . . or find on cassettes [in music stores] . . . The international circuit that Parisians talk about can take the rhythmic – really the polyrhythmic – complexity that African music does have and reduce it to French pop standards, to a kind of rock monotone. Unless a group is tough and confident . . . it can make that music as banal as elevator songs.[43]

A similar point has been made, with a qualified nod toward Horkheimer and Adorno, by the South African musician, Johnny Clegg. In *The Sounds of Soweto*, a television interview recorded in 1988, Clegg drew attention to the homogenizing effects of the commodification of African music, referring to the "Western cultural monster which feeds off anything new, takes it, perverts it and reduces it to a common denominator, and then markets and sells it."[44]

Yet one needs to proceed carefully here. For many Western-based popular music critics, anxious, no doubt, to establish their credentials by parading their hostility to the culture industry, have responded to such formulations as these by taking up a "Third Worldist" position that is not only undialectical but even reactionary. Consider, for instance, the terms of Richard Gehr's recent critique of Johnny Clegg himself. Writing in the avant-gardist *New Trouser Press Record Guide,* Gehr trashes Clegg's music with the band Juluka, dismissing it as "a mush of sweet, laid-back California style harmonies over a loping backbeat, with mild anti-apartheid sentiments."[45] And Clegg's subsequent music with his band Savuka receives still harsher treatment: according to Gehr, it is

even more Western-oriented. The slicker production of *Third World Child* relieves it of the simple, unassuming emotionality of township music. The self-conscious, breast-beating lyrics of the title track and "Berlin Wall" suggest that Clegg's gunning for the Nobel peace prize while attempting to forge a calculated commercial sound. Too bad Paul Simon beat him to the bank.[46]

This is a deplorable piece of criticism, displaying a profound ignorance of Clegg's work and of South African culture and society generally. Against Gehr, it seems worthwhile to record that during the several years that Juluka was made up only of Clegg and Sipho Mchunu, it had an almost exclusively black audience in South Africa. By the same token, it seems necessary to insist that there has been nothing "mild" about the "anti-apartheid sentiments" of Clegg's music over the course of the past fifteen years. On the contrary, such tracks as *"Asimbonanga* (Mandela)" ("We Have Not Seen [Mandela]"), off Savuka's *Third World Child* album (EMI, 1986) – with its recitation of the names of Mandela, Steven Biko, Victoria Mxenge, and Neil Aggett, political activists silenced or murdered by the apartheid regime – or "One (Hu)Man One Vote," off *Cruel, Crazy, Beautiful World* (EMI, 1989) – written in memory of the assassinated university lecturer David Webster – are as tough, politically committed, resourceful, and Afrocentric as any of Bob Marley's reggae tracks or Thomas Mapfumo's *chimurenga* releases.

Yet my purpose in quoting Gehr's broadside is not so much to protest its insufficiency as criticism, patent in any event, as to draw attention to the inadequacy of the way of thinking about African popular music that it exemplifies. For it is clear that what Gehr dislikes above all else about Clegg's music is its active embrace of certain "Western" musical idioms. Gehr does not complain about the fact that Savuka, a South African band, has added guitar techniques from Zimbabwe, Malawi, and elsewhere on the continent to its fundamentally South African mix. But he strongly objects to the "Western-orientation" that he sees as being the necessary consequence of Savuka's use of synthesizers, folk-rock harmonies, and multi-track recording facilities. It seems that there is a little bit of the ethnomusicological purist – and, indeed, of the Orientalist – in Gehr. He likes his Afropop not only "simple" and "unassuming," but also uncontaminated by "Western" pop harmonies, rhythms, and modes of production.

In its dogmatism, this way of thinking is unhistorical and does violence to the essentially syncretic form of *all* African pop music today. Celebrating the African pop music that he *does* like for its authenticity, its radical otherness from Western pop, Gehr paradoxically exoticizes it, thereby contributing to a situation in which African pop music is afforded only ghettoized airplay on specialty radio and television programs, or written about only in isolated feature articles. The existence of shelves marked "International" or "World Music" in music stores throughout Europe and the United States testifies to the pervasiveness of this latently essentialist conception. "World" music, it would seem, is to be categorized above all through reference to its *difference* from the prevailing "Western" forms: it is not rock, not rhythm-'n-blues, not soul, not reggae (a rich irony here, of course, given the fact that most reggae music is still produced in Jamaica by Jamaicans), not punk, and not jazz.

In Gehr's view, the "Western-orientation" of Savuka's *Third World Child* is the motor behind both the album's "commercialism" and its allegedly opportunistic politics. The clear inference is that an "authentic" African popular music would be less market-aware and more explicitly militant in its lyrics. The truth, however, turns out to be rather more complicated than this. For the lyrics of such different forms of African popular music as *juju*, *makossa*, *fuji*, highlife, *mbaqanga*, and *soukous* are, in general, squarely accommodationist. Chernoff points out that, "like their traditional counterparts," African pop musicians tend to "tell . . . the people who support them what they want to hear"; and, with such critics as Gehr in mind, perhaps, he allows himself to wonder what Western listeners would do "if they found out that they were dancing to Nigerian *juju* music whose lyrics praise the bourgeois or corporate sponsors of the gigs" ("Foreword," p. xii). The same general point is made by Waterman in his ethnographic study of *juju*. Waterman suggests that *juju* tends to "emphasize . . . the common interests of, rather than conflicts between, the rich and the poor" (*Juju*, p. 132). His conclusion is that when "[v]iewed as a system of rhetoric arguing for a particular vision of society, juju simultaneously legitimates inequality and argues that all actors may become wealthy and powerful, a kind of African Horatio Alger ideology. In the face of widening disparities in wealth, education, and health, music plays a role in the reproduction of hegemonic values" (p. 227).

Revealingly, Johnny Clegg himself has provided one appropriate response to what I have been describing as the "First Worldist" way of conceptualizing African pop music. In a 1988 television interview, Clegg described his musical "vision for the future" as being "to create and construct a music which is based in the African experience . . . My personal project is to define my African identity in the continent . . . and to communicate this with the world and my fellow Africans."[47] A skeptic could, of course, argue that as a *white* South African, however committed to a nonracial South Africa, Clegg's "African identity" is scarcely likely to be generalizable. The partial validity of this objection should be conceded. Tracks by Savuka like "Third World Child" (off the album of that name), and "African Shadow Man" and "Human Rainbow" (off the album *Shadow Man* [EMI, 1988]) clearly bespeak a restricted and, in the context of Africa at large, ungeneralizable subject position. Yet elsewhere Clegg has insisted that the cosmopolitan dimension of "African experience" is a daily reality not only for himself, but for all African musicians. Referring specifically to the South African scene – but to the South African scene *tout court*, not merely to the *white* South African scene – he argued that "what the new music is drawing on is not only, any more, the South African music experience, but the international one. People must understand and realize that we are exposed day and night to international music." Musicians in South Africa today, he continued, tend to celebrate, rather than deplore, their global perspective, which they do not in the least regard as corresponding to their subordination to imperialist social imperatives or to the logic of consumerist capitalism:

We do not want to be straitjacketed politically by apartheid . . . So there's been a reaction against this . . . Young people now [are saying], we speak English, we sing in English, and we're part of that whole, international culture. And . . . our music is reaching out to touch the soul and the spirit of that international music community, to be part of it.[48]

This formulation of the aspirations of *producers* of African pop music – echoed, incidentally, in the thinking of such other musicians as Aster Aweke of Ethiopia and Ray Lema of Zaire – seems compelling, not least because it accords neatly with the views of many of the music's Western-based *listeners*, enthusiastic followers of Afropop. Most Western listeners, of course, tend at the outset to know little about African cultural production, or even about social developments in Africa. "[W]hat a type of music is about in its own environment is often quite different from anything [they] can understand" (Chernoff, "Foreword," p. xii). Western listeners are initially attracted to African pop music because they find its sound exciting. What particularly stimulates them, I want to suggest, what enables them to find enjoyment in Afropop, is precisely its syncretism. Because it is a syncretic form, Afropop typically strikes Western listeners as simultaneously strange and familiar, accessible and inaccessible, opaque and immediately intelligible. This simultaneity – the relative alterity of Afropop, on the one hand, and the fact that it is "Euro-friendly," on the other – is arguably the source of a pleasing intellectual challenge to Western enthusiasts, who endeavor, in exploring and sampling different Afropop sounds, to render these more and more comprehensible.[49]

The music industry in the West attempts to exploit this passion on the part of Western consumers of Afropop – or, more generally, world music – by promoting world music as a new cultural resource waiting to be "discovered." It invites Western consumers to exoticize world music, to transform it into the musical equivalent of the "new" international cuisines, to which we in the West have been introduced as a direct consequence of our various imperial misadventures, and which we like to sample once every now and then for a culinary change of pace. One code name for this quasi-mechanical "strategy" is "cultural pluralism," which, as Abdul JanMohamed and David Lloyd have argued with particular reference to the American context, is

the Great White Hope of conservatives and liberals alike. The semblance of pluralism disguises the perpetuation of exclusion insofar as it is enjoyed only by those who have already assimilated the values of the dominant culture. For this pluralism, ethnic or cultural difference is merely an exoticism, an indulgence that can be relished without significantly modifying the individual who is securely embedded in the protective body of dominant ideology. Such pluralism tolerates the existence of salsa, it even enjoys Mexican restaurants, but it bans Spanish as a medium of instruction in American schools. Above all, it refuses to acknowledge the class basis of discrimination and the systematic economic exploitation of minorities that underlie postmodern culture.[50]

In his essay on world music, Martin Roberts criticizes this kind of analysis – which he terms "materialist," although it is obvious that the real object of his critique is Marxism – as reductionistic. The "materialist" reading, he suggests, tends to construe the world music phenomenon as "an entirely predictable outgrowth of the system of global capitalism and the commodity culture on which it depends" ("'World Music'," p. 233). Against this "materialist" understanding, he advocates instead a postmodernist conception of "musical landscapes," modeled on the work of Arjun Appadurai. "[G]lobal cultural phenomena," Roberts writes, "are no longer explicable today in terms of any one determinant alone (political, social, economic, etc.) but only in terms of the tension between a large number of such determinants" (p. 240). I do not find this formulation at all helpful. On the one hand, it says nothing that would not already be transparent to any but the most single-minded and mechanistic of contemporary "materialist" critics. And, on the other hand, it leads Roberts himself to proffer an analysis that seems – on my reading at least – so radically contingent as to render the sedimented and deeply layered structurality of cultural (and social) phenomena more or less unthinkable in any sustained or methodologically rigorous manner.

"Cultural pluralism" exists on the definition provided by Jan-Mohamed and Lloyd as the strict ideological correlate of transnational capitalism. The big companies that dominate the music industry world-wide tend to manufacture and market world music in the Western world as a stream of commodities whose production, distribution, and consumption are geared, to the greatest extent possible, toward profit maximization. It is clear that at the level of *production*, many of the musicians involved try to combat – or at least ameliorate – the industry's domination of their labor power and its fruits. (In some cases, independent labels have proved themselves to be valuable allies in this struggle.) But resistance to the homogenizing logic of commodity exchange also manifests itself, assuredly, at the level of *consumption*. To speak in this context of world music as "a kind of Trojan horse for disrupting the system from within," as Martin Roberts does ("'World Music'," p. 239), is, I think, to claim rather too much. Yet some registration needs to be made of the fact that listening to music is a cultural practice, and that, as such, it involves the taking up of positions which are distinctly different from one another in tendency and effect. As John Tomlinson has argued in his study of cultural imperialism, it does not follow from the fact that "capitalism is an homogenising cultural force" that the ideological valence (or symbolic value) of specific cultural phenomena produced under capitalist social relations is predetermined – even if "[t]he evidence of a general drift towards cultural convergence at certain levels is undeniable."[51]

There can, of course, be no substitute for empirical research on this question. Yet some speculations might be risked in advance of such research. In an essay, "Reading, Readers, the Literate, Literature," Pierre Bourdieu asks whether it is possible to "read anything at all without wondering what it is that reading means; without asking what are the social conditions of the possibility of reading."[52] He adds that

Inquiring into the conditions of possibility of reading means inquiring into the social conditions which make possible the situations in which one reads (and it is immediately clear that one of these conditions is the *scholé*, leisure in its educational form, that is, the time of reading, the time of learning how to read) and inquiring also into the social conditions of production of *lectores*.[53]

Transposing Bourdieu's commentary to the field of world music, we can speculate that *some* Western-based listeners, at least, (come to) occupy positions corresponding to those of *lectores*. For *these* listeners, arguably – those enthusiasts, say, who, following the lead of British rock musician and producer Peter Gabriel,[54] have heard enough to embrace the concept underlying it – world music is not to be thought of merely as a convenient name for a sprawling body of music deriving from Yemen or New Zealand or Brazil or Cameroon – in short, from anywhere but "here." It is, rather, the name of a movement that carries the potential to subvert the ideological parochialism of Euro-American popular music. For what makes it "world music" to these listeners, I want to propose, is precisely its latent capacity to contribute to the dismantling of the cultural logic of Western popular music, a cultural logic resting squarely upon the political economy of empire. To listen to world music dialogically, as these listeners arguably do, seems to me a distinctly subversive practice: for it is to allow oneself to take seriously the suggestion of a world free of imperial domination. Free of imperial domination, note – not "on the other side of the imperial divide"; the implicit proposal is not that we (in the West) listen to world music for what it can tell us about life "over there," but that we listen to it for what it can suggest to us about radically different ways of living "over here," ways of living that are unimaginable under prevailing social conditions.

Notes

Introduction: hating tradition properly

1 Theodor W. Adorno, *Minima Moralia: Reflections from Damaged Life*, trans. E.F.N. Jephcott (London: Verso, 1978), 52.
2 Edward W. Said, *Culture and Imperialism* (New York: Alfred A. Knopf, 1993), 316.
3 Theodor W. Adorno, "Cultural Criticism and Society," in *Prisms*, trans. Samuel and Shierry Weber (Cambridge: The MIT Press, 1983), 19.
4 He suggests, indeed, that nearly all of what passes for cultural criticism is itself to be criticized precisely for its failure to assume this task. "[W]hat makes the content of cultural criticism inappropriate is not so much lack of respect for that which is criticized as the dazzled and arrogant recognition which criticism surreptitiously confers on culture . . . [The critic's] vanity aids that of culture." *Ibid.*
5 See, for instance, Williams's critique of modernism in *The Politics of Modernism: Against the New Conformists* (London: Verso, 1989).
6 Theodor W. Adorno, *Negative Dialectics*, trans. E.B. Ashton (New York: Continuum, 1987), 41.
7 Pierre Bourdieu, "Universal Corporatism: the Role of Intellectuals in the Modern World," trans. Gisele Sapiro, *Poetics Today* 12.4 (1991), 669.
8 For commentaries on the historical emergence of the modern figure of the intellectual, see Jean-Paul Sartre, "A Plea for Intellectuals," in *Between Existentialism and Marxism: Sartre on Philosophy, Politics, Psychology, and the Arts*, trans. Joan Matthews (New York: Pantheon, 1983), 226–85; Zygmunt Bauman, *Legislators and Interpreters: On Modernity, Post-Modernity and Intellectuals* (Oxford: Polity Press, 1987); Edward W. Said, *Representations of the Intellectual: The 1993 Reith Lectures* (New York: Pantheon Books, 1994); Jürgen Habermas, "Heinrich Heine and the Role of the Intellectual in Germany," in *The New Conservatism: Cultural Criticism and the Historians' Debate*, ed. and trans. Shierry Weber Nicholsen (Cambridge: The MIT Press, 1989), 71–99; Habermas, *The Structural Transformation of the Public Sphere: An*

Inquiry into a Category of Bourgeois Society, trans. Thomas Burger (Cambridge: The MIT Press, 1993); and the relevant essays or sections in Pierre Bourdieu, *The Field of Cultural Production: Essays on Art and Literature*, ed. Randal Johnson, trans. Richard Nice (New York: Columbia University Press, 1993), *In Other Words: Essays Towards a Reflexive Sociology*, trans. Matthew Aronson (Stanford: Stanford University Press, 1990), and *The Rules of Art: Genesis and Structure of the Literary Field*, trans. Susan Emanuel (Stanford: Stanford University Press, 1996).

9 Theodor W. Adorno, "On Tradition," *Telos* 94 (1993–94), 75.

10 Anthony Giddens, *The Nation-State and Violence*, vol. II of *A Contemporary Critique of Historical Materialism* (Berkeley and Los Angeles: University of California Press, 1987), 12.

11 Anthony Giddens, *The Consequences of Modernity* (Stanford: Stanford University Press, 1990), 38.

12 Jürgen Habermas, *The Philosophical Discourse of Modernity: Twelve Lectures*, trans. Frederick Lawrence (Cambridge: The MIT Press, 1987), 84.

13 Georg Lukács, *History and Class Consciousness: Studies in Marxist Dialectics*, trans. Rodney Livingstone (Cambridge: The MIT Press, 1983), 229.

14 Fredric Jameson, "Actually Existing Marxism," *Polygraph* 6/7 (1993), 174–75.

15 See Samir Amin, who writes as follows: "Undoubtedly, the aspiration for rationality and universalism is not the product of the modern world. Not only has rationality always accompanied human action, but the universal concept of the human being, transcending the limits of his or her collective membership (in a race, a people, a gender, a social class) had already been produced by the great tributary ideologies . . . However, despite this, universalism had remained only a potential before the development of European capitalism, because no society had succeeded in imposing itself and its values on a worldwide scale." *Eurocentrism*, trans. Russell Moore (New York: Monthly Review Press, 1989), 72.

16 Jürgen Habermas, *The Theory of Communicative Action*, vol. II: *Lifeworld and System: A Critique of Functionalist Reason*, trans. Thomas McCarthy (Boston: Beacon Press, 1989), 352.

17 See Ernest Mandel's very telling critique of Adorno along these lines in *Late Capitalism*, trans. Joris De Bres (London and New York: Verso, 1993), 505–07.

18 Said, *Culture and Imperialism*, 279. Said's work is exceptional in its identification of Adorno as a figure relevant to the field of postcolonial studies. Among the very few other postcolonial theorists who share this perspective is Asha Varadharajan: see her *Exotic Parodies: Subjectivity in Adorno, Said, and Spivak* (Minneapolis: University of Minnesota Press, 1995).

19 George Orwell, *The Road to Wigan Pier* (New York: Harcourt, Brace, Jovanovich, 1958), 144.

20 Homi K. Bhabha, "Freedom's Basis in the Indeterminate," *October* 61

(1992), 47–48.

21 Homi K. Bhabha, *The Location of Culture* (London and New York: Routledge, 1994); Sara Suleri, *The Rhetoric of English India* (Chicago and London: University of Chicago Press, 1992); Trinh T. Minh-ha, *Woman, Native, Other: Writing Postcoloniality and Feminism* (Bloomington and Indianapolis: Indiana University Press, 1989); Robert Young, *White Mythologies: Writing History and the West* (London and New York: Routledge, 1990).

22 Edward W. Said, "East Isn't East," *Times Literary Supplement* 4792 (3 February 1995), 5. See also Kwame Anthony Appiah's chapter, "The Postcolonial and the Postmodern," in *In My Father's House: Africa in the Philosophy of Culture* (New York and Oxford: Oxford University Press, 1992).

23 Henry Louis Gates, Jr., "Critical Fanonism," *Critical Inquiry* 17.3 (1991), 458.

24 Among a very large number of sources that could be cited here, see in particular the following: J.M Bernstein, *Recovering Ethical Life: Jürgen Habermas and the Future of Critical Theory* (London and New York: Routledge, 1995); Steven Best and Douglas Kellner, *Postmodern Theory: Critical Interrogations* (New York: The Guilford Press, 1991); Roy Bhaskar, *Philosophy and the Idea of Freedom* (Oxford: Blackwell, 1991); Craig Calhoun, *Critical Social Theory: Culture, History, and the Challenge of Difference* (Oxford: Blackwell, 1995); Alex Callinicos, *Against Postmodernism: A Marxist Critique* (Oxford: Polity Press, 1990); Peter Dews, *Logics of Disintegration: Post-Structuralist Thought and the Claims of Political Theory* (London: Verso, 1987); Terry Eagleton, *Ideology: An Introduction* (London and New York: Verso, 1991), *The Ideology of the Aesthetic* (Oxford: Blackwell, 1990), and *The Illusions of Postmodernism* (Oxford: Blackwell, 1996); Nancy Fraser, *Unruly Practices: Power, Discourse, and Gender in Contemporary Social Theory* (Minneapolis: University of Minnesota Press, 1989); Norman Geras, *Discourses of Extremity: Radical Ethics and Post-Marxist Extravagances* (London: Verso, 1990); Habermas, *Philosophical Discourse*; Pauline Johnson, *Feminism as Radical Humanism* (Boulder and San Francisco: Westview, 1994); Jorge Larrain, *Ideology and Cultural Identity: Modernity and the Third World Presence* (Oxford: Polity Press, 1994); Sabina Lovibond, "Feminism and the 'Crisis of Rationality'," *New Left Review* 207 (1994), 72–102, and "Feminism and Postmodernism," in Thomas Docherty, ed., *Postmodernism: A Reader* (New York: Columbia University Press, 1993), 390–414; Christopher Norris, *Truth and the Ethics of Criticism* (Manchester and New York: Manchester University Press, 1994), and *The Truth about Postmodernism* (Oxford: Blackwell, 1993); Gillian Rose, *Dialectic of Nihilism: Post-Structuralism and Law* (Oxford: Blackwell, 1984); and Richard Wolin, *The Terms of Cultural Criticism: The Frankfurt School, Existentialism, Poststructuralism* (New York: Columbia University Press, 1992).

25 See for instance Partha Chatterjee, *The Nation and Its Fragments: Colonial and Postcolonial Histories* (Princeton: Princeton University Press, 1993), and *The Present History of West Bengal: Essays in Political Criti-*

cism (Delhi and New York: Oxford University Press, 1997); Nicholas Dirks, ed., *Colonialism and Culture* (Ann Arbor: University of Michigan Press, 1992); Timothy Mitchell, *Colonising Egypt* (Berkeley, Los Angeles, Oxford: University of California Press, 1991); Gyan Prakash, ed., *After Colonialism: Imperial Histories and Postcolonial Displacements* (Princeton: Princeton University Press, 1995); Mary Louise Pratt, *Imperial Eyes: Travel Writing and Transculturation* (New York and London: Routledge, 1992); Ann Laura Stoler, *Race and the Education of Desire: Foucault's History of Sexuality and the Colonial Order of Things* (Durham: Duke University Press, 1995).

26 Spivak's *Outside in the Teaching Machine* (London and New York: Routledge, 1993) and Bhabha's *The Location of Culture* are not, as Bart Moore-Gilbert claims in his *Postcolonial Theory: Contexts, Practices, Politics* (London and New York: Verso, 1997), "substantial volume[s] of new work" (3), but are instead collections of previously published essays.

27 Paul Gilroy, *"There Ain't No Black in the Union Jack": The Cultural Politics of Race and Nation* (London: Hutchinson, 1987), 49–50. See my discussion of this argument in Gilroy in Chapter One, below.

28 Fredric Jameson, "Third World Literature in the Era of Multinational Capitalism," *Social Text* 15 (1986), 65–88.

29 Aijaz Ahmad, "The Politics of Literary Postcoloniality," *Race & Class* 36.3 (1995), 1.

30 *Ibid.*

31 See my essay, "Postcolonialism and the Dilemma of Nationalism: Aijaz Ahmad's Critique of Third-Worldism," *Diaspora* 2.3 (1993), 373–400.

32 *Public Culture* 6.1 (1993).

33 Said, "East Isn't East," 5.

34 See Timothy Brennan, *At Home in the World: Cosmopolitanism Now* (Cambridge and London: Harvard University Press, 1997); Laura Chrisman, "Gendering Imperial Culture: *King Solomon's Mines* and Feminist Criticisms," in Keith Ansell-Pearson, Benita Parry, and Judith Squires, eds., *Cultural Readings of Imperialism: Edward Said and the Gravity of History* (London: Lawrence and Wishart, 1997), 290–304, and "Theorising 'Race,' Racism and Culture: Some Pitfalls in Idealist Critiques," *Paragraph: A Journal of Modern Critical Theory* 16.1 (1993), 78–90; Annie Coombes, "The Distance Between Two Points: Globalism and the Liberal Dilemma," in George Robertson et al., eds., *Travellers' Tales: Narratives of Home and Displacement* (London and New York: Routledge, 1994), 177–86, and "The Recalcitrant Object: Culture Contact and the Question of Hybridity," in Francis Barker, Peter Hulme, and Margaret Iversen, eds., *Colonial Discourse/Postcolonial Theory* (Manchester and New York: Manchester University Press, 1994), 89–114; Arif Dirlik, "The Postcolonial Aura: Third World Criticism in the Age of Global Capitalism," *Critical Inquiry* 20.2 (1994), 328–56; Peter Hulme, "The Locked Heart: the Creole Family Romance of *Wide Sargasso Sea*," in Barker, et al., eds., *Colonial Discourse/Postcolonial Theory*, 72–88, and "The Profit of Language: George Lamming

and the Postcolonial Novel," in Jonathan White, ed., *Recasting the World: Writing after Colonialism* (Baltimore and London: Johns Hopkins University Press, 1993), 120–36; Geeta Kapur, "Globalisation and Culture," *Third Text* 39 (1997), 21–38; Neil Larsen, *Reading North by South: On Latin American Literature, Culture and Politics* (Minneapolis: University of Minnesota Press, 1995); Satya P. Mohanty, *Literary Theory and the Claims of History: Postmodernism, Objectivity, Multicultural Politics* (Ithaca: Cornell University Press, 1997); Supriya Nair, *Caliban's Curse: George Lamming and the Revisioning of History* (Ann Arbor: University of Michigan Press, 1996), and "Expressive Countercultures and Postmodern Utopia: A Caribbean Context," *Research in African Literatures* 27.4 (1996), 71–87; Benita Parry, "Problems in Current Theories of Colonial Discourse," *Oxford Literary Review* 9.1–2 (1987), 27–58, "Resistance Theory/Theorising Resistance, or Two Cheers for Nativism," in Barker, et al., eds., *Colonial Discourse/Postcolonial Theory*, 172–96, "Signs of Our Times: A Discussion of Homi Bhabha's *The Location of Culture*," *Third Text* 28/29 (1994), 5–24; Modhumita Roy, "Writers and Politics/Writers in Politics: Ngugi and the Language Question," in Charles Cantalupo, ed., *Ngugi: Texts and Contexts* (Trenton, NJ: Africa World Press, 1995) and "'Englishing' India: Reinstituting Class and Social Privilege," *Social Text* 39 (1994), 83–109; E. San Juan, Jr., *Beyond Postcolonial Theory* (New York: St. Martin's Press, 1998); Michael Sprinker, "The National Question: Said, Ahmad, Jameson," *Public Culture* 6.1 (1993), 3–29; Achin Vanaik, *The Furies of Indian Communalism: Religion, Modernity and Secularization* (London and New York: Verso, 1997).

1   Modernity, globalization, and the "West"

1 Fredric Jameson, *Postmodernism, or, The Cultural Logic of Late Capitalism* (Durham: Duke University Press, 1992), 379. Further references to this work (hereafter *Postmodernism*) will be given in the body of the text.

2 I follow fairly conventional Marxist precedent in understanding capitalism as a globally dominant (if unevenly articulated) mode of production characterized by private ownership (or control) of the means of production, exploitation of labor power through the mediations of wage labor and the market, competition between capitals, and the priority of profit over need in the determination of the protocols of production.

3 Stuart Hall, "The Meaning of New Times," in Stuart Hall and Martin Jacques, eds., *New Times: The Changing Face of Politics in the 1990s* (London: Lawrence and Wishart, 1989), 123.

4 Within the Marxist tradition, Georg Lukács's theory of reification represents perhaps the most celebrated attempt to substantiate the claim that the advent of capitalism marks a qualitative transformation in intersubjective relations. Lukács speaks of the propensity of "commodity exchange together with its structural consequences . . . to influence the total outer and inner life of society." *History and Class*

Consciousness: Studies in Marxist Dialectics, trans. Rodney Livingstone (Cambridge: The MIT Press, 1983), 84. He adds that in societies in which the commodity form is dominant, the commodity-structure (or logic of the market) is actually "constitutive of that society," inasmuch as it contrives to "penetrate society in all its aspects and to remould it in its own image" (p. 85). For a critical reconstruction of Lukács's concept of reification, see Jürgen Habermas, *The Theory of Communicative Action*, vol. I, trans. Thomas McCarthy (Boston: Beacon Press, 1984), 339–99.

5 See Agnes Heller and Ferenc Feher, *The Grandeur and Twilight of Radical Universalism* (New Brunswick: Transaction Publishers, 1991).

6 Gregory Elliott, *Labourism and the English Genius: The Strange Death of Labour England?* (London and New York: Verso, 1993), 146.

7 Jürgen Habermas, *The Philosophical Discourse of Modernity: Twelve Lectures*, trans. Frederick Lawrence (Cambridge: The MIT Press, 1987), 6–7. Further references to this work (hereafter *Philosophical Discourse*) will be given in the body of the text.

8 Walter Benjamin, "Theses on the Philosophy of History," in *Illuminations*, trans. Harry Zohn (New York: Schocken Books, 1969), 253–64.

9 Martin Albrow, *The Global Age: State and Society Beyond Modernity* (Oxford: Polity Press, 1996), 6.

10 *Ibid.*, 101.

11 Eric J. Hobsbawm, "The Crisis of Today's Ideologies," *New Left Review* 192 (1992), 56–57. Compare Benjamin on the material and existential changes wrought by the events of the First World War: "Was it not noticeable at the end of the war that men returned from the battlefield grown silent – not richer, but poorer in communicable experience? What ten years later was poured out in the flood of war books was anything but experience that goes from mouth to mouth. And there was nothing remarkable about that. For never has experience been contradicted more thoroughly than strategic experience by tactical warfare, economic experience by inflation, bodily experience by mechanical warfare, moral experience by those in power. A generation that had gone to school on a horse-drawn streetcar now stood under the open sky in a countryside in which nothing remained unchanged but the clouds, and beneath these clouds, in a field of force of destructive torrents and explosions, was the tiny, fragile human body." "The Storyteller: Reflections on the Works of Nikolai Leskov," in *Illuminations*, 84.

12 Hobsbawm, "The Crisis of Today's Ideologies," 58.

13 Karl Marx and Friedrich Engels, *The Communist Manifesto*, trans. Samuel Moore (New York: Penguin, 1967), 83.

14 Among the vast body of writings that could be cited here, see Alex Callinicos, John Rees, Mike Haynes, and Chris Harman, *Marxism and the New Imperialism* (London, Chicago, Melbourne: Bookmarks, 1994); Jeremy Brecher and Tim Costello, *Global Village or Global Pillage: Economic Reconstruction From the Bottom Up* (Boston: South End Press, 1994); Folker Fröbel, Jürgen Heinrichs, and Otto Kreye, *The New International Division of Labour: Structural Unemployment in Indus-*

trialised Countries and Industrialisation in Developing Countries, trans. Pete Burgess (Cambridge: Cambridge University Press, 1980); and June Nash and María Fernández-Kelly, eds., *Women, Men and the International Division of Labor* (Albany: State University of New York Press, 1983).

15 Anthony Giddens, *The Consequences of Modernity* (Stanford: Stanford University Press, 1990), 12. Further references to this work (hereafter *Consequences*) will be given in the body of the text.

16 Achin Vanaik, *The Furies of Indian Communalism: Religion, Modernity and Secularization* (London and New York: Verso, 1997), 12.

17 Anthony Giddens, *The Nation-State and Violence*, vol. ii of *A Contemporary Critique of Historical Materialism* (Berkeley and Los Angeles: University of California Press, 1987), 33.

18 Max Weber, *The Protestant Ethic and the Spirit of Capitalism*, trans. Talcott Parsons (London: Unwin Hyman, 1989), 13.

19 Jeffrey Alexander, *Fin de Siècle Social Theory: Relativism, Reduction, and the Problem of Reason* (London and New York: Verso, 1995), 37.

20 S.N. Eisenstadt, quoted in *ibid.*

21 V[ictor] G. Kiernan, *Imperialism and Its Contradictions* (New York and London: Routledge, 1995), 47.

22 Jan Nederveen Pieterse, "Globalization as Hybridization," in Mike Featherstone, Scott Lash, and Roland Robertson, eds., *Global Modernities* (London, Thousand Oaks, CA, New Delhi: Sage, 1995), 46–47. Pieterse, it should be noted, directs this critique equally against the *Marxist* theory of capitalist modernity. As I shall attempt to show in the pages that follow, this extended critique strikes me as being unwarranted.

23 Giddens, *The Nation-State and Violence*, 162.

24 Ranajit Guha, "Colonialism in South Asia: A Dominance without Hegemony and Its Historiography," in *Dominance without Hegemony: History and Power in Colonial India* (Cambridge: Harvard University Press, 1997), 1–99. Further references to this article (hereafter "Dominance") will be given in the body of the text. "Dominance without Hegemony and Its Historiography" was first published in Guha, ed., *Subaltern Studies VI. Writings on South Asian History and Society* (Delhi: Oxford University Press, 1989), 210–309.

25 Samir Amin, *Eurocentrism*, trans. Russell Moore (New York: Monthly Review Press, 1989), 77.

26 See Vanaik's critique of Subaltern Studies in *The Furies of Indian Communalism*, esp. 180–92.

27 Dipesh Chakrabarty, "Postcoloniality and the Artifice of History: Who Speaks for 'Indian' Pasts?" *Representations* 37 (1992), 1. Further references to this article (hereafter "Postcoloniality") will be given in the body of the text.

28 Abdelkebir Khatibi, "Double Criticism: The Decolonization of Arab Sociology," in Halim Barakat, ed., *Contemporary North Africa: Issues of Development and Integration* (Washington, DC: Center for Contemporary Arab Studies, 1985), 9–19.

29 Compare Chakrabarty's reading here with that advanced by Arif

Dirlik in his book, *After the Revolution: Waking to Global Capitalism* (Hanover and London: Wesleyan University Press, 1994). Very like Chakrabarty, Dirlik argues that Marx's work is "limited by a conceptualization of the world in which the capitalist mode of production provides the principles for ordering time and space" (p. 11). He subsequently explains that his point "is not that Marx was an apologist for capitalism but that his critique of capitalism (and expectation of its demise) presupposed the spatial and temporal restructuring of the globe by capitalism. This presumption made the spatiality and temporality of the capitalist mode of production into the structuring principle of historical materialism" (pp. 23–24). And this leads Dirlik to conclude that "[w]hether or not Marx (or later Marxists) was Eurocentric by inclination, by turning a historical phenomenon into a universal prerequisite of liberation, historical materialism in its very structure presupposed Eurocentrism" (p. 24).

30 Karl Marx, *Grundrisse: Foundations of the Critique of Political Economy*, trans. Martin Nicolaus (London: Penguin, 1993), 105. Further references to this work (hereafter *Grundrisse*) will be given in the body of the text.

31 Zygmunt Bauman, "Searching for a Centre that Holds," in Featherstone, Lash, and Robertson, eds., *Global Modernities*, 144. See also Bauman, "Morality without Ethics," *Theory, Culture and Society* 11 (1994), 1–34.

32 Compare Kwame Anthony Appiah, *In My Father's House: Africa in the Philosophy of Culture* (New York and Oxford: Oxford University Press, 1992), who notes perceptively that if we wish to understand "our human modernity," "we must first understand why the rationalization of the world can no longer be seen as the tendency either of the West or of history; why, simply put, the modernist characterization of modernity must be challenged" (pp. 144–45).

33 Immanuel Wallerstein, *Geopolitics and Geoculture: Essays on the Changing World-System* (Cambridge: Cambridge University Press, 1992), 123–24.

34 *Ibid.*, 124.

35 Alain Lipietz, *Miracles and Mirages: The Crises of Global Fordism*, trans. David Macey (London: Verso, 1987), 15. The paradigm text of the regulationist school is Michel Aglietta, *A Theory of Capitalist Regulation: The US Experience*, trans. David Fernbach (London: New Left Books, 1979). Robert Boyer, *The Regulation School: A Critical Introduction*, trans. Craig Charney (New York: Columbia University Press, 1990), provides a good overview. Among the works reflecting the Anglo-American recuperation of regulationist theory, the two best known are probably Mike Davis, *Prisoners of the American Dream* (London: Verso, 1986) and David Harvey, *The Condition of Postmodernity: An Enquiry into the Origins of Cultural Change* (Oxford: Blackwell, 1989). For a review and searching critique of regulationist theory, see Robert Brenner and Mark Glick, "The Regulationist Approach: Theory and History," *New Left Review* 188 (1991), 45–119.

36 Simon Clarke, "The Crisis of Fordism or the Crisis of Social

Democracy?" *Telos* 83 (1990), 73.

37 This reading is predicated upon a set of assumptions, which Michael J. Piore and Charles F. Sabel characterize as follows: "In the neo-Marxist view, the Keynesian welfare state is the political expression of a stalemate between the bourgeoisie and the working class. The latter has not proved strong enough to impose socialism, and the former is too weak to defend successfully all the principles of market capitalism. The result is a situation in which the working class has used its political power to redistribute income in its own favor, to secure minimal guarantees of its welfare, and – by such measures as health-and-safety legislation – to circumscribe capital's rights to dispose of property. The economy has been slowly and partially democratized, in the sense that the right to vote can be used to control the market in limited ways." *The Second Industrial Divide: Possibilities for Prosperity* (New York: Basic Books, 1984), 10.

38 Nicholas Costello, Jonathan Michie, and Seumas Milne, *Beyond the Casino Economy: Planning for the 1990s* (London: Verso, 1989), 62.

39 Michael Rustin, "The Politics of Post-Fordism: or, the Trouble with 'New Times'," *New Left Review* 175 (1989), 55.

40 Harvey, *The Condition of Postmodernity*, 124, 147. "Flexible accumulation," he writes, "is characterized by the emergence of entirely new sectors of production, new ways of providing financial services, new markets, and, above all, greatly intensified rates of commercial, technological, and organizational innovation. It has entrained rapid shifts in the patterning of uneven development, both between sectors and between geographical regions . . . It has also entailed a new round of . . . 'time-space compression' . . . in the capitalist world – the time horizons of both private and public decision-making have shrunk, while satellite communication and declining transport costs have made it increasingly possible to spread those decisions immediately over an ever wider and variegated space" (p. 147).

41 Samir Amin, *Capitalism in the Age of Globalization: The Management of Contemporary Society* (London and Atlantic Highlands, NJ: Zed Books, 1997), 94. Further references to this work (hereafter *Capitalism*) will be given in the body of the text. Amin affirms the regulationist theorists' construction of the welfare state as "an historic compromise between capital and labour," but disputes their representation of this compromise under the rubric of "Fordism," arguing that this designation is "questionable . . . because Fordism was introduced in the United States before, and in opposition to, the Roosevelt New Deal" (p. 94).

42 Immanuel Wallerstein, *Historical Capitalism with Capitalist Civilization* (London and New York: Verso, 1996), 34–35.

43 Paul Smith, *Millennial Dreams: Contemporary Culture and Capital in the North* (London and New York: Verso, 1997), 20–21. Further references to this work (hereafter *Dreams*) will be given in the body of the text.

44 Martin Jacques, "New Times," *Marxism Today* (October 1988), 1.

45 A. Sivanandan, "All That Melts Into Air Is Solid: The Hokum of New Times," *Race & Class* 31.3 (1990), 6. For Sivanandan's own contrasting representation of the current conjuncture, see "New Circuits of Im-

perialism," in *Communities of Resistance: Writings on Black Struggles for Socialism* (London and New York: Verso, 1990), 169–95, and "Heresies and Prophecies: the Social and Political Fall-Out of the Technological Revolution: an Interview," *Race & Class* 37.4 (1996), 1–11.

46 Jacques, "New Times," 1.

47 Stuart Hall, *The Hard Road to Renewal: Thatcherism and the Crisis of the Left* (London: Verso, 1988), 246–47. Further references to this work (hereafter *Hard Road*) will be given in the body of the text.

48 A much better account than Hall's of the failures of Labour ideology in the post-1968 period is to be found in the relevant sections of Gregory Elliott's *Labourism and the English Genius*.

49 Hall charges, in this context, that "the culture of patriarchalism is nowhere so deeply embedded as within the left itself" (*Hard Road*, 249). "*Nowhere* so deeply embedded"? Is it really necessary here to do more than reference the cultures of fundamentalist Christianity or Tory familialism or the military? Even allowing for exaggeration for effect, Hall's allegation is patently too strong.

50 Ernesto Laclau and Chantal Mouffe, "Post-Marxism without Apologies," *New Left Review* 166 (1987), 80.

51 Ernesto Laclau and Chantal Mouffe, *Hegemony and Socialist Strategy: Towards a Radical Democratic Politics* (London and New York: Verso, 1987).

52 Costello, Michie, and Milne, *Beyond the Casino Economy*, 29.

53 Norman Geras offers a useful critique of the abuse of the concept of "Socialist Man" in contemporary social theory in his essay, "Seven Types of Obloquy: Travesties of Marxism," in Ralph Miliband, Leo Panitch, and John Saville, eds., *Socialist Register 1990: The Retreat of the Intellectuals* (London: Merlin, 1990), 1–34.

54 See Bob Jessop, Kevin Bonnett, Simon Bromley, and Tom Ling, "Authoritarian Populism, Two Nations, and Thatcherism," *New Left Review* 147 (1984), 32–60, and "Thatcherism and the Politics of Hegemony: A Reply to Stuart Hall," *New Left Review* 153 (1985), 87–101.

55 Rustin, "The Politics of Post-Fordism," 61.

56 *Ibid.*, 69.

57 Ernest Mandel, *Late Capitalism*, trans. Joris De Bres (London and New York: Verso, 1993), 194–97.

58 Paul Hirst and Grahame Thompson, *Globalization in Question: The International Economy and the Possibilities of Governance* (Oxford: Polity Press, 1996), 1.

59 William K. Tabb, "Globalization Is *An* Issue, the Power of Capital Is *The* Issue," *Monthly Review* 49.2 (1997), 20.

60 See the critical discussion of this corporate conception in Brecher and Costello, *Global Village or Global Pillage*, 15ff.

61 Gregory Jusdanis, "Culture, Culture Everywhere: the Swell of Globalization Theory," *Diaspora* 5.1 (1996), 141.

62 Craig Calhoun, *Critical Social Theory: Culture, History, and the Challenge of Difference* (Oxford: Blackwell, 1995), 111.

63 See Ellen Meiksins Wood, "Capitalism, Globalization, and Epochal Shifts: An Exchange," *Monthly Review* 48.9 (1997), 21–32, "Labor, the

State, and Class Struggle," *Monthly Review* 49.3 (1997), 1–17, "A Note on Du Boff and Herman," *Monthly Review* 49.6 (1997), 39–43, and "Class Compacts, the Welfare State, and Epochal Shifts (A Reply to Frances Fox Piven and Richard A. Cloward)," *Monthly Review* 49. 8 (1998), 24–43.

64 See Stuart Hall, "The Question of Cultural Identity," in Stuart Hall, David Held, Don Hubert, and Kenneth Thompson, eds., *Modernity: An Introduction to Modern Societies* (Oxford: Blackwell, 1996), 595–634; Nestor Garcia Canclini, *Hybrid Cultures: Strategies for Entering and Leaving Modernity*, trans. Christopher L. Ciappari and Silvia L. Lopez (Minneapolis and London: University of Minnesota Press, 1995); Arjun Appadurai, *Modernity at Large: Cultural Dimensions of Globalization* (Minneapolis and London: University of Minnesota Press, 1996); Pieterse, "Globalization as Hybridization"; Albrow, *The Global Age*; and Scott Lash and John Urry, *The End of Organized Capitalism* (Madison: University of Wisconsin Press, 1987).

65 Among writers in this category actively hostile to postmodernism, I would list Hobsbawm, "The Crisis of Today's Ideologies"; Brecher and Costello, *Global Village or Global Pillage*; Dirlik, *After the Revolution*; Masao Miyoshi, "A Borderless World? From Colonialism to Transnationalism and the Decline of the Nation-State," *Critical Inquiry* 19 (1993), 726–51; and William I. Robinson, "Globalisation: Nine Theses on Our Epoch," *Race & Class* 38.2 (1996), 13–31. Progressive writers with a more accommodating, but by no means uncritical, relationship to postmodernism would include Roland Robertson, *Globalization: Social Theory and Global Culture* (Newbury Park and London: Sage, 1992); David Harvey, *The Condition of Postmodernity*, and "Globalization in Question," *Rethinking Marxism* 8.4 (1995), 1–17; and Anthony McGrew, "A Global Society?" in Hall, Held, Hubert, and Thompson, eds., *Modernity: An Introduction to Modern Societies*, 466–503.

66 Robinson, "Globalisation," 14–15.

67 See Barrie Axford, *The Global System: Economics, Politics and Culture* (Oxford: Polity Press, 1995), who notes that "[b]y the early 1990s over 80 per cent of world trade was conducted between the 'Western' members of the OECD, with the newly market-oriented countries of the former Soviet bloc, the less developed countries (LDCs) and even the dynamic economies of the newly industrialized countries (NICs) accounting for only a small part of these overall transactions. The global trading economy is still largely confined to the richer nations, and the volume of intra-core trade continues the pattern of unequal exchange as a mechanism for the reproduction of global inequalities" (p. 104).

68 *Ibid.*, 97, where Axford points out that "there is a definitional world of difference between the concept of a multinational corporation, which implies that a corporation may be very 'national' in key aspects of its functioning and governance, and that of a transnational corporation ... or global corporation, which suggests that the company has broken free from or transcended the bounds of nationality." See also Chris Harman, "The State and Capitalism Today," *International Socialism* 51

(1991): 3–54.

69 Axford, *The Global System*, 106.

70 Bauman, "Searching for a Centre That Holds," 152.

71 Robinson, "Globalisation," 15.

72 Alex Callinicos, "Marxism and Imperialism Today," in Callinicos, et al., *Marxism and the New Imperialism*, 54.

73 Robinson, "Globalisation," 13–16.

74 Albrow, *The Global Age*, 4.

75 Dirlik, *After the Revolution*, 40.

76 Calhoun, *Critical Social Theory*, 98–99.

77 Harvey, "Globalization in Question," 11.

78 Paul Gilroy, *The Black Atlantic: Modernity and Double Consciousness* (Cambridge: Harvard University Press, 1993), 5. Further references to this work (hereafter *Black Atlantic*) will be given in the body of the text.

79 Robinson, "Globalisation," 15.

80 Paul Gilroy, *"There Ain't No Black in the Union Jack": The Cultural Politics of Race and Nation* (London: Hutchinson, 1987). Further references to this work (hereafter *"There Ain't No Black"*) will be given in the body of the text. Centre for Contemporary Cultural Studies, *The Empire Strikes Back: Race and Racism in 70s Britain* (London: Hutchinson, 1982).

81 He adds that "though seldom overtly named, the misplaced idea of a national interest gets invoked as a means to silence dissent and censor political debate when the incoherences and inconsistencies of Africalogical discourse are put on display" (*Black Atlantic*, 33).

82 Paul Gilroy, *Small Acts: Thoughts on the Politics of Black Cultures* (New York and London: Serpent's Tail, 1993), 70. Further references to this work (hereafter *Small Acts*) will be given in the body of the text.

83 Edward W. Said, *Culture and Imperialism* (New York: Alfred A. Knopf, 1993), 278. The Habermas citation is drawn from Jürgen Habermas, *Autonomy and Solidarity: Interviews*, trans. and ed. Peter Dews (London: Verso, 1986), 187.

84 Since my intention at this point is simply to provide a sense of the thrust and tendency of Gilroy's critique of Habermas, I will not engage the terms of this critique in any detail here. I do want to indicate, however, that there are grounds to question the validity of Gilroy's representation of Habermas's position. To accuse Habermas of logocentrism is, in my view, to fail to understand the significance of the critique of subject-centered reason that he advances in elaborating his theory of communicative action as an *intersubjective* process. By the same token, it seems to me that such passages as the following demonstrate that Habermas is very much attuned to the emancipatory potentials of aesthetic practice (a zone of practice that he theorizes as being quite distinct from that of philosophical discourse). Habermas refers, thus, to "the productivity and explosive power of basic aesthetic experiences that a subjectivity liberated from the imperatives of purposive activity and from conventions of quotidian perception gains from its own decentering – experiences that are presented in works of avant-garde art, that are articulated in the

discourses of art criticism, and that also achieve a *certain measure* of illuminating effect . . . in the innovatively enriched range of values proper to self-realization" (*Philosophical Discourse*, 113).

85 Samir Amin, *Empire of Chaos*, trans. W.H. Locke Anderson (New York: Monthly Review Press, 1992), 29.

86 Eric Williams, *Capitalism and Slavery* (New York: Russell and Russell, 1961). See Helen Scott's discussion of "race," racism, and capitalist development in her unpublished doctoral dissertation, "Ideologies of Postcolonialism: How Postmodernism Mystifies the History and Persistence of Imperialism" (Brown University, 1996).

87 Raymond Williams, "Culture is Ordinary," in *Resources of Hope: Culture, Democracy, Socialism*, ed. Robin Gable (London: Verso, 1989), 5.

88 See Laura Chrisman's "Journeying to Death: Gilroy's *Black Atlantic*," *Race & Class* 39.2 (1997), 51–64, which grounds its impressive challenge to Gilroy on precisely this point. See also Supriya Nair, "Expressive Countercultures and Postmodern Utopia: A Caribbean Context," *Research in African Literatures* 27.4 (1996), 71–87.

2 Disavowing decolonization: nationalism, intellectuals, and the question of representation in postcolonial theory

1 Hence Julia Kristeva's recent reflection that, to the members of her own intellectual cohort (the "generation of 1968"), the nation-form increasingly appeared an "archaism" which it was necessary to reject, "whether in favor of an egalitarianism, a Third-Worldism, or a belief in the homogenization of the world by virtue of economic or communications changes." "Foreign Body," *Transition* 59 (1993), 174.

2 Cf. Peter Worsley, who notes that the liberal nineteenth-century conception of nationalism associated with such figures as John Stuart Mill "did not survive the First World War." After 1918, "nationalism was seen as a problem, even a catastrophe; a reason for pessimism, not hope. To intellectuals, it had now become supremely illogical and supremely irrational. The subsequent emergence of fascism, which was launched upon the total elimination of dissent at home and military expansion abroad, seemed the final confirmation of the inherently evil nature of nationalist thinking pushed to its ultimate extremes." *The Three Worlds: Culture and World Development* (Chicago: University of Chicago Press, 1984), 272.

3 Timothy Brennan, "The National Longing for Form," in Homi K. Bhabha, ed., *Nation and Narration* (London and New York: Routledge, 1990), 57.

4 Partha Chatterjee, *The Nation and Its Fragments: Colonial and Postcolonial Histories* (Princeton: Princeton University Press, 1993), 4. Further references to this work (hereafter *Nation*) will be given in the body of the text. See also Jeffrey Alexander, who suggests that "Nationalism is the name intellectuals and publics are now increasingly giving to the negative antinomies of civil society. The categories of the 'irrational,' 'conspiratorial,' and 'repressive' are taken to be synonymous with forceful expressions of nationality, and equated with pri-

mordiality and uncivilized social forms." *Fin de Siècle Social Theory: Relativism, Reduction, and the Problem of Reason* (London and New York: Verso, 1995), 39.

5 Eric J. Hobsbawm, *Nations and Nationalism Since 1780: Programme, Myth, Reality* (Cambridge: Cambridge University Press, 1991), 14. Further references to this work (hereafter *Nations*) will be given in the body of the text.

6 Ernest Gellner, "Nationalism and Politics in Eastern Europe," *New Left Review* 189 (1991), 128.

7 Ernest Gellner, *Nations and Nationalism* (Ithaca: Cornell University Press, 1992), 48.

8 Michael Löwy, "Why Nationalism?" in Ralph Miliband and Leo Panitch, eds., *Real Problems, False Solutions: Socialist Register* (London: Merlin Press, 1993), 129.

9 *Ibid.*, 129–30.

10 Immanuel Wallerstein, *Geopolitics and Geoculture: Essays on the Changing World-System* (Cambridge: Cambridge University Press, 1992), 139.

11 See Gregory Jusdanis's useful gloss on the tendential logic of contemporary capitalist development: "[T]he concepts of universalism and particularity are neither new nor diametrically opposed but bound by a cord stretched in both directions. This is why we are witnessing not only the creation of federal political systems and free trade zones but also a renewed emphasis on ethnicity and a bloody 'tribalism': the Maastricht Treaty for European integration and the North American Free Trade Agreement, on the one hand, and ethnic cleansing in the former Yugoslavia and bloodletting in the Caucasus, on the other. The transnational conversations conducted by e-mail and fax are disrupted by the trumpets' blare of enmity." "Beyond National Culture?" *Boundary 2* 22.1 (1995), 51.

12 Chris Harman, "The State and Capitalism Today," *International Socialism* 51 (1991), 33.

13 Compare Basil Davidson, who provides a necessary corrective to Hobsbawm here: "Dositej Obradovic had certainly not envisaged a Serbian nationalism that would turn patriotism into an all-purpose chauvinism and duly ruin every political structure to which it put its hand. The early nationalists of Croatia would assuredly have drawn back in loathing if they could have foreseen the murderous brutalities of the so-called Croatian Independent State, Nezavisna Drzava Hrvatska, set up in 1941 by Croat servants of German Nazism and Italian Fascism. Not even Lajos Kossuth in his most nationalistic mood would have thought so much as possible the mass murder of the Jews of the Vojvodina by Hungarians in and after that terrible year of 1941." *The Black Man's Burden: Africa and the Curse of the Nation-State* (New York: Times Books, 1992), 161. Further references to this work (hereafter *Burden*) will be given in the body of the text.

14 Brennan, "The National Longing," 58.

15 *Ibid.*

16 V.I. Lenin, *The Right of Nations to Self-Determination* (Moscow: Progress

Publishers, 1979), 24. Italics in original.

17 See also the following: "*Insofar as* the bourgeoisie of the oppressed nation fights the oppressor, we are always, in every case, and more strongly than anyone else, *in favour*, for we are the staunchest and the most consistent enemies of oppression. But insofar as the bourgeoisie of the oppressed nations stands for *its own* bourgeois nationalism, we stand against. We fight against the privileges and violence of the oppressor nation, and do not in any way condone strivings for privileges on the part of the oppressed nation" (*ibid.*, 23; italics in original).

18 Michael Löwy, "Democrats and Demagogues," *Red Pepper* (July 1996), 14.

19 *Ibid.* The text of the passage in which Lenin likens the principle of the self-determination of nations to divorce reads as follows: "The reactionaries are opposed to freedom of divorce; they say that it must be 'handled carefully', and loudly declare that it means the 'disintegration of the family'. The democrats, however, believe that the reactionaries are hypocrites, and that they are actually defending the omnipotence of the police and the bureaucracy, the privileges of one of the sexes, and the worst kind of oppression of women. They believe that in actual fact freedom of divorce will not cause the 'disintegration' of family ties, but, on the contrary, will strengthen them on a democratic basis, which is the only possible and durable basis in civilised society" (*Right of Nations*, 33).

20 Aijaz Ahmad, *In Theory: Classes, Nations, Literatures* (London and New York: Verso, 1992), 11. Further references to this work (hereafter *In Theory*) will be given in the body of the text.

21 Ahmad's sentence actually continues: " . . . and it [i.e., "this way of viewing things"] does not characterize nations and states as coercive entities *as such.*" In his denunciatory review of *In Theory*, Partha Chatterjee seizes upon this clause and proclaims rather condescendingly that it shows that Ahmad does not know his Marx. "It would," he writes, "have to be a very strange Marxist-Leninist indeed who would suggest that . . . some nations and some states might be noncoercive. What would a state do if it did not coerce?" "The Need to Dissemble," *Public Culture* 6.1 (1993), 60. With respect to the Marxist theory of the *state*, this objection must, I think, be upheld: Ahmad does indeed commit himself to what I regard as an unsustainable position, namely that states are not necessarily the instruments of class domination. But Ahmad also claims that it is wrong to characterize *nations and nationalisms* as inherently coercive forces. And here, it seems to me, his Marxist credentials are impeccable, and tell decisively against the idealism of Chatterjee's own recent scholarship. Ahmad offers a defense of his own position against Chatterjee's strictures in "A Response," *Public Culture* 6.1 (1993), esp. 167–68.

22 Eric Hobsbawm, "Barbarism: A User's Guide," *New Left Review* 206 (1994), 45–46. I cite this passage not in the first instance to endorse (or, for that matter, to criticize) it, but simply to draw attention to the vast differences that exist between the general assumptions informing Hobsbawm's work and those informing the work of today's post-

structuralist and/or postmodernist critics. The sentiments to which Hobsbawm here declares his allegiance would be anathema to such writers as – say – Partha Chatterjee or Judith Butler or Jean-François Lyotard. However, with respect to the cited passage itself, let me add that while I do endorse – and fully – Hobsbawm's emphasis upon the indispensability of Enlightenment rationality to any adequate conception of social freedom, I find his contention that the long nineteenth century bore "material and moral" witness to "the progress of civility" quite unconvincing. It seems to me that nobody who takes proper cognizance of slavery or colonialism could construe the years between 1789 and 1914 in these terms. Aimé Césaire, Frantz Fanon, and C.L.R. James all provide necessary correctives to such a Eurocentrically limited understanding.

23 Anne McClintock, *Imperial Leather: Race, Gender and Sexuality in the Colonial Contest* (New York and London: Routledge, 1995), 353.

24 *Ibid.*, 352.

25 Benedict Anderson, *Imagined Communities: Reflections on the Origin and Spread of Nationalism* (London: Verso, 1983), 129. Further references to this work (hereafter *Imagined*) will be given in the body of the text. Although most contemporary commentators view nationalism as being constitutively racist in character, few have provided intellectually rigorous arguments in support of this assumption. One of the very few who has is Etienne Balibar, who argues in general that "in the historical 'field' of nationalism, there is always a reciprocity of determination between this and racism." ("Racism and Nationalism," in Balibar and Immanuel Wallerstein, *Race, Nation, Class: Ambiguous Identities*, trans. [of Balibar] Chris Turner [London and New York: Verso, 1991], 52.) For socialists especially, Balibar maintains, it is essential to reflect upon this "reciprocity of determination," for one cannot "simply ignore the fact that there is a common element – if only the logic of a situation, the structural inscription in the political forms of the modern world – in the nationalism of the Algerian FLN and that of the French colonial army, or today in the nationalism of the ANC and that of the Afrikaners. Let us take this to its extreme conclusion and say that this formal symmetry is not unrelated to the painful experience we have repeatedly undergone of seeing nationalism of liberation transformed into nationalisms of domination (just as we have seen socialist revolutions turn around to produce state dictatorships), which has compelled us at regular intervals to inquire into the oppressive potentialities contained within every nationalism" (pp. 45–46). In implicit accord with the Leninist doctrine, Balibar concedes that "[w]e have no right whatever to equate the nationalism of the dominant with that of the dominated, the nationalism of liberation with the nationalism of conquest . . . Fichte or Gandhi are not Bismarck; Bismarck or De Gaulle are not Hitler" (p. 45). Yet, speculating further on the all-too-frequently revealed racism of nationalist movements, Balibar develops the thesis that "racism is not an 'expression' of nationalism but *a supplement of nationalism* or more precisely *a supplement internal to nationalism*" (p. 54). I find Balibar's argument

plausible but not conclusive; and the provisional case that Anderson puts for the *separability* of racism and nationalism in *Imagined Communities* seems to me to be rather more compelling. See also James M. Blaut, *The National Question: Decolonizing the Theory of Nationalism* (London: Zed Press, 1987).

26 Frantz Fanon, *The Wretched of the Earth*, trans. Constance Farrington (New York: Grove Press, 1968), 36. Further references to this work (hereafter *Wretched*) will be given in the body of the text.

27 Homi K. Bhabha, "A Question of Survival: Nations and Psychic States," in James Donald, ed., *Psychoanalysis and Cultural Theory: Thresholds* (New York: St. Martin's Press, 1991), 102. Further references to this article (hereafter "Question") will be given in the body of the text.

28 Benita Parry, "Problems in Current Theories of Colonial Discourse," *Oxford Literary Review* 9.1–2 (1987), 31. Further references to this essay (hereafter "Problems") will be given in the body of the text.

29 I use this phrase, "nationalist internationalism," to indicate Fanon's dual revolutionary commitments to the national liberation struggle *and* the wider struggle for socialist internationalism – both, for him, entailed in the concept of anti-imperialism. In coining the phrase, I was not initially aware that it had a history. However, Balibar notes that it was first used by Wilhelm Reich, whose concern, Balibar writes, "was to understand the mimetic effects" both of the "paradoxical internationalism" of Marxism and of "another" paradoxical internationalism, "which was increasingly tending to realize itself in the form of an 'internationalist nationalism' just as, following the example of the 'socialist homeland' and around it and beneath, the Communist parties were turning into 'national parties', a development which in some cases drew upon anti-Semitism." "Racism and Nationalism," in Balibar and Wallerstein, *Race, Nation, Class*, 62–63. Balibar uses Reich's concept to further his thesis concerning the supplementarity of racism to nationalism. Since, as I have already indicated above, I do not accept this thesis, my own use of the concept is rather different: for me it emphasizes the indispensability (and relative privilege) of the national liberation struggle to the wider struggle for socialism.

30 "[The] nationalitarian phenomenon . . . has as its object, beyond the clearing of the national territory, the independence and sovereignty of the national state, uprooting in depth the positions of the ex-colonial power – the reconquest of the power of decision in all domains of national life . . . Historically, fundamentally, the struggle is for national liberation, the instrument of that reconquest of identity which . . . lies at the center of everything." Anouar Abdel-Malek, *Nation and Revolution*, trans. Mike Conzalez (Albany: State University of New York Press, 1981), 13. See also Amilcar Cabral, *Return to the Source: Selected Speeches by Amilcar Cabral*, Africa Information Service, ed. (New York: Monthly Review Press, 1973): "[T]he chief goal of the liberation movement goes beyond the achievement of political independence to the superior level of complete liberation of the productive forces and the construction of economic, social and cultural

progress of the people" (p. 52). Further references to this work (here-after *Return*) will be given in the body of the text.

31 Homi K. Bhabha, "Remembering Fanon: Self, Psyche, and the Colo-nial Condition," in Barbara Kruger and Phil Mariani, eds., *Remaking History* (Seattle: Bay Press, 1989), 146. Further references to this essay (hereafter "Remembering") will be given in the body of the text.

32 In her essay, "Signs of Our Times: A Discussion of Homi Bhabha's *The Location of Culture*," *Third Text* 28/29 (1994), Benita Parry juxtaposes Bhabha's repeated insistence on the agonistic – as distinct from antag-onistic – quality of colonial relations with Fanon's "stark definition" of decolonization as "the meeting of two forces, opposed to each other by their very nature" (p. 13). "It would seem," she continues, "that the contestation of colonialism's claims in an idiom avowing a struggle between polarised forces, fought against a decidable oppo-nent across binary battle lines, makes present-day postcolonialist theorists embarrassed by anti-colonialist forebears who failed to con-form to their rules about discursive radicalism, and who, by projec-ting the making of an insurgent subjectivity, committed what Bhabha considers the solecism of introducing 'restrictive notions of cultural identity with which we burden our visions of political change'."

33 Homi K. Bhabha, "Interrogating Identity: The Postcolonial Preroga-tive," in David Theo Goldberg, ed., *Anatomy of Racism* (Minneapolis: University of Minnesota Press, 1990), 198.

34 Homi K. Bhabha, "DissemiNation: Time, Narrative, and the Margins of the Modern Nation," in Bhabha, *Nation and Narration*, 302. Further references to this article (hereafter "DissemiNation") will be given in the body of the text.

35 Christopher Miller, *Theories of Africans: Francophone Literature and An-thropology in Africa* (Chicago and London: University of Chicago Press, 1990), 32. Further references to this work (hereafter *Theories*) will be given in the body of the text.

36 Miller regards such commitments and emphases as these in Fanon's thought as crippling liabilities. I believe them, on the contrary, to be for the most part not only correct but also indispensable. On my reading, thus, the nation *is* a decisive site of anti-imperialist struggle. Similarly, it seems to me that the trajectory of modernity *does* proceed from "history . . . to History, particular to universal, local to global" – it is precisely in this feature that the singularity and historical un-precedentedness of capitalism resides. I shall return to these points later in this chapter. My intention here, however, is solely to register that in his work Fanon merely *proclaims* these commitments, rather than justifying them. Miller is right, therefore, to point out that Fanon fails to subject them to critical scrutiny.

37 Terry Eagleton, "Nationalism: Irony and Commitment," in Terry Eagleton, Fredric Jameson, and Edward W. Said, *Nationalism, Colo-nialism, and Literature* (Minneapolis: University of Minnesota Press, 1990), 28. Romantic nationalist ideology is well exemplified in the following statement, drawn from Karl Renner's 1899 *State and Nation*: "[The people] become conscious of themselves as a force with a

historical destiny. They demand control over the state, as the highest available instrument of power, and strive for their political self-determination. The birthday of the political idea of the nation and the birth-year of this new consciousness, is 1789, the year of the French Revolution" (quoted in Hobsbawm, *Nations*, 101).

38 Frantz Fanon, *Black Skin, White Masks*, trans. Charles Lam Markmann (New York: Grove Press, 1977), 110. Further references to this work (hereafter *Black Skin*) will be given in the body of the text.

39 See also the revealing passage in which Fanon begins by speaking of "the town belonging to the colonized people," but then revises himself: " . . . or at least the native town, the Negro village, the medina, the reservation." The latter, he writes, is "a place of ill fame, peopled by men of evil repute . . . The native town is a hungry town, starved of bread, of meat, of shoes, of coal, of light. The native town is a crouching village, a town on its knees, a town wallowing in the mire. It is a town of niggers and dirty Arabs" (*Wretched*, 39).

40 Patrick Taylor, *The Narrative of Liberation: Perspectives on Afro-Caribbean Literature, Popular Culture, and Politics* (Ithaca: Cornell University Press, 1989), 60. Further references to this work (hereafter *Narrative*) will be given in the body of the text.

41 See also the following: "The native *rebuilds* his perceptions because he *renews* the purpose and dynamism of dancing and music, and of literature and the oral tradition. His world comes to lose its accursed character" (*Wretched*, 243–44; emphasis added).

42 See *An Antonio Gramsci Reader: Selected Writings, 1916–1935*, ed. David Forgacs (New York: Schocken Books, 1988), esp. 189–221, 306–07.

43 Abdul JanMohamed, "The Economy of Manichean Allegory: The Function of Racial Difference in Colonialist Literature," in Henry Louis Gates, Jr., ed., *"Race," Writing, and Difference* (Chicago and London: University of Chicago Press, 1986), 80.

44 *Ibid.*, 81.

45 In his book, *Manichean Aesthetics: The Politics of Literature in Colonial Africa* (Amherst: University of Massachusetts Press, 1983), Jan-Mohamed had earlier proposed that "in the colonial situation the function of class is replaced by race" (p. 5) – a reductive reading that works similarly to deny the pertinence of hierarchical divisions within colonized societies.

46 Ranajit Guha, "Colonialism in South Asia: A Dominance without Hegemony and Its Historiography," in *Dominance without Hegemony: History and Power in Colonial India* (Cambridge: Harvard University Press, 1997), 1–99. Further references to this essay (hereafter "Dominance") will be given in the body of the text.

47 Cedric Robinson offers a Marxist critique of the class address of *Black Skin, White Masks* in his essay, "The Appropriation of Frantz Fanon," *Race & Class* 35.1 (1993), 79–91.

48 Ranajit Guha, "On Some Aspects of the Historiography of Colonial India," in Guha, ed., *Subaltern Studies I. Writings on South Asian History and Society* (Delhi: Oxford University Press, 1986), 4. Further references to this essay (hereafter "On Some Aspects") will be given in the

body of the text.

49 See Neil Lazarus, *Resistance in Postcolonial African Fiction* (New Haven: Yale University Press, 1990), 8–17.

50 Ian Clegg, "Workers and Managers in Algeria," in Robin Cohen, Peter C.W. Gutkind, and Phyllis Brazier, eds., *Peasants and Proletarians: The Struggles of Third World Workers* (New York: Monthly Review Press, 1979), 239. Further references to this article (hereafter "Workers") will be given in the body of the text.

51 See, for example – among literally dozens of studies that could be cited – Ranajit Guha, *Elementary Aspects of Peasant Insurgency* (Delhi: Oxford University Press, 1983); Benedict J. Tria Kerkvliet, *Everyday Politics in the Philippines: Class and Status Relations in a Central Luzon Village* (Berkeley: University of California Press, 1990); Terence O. Ranger, *Peasant Consciousness and Guerrilla War in Zimbabwe* (Berkeley: University of California Press, 1985); and Peter Rigby, *Persistent Pastoralists: Nomadic Societies in Transition* (London: Zed Books, 1985). See also the excellent overviews of recent scholarship on peasant consciousness and insurgency in Africa and Latin America, respectively, by Allen F. Isaacman, "Peasants and Rural Social Protest in Africa," and William Roseberry, "Beyond the Agrarian Question in Latin America," in Frederick Cooper, Allen F. Isaacman, Florencia E. Mallon, William Roseberry, and Steve J. Stern, *Confronting Historical Paradigms: Peasants, Labor, and the Capitalist World System in Africa and Latin America* (Madison: University of Wisconsin Press, 1993), 205–317 and 318–68.

52 Isaacman, "Peasants and Rural Social Protest," 255.

53 *Ibid.*, 260.

54 James C. Scott, *Weapons of the Weak: Everyday Forms of Peasant Resistance* (New Haven: Yale University Press, 1985), 348–49. *Weapons of the Weak* is the second in a trio of books written by Scott over a ten-year period which, taken together, trace a disappointing if symptomatic trajectory from a broadly Marxist to a squarely post-Marxist standpoint on the questions of peasant revolution and anti-imperialist struggle. *Weapons* already begins to abandon the heterodox Marxist problematic of the earlier *The Moral Economy of the Peasant: Rebellion and Subsistence in Southeast Asia* (New Haven and London: Yale University Press, 1976), eschewing its concepts and vocabulary in favor of the cultural studies-inflected concepts of "hegemony" and "everyday resistance." By the time of *Domination and the Arts of Resistance: Hidden Transcripts* (New Haven: Yale University Press, 1990), the process is complete. As Tim Brennan has written, Scott now "openly contests not only ideology but hegemony as well. The logic of his argument [in *Domination and the Arts of Resistance*] is to heroize the oppressed and to cast the spokespeople for armed resistance or parliamentary strategies in the role of disrespectful paternalists, while at the same time portraying power relations as a closed circle in which resistance always complements repression." *At Home in the World: Cosmopolitanism Now* (Cambridge: Harvard University Press, 1997), 56–57.

55 Robert Young, *White Mythologies: Writing History and the West*

(London and New York: Routledge, 1990), 121.

56 *Ibid.*, 122.
57 Karl Marx, *Contribution to the Critique of Hegel's Philosophy of Right*, in T.B. Bottomore, ed. and trans. *Karl Marx: Early Writings* (New York: McGraw Hill, 1964), 59.
58 Gayatri Chakravorty Spivak, "Can the Subaltern Speak?" in Cary Nelson and Lawrence Grossberg, eds., *Marxism and the Interpretation of Culture* (Urbana and Chicago: University of Illinois Press, 1988), 295. Further references to this essay (hereafter "Subaltern") will be given in the body of the text.
59 Gayatri Chakravorty Spivak, "Practical Politics of the Open End," interview with Sarah Harasym, in Sarah Harasym, ed., *The Post-Colonial Critic: Interviews, Strategies, Dialogues* (New York and London: Routledge, 1990), 102. See also "Who Claims Alterity?" in Kruger and Mariani, *Remaking History*, in which Spivak writes that "[t]he master-words implicated in Indian decolonization offered four great legitimizing codes consolidated by the national bourgeoisie by way of the culture of imperialism: nationalism, internationalism, secularism, culturalism. If the privileged subject operated by these codes masquerades as the subject of an alternative history, we must meditate upon how they (we) are written, rather than simply read their masque as historical exposition" (pp. 269–70).
60 A telling critique of Miller's reading of Fanon – one that accords strongly with the argument I am developing in the present chapter – is to be found in Ato Sekyi-Otu, *Fanon's Dialectic of Experience* (Cambridge and London: Harvard University Press, 1996), 31–46. I have also drawn on Brennan, *At Home in the World*, 53–54; and Tamara Jakubowska, "The Ethics of Ethnicity: A Commentary on Christopher Miller's Theories on Mediating African Literature," unpublished paper, University of Essex, 1993.
61 G.W.F. Hegel, *The Philosophy of History*, trans. J. Sibree (New York: Dover Publications, 1956), 91, 93.
62 Hugh Trevor-Roper, *The Rise of Christian Europe* (New York: Harcourt Brace Jovanovich, 1965), 9.
63 Abdelkebir Khatibi, "Double Criticism: The Decolonization of Arab Sociology," in Halim Barakat, ed., *Contemporary North Africa: Issues of Development and Integration* (Washington, DC: Center for Contemporary Arab Studies, 1985), 12.
64 For a critical analysis of African socialism explicitly animated by Fanon's reading, see Ayi Kwei Armah, "African Socialism: Utopian or Scientific?" *Présence Africaine* 64.4 (1967), 6–30.
65 Two articles that usefully assess the politics of representation in contemporary cultural studies are Linda Alcoff, "The Problem of Speaking for Others," *Cultural Critique* 20 (1991–92), 5–32, and Ella Shohat, "The Struggle Over Representation: Casting, Coalitions, and the Politics of Identification," in Roman de la Campa, E. Ann Kaplan, and Michael Sprinker, eds., *Late Imperial Culture* (London and New York: Verso, 1995), 166–78. Alcoff observes, with particular reference to contemporary feminist theory (although the point is generalizable,

it seems to me), that "[a]s a type of discursive practice, speaking for others has come under increasing criticism, and in some communities it is being rejected. There is a strong, albeit contested, current within [critical theory] which holds that speaking for others is arrogant, vain, unethical, and politically illegitimate" (p. 6).

66 See R. Radhakrishnan's splendid critique of Foucault's delegitimation of representation in "Toward an Effective Intellectual: Foucault or Gramsci?" in *Diasporic Mediations: Between Home and Location* (Minneapolis and London: University of Minnesota Press, 1996), 27–61.

67 Trinh T. Minh-ha, *Woman, Native, Other: Writing Postcoloniality and Feminism* (Bloomington: Indiana University Press, 1989), 12–13.

68 Theodor W. Adorno, *Minima Moralia: Reflections from Damaged Life*, trans. E.F.N. Jephcott (London: Verso, 1978), 28.

69 Cf. Benita Parry, who perceptively notes that "[a]t a time when dialectical thinking is not the rage amongst colonial discourse theorists, it is instructive to recall how Fanon's dialogical interrogation of European power and native insurrection reconstructs a process of cultural resistance *and* cultural disruption, participates in writing a text that *can* answer colonialism back, *and* anticipates another condition beyond imperialism" ("Problems," 44).

70 Davidson himself has written widely on this subject. See, for instance, *The Fortunate Isles: A Study in African Transformation* (Trenton, NJ: Africa World Press; London: Century-Radius, 1989); *No Fist Is Big Enough to Hide the Sky* (London: Zed Books, 1984); and "On Revolutionary Nationalism: The Legacy of Cabral," *Race & Class* 27.3 (1986), 21–45.

71 I take for granted here the unsustainability of all formulations of the idea of "socialism in one country," no matter what their specific ideological provenance (Stalinist, Maoist, etc.) might be.

72 Radhakrishnan, *Diasporic Mediations*, 189.

73 Gayatri Chakravorty Spivak, "Woman in Difference: Mahasweta Devi's 'Douloti the Bountiful'," *Cultural Critique* 14 (1990), 107.

74 Pierre Bourdieu, "The Uses of the 'People'," in *In Other Words: Essays Towards a Reflexive Sociology*, trans. Matthew Aronson (Stanford: Stanford University Press, 1990), 150.

75 *Ibid.*, 152.

76 Ranajit Guha, "The Prose of Counter-Insurgency," in Ranajit Guha, ed., *Subaltern Studies II. Writings on South Asian History and Society* (Delhi: Oxford University Press, 1986), 1–2.

77 Gayatri Chakravorty Spivak, "How to Read a 'Culturally Different' Book," in Francis Barker, Peter Hulme, and Margaret Iversen, eds., *Colonial Discourse/Postcolonial Theory* (Manchester and New York: Manchester University Press, 1994), 143. See also the following: "Insofar as [the disenfranchised *female* in decolonized space] . . . can be represented among us . . . it is, first, as an object of knowledge, further, as a native-informant style subject of oral histories who is patronizingly considered incapable of strategy towards us, and finally, as imagined subject/object, in the real field of literature" ("Who Claims Alterity?" 273).

78 For further commentary on the debate between Spivak and Parry, see Jenny Sharpe, "Figures of Colonial Resistance," *Modern Fiction Studies* 35.1 (1989), 137–55.

79 Gayatri Chakravorty Spivak, "Feminism and Critical Theory," in *In Other Worlds: Essays in Cultural Politics* (New York: Methuen, 1987), 81.

80 See Silvia Tandeciarz, "Reading Gayatri Spivak's 'French Feminism in an International Frame': A Problem for Theory," *Genders* 10 (1991), 75–90. Tandeciarz charges that "Spivak falls precisely into that trap she seeks to avoid; she displaces both her purported political commitment and the possibility of addressing and learning from 'Third World women' in favor of exploring the pitfalls of French feminist theory and advancing in turn her own, seemingly 'more enlightened' perspective" (p. 76).

81 V.Y. Mudimbe, *Parables and Fables: Exegesis, Textuality, and Politics in Central Africa* (Madison: University of Wisconsin Press, 1991), 171. Further references to this work (hereafter *Parables*) will be given in the body of the text.

82 See Neil Lazarus, "Doubting the New World Order: Marxism and Postmodernist Social Theory," *differences. A Journal of Feminist Cultural Studies* 3.3 (1991), 94–138; and Neil Lazarus, Steven Evans, Anthony Arnove, and Anne Menke, "The Necessity of Universalism," *differences. A Journal of Feminist Cultural Studies* 7.1 (1995), 75–145.

83 Satya P. Mohanty, "Colonial Legacies, Multicultural Futures: Relativism, Objectivity, and the Challenge of Otherness," *PMLA* 110.1 (1995), 113.

84 The term "co-evality" (and its antonym, "allochrony") derives from Johannes Fabian's influential study, *Time and the Other: How Anthropology Makes Its Object* (New York: Columbia University Press, 1983).

85 Mohanty, "Colonial Legacies," 114–15.

86 For a definitive formulation of this liberal historiographic representation of nationalism in the European context, see Gellner, *Nations and Nationalism*, 19–52.

87 Edward W. Said, "Yeats and Decolonization," in Eagleton, Jameson, and Said, *Nationalism, Colonialism, and Literature*, 76. The phrasing is slightly revised in the version of "Yeats and Decolonization" that appears in Said's *Culture and Imperialism* (New York: Alfred A. Knopf, 1993), 220–38.

88 Radhakrishnan, *Diasporic Mediations*, 189.

89 See my treatment of this rhetorically apocalyptic but ideologically vapid discourse as it manifests itself in the work of the African novelist, Ayi Kwei Armah, in Chapters 5 and 6 of *Resistance in Postcolonial African Fiction*.

90 Masao Miyoshi, "Sites of Resistance in the Global Economy," *Boundary 2* 22.1 (1995), 76.

91 Gyan Prakash, "Writing Post-Orientalist Histories of the Third World: Perspectives from Indian Historiography," *Comparative Studies in Society and History* (1990), 390–91. Further references to this essay (hereafter "Post-Orientalist") will be given in the body of the text.

92 Michel Foucault, *The Order of Things: An Archaeology of the Human Sciences*, trans. Alan Sheridan-Smith (New York: Vintage, 1973), 261–62.

93 Dipesh Chakrabarty, "Marx After Marxism: Subaltern Histories and the Question of Difference," *Polygraph* 6/7 (1993), 10–11.

94 Foucault, *The Order of Things*, 262. One recalls, in this context, Fredric Jameson's wry comment that "it was always implicit in the theoreticians of the 'total system,' such as Foucault, that if the system was as tendentially totalizing as he said it was, then all local revolts, let alone 'revolutionary' impulses, remained inside that and were in reality a function of its immanent dynamic." *Postmodernism, or, The Cultural Logic of Late Capitalism* (Durham: Duke University Press, 1992), 203.

95 Partha Chatterjee, *Nationalist Thought and the Colonial World: A Derivative Discourse* (Minneapolis: University of Minnesota Press, 1993), 38. Further reference to this work (hereafter *Nationalist Thought*) will be given in the body of the text.

96 Dipesh Chakrabarty, "Postcoloniality and the Artifice of History: Who Speaks for 'Indian' Pasts?" *Representations* 37 (1992), 19.

97 The necessary corrective is provided by Roy Bhaskar, who points out that the mechanism of the Marxist dialectic "is not in general teleological, but even when it is, its teleology presupposes causality . . . The practical resolution of the contradiction here is the non-preservative transformative negation of the ground, which is the problem, not the solution. This involves what I am going to call '*transformed transformative totalizing transformist praxis*' in the struggle, presaged upon Marx's analysis of the dialectic processes of capitalism, for a sublation, traditionally known as 'socialism,' of the replaced social form." *Dialectic: The Pulse of Freedom* (Verso: London and New York, 1993), 60–61.

98 Halim Barakat, *The Arab World: Society, Culture, and State* (Berkeley: University of California Press, 1993), 161–62.

99 And see also Kwame Anthony Appiah, who points out in *In My Father's House: Africa in the Philosophy of Culture* (New York and Oxford: Oxford University Press, 1992) that "African and Asian intellectuals do not believe in national self-determination simply because it was forced upon them, because it was imposed as a tool of their continued neocolonial domination; rather, the idea of the nation provided – first for the local elite, then for the newly proletarianized denizens of the colonial city, and finally even for a peasantry attempting to come to terms with its increasing incorporation into the world system – a way to articulate a resistance both to the material domination of the world empires and to the more nebulous threat to precolonial modes of thought represented by the Western project of cultural ascendancy" (pp. 53–54).

100 Achin Vanaik, *The Furies of Indian Communalism: Religion, Modernity and Secularization* (London and New York: Verso, 1997), 187.

101 Homi K. Bhabha, "Articulating the Archaic: Notes on Colonial Nonsense," in Peter Collier and Helga Greyer-Ryan, eds., *Literary Theory*

Today (Ithaca: Cornell University Press, 1990), 210.

102 Homi K. Bhabha, "Signs Taken For Wonders: Questions of Ambivalence and Authority Under a Tree Outside Delhi, May 1817," in Gates, ed., *"Race," Writing, and Difference*, 169. Further references to this article (hereafter "Signs") will be given in the body of the text.

103 Homi K. Bhabha, "Of Mimicry and Man: The Ambivalence of Colonial Discourse," *October* 28 (1984), 126.

104 *Ibid.*, 130.

105 Bhabha, "A Question of Survival," 90.

106 Salman Rushdie, *Shame* (New York: Alfred A. Knopf, 1983), 89–90.

107 Brennan, *At Home in the World*, 123–24.

108 Vanaik, *The Furies of Indian Communalism*, 42. See also Gopal Balakrishnan's statement (in a commentary on Anderson's *Imagined Communities*) that "[i]f we cannot honestly prefer the nation to the International, Anderson's book is a reminder that, at its best, imagined nationhood in all its crudity has been the entry ticket for the wretched of the earth into world history." "The National Imagination," *New Left Review* 211 (1995), 69.

109 Jusdanis, "Beyond National Culture?" 31. Jusdanis adds that "[s]uch a conceptualization is peculiarly modern in that only nation-states aspire to a national consciousness, a collective history, and a common destiny."

110 Rogers Brubaker, "Rethinking Nationhood: Nation as Institutionalized Form, Practical Category, Contingent Event," *Contention* 4.1 (1994), 10. Brubaker continues as follows: "It is a world in which nation is widely, if unevenly, available and resonant as a category of social vision and division. It is a world in which nationness may suddenly, and powerfully, 'happen.' But none of this implies a world of nations – of substantial, enduring collectivities."

111 Edward W. Said, "Figures, Configurations, Transfigurations," *Race & Class* 32.1 (1990), 1–2.

112 In this essay, San Juan offers a suggestive analysis of Roque Dalton's extraordinary essay, "Poetry and Militancy in Latin America." Quoting directly from Dalton's essay, San Juan writes as follows: "Retrospectively noting the 'painful scars' left by his Jesuit education, his irresponsible lifestyle nurtured in the 'womb of the mean-spirited Salvadoran bourgeoisie,' Dalton's career exemplifies the predicament of the Third World artist bifurcated by his 'long and deep bourgeois formative period' and his 'Communist militancy.' His text registers the hesitancies, reservations, misgivings and scruples of this hybrid genealogy. The writer engages in self-criticism not by jettisoning the past, but by subsuming it in a dialectical mode of absorption/negation: he believes that far from exhausting its potential, the bourgeois outlook offers 'creative possibilities,' so by discarding its essentially negative aspects, the artist can 'use it as an instrument to create ideal conditions for the new people's art that will spring up' in the process of Salvadorans fashioning a new autonomous life for themselves." In *Ruptures, Schisms, Interventions: Cultural Revolution in the Third World* (Manila: De La Salle University

Press, 1988), 90.

113 Edward W. Said, *Representations of the Intellectual: The 1993 Reith Lectures* (New York: Pantheon Books, 1994), 43–44.

114 *Ibid.*, xviii.

115 Edward W. Said, "Nationalism, Human Rights, and Interpretation," *Raritan* 12.3 (1993), 41–42.

116 Bourdieu, *In Other Words*, 147.

117 Samir Amin, "The Social Movements in the Periphery: An End to National Liberation?" in Samir Amin, Giovanni Arrighi, André Gunder Frank, and Immanuel Wallerstein, *Transforming the Revolution: Social Movements and the World-System* (New York: Monthly Review Press, 1990), 136.

118 V.I. Lenin, *What Is To Be Done? Burning Questions of Our Movement* (New York: International Publishers, 1969), 25.

119 Henry Louis Gates, Jr., "Critical Fanonism," *Critical Inquiry* 17.3 (1991), 458.

3   Cricket, modernism, national culture: the case of C. L. R. James

1 Hazel V. Carby, "Proletarian or Revolutionary Literature: C.L.R. James and the Politics of the Trinidadian Renaissance," *South Atlantic Quarterly* 87.1 (1988), 51.

2 Since 1989, several new editions of works by James have been released: these include *American Civilization*, ed. Anna Grimshaw and Keith Hart (Oxford: Blackwell, 1993); *Beyond a Boundary* (Durham: Duke University Press, 1993); *The Black Jacobins* (New York: Vintage Books, 1989); and *World Revolution, 1917–1936: The Rise and Fall of the Communist International* (Atlantic Highlands, NJ: Humanities Press, 1993). Recent edited collections of James's writings include Scott McLemee and Paul Le Blanc, eds., *C.L.R. James and Revolutionary Marxism: Selected Writings of C.L.R. James, 1939–1949* (Atlantic Highlands, NJ: Humanities Press, 1994); Scott McLemee, ed., *C.L.R. James on the "Negro Question"* (Jackson: University Press of Mississippi, 1996); and Anna Grimshaw, ed., *The C.L.R. James Reader* (Oxford: Blackwell, 1992). Anna Grimshaw has also edited *Special Delivery: The Letters of C.L.R. James to Constance Webb, 1939–48* (Oxford: Blackwell, 1995). Recent studies of James's life, politics, and thought include Anthony Bogues, *Caliban's Freedom: The Early Political Thought of C.L.R. James* (London and Chicago: Pluto Press, 1997); Paul Buhle, *C.L.R. James: The Artist as Revolutionary* (London: Verso, 1988); Aldon Lynn Nielsen, *C.L.R. James: A Critical Introduction* (Jackson: University Press of Mississippi, 1997); and Kent Worcester, *C.L.R. James: A Political Biography* (Albany: State University of New York Press, 1996). Several recent collections of critical essays dedicated to James's work have also been published, among them Paul Buhle and Paget Henry, eds., *C.L.R. James's Caribbean* (Durham: Duke University Press, 1992); Selwyn Cudjoe and William E. Cain, eds., *C.L.R. James: His Intellectual Legacies* (Amherst: University of Massachusetts Press, 1995); and

Grant Farred, ed., *Rethinking C.L.R. James* (Oxford: Blackwell, 1996). See also the chapter devoted to James in Timothy Brennan, *At Home in the World: Cosmopolitanism Now* (Cambridge: Harvard University Press, 1997), 208–58.

3 Michael Manley, *A History of West Indies Cricket* (London, Sydney, and Auckland: Pan Books, 1988), 13. Further references to this work (hereafter *History*) will be given in the body of the text.

4 E.P. Thompson, "C.L.R. James at 80," *Urgent Tasks* 12 (1981), back cover.

5 Mike Marqusee, *Anyone But England: Cricket and the National Malaise* (London and New York: Verso, 1994), 1. Further references to this work (hereafter *Anyone*) will be given in the body of the text.

6 C.L.R. James, *The Future in the Present: Selected Writings* (London: Allison and Busby, 1977), 214. Further references to this work (hereafter *Future*) will be given in the body of the text.

7 C.L.R. James, *Cricket*, ed. Anna Grimshaw (London: Allison and Busby, 1986), 165–66. Further references to this work will be given in the body of the text.

8 C.L.R. James, *Beyond a Boundary*, 66. Further references to this text (hereafter *Beyond*) will be given in the body of the text.

9 Walter Benjamin, *Illuminations*, trans. Harry Zohn (New York: Schocken Books, 1969), 201.

10 See for instance Roland Barthes's discussion of "The World of Wrestling" in *Mythologies*, trans. Annette Lavers (New York: Hill and Wang, 1987), 15–25.

11 A Test match is a match between the representative teams of two nations. The duration of such a match is five days (although six days are sometimes allotted). Test match cricket is the highest level at which the game is played.

12 James cites with approval the following comment by Cardus: "Why do we deny the art of a cricketer, and rank it lower than a vocalist's or a fiddler's? If anybody tells me that R.H. Spooner did not compel a pleasure as aesthetic as any compelled by the most cultivated Italian tenor that ever lived I will write him down a purist and an ass" (*Beyond*, 195).

13 In using the term "ordinarily" here, I have in mind Raymond Williams's great essay of 1958, "Culture is Ordinary," with its emphasis upon culture as a shared inheritance, held in common by the members of any given society. In *Resources of Hope: Culture, Democracy, Socialism*, ed. Robin Gable (London: Verso, 1989), 3–18.

14 See, for instance, his comments in an essay on "The 1963 West Indians," published just one year later than *Beyond a Boundary*, and reprinted in *Cricket*, 134–46.

15 Adorno himself freely acknowledges this commonality: hence his suggestion that "[n]ot least among the tasks now confronting thought is that of placing all the reactionary arguments against Western culture in the service of progressive enlightenment." *Minima Moralia. Reflections from Damaged Life*, trans. E.F.N. Jephcott (London: Verso, 1978), 192.

16 I derive the concept of "ideologeme" from M.M. Bakhtin and P.N. Medvedev, *The Formal Method in Literary Scholarship: A Critical Intro-duction to Sociological Poetics*, trans. Albert J. Wehrle (Cambridge: Harvard University Press, 1985), esp. 16–37.

17 See Andreas Huyssen, *After the Great Divide. Modernism, Mass Culture, Postmodernism* (Bloomington: Indiana University Press, 1986).

18 There were of course exceptions to this general tendency – among them the avant-gardist practice of such Marxists as Walter Benjamin, with his insistence upon the emancipatory capabilities of the mechan-ically reproduced artwork, and of such fascist artists as the vorticist Wyndham Lewis and the futurist Emilio Marinetti, with their profoundly fetishistic technologism.

19 Max Horkheimer and Theodor W. Adorno, *Dialectic of Enlightenment*, trans. John Cumming (New York: Continuum, 1987), 124. Further references to this work (hereafter *Dialectic*) will be given in the body of the text.

20 For Horkheimer and Adorno, the autonomy of the modern(ist) art-work is not only tenuous. It is also achieved at the definitive price of art's innocence, if not its ingenuousness. The condition of possibility of art is class domination: no matter how hard it tries, art can never wash the stain of its complicity in this domination from its hands. Thus: "[t]he purity of bourgeois art, which hypostasized itself as a world of freedom in contrast to what was happening in the material world, was from the beginning bought with the exclusion of the lower classes – with whose cause, the real universality, art keeps faith precisely by its freedom from the ends of the false universality" (*Dialectic*, 135).

21 See Theodor W. Adorno, "On the Fetish-Character in Music and the Regression of Listening," in Andrew Arato and Eike Gebhardt, eds., *The Essential Frankfurt School Reader* (New York: Continuum, 1985), 270–99.

22 See Adorno's further elaboration of this point in "Culture Industry Reconsidered," trans. Anson Rabinbach, in J.M. Bernstein, ed., *The Culture Industry: Selected Essays on Mass Culture* (London: Routledge, 1992), 85–92.

23 Raymond Williams, *The Politics of Modernism: Against the New Con-formists* (London: Verso, 1989), 33. Further references to this work (hereafter *Politics*) will be given in the body of the text. Williams adds that "[w]e have only to review the names in the real history to see the open ideologizing which permits the selection."

24 I am here rehearsing the terms of Williams's critique: "After Modern-ism is canonized ... there is then the presumption that since Modern-ism is *here* in this specific phase or period, there is nothing beyond it ... . 'Modernism' is confined to this highly selective field and denied to everything else in an act of pure ideology, whose first, unconscious irony is that, absurdly, it stops history dead. Modernism being the terminus, everything afterwards is counted out of development. It is *after*; stuck in the post ... [T]he innovations of what is called Modern-ism have become the new but fixed forms of our present moment. If

we are to break out of the non-historical fixity of *post*-modernism, then we must search out and counterpose an alternative tradition taken from the neglected works left in the wide margin of the century, a tradition which may address itself not to this by now exploitable because quite inhuman rewriting of the past but, for all our sakes, to a modern future in which community may be imagined again" (*ibid.*, 34–35).

25 See Edward W. Said, "Zionism from the Standpoint of Its Victims," in *The Question of Palestine* (New York: Vintage Books, 1992), 56–114. And compare Paul Gilroy's suggestion that "[t]he time has come for the primal history of modernity to be reconstructed from the slaves' points of view." *The Black Atlantic: Modernity and Double Consciousness* (Cambridge: Harvard University Press, 1993), 55. Gilroy explicitly develops his notion of black Atlanticism by way of countering the Eurocentrism of received theories of modernity and modern cultural practice.

26 Adorno, *Minima Moralia*, 15.

27 See Georg Lukács, *History and Class Consciousness: Studies in Marxist Dialectics*, trans. Rodney Livingstone (Cambridge: The MIT Press, 1983), 83–222; and Jürgen Habermas, *The Theory of Communicative Action*, trans. Thomas McCarthy. Two vols.: vol. I: *Reason and the Rationalization of Society* (Boston: Beacon Press, 1984); vol. II: *Lifeworld and System: A Critique of Functionalist Reason* (Boston: Beacon Press, 1989).

28 Charles Williams has recently published a biography of Bradman that comes close to meeting this Jamesian requirement. See *Bradman: An Australian Hero* (London: Little, Brown and Co., 1996).

29 Situated in northwest London, Lord's is the most famous cricket ground in the world. It is a Test match site, home of the Middlesex county side and of the Marylebone Cricket Club, and headquarters of cricket world-wide. For a celebratory history of Lord's, see Sir Pelham Warner, *Lord's: 1787–1945* (London: George G. Harrap, 1946); for a more critically informed perspective, see Marqusee, *Anyone*, 41ff.

30 Ashis Nandy, *The Tao of Cricket: On Games of Destiny and the Destiny of Games* (Calcutta: Penguin Books, 1989), 15. Further references to this work (hereafter *Tao*) will be given in the body of the text.

31 Kenneth Surin, "C.L.R. James's Materialist Aesthetics of Cricket," *Polygraph* 4 (1990), 141–42. Further references to this article (hereafter "Materialist") will be given in the body of the text.

32 Compare Manley, who succumbs here, surprisingly, to the pastoralist myth of pre-industrial England as a world free of class struggle: "Cricket . . . is a game conceived to occupy rather than defeat time. Clearly baseball is a function of urban industrial societies with their time clocks and fiercely concentrated energy. Cricket, however, evolved as a rural entertainment contrived to fill long summer days in which the sun would not disappear from some English meadow till perhaps nine at night. It was a game to occupy the whole of a Sunday or a festive day, designed for picnic lunches and that spacious view of time which is peculiarly of the rural tradition" (*History*, 2).

33 For more on this era, see John Simons, "The Golden Age of Cricket," in Gary Day, ed., *Readings in Popular Culture: Trivial Pursuits?* (New York: St. Martin's Press, 1990), 151–63.

34 The best study of Indian cricket to have appeared to date is arguably Richard Cashman's *Patrons, Players and the Crowd: The Phenomenon of Indian Cricket* (New Delhi: Longman Orient, 1980). See also Cashman, "Cricket and Colonialism: Colonial Hegemony and Indigenous Subversion," in James A. Mangan, ed., *Pleasure, Profit, Proselytism* (London: Frank Cass, 1988), 258–72. For more on the origins and cultural transmission of cricket, see Allen Guttmann, *Games and Empires: Modern Sports and Cultural Imperialism* (New York: Columbia University Press, 1994), 15–40.

35 Hilary Beckles, "The Origins and Development of West Indies Cricket Culture in the Nineteenth Century: Jamaica and Barbados," in Hilary McD. Beckles and Brian Stoddart, eds., *Liberation Cricket: West Indies Cricket Culture* (Manchester and New York: Manchester University Press, 1995), 34–35.

36 Manthia Diawara, "Englishness and Blackness: Cricket as Discourse on Colonialism," *Callaloo* 13.4 (1991), 835.

37 "Creolization" is the term favored in Beckles and Stoddart, eds., *Liberation Cricket*. See especially the essays in Part II of this volume, entitled "Creolisation, Ideology and Popular Culture." But contrast Jonathan Friedman, who suggests that the notion of "creolization" typically proceeds from an idealist "substantialization" of culture: the idea of a "mingling of cultures . . . is a metaphor that can only succeed in terms of a previous metaphor, that of culture as matter, in this case, apparently, a fluid. In strictly formal terms this substantialization of culture also leads to an understanding of the latter in terms of products rather than production. Thus, while allusion is made to the 'social organization of meaning,' the social organization as such all but disappears in references to *flows* of meaning, from the centre to the periphery and back." "Global System, Globalization and the Parameters of Modernity," in Mike Featherstone, Scott Lash and Roland Robertson, eds., *Global Modernities* (London, Thousand Oaks, CA, New Delhi: Sage, 1995), 82.

38 Orlando Patterson, "The Ritual of Cricket," in Beckles and Stoddart, eds., *Liberation Cricket*, 144. In what might appear a counter-intuitive but strikes me instead as a symptomatic gesture, the contemporary anti-foundationalist theorist of "postcoloniality," Helen Tiffin, confesses herself in agreement with Patterson's essentialist critique of James's dialectical argument in her article, "Cricket, Literature and the Politics of De-Colonisation: the Case of C.L.R. James," in Beckles and Stoddart, eds., *Liberation Cricket*, 364–66.

39 Keith Sandiford and Brian Stoddart, "The Elite Schools and Cricket in Barbados: a Study in Colonial Continuity," in Beckles and Stoddart, eds., *Liberation Cricket*, 57.

40 Mark Kingwell, "Keeping a Straight Bat: Cricket, Civility, and Postcolonialism," in Selwyn Cudjoe and William E. Cain, eds., *C.L.R. James: His Intellectual Legacies* (Amherst: University of Massachusetts

Press, 1995), 379–80.

41 The scarcely disguised racism of this report does not, of course, escape
James. Throughout his writing career he attempted to combat the
(still) pervasive stereotypes about "natural" black athleticism. For a
representative treatment of this question, see his "Cricket and Race"
(1975), reprinted in *Cricket*, 278–79. In this context see also Chris
Searle, "Cricket and the Mirror of Racism," *Race & Class* 34.3 (1993),
45–54; and "Race Before Wicket: Cricket, Empire and the White
Rose," *Race & Class* 31.3 (1990), 31–48.

42 Diawara, "Englishness and Blackness," 831. Although in this essay
Diawara tends to privilege the problematic of race – what Fanon calls
"the fact of blackness" – in his consideration of modern African-
diasporic cultural production, he occasionally subordinates race to a
(nationalist) problematic of anti-colonialism. In this respect, his approach differs from that taken by Paul Gilroy in *The Black Atlantic*.
Certainly, the wider intent of Diawara's essay – which is to argue for a
conception of "black performance in contemporary sports and arts"
as a (black) discourse on (white) modernity (p. 835) – is in full accord
with Gilroy's position. I do not know whether Diawara intends to
follow Gilroy in arguing that nationality in the modern world is
always-already racialized. I find suggestive, however, the countervailing indication in at least some passages in his essay that the
question of modernity might need to be situated in the first instance
relative to the formations of *class* and *nation* rather than to that of race;
that the first term in a plausible counter-discourse of modernity might
still be the nationalist concept of "the Caribbean" rather than the
racialized concept of "the *black* Atlantic." Consider, for instance, the
following formulation, in which Diawara attempts to locate the specificity of the West Indian appropriation of cricket: West Indian
cricketers, he writes, "wrested cricket away from Englishness and
made it pliable enough to serve the needs of people in [the Caribbean].
Such a capturing of the game, which destabilized the monolithic
structure of Englishness, constituted the mode of weaving a Caribbean identity in modernist instruments which had hitherto made the
colonized subject into an object. The Caribbean appropriation of modernization, i.e., cricket, literacy, Christianity and industrialization,
demonstrated that there was more than one way, the English way, of
apprehending modernity" (p. 841).

43 In *Beyond a Boundary*, he observes that: "I did not merely play cricket. I
studied it. I analysed strokes, I studied types, I read its history, its
beginnings, how and when it changed from period to period, I read
about it in Australia and in South Africa. I read and compared statis-
tics, I made clippings, I talked to all cricketers, particularly the inter-
colonial cricketers and those who had gone abroad. I compared what
they told me with what I read in old copies of *Wisden*. I looked up the
play of the men who had done well or badly against the West Indies. I
read and appreciated the phraseology of laws" (pp. 32–33).

44 Tim Hector, "West Indian Nationhood, Integration, and Cricket Politics," in Hilary Beckles, ed., *An Area of Conquest: Popular Democracy and*

West Indies Cricket Supremacy (Kingston, Jamaica: Ian Randle Publishers, 1994), 123. Further references to this article (hereafter "West Indian") will be given in the body of the text.

45 "The Welfare State of Mind" is the title of a chapter in *Beyond a Boundary*.

46 Hector also notes that the final day of the fateful Fourth Test in 1968 coincided with the staging of a General Strike in Antigua, in defiance of a State of Emergency that had been imposed there by the oligarchic Prime Minister V.C. Bird ("West Indian," 122).

47 For an eloquent statement of the enduring popular support for the idea of pan-West Indianism, see "Caribbean Unity," a 1979 composition by soca musician Black Stalin (reissued on the album *Roots, Rock, Soca* [Rounder, 1991]):

You try with a Federation, the whole thing end in confusion
Caricom and then Carifta, but somehow I smellin' disaster
Mr. West Indian Politician, I mean you went to big institution
And how come you can't unite seven million
When a West Indian unity I know is very easy
If you only rap to your people and tell them like me

Dem is one race . . . the Caribbean Man
From de same place . . . the Caribbean Man
That make de same trip . . . the Caribbean Man
On de same ship . . . the Caribbean Man
So we must push one common intention
Is for a better life in de region
For we woman and we children
That must be the ambition of the Caribbean Man

48 For commentary on the West Indies–South Africa Test and its subsequent registration in calypso music, see Gordon Rohlehr, "Music, Literature, and West Indian Cricket Values," in Beckles, ed., *An Area of Conquest*, 96ff.

49 For an assessment of the social and historical significance of Lara's Test match innings, see Chris Searle, "Lara's Innings: A Caribbean Moment," *Race & Class* 36.4 (1995), 31–42.

50 I insert the "more or less" here to indicate that both Surin and Nandy do take a critical distance from James even with respect to his broad conceptualization of the game and his narrative of its earlier development. Surin, for instance, faults James both for what he takes to be his idealism and for what he reads as a latent Weberianism. Still, he goes on to note that "[t]o make this criticism is not . . . to dismiss James. All subsequent social and cultural historians of cricket, whether they profess themselves to be Marxists or not, will have to engage with his analyses and proposals. We will have to work through James, not circumvent him. Besides, he was right, deeply right, most of the time" ("Materialist," 135).

51 Bradman himself retired from cricket at the end of the 1940s, at the age of 40. But the kind of play that he was so instrumental in consolidating has continued to represent one of the game's dominant axes ever since

the late 1920s.

52 See his reference to cricket's "culture of anarchic individualism and
. . . peculiar, non-repressive collectivism based on that anarchy" (*Tao*,
2).

53 He adds that it is conceivable that cricket will "survive . . . the
vicissitudes of our time," and that if it does so it "will perhaps survive
as a defiance and critique of modernity in a world moving towards
post-modernity"; but to hope for this is really to "hope against hope,"
in his view.

54 Fredric Jameson, *Postmodernism, or, The Cultural Logic of Late Capitalism* (Durham: Duke University Press, 1992), 307.

55 *Ibid.*, 309–10.

56 In his most recent work, in fact, Nandy has come to champion an
avowedly anti-modernist, "indigenist" neo-traditionalism. See Achin
Vanaik's critique in *The Furies of Indian Communalism: Religion, Modernity and Secularization* (London and New York: Verso, 1997),
130–233.

57 For further commentary on Nandy – which, however, accepts the
terms of his argument in *The Tao of Cricket* – see Kingwell, "Keeping a
Straight Bat."

58 See the entry on Haynes in Jack Bannister's compilation, *The Innings of
My Life* (London: Headline Book Publishing, 1993), 106–09.

59 See also Manley, who offers the following snapshot summary of the
West Indies pace attack: "Holding, all fluid menace; Roberts of the
padding approach and fierce body action; Croft, with his angular,
utilitarian hostility, cutting the ball off the seam and forcing the
batsman to defend his chest and armpits; Garner, delivering from a
great height, obliging batsmen to attempt new and unfamiliar techniques to deal with the extent of deviation and bounce; finally, Marshall, compact, direct and uncompromisingly fast" (*History*, 392).

60 Manley offers a useful corrective to Surin's reading of Lloyd in the
relevant chapters of *A History of West Indies Cricket*. See also John
Arlott, *The Essential Arlott on Cricket: Forty Years of Classic Writing on
the Game*, ed. David Rayvern Allen (London: Fontana, 1989), 109–12.

61 A useful corrective to Surin is provided by Ramachandra Guha in his
chapter on Gavaskar in *Spin and Other Turns: Indian Cricket's Coming of
Age* (New Delhi: Penguin, 1994).

62 English translations of Negri's writings include *Marx Beyond Marx:
Lessons on the Grundrisse*, ed. Jim Fleming, trans. Harry Cleaver,
Michael Ryan, and Maurizio Viano (South Hadley, MA: Bergin and
Garvey, 1984); *The Politics of Subversion: A Manifesto for the Twenty-First
Century*, trans. James Newell (Oxford: Polity Press, 1989); "Twenty
Theses on Marx: Interpretation of the Class Situation Today," trans.
Michael Hardt, *Polygraph* 5 (1992), 136–70; and (with Felix Guattari)
Communists Like Us: New Spaces of Liberty, New Lines of Alliance, trans.
Michael Ryan (New York: Semiotext(e), 1990).

63 Kenneth Surin, "'The Continued Relevance of Marxism' as a Question: Some Propositions," *Polygraph* 6–7 (1993), 52.

64 See my essay "Doubting the New World Order: Marxism and Post-

modernist Social Theory," *differences. A Journal of Feminist Cultural Studies* 3.3 (1991), 94–138. See also Alex Callinicos, who offers a succinct rebuttal of postmodernist and "post-Fordist" theories in *Against Postmodernism: A Marxist Critique* (Oxford: Polity, 1990).

65 See also the following: "About a hundred of the world's top cricketers play each other repeatedly in twenty or so major international cricketing venues . . . year after year, and with the unrelenting 'internationalization' of commercial cricket, they no more express a 'national' spirit or identity than do tennis players domiciled in Monte Carlo but who continue to represent their 'home countries' in the Davis Cup" ("Materialist," 121).

66 Frantz Fanon, *The Wretched of the Earth*, trans. Constance Farrington (New York: Grove Press, 1968), 148.

67 Ambrose took 6–22 in England's second innings, reducing the tourists to 46 all out, their lowest total in a Test since 1887.

68 As mentioned above, Sobers's record was broken early in 1994 by Brian Lara, who scored 375 for the West Indies against England at St. John's, Antigua.

69 A very useful commentary on the "popular ideology" of the crowd in West Indies cricket is provided in Hilary Beckles and Harclyde Walcott, "Redemption Sounds: Music, Literature and the Popular Ideology of West Indian Cricket Crowds," in Beckles and Stoddart, eds., *Liberation Cricket*, 370–83.

70 In this respect, see also Ashis Nandy, who writes in *The Tao of Cricket* that "[t]he West Indian fanaticism in cricket may look forbidding, but the West Indian team is a multinational team and the collective militant enthusiasm of the West Indies is moderated by the absence of a good fit between national, racial and cultural responsibilities" (p. 105). Again, the national sovereignty of existing states is taken for granted. This leads Nandy to misrecognize – indeed, not even to notice – the *utopian* dimension of the pan-West Indian consciousness mobilized by the West Indian team in its Test match encounters.

71 Cf. "'The Continued Relevance of Marxism' as a Question," in which Surin argues both that "[t]he restructuring of capital in its current phase of development necessitates a recasting of the marxist paradigm" (p. 41), and that "it is now evident that the dialectic is too simple and clumsy an instrument to account for the kinds of antagonism which prevail in contemporary capitalism" (p. 61).

72 C.L.R. James, *Spheres of Existence: Selected Writings* (Westport, CT: Lawrence Hill and Co., 1980), 177. Further reference to this work (hereafter *Spheres*) will be given in the body of the text.

73 See for instance Jamaican novelist Andrew Salkey's assessment, cited in Walton Look Lai, "C.L.R. James and Trinidadian Nationalism," in Buhle and Henry, eds., *C.L.R. James's Caribbean*, 181.

74 Henry Louis Gates, Jr, "Critical Fanonism," *Critical Inquiry* 17.3 (1991), 458.

75 Edward W. Said, *Culture and Imperialism* (New York: Alfred A. Knopf, 1993), 274.

4 "Unsystematic fingers at the conditions of the times": Afropop and the paradoxes of imperialism

The title of this chapter is derived from the Zimbabwean writer Tsitsi Dangarembga's novel, *Nervous Conditions* (Harare: Zimbabwe Publishing House, 1988), in which a reference is made to "the new rumba that, as popular music will, pointed unsystematic fingers at the conditions of the times" (p. 4).

1 Ayi Kwei Armah, *The Healers* (London: Heinemann, 1979), 308–09.

2 Armah's historical reference here is characteristically precise. In his book, *Popular Musics of the Non-Western World* (Oxford: Oxford University Press, 1988), Peter Manuel notes that "[r]egimental bands were introduced in Western Africa as early as the seventeenth century, and by 1750 a number of British-style bands with native musicians were extant. Significantly, as early as the 1840s the native bands were playing contemporary popular songs as well as marches. A gradual process of Africanization subsequently transpired in the brass bands. In the early years of this century, the European marches and dance songs were enlivened with indigenous syncopations, giving birth to hybrid dance forms like the Ghanaian *adaha*" (p. 86). Further references to this work (hereafter *Popular*) will be given in the body of the text.

3 Deborah James, "Musical Form and Social History: Research Perspectives on Black South African Music," *Radical History Review* 46/7 (1990), 309.

4 *Ibid.*, 313.

5 Francis Bebey, *African Music: A People's Art*, trans. Josephine Bennett (Westport, CT: Lawrence Hill and Company, 1975), 1.

6 See David Coplan, *In Township Tonight! South Africa's Black City Music and Theatre* (London and New York: Longman, 1986); John Storm Roberts, *Black Music of Two Worlds* (New York: Praeger Publishers, 1972). Further references to this work (hereafter *Black Music*) will be given in the body of the text.

7 Roberts, *Black Music*, 259. See also John Collins, *West African Pop Roots* (Philadelphia: Temple University Press, 1992); and John Collins and Paul Richards, "Popular Music in West Africa," in Simon Frith, ed., *World Music, Politics and Social Change* (Manchester and London: Manchester University Press, 1989), 12–46.

8 Manuel cautions, however, that not all "Western-like features in ethnic pop musics are . . . necessarily borrowed from the West"; in many cases, they may "have originated out of indigenous precedents or processes . . . [D]iffusion should not be confused with polygenesis" (*Popular*, 22).

9 Andrew Tracey, qtd. in Billy Bergman, *Goodtime Kings: Emerging African Pop* (New York: Quill, 1985), 32. Further references to this work (hereafter *Goodtime*) will be given in the body of the text.

10 Simon Frith, "Introduction," in Frith, ed., *World Music*, 3.

11 Andrew Goodwin and Joe Gore, "World Beat and the Cultural Imperialism Debate," *Socialist Review* 20.3 (1990), 70.

12 In thinking about the relationship between "traditional" African music and Afropop, Manuel urges us to bear in mind "that in many areas, modern synthetic musics continue to play only a limited role in musical life. Thus, for example, even in Ghana – a small country with a lively pop music scene – a large percentage of the population has only limited access to radios or cassettes, not to mention live performances of popular musics; this is true especially in the less developed northern regions. For such peoples, while popular music styles may not be unfamiliar, it is the traditional, communally performed songs and dances which constitute musical culture" (*Popular*, 89).

13 Salif Keita, qtd. in Chris Stapleton and Chris May, *African All-Stars: The Pop Music of a Continent* (London: Paladin, 1989), 111. Further references to this work will be given in the body of the text. For a discussion of the social relationship between nobles and griots in Mande culture, see Christopher Miller, *Theories of Africans: Francophone Literature and Anthropology in Africa* (Chicago and London: University of Chicago Press, 1990), 68–113.

14 Nii Yamotei, liner notes to *Soro*.

15 For further commentary on Salif Keita, and Malian popular music generally, see Lucy Duran, "Music Created By God: The Art of the Manding Jalis of Mali and Guinea," in Simon Broughton, Mark Ellingham, David Muddyman, and Richard Trillon, eds., *World Music: The Rough Guide* (London: Rough Guides/Penguin, 1994), 243–60; and Wolfgang Bender, *Sweet Mother: Modern African Music*, trans. Wolfgang Freis (Chicago: University of Chicago Press, 1991), 21–31. These discussions are significant not least because they focus in some detail on the work of such popular *female* singers as Fanta Damba, Fanta Sacko, and Tata Bambo Kouyate. The importance and popularity of women musicians has only recently begun to be reflected in the marketing of Malian popular music to a metropolitan audience. An initial compilation featuring Sali Sidibe, Oumou Sangare, Coumba Sidibe, Dienaba Diakite, and Kagbe Sidibe was published by Sterns under the title *Women of Mali: The Wassoulou Sound* only in the early 1990s. But following the publication of this album, a number of other albums showcasing individual Malian women singers have been released.

16 Ella Shohat, "Notes on the 'Post-Colonial'," *Social Text* 31/32 (1992), 109.

17 Chinua Achebe, *Hopes and Impediments: Selected Essays* (New York: Doubleday, 1989), 22–23.

18 Martin Roberts, "'World Music' and the Global Cultural Economy," *Diaspora* 2.2 (1992), 236. Further references to this article (hereafter "'World Music'") will be given in the body of the text.

19 Christopher Alan Waterman, *Juju: A Social History and Ethnography of an African Popular Music* (Chicago: University of Chicago Press, 1990), 117. Further references to this work (hereafter *Juju*) will be given in the body of the text. See also Collins, *West African Pop Roots*, 253–54; and Manuel, *Popular*, 89. Manuel contrasts the Nigerian situation with that prevailing in Tanzania. In the mid-1970s, the Tanzanian state "sup-

ported an attempt to oust Zairian bands" from their position of privilege within Tanzania itself. "More significantly, it barred the import of records and blank tapes and . . . effectively prohibited multinationals from setting up record businesses in the country." Today, "[t]he government-run radio and television broadcast only Tanzanian music . . . Tanzania, then, has no record industry. Such conditions have prevented Tanzanian music from gaining an international audience, but they have contributed to a lively local music scene in which national music is far better prepared to compete with imported music than, for example in neighboring Kenya" (p. 102).

20 John Miller Chernoff, "Foreword" to Bender, *Sweet Mother*, xii. Further references to this article will be given in the body of the text.

21 Johnny Clegg, interviewed on the television documentary production *The Sounds of Soweto*, dir. Barry Coetzee (Picture Music International, 1988).

22 For more on the structure of the South African recording industry, see Coplan, *In Township Tonight!*; see also Collins, *West African Pop Roots*, 248–49.

23 Helen Kivnick, *Where Is the Way: Song and Struggle in South Africa* (New York: Penguin Books, 1990), 229. Kivnick adds that it is the music produced "at this end of the spectrum, under white control," that some musicologists have seen as giving *mbaqanga* its name. She cites Collins, who "translates *mbaqanga* as 'quickly made steamed mealie porridge,' and [who] identifies it with music that is nondescript and manufactured quickly and cheaply" (pp. 229–30).

24 See also Abiola Irele, who argues that "in their creative transformation of foreign models, and, even more strikingly, their manipulation of foreign instruments, our popular musicians have evolved a musical idiom that is both original and adapted to a new, modern African sensibility. In this idiom, the determining factor is the recognizable indigenous element in which it is rooted." "Is African Music Possible?" *Transition* 61 (1993), 71. Irele goes on to suggest that "it is the wide appeal of our popular music that makes it the most important single source of moral sustenance for millions on our continent, faced today with the harsh realities of what Ali Mazrui has called 'the African condition'."

25 The general methodological reference here is to Pierre Bourdieu's analysis of cultural production as a field of sociological inquiry. See especially *The Field of Cultural Production: Essays on Art and Literature*, ed. Randal Johnson, trans. Richard Nice (New York: Columbia University Press, 1993) and (with Alain Darbel and Dominique Schnapper), *The Love of Art: European Art Museums and their Public*, trans. Caroline Beattie and Nick Merriman (Stanford: Stanford University Press, 1990).

26 One needs the insertion of the majoritarian racial category – "black" – here, since *Graceland* did enjoy considerable success among one sector of the South African population: that of the whites, both English and Afrikaans speaking. Given the segregated structure of apartheid society, this is easy to understand. Because most white South Africans

were more or less wholly unfamiliar with African expressive culture, *Graceland* would have sounded as exotic and intriguingly different to them as it sounded to its Western-based audiences.

27 This play is overdetermined by the design of the album cover, which features a framed portrait of a chimpanzee (the frame signifying "culture" and the chimp "nature"), and by the album's title, which gestures toward the distinction, made famous by John Berger, between nakedness and nudity. See *Ways of Seeing* (London: British Broadcasting Service and Penguin Books, 1986), 45–64.

28 Nigerian pedal steel-guitarist Demola Adepoju plays on the title track and the renowned Senegalese performer Youssou N'Dour is featured on "Diamonds on the Soles of Her Shoes."

29 John Pareles, "Righteous Rock: Issues You Can Dance To," *New York Times* (26 August 1990), 23.

30 Ronnie Graham, *The Da Capo Guide to Contemporary African Music* (New York: Da Capo Press, 1988), 20–22.

31 "Bhundu" is a colloquial term for "bush" in Southern Africa.

32 Paul Berliner, *The Soul of Mbira: Music and Traditions of the Shona People of Zimbabwe* (Berkeley: University of California Press, 1981), 4–10. Further references to this work (hereafter *Soul*) will be given in the body of the text.

33 "*Muka! Muka!,*" qtd. in Julie Frederickse, *None But Ourselves: Masses vs. Media in the Making of Zimbabwe* (Johannesburg: Ravan Press, 1982), 104. Further references to this work (hereafter *None*) will be given in the body of the text. I have drawn extensively on Frederickse's indispensable study in my account of Zimbabwean music in the national liberation struggle. Equally indispensable is Alex Pongweni's compilation, *Songs that Won the Liberation War* (Harare: The College Press, n.d. [1982?]). Further references to this work (hereafter *Songs*) will be given in the body of the text.

34 Thomas Mapfumo and the Blacks Unlimited, "*Ndamutswa Nengoma,*" on the compilation album, *Viva Zimbabwe!* (Carthage, 1983).

35 Both tracks are included on Thomas Mapfumo, *The Chimurenga Singles 1976–1980* (Meadowlark, 1985). See also the analysis of "*Nyaya Huru*" ("A Serious Issue") in Pongweni, *Songs*, 158–62.

36 For more on Mapfumo and *chimurenga*, see Bender, *Sweet Mother*, 160–65; Manuel, *Popular*, 104–06; Judy Kendall, "Put More Zesa!: Jit, Mbira and Chimurenga – Music of Zimbabwe," in Broughton, Ellingham, Muddyman, and Trillo, eds., *World Music: The Rough Guide*, 396–407; and Banning Eyre, "On the Road With Thomas Mapfumo," *The Beat* 10.6 (1991): 48–53, 78.

37 Florian Hetze, liner notes to *Ambuya?* (Shanchie/Piranha, 1990). Chiweshe has also worked as a session musician in Germany. Her *mbira* playing is featured, for example, on *Life at the Pyramids*, the first album by the influential Berlin band Dissidenten. See Peter Spencer, *World Beat: A Listener's Guide to Contemporary World Music on CD* (Pennington, NJ: A Cappella Books, 1992), 45.

38 Stella Chiweshe, liner notes to *Ambuya?*

39 Mukwesha has now released *jit* albums under her own name: *Farai*

("Be Happy") (Piranha, n.d.), and *Chamu* (Shava, n.d.).

40 For an excellent treatment of the sociology of *rai* music, see Joan Gross, David McMurray, and Ted Swedenburg, "Arab Noise and Ramadan Nights: Rai, Rap, and Franco-Maghrebi Identity," *Diaspora* 3.1 (1994), 3–39. Gross et al. observe that "during the independence struggle, rai artists participated in the nationalist glorification of Algeria." Of course, for the most part, "the main subjects of rai singers were wine, love, and the problems and pleasures of marginal life, expressions of a rather libertine sensibility." Yet even such apparently non-political material had profoundly political effects. For "[w]omen singers played a prominent role in rai from the beginning. In addition, unlike those of other Algerian musical genres, rai performances were associated with dancing, often in mixed-gender settings." "By the early '80s," *rai* "had become a *national* music for Algerian youth. Its popularity depended not only on its updated sounds but on its reputation as a racy music whose singers treated subjects like sex and alcohol frankly and challenged official puritanism and patriarchal authority within the family. The modernity of rai's musical texture and its social messages was what won over a new generation of disaffected, often unemployed, youth, who were chafing at traditional social constraints" (pp. 6–7).

41 For more on Chiweshe, see Judy Kendall, "Put More Zesa!" and Moreblessings Chitauro, Caleb Dube, and Liz Gunner, "Song, Story and Nation: Women as Singers and Actresses in Zimbabwe," in Gunner, ed., *Politics and Performance: Theatre, Poetry and Song in Southern Africa* (Johannesburg: Witwatersrand University Press, 1994), 111–38. For commentary on Djura (as well as on Angelique Kidjo of Benin and Marie Dualne of Zaire), see Ty Burr, "From Africa, Three Female Rebels With a Cause," *New York Times* (10 July 1994), 26, 28.

42 Tunde Jegede and Galina Chester, "Walking Away With the Music," in Kwesi Owusu, ed., *Storms of the Heart: An Anthology of Black Arts and Culture* (London: Camden Press, 1988), 108.

43 Jane Kramer, "Letter From Europe," *New Yorker* (19 May 1986), 112.

44 *The Sounds of Soweto*.

45 Richard Gehr, Entry on Savuka/Juluka/Johnny Clegg, in Ira A. Robbins, ed., *The New Trouser Press Record Guide* (New York: Macmillan, 1989), 304.

46 *Ibid.*, 305.

47 Johnny Clegg, interviewed on the television documentary production *Johnny Clegg*, dir. Julian Caidan (Picture Music International, 1988).

48 Johnny Clegg in *The Sounds of Soweto*.

49 Cf. Brad Weiss's observation, in an article about the social meanings of coffee as a commodity in Tanzania and Europe, that coffee in the West "is marked as a distinctly foreign good, one that is differentiated, marketed, and indeed known through a symbolic code of internationalism. Variety, as it presents itself to the [Western] coffee consumer, is not formulated in terms of flavour, age, heritage, or botanical stocks, but of countries of origin . . . Whether downing a cup of Java, or lingering over a mug of Kenya AA, the coffee drinker

always selects from among an array of place names that gives him or her a place in an international world of goods. The sensibilities of coffee drinking in the West, whether the desired effect is one of distinction, or camaraderie, are therefore inherently cosmopolitan. The social life of coffee – as commodity, stimulant, and lexical item – 'grounds' the forms and practices of the public sphere, and the subjective dispositions of its habitus, in a wider transnational nexus of signs and transactions." "Coffee Breaks and Coffee Connections: The Lived Experience of a Commodity in Tanzanian and European Worlds," in David Howes, ed., *Cross-Cultural Consumption: Global Markets, Local Realities* (London and New York: Routledge, 1996), 101–02.

50 Abdul R. JanMohamed and David Lloyd, "Toward a Theory of Minority Discourse: What Is To Be Done?" in Abdul R. JanMohamed and David Lloyd, eds., *The Nature and Context of Minority Discourse* (New York and Oxford: Oxford University Press, 1990), 8.

51 John Tomlinson, *Cultural Imperialism: A Critical Introduction* (London: Pinter Publishers, 1991), 26.

52 Pierre Bourdieu, *In Other Words: Essays Towards a Reflexive Sociology*, trans. Matthew Aronson (Stanford: Stanford University Press, 1990), 94.

53 Bourdieu explains that in the medieval tradition from which he derives the terms, the *lector*, who "comments on an already-established discourse," is contrasted with the *auctor*, "who produces new discourse."

54 Goodwin and Gore note the extent of Gabriel's commitment to the promotion of world music, citing, for instance, "his support for Britain's WOMAD organization, and more recently . . . his participation with the Real World record label and recording studio" ("World Beat," 67). Gabriel is one of the very few Western pop performers whose appropriation of world music has been culturally sensitive and genuinely dialogical.

Bibliography

Abdel-Malek, Anouar. *Nation and Revolution*. Trans. Mike Conzalez. Albany: State University of New York Press, 1981.

Achebe, Chinua. *Hopes and Impediments: Selected Essays*. New York: Doubleday, 1989.

Adorno, Theodor W. "Culture Industry Reconsidered." Trans. Anson Rabinbach. In *The Culture Industry: Selected Essays on Mass Culture*. Ed. J.M. Bernstein. London: Routledge, 1992: 85–92.

"Cultural Criticism and Society." In *Prisms*. Trans. Samuel and Shierry Weber. Cambridge: The MIT Press, 1983: 17–34.

"On the Fetish-Character in Music and the Regression of Listening." In *The Essential Frankfurt School Reader*. Eds. Andrew Arato and Eike Gebhardt. New York: Continuum, 1985: 270–99.

Minima Moralia: Reflections from Damaged Life. Trans. E.F.N. Jephcott. London: Verso, 1978.

Negative Dialectics. Trans. E.B. Ashton. New York: Continuum, 1987.

"On Tradition." *Telos* 94 (1993–94): 75–82.

Aglietta, Michel. *A Theory of Capitalist Regulation: The US Experience*. Trans. David Fernbach. London: New Left Books, 1979.

Ahmad, Aijaz. *In Theory: Classes, Nations, Literatures*. London and New York: Verso, 1992.

"The Politics of Literary Postcoloniality." *Race & Class* 36.3 (1995): 1–20.

"A Response." *Public Culture* 6.1 (1993): 143–91.

Albrow, Martin. *The Global Age: State and Society Beyond Modernity*. Oxford: Polity Press, 1996.

Alcoff, Linda. "The Problem of Speaking for Others." *Cultural Critique* 20 (1991–92): 5–32.

Alexander, Jeffrey C. *Fin de Siècle Social Theory: Relativism, Reduction, and the Problem of Reason*. London and New York: Verso, 1995.

Amin, Samir. *Capitalism in the Age of Globalization: The Management of Contemporary Society*. London and Atlantic Highlands, NJ: Zed Books, 1997.

Empire of Chaos. Trans. W.H. Locke Anderson. New York: Monthly Review Press, 1992.

Eurocentrism. Trans. Russell Moore. New York: Monthly Review Press, 1989.

"The Social Movements in the Periphery: An End to National Liberation?" In *Transforming the Revolution: Social Movements and the World-System*. Samir Amin, Giovanni Arrighi, André Gunder Frank, Immanuel Wallerstein. New York: Monthly Review Press, 1990: 96–138.

Anderson, Benedict. *Imagined Communities: Reflections on the Origin and Spread of Nationalism*. London: Verso, 1983.

"The New World Disorder." *New Left Review* 193 (1992): 3–13.

Appadurai, Arjun. *Modernity at Large: Cultural Dimensions of Globalization*. Minneapolis and London: University of Minnesota Press, 1996.

Appiah, Kwame Anthony. *In My Father's House: Africa in the Philosophy of Culture*. New York and Oxford: Oxford University Press, 1992.

Arlott, John. *The Essential Arlott on Cricket: Forty Years of Classic Writing on the Game*. Ed. David Rayvern Allen. London: Fontana, 1989.

Armah, Ayi Kwei. "African Socialism: Utopian or Scientific?" *Présence Africaine* 64.4 (1967): 6–30.

The Healers. London: Heinemann, 1979.

Axford, Barrie. *The Global System: Economics, Politics and Culture*. Oxford: Polity Press, 1995.

Bakhtin, M.M. and P.N. Medvedev. *The Formal Method in Literary Scholarship: A Critical Introduction to Sociological Poetics*. Trans. Albert J. Wehrle. Cambridge: Harvard University Press, 1985.

Balakrishnan, Gopal. "The National Imagination." *New Left Review* 211 (1995): 56–69.

Balibar, Etienne and Immanuel Wallerstein. *Race, Nation, Class: Ambiguous Identities*. Trans. (of Balibar) Chris Turner. London and New York: Verso, 1991.

Bannister, Jack. Compiler. *The Innings of My Life*. London: Headline Book Publishing, 1993.

Barakat, Halim. *The Arab World: Society, Culture, and State*. Berkeley: University of California Press, 1993.

Barthes, Roland. *Mythologies*. Trans. Annette Lavers. New York: Hill and Wang, 1987.

Bauman, Zygmunt. *Legislators and Interpreters: On Modernity, Post-Modernity and Intellectuals*. Oxford: Polity Press, 1987.

"Morality without Ethics." *Theory, Culture and Society* 11 (1994): 1–34.

"Searching for a Centre that Holds." In *Global Modernities*. Eds. Mike Featherstone, Scott Lash, and Roland Robertson. London, Thousand Oaks, CA, New Delhi: Sage, 1995: 140–54.

Bebey, Francis. *African Music: A People's Art*. Trans. Josephine Bennett. Westport, CT: Lawrence Hill and Company, 1975.

Beckles, Hilary McD. "The Origins and Development of West Indies Cricket Culture in the Nineteenth Century: Jamaica and Barbados." In *Liberation Cricket: West Indies Cricket Culture*. Eds. Hilary McD. Beckles and Brian Stoddart. Manchester and New York: Manchester University Press, 1995: 33–43.

Beckles, Hilary McD. and Brian Stoddart. Eds. *Liberation Cricket: West*

Indies Cricket Culture. Manchester and New York: Manchester University Press, 1995.

Beckles, Hilary McD. and Harclyde Walcott. "Redemption Sounds: Music, Literature and the Popular Ideology of West Indies Cricket Crowds." In *Liberation Cricket: West Indies Cricket Culture*. Eds. Hilary McD. Beckles and Brian Stoddart. Manchester and New York: Manchester University Press, 1995: 370–83.

Bender, Wolfgang. *Sweet Mother: Modern African Music*. Trans. Wolfgang Freis. Chicago: University of Chicago Press, 1991.

Benjamin, Walter. *Illuminations*. Trans. Harry Zohn. New York: Schocken Books, 1969.

Berger, John. *Ways of Seeing*. London: British Broadcasting Service and Penguin Books, 1986.

Bergman, Billy. *Goodtime Kings: Emerging African Pop*. New York: Quill, 1985.

Berliner, Paul. *The Soul of Mbira: Music and Traditions of the Shona People of Zimbabwe*. Berkeley: University of California Press, 1981.

Bernstein, J.M. *Recovering Ethical Life: Jürgen Habermas and the Future of Critical Theory*. London and New York: Routledge, 1995.

Best, Steven and Douglas Kellner. *Postmodern Theory: Critical Interrogations*. New York: The Guilford Press, 1991.

Bhabha, Homi K. "Articulating the Archaic: Notes on Colonial Nonsense." In *Literary Theory Today*. Eds. Peter Collier and Helga Greyer-Ryan. Ithaca: Cornell University Press, 1990: 203–18.

"DissemiNation: Time, Narrative, and the Margins of the Modern Nation." In *Nation and Narration*. Ed. Homi K. Bhabha. London and New York: Routledge, 1990: 291–322.

"Freedom's Basis in the Indeterminate." *October* 61 (1992): 46–57.

"Interrogating Identity: The Postcolonial Prerogative." In *Anatomy of Racism*. Ed. David Theo Goldberg. Minneapolis: University of Minnesota Press, 1990: 183–209.

The Location of Culture. London and New York: Routledge, 1994.

"Of Mimicry and Man: The Ambivalence of Colonial Discourse." *October* 28 (1984): 125–33.

"A Question of Survival: Nations and Psychic States." In *Psychoanalysis and Cultural Theory: Thresholds*. Ed. James Donald. New York: St. Martin's Press, 1991: 89–103.

"Remembering Fanon: Self, Psyche, and the Colonial Condition." In *Remaking History*. Eds. Barbara Kruger and Phil Mariani. Seattle: Bay Press, 1989: 131–48.

"Signs Taken For Wonders: Questions of Ambivalence and Authority Under a Tree Outside Delhi, May 1817." In *"Race," Writing, and Difference*. Ed. Henry Louis Gates, Jr. Chicago and London: University of Chicago Press, 1986: 163–84.

Bhaskar, Roy. *Dialectic: The Pulse of Freedom*. Verso: London and New York, 1993.

Philosophy and the Idea of Freedom. Oxford: Blackwell, 1991.

Blaut, James M. *The National Question: Decolonizing the Theory of Nationalism*. London: Zed Press, 1987.

Bogues, Anthony. *Caliban's Freedom: The Early Political Thought of C.L.R. James*. London and Chicago: Pluto Press, 1997.

Bourdieu, Pierre. *The Field of Cultural Production: Essays on Art and Literature*. Ed. Randal Johnson. Trans. Richard Nice. New York: Columbia University Press, 1993.

In Other Words: Essays Towards a Reflexive Sociology. Trans. Matthew Aronson. Stanford: Stanford University Press, 1990.

The Rules of Art: Genesis and Structure of the Literary Field. Trans. Susan Emanuel. Stanford: Stanford University Press, 1996.

"Universal Corporatism: the Role of Intellectuals in the Modern World." Trans. Gisele Sapiro. *Poetics Today* 12.4 (1991): 655–69.

Bourdieu, Pierre and Alain Darbel, with Dominique Schnapper. *The Love of Art: European Art Museums and their Public*. Trans. Caroline Beattie and Nick Merriman. Stanford: Stanford University Press, 1990.

Boyer, Robert. *The Regulation School: A Critical Introduction*. Trans. Craig Charney. New York: Columbia University Press, 1990.

Brecher, Jeremy and Tim Costello. *Global Village or Global Pillage: Economic Reconstruction From the Bottom Up*. Boston: South End Press, 1994.

Brennan, Timothy. *At Home in the World: Cosmopolitanism Now*. Cambridge: Harvard University Press, 1997.

"The National Longing For Form." In *Nation and Narration*. Ed. Homi K. Bhabha. London and New York: Routledge, 1990: 44–70.

Brenner, Robert and Mark Glick. "The Regulationist Approach: Theory and History." *New Left Review* 188 (1991): 45–119.

Brubaker, Rogers. "Rethinking Nationhood: Nation as Institutionalized Form, Practical Category, Contingent Event," *Contention* 4.1 (1994): 3–14.

Buell, Frederick. *National Culture and the New Global System*. Baltimore and London: The Johns Hopkins University Press, 1994.

Buhle, Paul. *C.L.R. James: The Artist as Revolutionary*. London: Verso, 1988.

Buhle, Paul and Paget Henry. Eds. *C.L.R. James's Caribbean*. Durham: Duke University Press, 1992.

Burr, Ty. "From Africa, Three Female Rebels With a Cause." *New York Times* (10 July 1994): 26, 28.

Cabral, Amilcar. *Return to the Source: Selected Speeches by Amilcar Cabral*. Ed. Africa Information Service. New York: Monthly Review Press, 1973.

Calhoun, Craig. *Critical Social Theory: Culture, History, and the Challenge of Difference*. Oxford: Blackwell, 1995.

Callinicos, Alex. *Against Postmodernism: A Marxist Critique*. Oxford: Polity Press, 1990.

Callinicos, Alex, John Rees, Mike Haynes, and Chris Harman. *Marxism and the New Imperialism*. London, Chicago, Melbourne: Bookmarks, 1994.

Canclini, Nestor Garcia. *Hybrid Cultures: Strategies for Entering and Leaving Modernity*. Trans. Christopher L. Ciappari and Silvia L. Lopez. Minneapolis and London: University of Minnesota Press, 1995.

Carby, Hazel V. "Proletarian or Revolutionary Literature: C.L.R. James and the Politics of the Trinidadian Renaissance." *South Atlantic*

Quarterly 87.1 (1988): 39–52.

Cashman, Richard. "Cricket and Colonialism: Colonial Hegemony and Indigenous Subversion." In *Pleasure, Profit, Proselytism*. Ed. James A. Mangan. London: Frank Cass, 1988: 258–72.

Patrons, Players and the Crowd: The Phenomenon of Indian Cricket. New Delhi: Longman Orient, 1980.

Centre for Contemporary Cultural Studies. *The Empire Strikes Back: Race and Racism in 70s Britain*. London: Hutchinson, 1982.

Césaire, Aimé. *Discourse on Colonialism*. Trans. Joan Pinkham. London and New York: Monthly Review Press, 1972.

Chakrabarty, Dipesh. "Marx After Marxism: Subaltern Histories and the Question of Difference." *Polygraph* 6/7 (1993): 10–16.

"Postcoloniality and the Artifice of History: Who Speaks for 'Indian' Pasts?" *Representations* 37 (1992): 1–26.

Chatterjee, Partha. *The Nation and Its Fragments: Colonial and Postcolonial Histories*. Princeton: Princeton University Press, 1993.

Nationalist Thought and the Colonial World: A Derivative Discourse. Minneapolis: University of Minnesota Press, 1993.

"The Need to Dissemble." *Public Culture* 6.1 (1993): 55–64.

The Present History of West Bengal: Essays in Political Criticism. Delhi and New York: Oxford University Press, 1997.

Chernoff, John Miller. "Foreword" to Wolfgang Bender, *Sweet Mother: Modern African Music*. Chicago: University of Chicago Press, 1991: ix–xvii.

Chitauro, Moreblessings, Caleb Dube, and Liz Gunner. "Song, Story and Nation: Women as Singers and Actresses in Zimbabwe." In *Politics and Performance: Theatre, Poetry and Song in Southern Africa*. Ed. Liz Gunner. Johannesburg: Witwatersrand University Press, 1994: 111–38.

Chrisman, Laura. "Gendering Imperial Culture: *King Solomon's Mines* and Feminist Criticisms." In *Cultural Readings of Imperialism: Edward Said and the Gravity of History*. Eds. Keith Ansell-Pearson, Benita Parry, and Judith Squires. London: Lawrence and Wishart, 1997: 290–304.

"Journeying to Death: Gilroy's *Black Atlantic*." *Race & Class* 39.2 (1997): 51–64.

"Theorising 'Race,' Racism and Culture: Some Pitfalls in Idealist Critiques." *Paragraph: A Journal of Modern Critical Theory* 16.1 (1993): 78–90.

Clarke, Simon. "The Crisis of Fordism or the Crisis of Social Democracy?" *Telos* 83 (1990): 71–98.

Clegg, Ian. "Workers and Managers in Algeria." In *Peasants and Proletarians: The Struggles of Third World Workers*. Eds. Robin Cohen, Peter C.W. Gutkind, and Phyllis Brazier. New York: Monthly Review Press, 1979: 223–47.

Collins, John. *West African Pop Roots*. Philadelphia: Temple University Press, 1992.

Collins, John and Paul Richards. "Popular Music in West Africa." In *World Music, Politics and Social Change*. Ed. Simon Frith. Manchester and London: Manchester University Press, 1989: 12–46.

Coombes, Annie. "The Distance Between Two Points: Globalism and the Liberal Dilemma." In *Travellers' Tales: Narratives of Home and Displacement*. Eds. George Robertson et al. London and New York: Routledge, 1994: 177–86.

"The Recalcitrant Object: Culture Contact and the Question of Hybridity." In *Colonial Discourse/Postcolonial Theory*. Eds. Francis Barker, Peter Hulme, and Margaret Iversen. Manchester and New York: Manchester University Press, 1994: 89–114.

Coplan, David. *In Township Tonight! South Africa's Black City Music and Theatre*. London and New York: Longman, 1986.

Costello, Nicholas, Jonathan Michie, and Seumas Milne. *Beyond the Casino Economy: Planning for the 1990s*. London: Verso, 1989.

Cudjoe, Selwyn and William E. Cain. Eds. *C.L.R. James: His Intellectual Legacies*. Amherst: University of Massachusetts Press, 1995.

Dangarembga, Tsitsi. *Nervous Conditions*. Harare: Zimbabwe Publishing House, 1988.

Davidson, Basil. *The Black Man's Burden: Africa and the Curse of the Nation-State*. New York: Times Books, 1992.

The Fortunate Isles: A Study in African Transformation. Trenton, NJ: Africa World Press; London: Century-Radius, 1989.

No Fist Is Big Enough to Hide the Sky. London: Zed Books, 1984.

"On Revolutionary Nationalism: The Legacy of Cabral." *Race & Class* 27.3 (1986): 21–45.

Davis, Mike. *Prisoners of the American Dream*. London: Verso, 1986.

Dews, Peter. *Logics of Disintegration: Post-Structuralist Thought and the Claims of Political Theory*. London: Verso, 1987.

Diawara, Manthia. "Englishness and Blackness: Cricket as Discourse on Colonialism." *Callaloo* 13.4 (1991): 830–44.

Dirks, Nicholas. Ed. *Colonialism and Culture*. Ann Arbor: University of Michigan Press, 1992.

Dirlik, Arif. *After the Revolution: Waking to Global Capitalism*. Hanover and London: Wesleyan University Press, 1994.

"The Postcolonial Aura: Third World Criticism in the Age of Global Capitalism." *Critical Inquiry* 20.2 (1994): 328–56.

Duran, Lucy. "Music Created By God: The Art of the Manding Jalis of Mali and Guinea." In *World Music: The Rough Guide*. Eds. Simon Broughton, Mark Ellingham, David Muddyman, and Richard Trillo. London: Rough Guides/ Penguin, 1994: 243–60.

Eagleton, Terry. *Ideology: An Introduction*. London and New York: Verso, 1991.

The Ideology of the Aesthetic. Oxford: Blackwell, 1990.

The Illusions of Postmodernism. Oxford: Blackwell, 1996.

"Nationalism: Irony and Commitment." In *Nationalism, Colonialism, and Literature*. Terry Eagleton, Fredric Jameson, and Edward W. Said. Minneapolis: University of Minnesota Press, 1990: 23–39.

Elliott, Gregory. *Labourism and the English Genius: The Strange Death of Labour England?* London and New York: Verso, 1993.

Eyre, Banning. "On the Road With Thomas Mapfumo." *The Beat* 10.6

Bibliography

(1991): 48–53, 78.
Fabian, Johannes. *Time and the Other: How Anthropology Makes Its Object.* New York: Columbia University Press, 1983.
Fanon, Frantz. *Black Skin, White Masks.* Trans. Charles Lam Markmann. New York: Grove Press, 1977.
The Wretched of the Earth. Trans. Constance Farrington. New York: Grove Press, 1968.
Farred, Grant. Ed. *Rethinking C.L.R. James.* Oxford: Blackwell, 1996.
Foucault, Michel. *The Order of Things: An Archaeology of the Human Sciences.* Trans. Alan Sheridan-Smith. New York: Vintage, 1973.
Fraser, Nancy. *Unruly Practices: Power, Discourse, and Gender in Contemporary Social Theory.* Minneapolis: University of Minnesota Press, 1989.
Frederickse, Julie. *None But Ourselves: Masses vs. Media in the Making of Zimbabwe.* Johannesburg: Ravan Press, 1982.
Friedman, Jonathan. "Global System, Globalization and the Parameters of Modernity." In *Global Modernities.* Eds. Mike Featherstone, Scott Lash, and Roland Robertson. London, Thousand Oaks, CA, New Delhi: Sage, 1995: 69–90.
Frith, Simon. "Introduction." In *World Music, Politics and Social Change.* Ed. Frith. Manchester and London: Manchester University Press, 1989: 1–6.
Fröbel, Folker, Jürgen Heinrichs, and Otto Kreye. *The New International Division of Labour: Structural Unemployment in Industrialised Countries and Industrialisation in Developing Countries.* Trans. Pete Burgess. Cambridge: Cambridge University Press, 1980.
Gates, Henry Louis, Jr. "Critical Fanonism." *Critical Inquiry* 17.3 (1991): 457–70.
Gehr, Richard. Entry on Savuka/Juluka/Johnny Clegg. In *The New Trouser Press Record Guide.* Ed. Ira A. Robbins. New York: Macmillan, 1989: 304–05.
Gellner, Ernest. "Nationalism and Politics in Eastern Europe." *New Left Review* 189 (1991): 127–34.
Nations and Nationalism. Ithaca: Cornell University Press, 1992.
Geras, Norman. *Discourses of Extremity: Radical Ethics and Post-Marxist Extravagances.* London: Verso, 1990.
"Seven Types of Obloquy: Travesties of Marxism." In *Socialist Register: The Retreat of the Intellectuals.* Eds. Ralph Miliband, Leo Panitch, and John Saville. London: Merlin, 1990: 1–34.
Giddens, Anthony. *The Consequences of Modernity.* Stanford: Stanford University Press, 1990.
The Nation-State and Violence. Vol. II of *A Contemporary Critique of Historical Materialism.* Berkeley and Los Angeles: University of California Press, 1987.
Gilroy, Paul. *The Black Atlantic: Modernity and Double Consciousness.* Cambridge: Harvard University Press, 1993.
"There Ain't No Black in the Union Jack": The Cultural Politics of Race and Nation.* London: Hutchinson, 1987.
Small Acts: Thoughts on the Politics of Black Cultures. New York and London: Serpent's Tail, 1993.

Goodwin, Andrew and Joe Gore. "World Beat and the Cultural Imperialism Debate." *Socialist Review* 20.3 (1990): 63–80.

Graham, Ronnie. *The Da Capo Guide to Contemporary African Music.* New York: Da Capo Press, 1988.

Gramsci, Antonio. *An Antonio Gramsci Reader: Selected Writings, 1916–1935.* Ed. David Forgacs. New York: Schocken Books, 1988.

Gross, Joan, David McMurray, and Ted Swedenburg. "Arab Noise and Ramadan Nights: Rai, Rap, and Franco-Maghrebi Identity." *Diaspora* 3.1 (1994): 3–39.

Guha, Ramachandra. *Spin and Other Turns: Indian Cricket's Coming of Age.* New Delhi: Penguin, 1994.

Guha, Ranajit. *Dominance without Hegemony: History and Power in Colonial India.* Cambridge: Harvard University Press, 1997.

"Dominance Without Hegemony and Its Historiography." *Subaltern Studies* VI. *Writings on South Asian History and Society.* Ed. Ranajit Guha. Delhi: Oxford University Press, 1989: 210–309.

Elementary Aspects of Peasant Insurgency. Delhi: Oxford University Press, 1983.

"The Prose of Counter-Insurgency." *Subaltern Studies* II. *Writings on South Asian History and Society.* Ed. Ranajit Guha. Delhi: Oxford University Press, 1986: 1–42.

"On Some Aspects of the Historiography of Colonial India." *Subaltern Studies* I. *Writings on South Asian History and Society.* Ed. Ranajit Guha. Delhi: Oxford University Press, 1986: 1–8.

Guttmann, Allen. *Games and Empires: Modern Sports and Cultural Imperialism.* New York: Columbia University Press, 1994.

Habermas, Jürgen. *Autonomy and Solidarity: Interviews.* Ed. and trans. Peter Dews. London: Verso, 1986.

"Heinrich Heine and the Role of the Intellectual in Germany." In *The New Conservatism: Cultural Criticism and the Historians' Debate.* Ed. and trans. Shierry Weber Nicholsen. Cambridge: The MIT Press, 1989: 71–99.

The Philosophical Discourse of Modernity: Twelve Lectures. Trans. Frederick Lawrence. Cambridge: The MIT Press, 1987.

The Structural Transformation of the Public Sphere: An Inquiry into a Category of Bourgeois Society. Trans. Thomas Burger. Cambridge: The MIT Press, 1993.

The Theory of Communicative Action. Trans. Thomas McCarthy. 2 vols.: vol. I: *Reason and the Rationalization of Society.* Boston: Beacon Press, 1984; vol. II: *Lifeworld and System: A Critique of Functionalist Reason.* Boston: Beacon Press, 1989.

Hall, Stuart. *The Hard Road to Renewal: Thatcherism and the Crisis of the Left.* London: Verso, 1988.

"The Meaning of New Times." In *New Times: The Changing Face of Politics in the 1990s.* Eds. Stuart Hall and Martin Jacques. London: Lawrence and Wishart, 1989: 116–34.

"The Question of Cultural Identity." In *Modernity: An Introduction to Modern Societies.* Eds. Stuart Hall, David Held, Don Hubert, and Kenneth Thompson. Oxford: Blackwell, 1996: 595–634.

Harman, Chris. "The State and Capitalism Today." *International Socialism* 51 (1991): 3–54.

Harvey, David. *The Condition of Postmodernity: An Enquiry into the Origins of Cultural Change*. Oxford: Blackwell, 1989.

"Globalization in Question." *Rethinking Marxism* 8.4 (1995): 1–17.

Hector, Tim. "West Indian Nationhood, Integration, and Cricket Politics." In *An Area of Conquest: Popular Democracy and West Indies Cricket Supremacy*. Ed. Hilary Beckles. Kingston, Jamaica: Ian Randle Publishers, 1994: 113–26.

Hegel, Georg Wilhelm Friedrich. *The Philosophy of History*. Trans. J. Sibree. New York: Dover Publications, 1956.

Heller, Agnes and Ferenc Feher. *The Grandeur and Twilight of Radical Universalism*. New Brunswick: Transaction Publishers, 1991.

Hirst, Paul and Grahame Thompson. *Globalization in Question: The International Economy and the Possibilities of Governance*. Oxford: Polity Press, 1996.

Hobsbawm, Eric J. "Barbarism: A User's Guide." *New Left Review* 206 (1994): 44–54.

"The Crisis of Today's Ideologies." *New Left Review* 192 (1992): 55–64.

Nations and Nationalism Since 1780: Programme, Myth, Reality. Cambridge: Cambridge University Press, 1991.

Horkheimer, Max and Theodor W. Adorno. *Dialectic of Enlightenment*. Trans. John Cumming. New York: Continuum, 1987.

Hulme, Peter. "The Locked Heart: the Creole Family Romance of *Wide Sargasso Sea*." In *Colonial Discourse/Postcolonial Theory*. Eds. Francis Barker, Peter Hulme, and Margaret Iversen. Manchester and New York: Manchester University Press, 1994: 72–88.

"The Profit of Language: George Lamming and the Postcolonial Novel." In *Recasting the World: Writing after Colonialism*. Ed. Jonathan White. Baltimore and London: Johns Hopkins University Press, 1993: 120–36.

Huyssen, Andreas. *After the Great Divide. Modernism, Mass Culture, Postmodernism*. Bloomington: Indiana University Press, 1986.

Irele, Abiola. "Is African Music Possible?" *Transition* 61 (1993): 56–71.

Isaacman, Allen F. "Peasants and Rural Social Protest in Africa." In *Confronting Historical Paradigms: Peasants, Labor, and the Capitalist World System in Africa and Latin America*. Frederick Cooper, Allen F. Isaacman, Florencia E. Mallon, William Roseberry, and Steve J. Stern. Madison: University of Wisconsin Press, 1993: 205–317.

Jacques, Martin. "New Times." *Marxism Today* (October 1988): 1.

Jakubowska, Tamara. "The Ethics of Ethnicity: A Commentary on Christopher Miller's Theories on Mediating African Literature." Unpublished paper, University of Essex, 1993.

James, C.L.R. *American Civilization*. Eds. Anna Grimshaw and Keith Hart. Oxford: Blackwell, 1993.

Beyond a Boundary. Durham: Duke University Press, 1993.

The Black Jacobins. New York: Vintage Books, 1989.

C.L.R. James and Revolutionary Marxism: Selected Writings of C.L.R. James, 1939–1949. Eds. Scott McLemee and Paul Le Blanc. Atlantic

Highlands, NJ: Humanities Press, 1994.

C.L.R. James on the "Negro Question." Ed. Scott McLemee. Jackson: University Press of Mississippi, 1996.

The C.L.R. James Reader. Ed. Anna Grimshaw. Oxford: Blackwell, 1992.

Cricket. Ed. Anna Grimshaw. London: Allison and Busby, 1986.

The Future in the Present: Selected Writings. London: Allison and Busby, 1977.

Special Delivery: The Letters of C.L.R. James to Constance Webb, 1939–48. Ed. Anna Grimshaw. Oxford: Blackwell, 1995.

Spheres of Existence: Selected Writings. Westport, CT: Lawrence Hill and Co., 1980.

World Revolution, 1917–1936: The Rise and Fall of the Communist International. Atlantic Highlands, NJ: Humanities Press, 1993.

James, Deborah. "Musical Form and Social History: Research Perspectives on Black South African Music." *Radical History Review* 46/7 (1990): 309–19.

Jameson, Fredric. "Actually Existing Marxism." *Polygraph* 6/7 (1993): 170–95.

Postmodernism, or, The Cultural Logic of Late Capitalism. Durham: Duke University Press, 1992.

"Third World Literature in the Era of Multinational Capitalism." *Social Text* 15 (1986): 65–88.

JanMohamed, Abdul. "The Economy of Manichean Allegory: The Function of Racial Difference in Colonialist Literature." In *"Race," Writing, and Difference.* Ed. Henry Louis Gates, Jr. Chicago and London: University of Chicago Press, 1986: 78–106.

Manichean Aesthetics: The Politics of Literature in Colonial Africa. Amherst: University of Massachusetts Press, 1983.

JanMohamed, Abdul R. and David Lloyd. Editors' Introduction: "Toward a Theory of Minority Discourse: What Is To Be Done?" In *The Nature and Context of Minority Discourse.* New York and Oxford: Oxford University Press, 1990: 1–16.

Jegede, Tunde and Galina Chester. "Walking Away With the Music." In *Storms of the Heart: An Anthology of Black Arts and Culture.* Ed. Kwesi Owusu. London: Camden Press, 1988: 107–10.

Jessop, Bob, Kevin Bonnett, Simon Bromley, and Tom Ling. "Authoritarian Populism, Two Nations, and Thatcherism." *New Left Review* 147 (1984): 32–60.

"Thatcherism and the Politics of Hegemony: A Reply to Stuart Hall." *New Left Review* 153 (1985): 87–101.

Johnson, Pauline. *Feminism as Radical Humanism.* Boulder and San Francisco: Westview, 1994.

Jusdanis, Gregory. "Beyond National Culture?" *Boundary 2* 22.1 (1995): 23–60.

"Culture, Culture Everywhere: the Swell of Globalization Theory." *Diaspora* 5.1 (1996): 141–61.

Kapur, Geeta. "Globalisation and Culture." *Third Text* 39 (1997): 21–38.

Kendall, Judy. "Put More Zesa!: Jit, Mbira and Chimurenga – Music of Zimbabwe." In *World Music: The Rough Guide.* Eds. Simon

Broughton, Mark Ellingham, David Muddyman, and Richard Trillo. London: Rough Guides/Penguin, 1994: 396–407.

Kerkvliet, Benedict J. Tria. *Everyday Politics in the Philippines: Class and Status Relations in a Central Luzon Village.* Berkeley: University of California Press, 1990.

Khatibi, Abdelkebir. "Double Criticism: The Decolonization of Arab Sociology." In *Contemporary North Africa: Issues of Development and Integration.* Ed. Halim Barakat. Washington, DC: Center for Contemporary Arab Studies, 1985: 9–19.

Kiernan, Victor G. *Imperialism and Its Contradictions.* New York and London: Routledge, 1995.

Kingwell, Mark. "Keeping a Straight Bat: Cricket, Civility, and Postcolonialism." In *C.L.R. James: His Intellectual Legacies.* Eds. Selwyn Cudjoe and William E. Cain. Amherst: University of Massachusetts Press, 1995: 359–87.

Kivnick, Helen Q. *Where Is the Way: Song and Struggle in South Africa.* New York: Penguin Books, 1990.

Kramer, Jane. "Letter From Europe." *New Yorker* (19 May 1986): 105–17.

Kristeva, Julia. "Foreign Body." *Transition* 59 (1993): 172–83.

Laclau, Ernesto and Chantal Mouffe. *Hegemony and Socialist Strategy: Towards a Radical Democratic Politics.* London and New York: Verso, 1987.

"Post-Marxism without Apologies." *New Left Review* 166 (1987): 79–106.

Larrain, Jorge. *Ideology and Cultural Identity: Modernity and the Third World Presence.* Oxford: Polity Press, 1994.

Larsen, Neil. *Reading North by South: On Latin American Literature, Culture and Politics.* Minneapolis: University of Minnesota Press, 1995.

Lash, Scott and John Urry. *The End of Organized Capitalism.* Madison: University of Wisconsin Press, 1987.

Lazarus, Neil. "Doubting the New World Order: Marxism and Postmodernist Social Theory." *differences. A Journal of Feminist Cultural Studies* 3.3 (1991): 94–138.

"Postcolonialism and the Dilemma of Nationalism: Aijaz Ahmad's Critique of Third-Worldism." *Diaspora* 2.3 (1993): 373–400.

Resistance in Postcolonial African Fiction. New Haven: Yale University Press, 1990.

Lazarus, Neil, Steven Evans, Anthony Arnove, and Anne Menke. "The Necessity of Universalism." *differences. A Journal of Feminist Cultural Studies* 7.1 (1995): 75–145.

Lenin, V.I. *The Right of Nations to Self-Determination.* Moscow: Progress Publishers, 1979.

What Is To Be Done? Burning Questions of Our Movement. New York: International Publishers, 1969.

Lipietz, Alain. *Miracles and Mirages: The Crises of Global Fordism.* Trans. David Macey. London: Verso, 1987.

Look Lai, Walton. "C.L.R. James and Trinidadian Nationalism." In *C.L.R. James's Caribbean.* Eds. Paul Buhle and Paget Henry. Durham: Duke University Press, 1992: 174–209.

Lovibond, Sabina. "Feminism and the 'Crisis of Rationality'." *New Left Review* 207 (1994): 72–102.

"Feminism and Postmodernism." In *Postmodernism: A Reader*. Ed. Thomas Docherty. New York: Columbia University Press, 1993: 390–414.

Löwy, Michael. "Democrats and Demagogues." *Red Pepper* (July 1996): 11–14.

"Why Nationalism?" In *Real Problems, False Solutions: Socialist Register*. Eds. Ralph Miliband and Leo Panitch. London: Merlin Press, 1993: 125–38.

Lukács, Georg. *History and Class Consciousness: Studies in Marxist Dialectics*. Trans. Rodney Livingstone. Cambridge: The MIT Press, 1983.

Mandel, Ernest. *Late Capitalism*. Trans. Joris De Bres. London and New York: Verso, 1993.

Manley, Michael. *A History of West Indies Cricket*. London, Sydney, and Auckland: Pan Books, 1988.

Manuel, Peter. *Popular Musics of the Non-Western World*. Oxford: Oxford University Press, 1988.

Marqusee, Mike. *Anyone But England: Cricket and the National Malaise*. London and New York: Verso, 1994.

Marx, Karl. *Contribution to the Critique of Hegel's Philosophy of Right*. In *Karl Marx: Early Writings*. Ed. and trans. T.B. Bottomore. New York: McGraw Hill, 1964: 41–59.

Grundrisse: Foundations of the Critique of Political Economy. Trans. Martin Nicolaus. London: Penguin, 1993.

Marx, Karl and Friedrich Engels. *The Communist Manifesto*. Trans. Samuel Moore. New York: Penguin, 1967.

McClintock, Anne. *Imperial Leather: Race, Gender and Sexuality in the Colonial Context*. New York and London: Routledge, 1995.

McGrew, Anthony. "A Global Society?" In *Modernity: An Introduction to Modern Societies*. Eds. Stuart Hall, David Held, Don Hubert, and Kenneth Thompson. Oxford: Blackwell, 1996: 466–503.

Miller, Christopher. *Theories of Africans: Francophone Literature and Anthropology in Africa*. Chicago and London: University of Chicago Press, 1990.

Mitchell, Timothy. *Colonising Egypt*. Berkeley, Los Angeles, Oxford: University of California Press, 1991.

Miyoshi, Masao. "A Borderless World? From Colonialism to Transnationalism and the Decline of the Nation-State." *Critical Inquiry* 19 (1993): 726–51.

"Sites of Resistance in the Global Economy." *Boundary 2* 22.1 (1995): 61–84.

Mohanty, Satya P. "Colonial Legacies, Multicultural Futures: Relativism, Objectivity, and the Challenge of Otherness." *PMLA* 110.1 (1995): 108–18.

Literary Theory and the Claims of History: Postmodernism, Objectivity, Multicultural Politics. Ithaca: Cornell University Press, 1997.

Moore-Gilbert, Bart. *Postcolonial Theory: Contexts, Practices, Politics*. London and New York: Verso, 1997.

Mudimbe, V.Y. *Parables and Fables: Exegesis, Textuality, and Politics in Central Africa.* Madison: University of Wisconsin Press, 1991.

Nair, Supriya. *Caliban's Curse: George Lamming and the Revisioning of History.* Ann Arbor: University of Michigan Press, 1996.

"Expressive Countercultures and Postmodern Utopia: A Caribbean Context." *Research in African Literatures* 27.4 (1996): 71–87.

Nandy, Ashis. *The Tao of Cricket: On Games of Destiny and the Destiny of Games.* Calcutta: Penguin Books, 1989.

Nash, June and María Fernández-Kelly. Eds. *Women, Men and the International Division of Labor.* Albany: State University of New York Press, 1983.

Negri, Antonio. *Marx Beyond Marx: Lessons on the Grundrisse.* Ed. Jim Fleming. Trans. Harry Cleaver, Michael Ryan, and Maurizio Viano. South Hadley, MA: Bergin and Garvey, 1984.

The Politics of Subversion: A Manifesto for the Twenty-First Century. Trans. James Newell. Oxford: Polity Press, 1989.

"Twenty Theses on Marx: Interpretation of the Class Situation Today." Trans. Michael Hardt. *Polygraph* 5 (1992): 136–70.

Negri, Antonio and Felix Guattari. *Communists Like Us: New Spaces of Liberty, New Lines of Alliance.* Trans. Michael Ryan. New York: Semiotext(e), 1990.

Nielsen, Aldon Lynn. *C.L.R. James: A Critical Introduction.* Jackson: University Press of Mississippi, 1997.

Norris, Christopher. *Truth and the Ethics of Criticism.* Manchester and New York: Manchester University Press, 1994.

The Truth about Postmodernism. Oxford: Blackwell, 1993.

Orwell, George. *The Road to Wigan Pier.* New York: Harcourt, Brace, Jovanovich, 1958.

Pareles, John. "Righteous Rock: Issues You Can Dance To." *New York Times* 26 August 1990.

Parry, Benita. "Problems in Current Theories of Colonial Discourse." *Oxford Literary Review* 9.1–2 (1987): 27–58.

"Resistance Theory/Theorising Resistance, or Two Cheers for Nativism." In *Colonial Discourse/Postcolonial Theory.* Eds. Francis Barker, Peter Hulme, and Margaret Iversen. Manchester and New York: Manchester University Press, 1994: 172–96.

"Signs of Our Times: A Discussion of Homi Bhabha's *The Location of Culture.*" *Third Text* 28/29 (1994): 5–24.

Patterson, Orlando. "The Ritual of Cricket." In *Liberation Cricket: West Indies Cricket Culture.* Eds. Hilary McD. Beckles and Brian Stoddart. Manchester and New York: Manchester University Press, 1995: 141–47.

Pieterse, Jan Nederveen. "Globalization as Hybridization." In *Global Modernities.* Eds. Mike Featherstone, Scott Lash, and Roland Robertson. London, Thousand Oaks, CA, New Delhi: Sage, 1995: 45–68.

Piore, Michael J. and Charles F. Sabel. *The Second Industrial Divide: Possibilities for Prosperity.* New York: Basic Books, 1984.

Pongweni, Alex J.C. *Songs that Won the Liberation War.* Harare: The College Press, n.d. (1982?).

278

Prakash, Gyan. "Writing Post-Orientalist Histories of the Third World: Perspectives from Indian Historiography." *Comparative Studies in Society and History* (1990): 383–408.

Prakash, Gyan. Ed. *After Colonialism: Imperial Histories and Postcolonial Displacements.* Princeton: Princeton University Press, 1995.

Pratt, Mary Louise. *Imperial Eyes: Travel Writing and Transculturation.* New York and London: Routledge, 1992.

Radhakrishnan, R. *Diasporic Mediations: Between Home and Location.* Minneapolis and London: University of Minnesota Press, 1996.

Ranger, Terence O. *Peasant Consciousness and Guerrilla War in Zimbabwe.* Berkeley: University of California Press, 1985.

Rigby, Peter. *Persistent Pastoralists: Nomadic Societies in Transition.* London: Zed Books, 1985.

Roberts, John Storm. *Black Music of Two Worlds.* New York: Praeger Publishers, 1972.

Roberts, Martin. "'World Music' and the Global Cultural Economy." *Diaspora* 2.2 (1992): 229–42.

Robertson, Roland. *Globalization: Social Theory and Global Culture.* Newbury Park and London: Sage, 1992.

Robinson, Cedric. "The Appropriation of Frantz Fanon." *Race & Class* 35.1 (1993): 79–91.

Robinson, William I. "Globalisation: Nine Theses on Our Epoch." *Race & Class* 38.2 (1996): 13–31.

Rohlehr, Gordon, "Music, Literature, and West Indian Cricket Values." In *An Area of Conquest: Popular Democracy and West Indies Cricket Supremacy.* Ed. Hilary Beckles. Kingston, Jamaica: Ian Randle Publishers, 1994: 55–102.

Rose, Gillian. *Dialectic of Nihilism: Post-Structuralism and Law.* Oxford: Blackwell, 1984.

Roseberry, William. "Beyond the Agrarian Question in Latin America." In *Confronting Historical Paradigms: Peasants, Labor, and the Capitalist World System in Africa and Latin America.* Frederick Cooper, Allen F. Isaacman, Florencia E. Mallon, William Roseberry, and Steve J. Stern. Madison: University of Wisconsin Press, 1993: 318–68.

Roy, Modhumita. "Writers and Politics/Writers in Politics: Ngugi and the Language Question." In *Ngugi: Texts and Contexts.* Ed. Charles Cantalupo. Trenton, NJ: Africa World Press, 1995: 165–85.

———. "'Englishing' India: Reinstituting Class and Social Privilege." *Social Text* 39 (1994): 83–109.

Rushdie, Salman. *Shame.* New York: Alfred A. Knopf, 1983.

Rustin, Michael. "The Politics of Post-Fordism: or, the Trouble with 'New Times'." *New Left Review* 175 (1989): 54–77.

Said, Edward W. *Culture and Imperialism.* New York: Alfred A. Knopf, 1993.

———. "East Isn't East." *Times Literary Supplement* 4792 (3 February 1995): 3–5.

———. "Figures, Configurations, Transfigurations." *Race & Class* 32.1 (1990): 1–16.

———. "Nationalism, Human Rights, and Interpretation." *Raritan* 12.3 (1993): 26–51.

Representations of the Intellectual: The 1993 Reith Lectures. New York: Pantheon Books, 1994.

"Yeats and Decolonization." In *Nationalism, Colonialism, and Literature.* Terry Eagleton, Fredric Jameson, and Edward W. Said. Minneapolis: University of Minnesota Press, 1990: 69–95.

"Zionism from the Standpoint of Its Victims." In *The Question of Palestine.* New York: Vintage Books, 1992: 56–114.

Sandiford, Keith A.P. and Brian Stoddart, "The Elite Schools and Cricket in Barbados: a Study in Colonial Continuity." In *Liberation Cricket: West Indies Cricket Culture.* Eds. Hilary McD. Beckles and Brian Stoddart. Manchester and New York: Manchester University Press, 1995: 44–60.

San Juan, Jr., E. *Beyond Postcolonial Theory.* New York: St. Martin's Press, 1998.

Ruptures, Schisms, Interventions: Cultural Revolution in the Third World. Manila: De La Salle University Press, 1988.

Sartre, Jean-Paul. "A Plea for Intellectuals." In *Between Existentialism and Marxism: Sartre on Philosophy, Politics, Psychology, and the Arts.* Trans. Joan Matthews. New York: Pantheon, 1983: 226–85.

Sayer, Derek. *Capitalism and Modernity: An Excursus on Marx and Weber.* London and New York: Routledge, 1991.

Scott, Helen. "Ideologies of Postcolonialism: How Postmodernism Mystifies the History and Persistence of Imperialism." Unpublished doctoral dissertation, Brown University, 1996.

Scott, James C. *Domination and the Arts of Resistance: Hidden Transcripts.* New Haven: Yale University Press, 1990.

The Moral Economy of the Peasant: Rebellion and Subsistence in Southeast Asia. New Haven and London: Yale University Press, 1976.

Weapons of the Weak: Everyday Forms of Peasant Resistance. New Haven: Yale University Press, 1985.

Searle, Chris. "Cricket and the Mirror of Racism." *Race & Class* 34.3 (1993): 45–54.

"Lara's Innings: A Caribbean Moment." *Race & Class* 36.4 (1995): 31–42.

"Race Before Wicket: Cricket, Empire and the White Rose." *Race & Class* 31.3 (1990): 31–48.

Sekyi-Otu, Ato. *Fanon's Dialectic of Experience.* Cambridge and London: Harvard University Press, 1996.

Sharpe, Jenny. "Figures of Colonial Resistance." *Modern Fiction Studies* 35.1 (1989): 137–55.

Shohat, Ella. "Notes on the 'Post-Colonial'." *Social Text* 31/32 (1992): 99–113.

"The Struggle Over Representation: Casting, Coalitions, and the Politics of Identification." In *Late Imperial Culture.* Eds. Roman de la Campa, E. Ann Kaplan, and Michael Sprinker. London and New York: Verso, 1995: 166–78.

Simons, John. "The Golden Age of Cricket." In *Readings in Popular Culture: Trivial Pursuits?* Ed. Gary Day. New York: St. Martin's Press, 1990: 151–63.

Sivanandan, A. "All That Melts Into Air Is Solid: The Hokum of New Times." *Race & Class* 31.3 (1990): 1–30.

"Heresies and Prophecies: the Social and Political Fall-Out of the Technological Revolution: an Interview." *Race & Class* 37.4 (1996): 1–11.

"New Circuits of Imperialism." In *Communities of Resistance: Writings on Black Struggles for Socialism*. London and New York: Verso, 1990: 169–95.

Smith, Paul. *Millennial Dreams: Contemporary Culture and Capital in the North*. London and New York: Verso, 1997.

Spencer, Peter. *World Beat: A Listener's Guide to Contemporary World Music on CD*. Pennington, NJ: A Cappella Books, 1992.

Spivak, Gayatri Chakravorty. "Can the Subaltern Speak?" In *Marxism and the Interpretation of Culture*. Eds. Cary Nelson and Lawrence Grossberg. Urbana and Chicago: University of Illinois Press, 1988: 271–313.

"Criticism, Feminism, and the Institution." Interview with Elizabeth Grosz. In *The Post-Colonial Critic: Interviews, Strategies, Dialogues*. Ed. Sarah Harasym. New York and London: Routledge, 1990: 1–16.

"How to Read a 'Culturally Different' Book." In *Colonial Discourse/Postcolonial Theory*. Eds. Francis Barker, Peter Hulme, and Margaret Iversen. Manchester and New York: Manchester University Press, 1994: 126–50.

In Other Worlds: Essays in Cultural Politics. New York: Methuen, 1987.

Outside in the Teaching Machine. London and New York: Routledge, 1993.

"Practical Politics of the Open End." Interview with Sarah Harasym. In *The Post-Colonial Critic: Interviews, Strategies, Dialogues*. Ed. Sarah Harasym. New York and London: Routledge, 1990: 95–112.

"Who Claims Alterity?" In *Remaking History*. Eds. Barbara Kruger and Phil Mariani. Seattle: Bay Press, 1989: 269–92.

"Woman in Difference: Mahasweta Devi's 'Douloti the Bountiful.'" *Cultural Critique* 14 (1990): 105–28.

Sprinker, Michael. "The National Question: Said, Ahmad, Jameson." *Public Culture* 6.1 (1993): 3–29.

Stapleton, Chris and Chris May. *African All-Stars: The Pop Music of a Continent*. London: Paladin, 1989.

Stoler, Ann Laura. *Race and the Education of Desire: Foucault's History of Sexuality and the Colonial Order of Things*. Durham: Duke University Press, 1995.

Suleri, Sara. *The Rhetoric of English India*. Chicago and London: University of Chicago Press, 1992.

Surin, Kenneth. "C.L.R. James's Materialist Aesthetics of Cricket." *Polygraph* 4 (1990): 114–59.

"'The Continued Relevance of Marxism' as a Question: Some Propositions." *Polygraph* 6–7 (1993): 39–71.

Tabb, William K. "Globalization Is *An* Issue, the Power of Capital Is *The* Issue." *Monthly Review* 49.2 (1997): 20–30.

Tandeciarz, Silvia. "Reading Gayatri Spivak's 'French Feminism in an International Frame': A Problem for Theory." *Genders* 10 (1991): 75–90.

Taylor, Patrick. *The Narrative of Liberation: Perspectives on Afro-Caribbean Literature, Popular Culture, and Politics.* Ithaca: Cornell University Press, 1989.

Thompson, E.P. "C.L.R. James at 80." *Urgent Tasks* 12 (1981): back cover.

Tiffin, Helen. "Cricket, Literature and the Politics of De-Colonisation: the Case of C.L.R. James." In *Liberation Cricket: West Indies Cricket Culture.* Eds. Hilary McD. Beckles and Brian Stoddart. Manchester and New York: Manchester University Press, 1995: 356–69.

Tomlinson, John. *Cultural Imperialism: A Critical Introduction.* London: Pinter Publishers, 1991.

Trevor-Roper, Hugh. *The Rise of Christian Europe.* New York: Harcourt Brace Jovanovich, 1965.

Trinh T. Minh-ha. *Woman, Native, Other: Writing Postcoloniality and Feminism.* Bloomington: Indiana University Press, 1989.

Vanaik, Achin. *The Furies of Indian Communalism: Religion, Modernity and Secularization.* London and New York: Verso, 1997.

Varadharajan, Asha. *Exotic Parodies: Subjectivity in Adorno, Said, and Spivak.* Minneapolis: University of Minnesota Press, 1995.

Wallerstein, Immanuel. *Geopolitics and Geoculture: Essays on the Changing World-System.* Cambridge: Cambridge University Press, 1992.

Historical Capitalism with Capitalist Civilization. London and New York: Verso, 1996.

Warner, Sir Pelham. *Lord's: 1787–1945.* London: George G. Harrap, 1946.

Waterman, Christopher Alan. *Juju: A Social History and Ethnography of an African Popular Music.* Chicago: University of Chicago Press, 1990.

Weber, Max. *The Protestant Ethic and the Spirit of Capitalism.* Trans. Talcott Parsons. London: Unwin Hyman, 1989.

Weiss, Brad. "Coffee Breaks and Coffee Connections: The Lived Experience of a Commodity in Tanzanian and European Worlds." In *Cross-Cultural Consumption: Global Markets, Local Realities.* Ed. David Howes. London and New York: Routledge, 1996: 93–105.

Williams, Charles. *Bradman: An Australian Hero.* London: Little, Brown and Co., 1996.

Williams, Eric. *Capitalism and Slavery.* New York: Russell and Russell, 1961.

Williams, Raymond. *The Politics of Modernism: Against the New Conformists.* London: Verso, 1989.

Resources of Hope: Culture, Democracy, Socialism. Ed. Robin Gable. London: Verso, 1989.

Wolin, Richard. *The Terms of Cultural Criticism: The Frankfurt School, Existentialism, Poststructuralism.* New York: Columbia University Press, 1992.

Wood, Ellen Meiksins. "Capitalism, Globalization, and Epochal Shifts: An Exchange." *Monthly Review* 48.9 (1997): 21–32.

"Class Compacts, the Welfare State, and Epochal Shifts (A Reply to

Frances Fox Piven and Richard A. Cloward)." *Monthly Review* 49.8 (1998): 24–43.

"Labor, the State, and Class Struggle." *Monthly Review* 49.3 (1997): 1–17.

"A Note on Du Boff and Herman." *Monthly Review* 49.6 (1997): 39–43.

Worcester, Kent. *C.L.R. James: A Political Biography*. Albany: State University of New York Press, 1996.

Worsley, Peter. *The Three Worlds: Culture and World Development*. Chicago: University of Chicago Press, 1984.

Young, Robert. *White Mythologies: Writing History and the West*. London and New York: Routledge, 1990.

Index

Index

Gellner, Ernest, 69, 131, 132, 239n.6, 239n.7, 248n.86

Georgia, 69

Geras, Norman, 228n.24, 235n.53

Germany, 1, 69, 263n.37

Ghana, 36, 196, 261n.12

Gibbs, Lance, 168, 180

Giddens, Anthony, 5, 26, 29; *The Consequences of Modernity*, 20, 22–24

Gilroy, Paul, 12; *The Black Atlantic*, 51–67, 237n.81, 237n.84, 254n.25, 256n.42; "There Aint No Black in the Union Jack," 53, 54, 62

Glick, Mark, 233n.35

Glissant, Eduoard, 195

globalization, 8, 25, 36, 42–51, 61; and cricket, 176–77, 184–85, 186, 187, 190–91; and the nation-state, 48, 71, 72; and neo-liberal ideology, 43–46; and postmodernism, 18–19, 47; and "world music," 221, 223

Goodwin, Andrew, 199, 265n.54

Gomes, Larry, 180

Gordimer, Nadine, 8

Gore, Joe, 199, 265n.54

Grace, W.G., 158–59, 162, 173, 178

Graham, Ronnie, 207

Gramsci, Antonio, 89

Great Britain, 14, 37, 41, 65, 69, 156

Greek society, classical, 149, 193

Greenberg, Clement, 150

Greenfeld, Liah, 69

Greenidge, Gordon, 179, 180

Griffith, Charlie, 180

Gross, Joan, 264n.40

Guadeloupe, 190

Guevara, Ché, 77

Guha, Ramachandra, 258n.61

Guha, Ranajit, 8, 26–27, 44, 91, 111, 117, 118, 119, 128, 133, 245n.51; "Dominance without Hegemony," 25–26, 90, 125–27

Guinea, 98, 99, 100, 200

Guinea-Bissau, 77, 104

Gunner, Liz, 264n.41

Guttmann, Allen, 255n.34

Guyana, 63, 190

Habermas, Jürgen, 6, 7, 15, 17–18, 21–22, 26, 57–58, 154, 226–27n.8, 228n.24, 237–38n.84

Hadlee, Richard, 183

Haiti, 190, 194

Hall, Stuart, 16, 47, 63; *The Hard Road to Renewal*, 36–40, 235n.49

Hall, Wesley, 147, 168, 180

Hammond, Walter, 147

Hanif Mohammad, 172, 185, 186

Harman, Chris, 72, 231n.14, 236n.68

Harris, Wilson, 8, 195

Harvey, David, 32, 49–51, 233n.35, 234n.40, 236n.65

Haynes, Desmond, 180, 258n.58

Haynes, Mike, 231n.14

Hazlitt, William, 147

Headley, George, 169, 183

Hector, Tim, 169–71, 257n.46

Hegel, G.W.F., 7, 51, 57, 97, 99, 127, 193, 194

Heinrichs, Jürgen, 231n.14

Heller, Agnes, 17

Henry, Paget, 251n.1

Hetze, Florian, 215

Hick, Graeme, 185, 186

Hirst, Paul, 43

Ho Chi Minh, 77

Hobsbawm, Eric, 19, 69, 76, 77, 111, 121, 122, 135, 236n.65, 240–41n.22; *Nations and Nationalism Since 1780*, 70–74

Holding, Michael, 179, 181, 182, 183

Horkheimer, Max, 5, 151, 152, 218, 253n.20

Hroch, Miroslav, 69

Hulme, Peter, 15

Huyssen, Andreas, 253n.17

hybridity, 53, 55, 56, 60–61, 133–34; in African music, 197, 198, 200, 203, 220, 222

Imran Khan, 183, 186

India, 68, 111, 112, 117, 118, 119, 121, 125, 156, 176

Index

Cultural Margins

Titles published in the series